C000197013

Famous Diamonds

Famous Diamonds

Ian Balfour

CHRISTIE'S

Contents

To Maria

Fourth edition, revised and
updated, published in 2000 by
Christie, Manson and Woods Ltd,
8 King Street, St James's
London SW1Y 6QT, England.

ISBN 0—903432—65—X

British Library Cataloguing-
in-Publication Data.

A catalogue record for this book is
available from the British Library.

© 2000 Ian Balfour – Christie,
Manson and Woods Ltd

First edition 1987
Second edition 1992
Third edition 1997

This edition produced
by Paul Holberton publishing.
Designed by Isambard Thomas.
Jacket design by Roger Davies.
Printed and bound in Italy.

Jacket illustration:
The De Beers Millennium Star
(see p. 184)

Preface to the Fourth Edition

Iam delighted that Christie's, which has had the privilege of valuing and offering some of the finest diamonds in the world, should now have the opportunity to publish the fourth edition of this indispensable reference work. Indeed, the success of this publication is proving all-enduring, as the greatly revised and expanded third edition, published by Christie's in 1997, quickly sold out.

Since the 1970s, numerous important stones weighing in excess of 80 carats have appeared on the market. However, the information surrounding them has never been available as a whole or in easily accessible form.

This updated version of *Famous Diamonds* presents not only the classic historic and legendary gems, but also the many new 'D' flawless stones which have made the headlines over the years. It includes the Millennium Star of 203.04 carats polished and exhibited by De Beers to celebrate the year 2000. It also provides examples of important coloured diamonds which have risen tremendously in value and interest recently. Finally, it introduces some of the renowned contemporary personalities who are foremost in the industry.

As we embark on the twenty-first century, these rare and beautiful gems continue to reach record prices at auction. With the advent of the internet and the many other developments which are having such a profound impact on our lives, it is reassuring that the diamond market remains so buoyant. While everything is changing at such a rapid pace, this particular industry is showing remarkable stability and strength.

Man's love affair with diamonds is eternal. Their beauty and mystery will continue to fascinate the world and transcend both time and value.

François Curiel
Christie's International Jewellery Director and Group Vice-Chairman
September 2000

Foreword

I am especially proud to be associated with this excellent revised edition of *Famous Diamonds*, which remains, in my mind, the most comprehensive work yet undertaken on important diamonds that I can recall. You might say that Lord Balfour has, with this book, carved his own unique niche, as the custodian and guardian of the narratives behind the most highly prized and rarest diamonds.

I have spent my lifetime being endlessly fascinated with the diamond business, and my interest in diamonds themselves remains as strong as it ever was. I get particular satisfaction from knowing that our trade still continues, to a great degree, to be dependent on family businesses throughout what we call the 'diamond pipeline'. The family element of entrepreneurship has been of particular importance in the evolution of our industry; this has made it the special business it is today and differentiated it from the usual norms of commerce. A myriad of skills in diamond polishing, trading in important stones and manufacturing fine jewellery has been passed down from generation to generation, and a number of individuals have become outstanding masters of their craft, as this book so vividly illustrates.

The discovery of a large outstanding gem diamond, a rare occurrence indeed, never fails to elicit in one a tingle of apprehension allied to a degree of suppressed excitement. One can anticipate the tension yet to come when the often fraught and challenging process is about to begin of turning such a rough diamond into a polished stone of outstanding brilliance and craftsmanship. Both of these elements were in my mind when I was shown the De Beers Millennium Star for the first time once its polishing was completed. This exquisite marvel of nature is a wonderfully fitting way to symbolize our hopes and aspirations at the dawn of this new millennium.

It is also worth reminding ourselves that diamonds have transformed the economic and social fortunes of a number of countries – dramatically in some instances, like Botswana – providing the bedrock for much-needed infrastructure in the most complete sense.

In South Africa's case, this was the catalyst over a hundred years ago that subsequently transformed its whole economic development. In more recent times the growth in other centres of diamond manufacturing and trading, allied to the creation of diamond jewellery and retail distribution, has added its own meaningful contribution.

I also want to mention that De Beers is still privileged to be associated with Historic Royal Palaces in the 'Crowns and Diamonds' permanent exhibition at the restored Martin Tower, which was the original jewel house at the Tower of London. This has a particular relevance in that two of the most important diamonds in history, namely the First Star of Africa and the Second Star of Africa, cut from the largest rough diamond so far discovered – the Cullinan – came from the Premier mine in South Africa and are both on display close by in the magnificent Jewel House at the Tower.

I have no doubt that Lord Balfour's latest edition will give the reader many hours of pleasure and will be returned to time and again. Just as the first attempt at cutting a diamond unlocked a secret fire hitherto unknown from within, so this volume, too, will unlock an immensely fascinating journey into the great historic, and other notable, diamonds of the world. This is a most memorable tribute to the greatest of all gems.

Harry Oppenheimer
Former Chairman, De Beers

Author's Preface

The world of famous diamonds places before us an extraordinary panorama of characters: it extends from kings and queens, emperors and empresses, other potentates, soldiers, statesmen, politicians, to the more mundane businessmen, bankers, brokers, diamond dealers, cutters, cleavers, and the shadowy world of paramours, parasites, swindlers, smugglers and other assorted criminals.

I have learned this since the day, more than a quarter of a century ago, when I was asked to revise some notes on famous diamonds. At that time my acquaintance with the subject was slight: I had once paid a cursory visit to the Tower of London to see the Crown Jewels; I retained memories of the fine exhibition 'The Ageless Diamond' held in London in 1959, and had been down the Premier mine, vaguely aware that it had been the source of a fine diamond known as the 'Cullinan'. Beyond that I was ignorant. Then I met with a stroke of fortune; I found in a second-hand bookshop a copy of Edwin Streeter's *The Great Diamonds of the World*. For a long time this was the only book in English on the subject and it still remains a fascinating and valuable source of information. However, it has two drawbacks: it was published at a time when the first discoveries in Africa, the principal diamondiferous continent, had only just been made; and its style is probably too verbose for most readers today. It was written for a more leisurely age, unlike ours when speed, including the speedy impartation of facts, is valued above all else. My acquisition of Streeter's work was followed by that of other publications so that in time I built up a small library and formed some general impressions on the subject. I was able to revise the notes, publish a booklet, and contribute a number of articles to various books and magazines.

In the late 1970s my old friend John Rudd, in his capacity as editor of the magazine *Indiaqua*, asked me whether I might contribute an article on a particular diamond to each issue. In his own words, he wanted to metamorphosize the magazine, then almost exclusively devoted to the field of industrial diamonds, to include more of the gem diamond world. I was happy to do so – and the work I began for *Indiaqua* started me on the trail that has led, eventually, to this book.

It has been difficult to decide exactly which diamonds to include and which to leave out, and I am sure some will disagree with my final choice. One or two publications have accounts of more than twice the number of diamonds that appear here, but I believe that some of the diamonds they have listed are noteworthy rather than notable.

As my researches progressed, I was struck by the very great confusion surrounding so many of these diamonds' histories. Often the facts about one stone in one publication had been substituted for those of another in a different one. It sometimes seemed as if one were groping in a minefield enveloped in a thick fog. The apparent disappearance of many exceptional diamonds following events such as the sack of Delhi in 1739 by the Persians or the theft of the French Crown Jewels from their place of safekeeping in 1792 contrived to make the position even more confused. Two major conflicts this century, contributing to the loss or disappearance of several notable diamonds, have further complicated matters; it is quite possible that some of these lost diamonds do exist today after having been recut to avoid detection. In addition there is the understandable reluctance of owners to admit ownership or to divulge information, both from the point of view of security and the fear of punitive measures being taken by a government. Such obstacles, therefore, make detection of the table-cut diamond of Shah Jahan and the identification of the Great Table diamond all the more remarkable achievements.

In the quest for accuracy there is a danger of throwing out the legends that have become attached to some of the most famous stones. But I believe there is sufficient romance left without resorting to spurious 'facts' to give 'colour' to certain histories. And there are those who maintain that diamonds are useless baubles, valueless and not worth a moment's attention. I shall merely reply by quoting Ruskin's words that we should 'remember that the most beautiful things in the world are the most useless'.

Fortunately, to judge from my own experience, there are enough individuals aware of the beauty of a fine diamond and the romance and history attached to many of the most celebrated specimens to justify a book on the subject.

This book is an attempt to give as straightforward and accurate an account as possible of the world's greatest diamonds. It will not be the last word on the subject. Since the publication of previous editions of this book, in 1987, 1992 and 1997, information concerning some of the older, historic diamonds has come to light which has resulted occasionally in complete rewriting and in numerous small changes. Furthermore, the whereabouts of one diamond, previously considered missing, has been established and new gems have been mined, cut and polished in recent years, in particular the De Beers Millennium Star. Some of these diamonds made their first public appearance in the salerooms so it is fitting that this new edition, like its predecessor, should be published under the aegis of a great auction house.

Introduction

The perfect octahedron was already considered the ideal shape for a rough diamond in the earliest Indian texts dating back to 321 BC.

De Beers Archives.

Previous page: the final polishing stage to achieve maximum brilliance of the diamond.

Photo © Michel Plassart.

An Early History

Diamonds date almost from the dawn of time. They have captivated mankind ever since it began to appreciate what nature had bequeathed – superstition and divine belief surrounding them in mystique long before they were chronicled in the fourth century BC.

The earliest known source of diamonds was India, where they were found among gravels in ancient river beds centuries before the first millennium began. Some believe the original 'discovery' may have been made by the Dravidians during the Indus Valley civilization, between 2500 and 1700 BC. These were alluvial diamonds that had been ejected from the earth by fierce volcanic activity, swept up by water and jostled along by companion rocks and sediments over millions of years, before reaching their final destinations.

Diamonds are often much older than the two host rocks – kimberlite or lamproite – which transported them to the surface. Crystallized from pure carbon under great heat and pressure in the earth's upper mantle at depths of up to 180 kilometres, their ages may vary between 660 and 3,300 million years. It was during the past 1,200 million years, however, during different episodes of volcanic activity, that the primary deposits – diamond 'pipes', dykes or flat-lying sills – were laid down. South Africa's Premier mine dates back to the earliest episode while others, such as the Orapa mine in Botswana, are of a much later period: 100 million years according to recent studies.

Later erosion of the earth's surface by rain, sun and wind released many diamonds from their primary location. Some, remaining relatively close to their host, formed secondary 'eluvial' deposits in

soil or surface rubble. Others travelled greater distances and were cached in 'alluvial' deposits, either in ancient river beds or spread along beach terraces. Those which were not returned in the surf became 'marine' deposits, settling into the ocean floor itself. Thus primary deposits were formed in the throats of ancient volcanoes where kimberlite or lamproite had acted as the diamonds' means of transportation to the surface, whilst secondary and, sometimes, tertiary deposits provide the further sources for diamond recovery today.

References to diamonds by name, rather than to hard and 'invincible' substances, began to appear in Sanskrit texts during the fourth century BC. To the Western world, 'diamond' is derived from the Greek word *adamas*, 'the unconquerable', *diamas* being its Latin equivalent. Together with *vairam* (Tamil), *vajra*, *hira*, *hirak* (Sanskrit), and *almas* (Arabic), these words were used as a general term to describe hard metals or minerals in ancient times. Not until the first century AD did they become precise in denoting a diamond, per se.

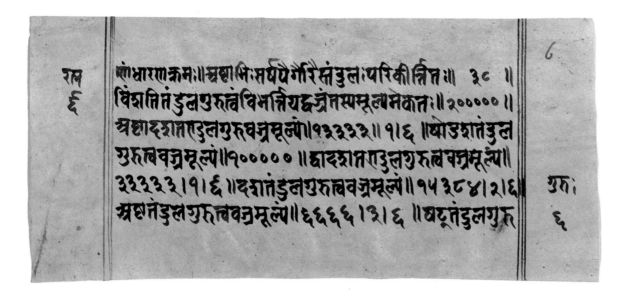

Consequently, it is now recognised that the Hebraic *jahalom* (stemming from 'to overcome') used in the Old Testament was incorrectly translated as diamond in the Authorized Version of the Bible of 1612. One authority considers earlier translators used the now archaic 'chrysolite' in its stead. This, he says, would have been applied to any yellow or green-yellowish gemstone, worn as an adornment.

Besides references in the Book of Exodus (circa 1200 BC), a later mention in the Prophet Jeremiah (17:1), dating from around 600 BC, describes a diamond as being used as a 'tool for engraving'. Although often quoted in the past, these useful descriptions in the Old Testament relating to the two parts of the diamond industry as it is today – the fashioning of cuttable diamonds into jewellery and the application of industrial diamonds – would now seem to have been premature.

Man's first recorded knowledge of diamonds appears in the Sanskrit text *Arthasastra* ('Science of Material Gain'), written shortly after 321 BC. These ancient texts indicate that diamonds were being traded in India and abroad, and produced further revenue through the imposition of customs duties and tax. Larger stones were retained in the rulers' exchequers, so evidently diamonds had not only been 'found', but also 'identified', long before this. In Sanskrit texts known as *Ratnapariksa* ('The Estimation and Valuation of Precious Stones'), there is a discourse on grading standards, with the provision that every diamond should be examined by 'experts'. Although these texts may have been edited and updated in the *Brhatsamhita* of the sixth century AD, the ancient myths were to persist:

He who wears a diamond will see dangers recede from him whether he be threatened by serpents, fire, poison, sickness, thieves, flood or evil spirits.

In both works, the diamond is described as 'the jewel above all others'. Although prized because of its unique hardness and extraordinary optical qualities, it embodied an ancient mystical concept which endowed it with magical powers. As a protector and benefactor, the diamond had no equal and came at the very forefront of ancient Indian desire. The 'ideal' rough diamond was octahedral in shape, requiring 'the six sharp points, the eight identical plane facets, the twelve narrow, straight edges', while the importance of its optical properties – clarity, transparency, colour, 'fire', and light refraction – were carefully explained. The extreme rarity of a diamond that met the highest standards had the effect of 'lighting up the room with the fire of the rainbow'.

Divine and mystical, white octahedral-shaped diamonds were consecrated to the god Indra, the deity of violent weather. Black 'diamonds' were sacred to Yama, god of death, and all crystal shapes of an unknown 'kadali' colour were dedicated to Vishnu, god of the heavens. Diamonds were further treasured for their remedial properties through their harmony with the solar system and for their interpretation in horoscopes. The Hindus fervently believed that swallowing the powder of the highest quality diamonds imparted energy, strength, beauty, happiness and long life. To this day, diamond ash is still considered in some medicinal circles to be cancer's most effective cure.

The single reference to *adamas* in classic Hellenic literature appears as the title to a list of 'fire-resistant' materials in Theophostratus' *Book of Stones* (315 BC). But one of the first recorded events in Indian history was the invasion by Alexander the Great, some 14 years earlier, which provoked a tremendous spirit of resistance and unity in India, and ended a long period of decline. Under Chandragupta Maurya (c.325–c.297 BC), the

Extract from the Sanskrit *Ratnapariksa* believed to be the first written account of diamonds: 'A diamond weighing 20 tandula is worth 200,000 rupakas... If a diamond possessing all these qualities floats on water, that is the stone to be desired above all other jewels.'

Mid-5th-century manuscript. Bibliothèque nationale de France, Paris.

powerful new kingdom of Magadha became established and extended over most of northern and central India, besides Afghanistan and the Hindu Kush. Initially, this brought reprisals from Seleucus Nicator, Alexander's successor in the region, but they were resisted and a marriage alliance later ensued, enabling India to enjoy a period of great cultural development, and through the *Arthashastra*, written under the supervision of Chandragupta's chief mentor and minister, Kautilya, it is clear that diamonds played an important part.

Legends have always surrounded diamonds, yet it does seem curious that Alexander the Great should be featured in one, having been in India for less than two years. This well-known story has evolved substantially in its re-telling, one of the best-known versions as a tale of 'Sindbad the Sailor' in the *Arabian Nights.* This extract was written 1,000 years after Alexander was in India by someone now described as the 'pseudo Aristotle':

Other than my pupil Alexander, no one has ever reached the valley where the diamonds are found. It lies in the East, along the great border of Khurasan, and it is so deep that a human eye cannot see to the bottom. When Alexander reached the valley, a multitude of serpents prevented him going farther, for their glance proved mortal to men. So he resorted to the use of mirrors; the serpents were caught by the reflection of their own eyes and so perished.

Alexander then adopted another ruse. Sheep were slaughtered, then flayed, and their flesh cast into the depths. Birds of prey from the neighbouring mountains swooped down and carried off in their claws the flesh, to which countless diamonds adhered. Alexander's warriors hunted the birds, which dropped their booty, and the men merely had to gather it where it fell.

Speculation concerning the history of the legend is of interest, as it is thought to have started in Asia during the first century BC, before being carried to China and back along the ancient trade routes. After being recounted frequently by Arab and Persian merchants, the story finally reached Europe two centuries later. However much it must have changed in the re-telling, the Western world would nonetheless have learned something about diamonds and the miraculous properties they were said to possess. This example highlights the difficulty researchers experience today in attempting to distinguish 'fact' from 'fiction', before the seventh century AD. It has even been suggested that the legend was deliberately encouraged by merchants in Golconda who wanted to hide the real source of the diamonds in the river-beds nearby!

Early Trade

Diamond merchants began 'to risk their lives on the high seas for the sake of high profits' from about the third century BC. Goods from India were shipped through the Red Sea or the Persian Gulf into the major Mediterranean and Black Sea ports, while others went overland to Taxila (Takshasila, now in Afghanistan). Following an ancient route, a road had been constructed from the Mauryan capital, Pataliputra, to Taxila. This latter, more northerly, city had long been a meeting point where India had traded with south-east Asia and China for centuries, and where the Persians and Greeks were later to join them.

Nonetheless, only minimal quantities of the diamonds being mined in India at the time ever filtered through into Europe. Those that were seen in Rome were small and insignificant stones ('*lapis parves atque indecori*'), as the larger sizes and better qualities had either remained in India or been purchased along the way. It was not until Vasco da Gama (c.1469–1524) opened the direct sea-route to India and returned to Portugal from a more successful, second, voyage in September 1503, that the situation changed.

The legendary Valley of Diamonds which was guarded by serpents. The birds of prey hovering above carry lumps of meat to which the diamonds adhered.

Miniature from a Turkish manuscript, 1582. Bibliothèque Nationale de France, Paris.

Indian Diamonds

To the Romans, the diamond was 'only a speck of a stone, but more precious than gold' and was 'known only to kings, and to very few of them', yet they believed in the 'mystical concept' almost as ardently as the Indians. The philosopher Pliny the Elder may never even have seen a diamond, but he drew attention to its usefulness: 'When an *adamas* is successfully broken, it disintegrates into splinters so small that they can hardly be seen. These are much sought after by engravers and are inserted into iron tools for making hollows in the hardest material without any difficulty.'

Certainly, this would not have surprised the Chinese, who used the diamond as a 'bit' in an iron holder for finishing jade and drilling pearls. This was well before learning it was considered a valuable gem elsewhere. With different beliefs, they could not appreciate any need for amulets, armbands and 'ring stones', and thought 'the foreigners quite mad' to wear them. To them, 'a diamond cut jade as if it were clay' and served solely that purpose. However, with the collapse of the Roman Empire and the spread of Christianity, European interest in diamonds began to falter. By the fourteenth century, they had been demoted to 18th place in the gemstone league, well behind rubies, red spinels (balas rubies) and sapphires.

In the *Agastimata*, written before or in the fourteenth century, it was stated that only rough diamonds would retain their magical powers and, if placed on a polishing wheel, they would become useless. Not until the seventeenth century was this stigma overcome to permit a rough diamond to be fashioned. While much of its original weight would have been retained, some of its inherent radiance was unleashed, enabling diamonds swiftly to regain the pre-eminent position they have held to this day.

The *Ratnapariksa* refers to eight diamond mines but does not state their locations. Flooding and erosion may easily have caused them to disappear, as with other deposits seen during the past 400 years. An observation by the Greek sailor, Eudoxus Cysici, around 120 BC, is thought to be the earliest reference in European literature to diamond mining. He saw 'diggings of deep galleries' next to river 'alluvions' which, if accurate, could indicate that these deposits were being worked from underground. Today it is known that five groups of secondary deposits were formed over a wide area, known as the 'diamond belt'. This extends for 1,600 km from Panna to the Penner River in the south; and for some 1,050 km from Panna in the east to the Ganges in the west. From primary deposits that have since been located, geologists now believe these may have been the original source of four of the five groups dating back to that volcanic episode of a billion years ago.

The celebrated French jeweller and traveller, Jean Baptiste Tavernier (1605–1689), did much to develop trade between India and France. Described as 'the father of the modern diamond trade', the books of his travels contain a wealth of information, alongside drawings and descriptions of some of India's most legendary diamonds. The first, *The Six Voyages of Jean Baptiste Tavernier*, completed in 1670, represents a compilation of his experiences in visiting India over 30 years.

A Protestant, whose father had fled from Antwerp to Paris to escape religious persecution, Tavernier visited Raolconda (Ramalakota, south of Karnul), Coulour (Kollur on the River Krishna) and Soumelpour on his third voyage (1643–49), returning again 'to the mines' on his fifth (1657–62). Each mine was some days' distance from the now deserted and ruined fortress of Golconda, which served as the commercial centre – the term 'Golconda' has survived to describe a type of diamond peculiar to India, one which is limpid, colourless, but may have a slight bluish tinge.

Raolconda must have astonished Tavernier, not only because the miners were almost naked and carefully watched, but also because they worked in pits no larger than six metres in length and nine metres deep. Using heavy tools, the men would break through four metres of earth, before hitting the yellowish clay they called the 'matrix'. Without the help of pulleys to hoist the earth, it was a laborious task, passing containers from hand to hand in relays of women and children, only to discard it in worked-out pits nearby. This matrix was all important, as it was this layer which

Six diamond crystals, illustrating some of the variety of shapes in which they can occur. The triangular crystal (bottom right) is a contact twin known as a 'maccle', where the two halves of the octahedron have grown together, but with one half being rotated through 180 degrees relative to the other.

Courtesy De Beers.

15

The diamond plate engraving text:

REPRESENTATION de Vingt des plus beaux DIAMENS choisis entre tous ceux que le S.ᵗ I.B. Tavernier a Vendus au ROY, a son dernier retour des Indes, qui a esté le 6.ᵉ Decembre 1668. ou il a fait Six Voyages par terre, Et en cette consideration, et des Services que ledit Tavernier a rendus a l'Estat, Sa Majesté la honnoré de la Qualité de Noble.

Le DIAMENT cotté A, est net et d'vn beau Violet.
Ceux cottéz B, et C, Sont de couleur de rose-pâle. Celuy cotté D, est d'vne Eau extraordinairement belle.

Tous les autres Sont blans et nets, et ont esté taillez aux Indes. Les trois d'Embas cottéz 1, 2, 3. Sont Bruts.

II. Partie. fol. 307.

16 Tavernier's drawings of twenty diamonds sold to King Louis XIV. The diamonds marked 'A', 'B', 'C' disappeared when the French Crown Jewels were stolen in 1792.

In *Les Six Voyages* de Jean Baptiste Tavernier, Paris, 1676 edition. Bibliothèque nationale de France, Paris.

Below: 'Father of the Modern Diamond Trade': Jean Baptiste Tavernier.

17th-century engraving.

contained the diamonds and, at best, can have only been 13 cm thick.

Next to where they worked, the miners would level off an area and enclose it within a 60 cm wall, with holes at appropriate intervals. These would then be covered, and the matrix would be dumped inside the enclosure. Water was then tipped in, bringing it to a thick mixture in one or two days. The holes would be unblocked to draw off the water and mud. More than one washing was often necessary, after which the hot sun would dry off the moisture, leaving only sand containing the diamonds. The smaller material would be fanned like corn in baskets to let the lighter material be blown away. The remainder was raked over, exposing many small rocks which were then broken up by pounding the area with large wooden mallets before the fanning process began all over again. Finally, on their hands and knees, all would work carefully to pick out any diamonds that were there.

Tavernier also reported that, at Raolconda, several diamond cutters were working on steel mills. 'If the stone be clean, they only give it a turn or two upon the wheel, not caring to shape it for fear of losing the weight. If there be any flaws, or any points… they cut all the stone into Fossets [facets]; or if there be only a little flaw, they work it under the ridge of one of the Fossets, to hide the defect.' He became very wary of purchasing facetted diamonds after seeing this, and went on to compare the differences in cutting and polishing techniques, noticing that the Indian wheel did not run quite so evenly as it did in Europe. 'Though a Diamond be naturally very hard, having a kind of a knot, as you see in wood, the Indian Lapidaries will cut the Stone, which our European Lapidaries find great difficulty to do, and usually will not undertake to perform; which makes the Indians require something more for the fashion.' Some Indian authorities maintain that Tavernier was providing the first description of the cleaving process, dividing a diamond along its natural grain, but others are not so certain. Tavernier would have been one of the last literate European travellers to have seen the mines in operation because, although still being fully worked when he was there, their production soon declined. By the end of the seventeenth century, they were no longer profitable and were soon considered 'exhausted'. Today, some 20,000 carats of diamonds are produced annually from the Majhgawan mine in the Panna district of Madhya Pradesh; however, alluvial production has all but ceased. Plans for much wider exploration of the country have been under consideration for some time and may be put into effect.

Borneo

In the *Six Voyages*, Tavernier also referred to the existence of the diamonds in Borneo, thus revealing this – now Indonesian – island to be their second earliest known source. Although the date of their discovery is similarly unknown – suggested variously at between 600 and 1500 AD – Tavernier reported that, in his time, the annual tribute paid to the Chinese emperor was exclusively in diamonds. These alluvial deposits, situated in the regions of western and southern Kalimantan, have continued to yield small quantities of diamonds.

Brazil

At a time when the Indian production had declined so rapidly, diamonds were identified in the Tejuco region of Minas Gerais, Brazil. As the story goes, it was in 1725 that a Portuguese settler, who had once lived in India, first noticed gold prospectors using them as betting chips in games of cards. Within five feverish years, the Portuguese administration had established the 'Serra do Frio' diamond district, in the province of Minas Gerais (General Mines) some 500 km north of Rio de Janeiro. The new settlement, later to be re-named Diamantina, was fenced-off, placed under military protection, and declared Crown property.

But the impact of these new supplies on world markets proved catastrophic. Between 1730 and 1735, rough diamond prices fell by 75 per cent. Not only was there considerable over-supply, but trade confidence was shattered by the illusion that inexhaustible deposits now existed. In an attempt to rectify the situation, international merchants spread rumours that the Brazilian diamonds were inferior quality Indian stones which had been shipped to South America before being sent across to Portugal. In a retaliatory move, the Portuguese responded by shipping their diamonds to Goa, before re-exporting them to Europe as 'first quality Indian' stones.

The colonial administrators in Brazil also had little chance of preventing the *garimpeiros* – 'who flee at the approach of soldiers and seek shelter in the mountains' – from prospecting the widely scattered deposits in the inhospitable climate and difficult terrain. Illicit mining and dealing became rife and, in 1775, official lease-holders were restricted to employing no more than 600 slaves. As their rents were so high, they needed to intensify their efforts, which only softened diamond prices more.

Nonetheless Brazil remained the foremost producer until diamonds were found in Africa, but by that time the alluvial deposits at Diamantina were nearing exhaustion. Between 1725 and 1870, some 17 million carats were officially recorded as having been mined in the country, but illicit operations and theft may have more than doubled this figure. Since then, numerous kimberlitic and lamproitic occurrences as well as several alluvial deposits have been identified in Brazil, but a primary source of economic value has yet to be discovered. Large diamonds are still occasionally found in Minas Gerais, while, in the southern province of Bahia, a type of diamond known as 'carbonado', a black, grey or brown stone, considered the hardest kind of natural industrial diamond, often comes to light. Venezuela and Guyana are two other countries in South America where diamonds are produced. In the more important of the two, Venezuela, alluvial deposits in the eastern part of the country are worked by small dredging concerns or by individual diggers.

Southern Africa

There are indications that diamonds were being picked up in southern Africa in the middle of the last century. It is thought that Bushmen may also have found a use for them. But the first in a chain of events that, ultimately, was to transform large areas of the African continent is believed to have occurred late in 1866.

Then the child of a poor farmer picked up a pebble close to the Orange River in the Hopetown district of Cape Colony, 800 km north of Cape Town. Eventually the curiosity was sent to an amateur mineralogist who verified it to be a diamond, approximating its weight at 21 carats. The Eureka, as the diamond became known, was shipped to London where it attracted little interest. Subsequently, further finds were made before events took a dramatic turn in March 1869.

A Griqua shepherd boy found a diamond of 83½ carats which a farmer, previously involved in the discovery of the Eureka, bought for 500 sheep, ten oxen and a horse. While it may have represented undreamed-of wealth to the boy, the farmer soon sold it for £11,200. The discovery of this diamond, the Star of South Africa, set the whole scene alight.

As news of its discovery spread, fortune seekers and prospectors swarmed to Hopetown and the Vaal River, many of them travelling hundreds of kilometres across the Karoo desert.

In November 1869 the first of the 'dry diggings' was located on a farm, known as Bultfontein. This was soon to be followed by easier and richer alluvial finds at Klipdrift (later Barkly West) in the 'river diggings'. Then, when a transport driver arrived at the Vaal to have his pebble confirmed as a diamond, he quietly made the 200 km journey back to the Koffiefontein farm, near Fauresmith in the then Orange Free State, to start on the second dry digging. A month later, August 1870, a fine 50-carat diamond was found on the nearby farm of Jagersfontein – another 'dry digging'. This was to see the start of the famous Jagersfontein mine, destined to yield many fine gems. Next in this rapid succession came a discovery on the farm, Dorstfontein (later Dutoitspan), bordering Bultfontein, in September 1870.

At the dry diggings the early claimholders were merely scratching the surface. A year later, a digger broke through the limestone overburden to find the decomposed kimberlite or 'yellow ground'. By then, two more primary deposits had been located on the farm Vooruitzigt, which had been purchased for £50 ten years earlier by the two brothers, Johannes Nicolaas and Diederik Arnoldus de Beer. These were later to become the De Beers (May 1871) and Kimberley (July 1871) mines. As with other owners of farms where diamonds were discovered, the brothers could not prevent the growing numbers of intruders coming onto their land. Rather than be overrun in a diamond rush that was to attract not only hundreds of local diggers but thousands of people from different countries, they moved out. Accepting an offer for Vooruitzigt (meaning Foresight), the de Beer brothers sold the farm to a Port Elizabeth firm for £6,300. By 1872 more than 50,000 had descended on an area where once only hardy cattle could graze. Now an enormous mining camp existed, complete with hotels, offices and saloons built of mud-

bricks, or from canvas and tin. Known as 'New Rush', it was proclaimed as the town of Kimberley in 1873, after the British Secretary of State for the Colonies at the time. The Kimberley deposits were mined by thousands of individual claimholders and small syndicates so that, within ten years, diggers were working at varying speeds and at different levels in what had become gigantic craters. Caving-in of the side walls, falling rock, flooding, and several accidents took their toll of men and equipment. It was then that a young Englishman, Cecil John Rhodes, perceived the path that South Africa was to pursue.

The sickly son of a country parson, Rhodes, then 17, had arrived in 1870 to join his eldest brother, Herbert, who had begun by cotton farming at Umkomaas in Natal. After harvesting a second crop, the water supplies dried up, and the young Cecil took the month-long trek in an ox-cart to the diggings where his brother had already acquired three claims. Between 1871 and 1873 the younger Rhodes demonstrated considerable initiative in his partnership with another Englishman, Charles Rudd, when together they ordered an ice-making machine from Britain to supply ice to the ever thirsty digging community. At the end of its first successful season, the machine was sold for £1,500, enabling the partners to purchase more claims in the rich Baxter's Gully block of the De Beers mine.

The years 1874–1878 saw other intuitive moves. The young men won the contract from the Mining Board to pump out floodwater from the De Beers and Dutoitspan mines. Together with others, Rhodes realized that the sole hope for a stable and prosperous future for the Kimberley mines lay in their consolidation as one concern. With the finance they had acquired from their various enterprises, Rhodes and Rudd continued to acquire claims within the De Beers mine. In 1880, they were instrumental in forming the De Beers Mining Company, with a capital of £200,000.

Next they concentrated their attention on the much richer Kimberley mine, largely controlled by their great rival, Barney Barnato. After a titanic financial struggle, they won sufficient shareholders over to ensure it could be mined as a single unit. On 12 March 1888, De Beers Consolidated Mines Limited was registered and victory had been achieved. The new Company possessed the whole share capital of the De Beers mine, 75 per cent of the Kimberley mine, and the majority interest in the Bultfontein and Dutoitspan mines.

The Company's Articles of Association became the widest ranging of any concern since the founding of the English East India Company almost 300 years earlier. They signified Rhodes's

Above: Johannes Nicolaas de Beer who, with his brother, owned the farm on which the De Beers and Kimberley pipes were located in 1871. Their reaction was one of panic; they sold up and left the area altogether.

De Beers Archives.

Below: the Kimberley mine in 1878. 'Out of the dry dusty ground, which looked so parched that one was driven to think that it had never yet rained in those parts... soil is taken out to some place where it is washed and the debris examined.' Anthony Trollope.

De Beers Archives.

aspirations for the future of the whole of southern Africa. De Beers was to help finance railways, road building projects and the gold industry, paving the way for the sub-continent's future industrialization, before the twentieth century was under way. The discovery of diamonds in South Africa had introduced a new dimension to the world-wide diamond trade. Cecil Rhodes believed that the necessary adjunct to the mines' amalgamation now lay in the sales of its production through a single channel.

In the aftermath of the 1888 consolidation, a market downturn occurred. Several merchants were left holding large stocks and stared bankruptcy in the face. Both to restore confidence and avoid serious disruption of the industry, a system of co-ordinated selling was introduced. This was to prove successful and, in 1890, the first single selling channel emerged, known as the 'London Diamond Syndicate'. Supply and demand were balanced among ten member firms, each of which purchased a specific percentage, or quota, of the entire production from De Beers. Soon after, the Syndicate made a similar arrangement with the Jagersfontein mine.

London was the natural location for the Diamond Syndicate. In 1650 the English East India Company had secured the right to export all of the Indian diamond production from its offices in Madras to London. This had made it the trading centre for most of the world's rough diamonds. For a time the Syndicate operated satisfactorily, but a series of diamond discoveries throughout Africa before 1930 was to overwhelm it. With a structure that had only been designed to purchase the output of the De Beers mines, it was understandable that the new producers might wish to seek other buyers whose interests and financial arrangements were not so committed to one supplier. The first of these discoveries took place in 1902 when a substantial pipe near Pretoria, which had been known for some time, was finally proved. It became the Premier mine.

There is an apocryphal story that the size of this deposit and the potential threat it posed to the stability of the trade caused one of the De Beers directors, on a visit to the mine early in 1903, to suffer a heart attack. (It was a mild stroke, caused by the warmth of the welcoming breakfast and over-exertion in the heat of the mid-day sun!)

But having started by selling to the Syndicate, the newly formed Premier (Transvaal) Diamond Mining Company decided to change its arrangements in 1906. This was after the Cullinan diamond had been discovered and the directors had been assured that the market was strong and prices were rising sharply. In reaching this decision,

however, they had neglected to consider the cyclical nature of the fortunes of the diamond industry. A year later, the market went into reverse as a financial crisis loomed in America. To protect its share of the market, Premier then competed with De Beers by stepping up its production and, in doing so, saw a loss of nearly 50 per cent on its sales. Later, Premier was to revert to the Syndicate and, in 1917, become part of the De Beers group of mines. The depressed state of the market in 1932 resulted in a further closure, but as 80 per cent of the mine's production consisted of strategic industrial diamonds, it was granted a new lease of life in the 1940s. The Premier mine's record in yielding large gem diamonds remains outstanding, having produced a quarter of the world's great diamonds weighing more than 400 carats.

A little-known photograph of a claim within the Kimberley mine, c. 1878. *'At first the bottom of the bowl seems small. Gradually it becomes enormously large as your eye dwells on the energetic business going on in subdivided claims. Should you be a lady I would advise you to stay where you are... everything is dirty, and the place below is not nearly so interesting as it is above.'* Anthony Trollope.

De Beers Archives.

The next major find took place in one of the most inhospitable and inaccessible parts of the continent – the German colony of South-West Africa, now Namibia. In 1908 a German railway inspector working on the line near Kolmanskop, south of Lüderitz, was handed some shiny pebbles by a labourer, who had once worked in Kimberley. Satisfying himself that they were diamonds, he tendered his resignation and obtained the prospecting rights. This initial discovery led to finds of several alluvial deposits nearby, in a region locked between the ice-cold currents of the sea to the west and barriers of sand dunes and mountains to the east.

Between 1908 and the outbreak of the First World War, diamond production from this area was immense, with sales being handled by the Diamond Regie, a German government body headquartered in Lüderitz. But the war brought mining to a halt. After General Botha's successful invasion in 1915, the area that had previously been declared a *Sperrgebiet* or 'Forbidden territory' fell into the hands of South Africa's Custodian of Enemy Property. Five years later, the German companies sold their interests and were amalgamated into the Consolidated Diamond Mines of South-West Africa (CDM) by Ernest Oppenheimer.

Further discoveries followed in this region. In 1925 a German geologist noticed that diamonds were being found together with a line of fossilized oyster shells running parallel to the sea. These diggings, situated at Alexander Bay, south of the Orange River in South Africa, became known as the 'Oyster Line'. Then, immediately to the north of the river, rich diamond-bearing terraces were discovered. In terms of quality, this has proved to be the finest producer of them all, with almost 90 per cent of the diamonds recovered being classified into superior categories. Namdeb Diamond Corporation, formed as the successor to CDM in 1994, also mines part of the foreshore along the coastal beach. An accepted theory as to how these diamonds arrived on this desolate coast is that they came from eroded volcanic pipes in the southern African interior. Borne by ancient rivers down to the sea on a water course that closely follows that of the Orange River today, powerful currents swept them northwards up the coast before storm surf deposited them onto prehistoric marine terraces. Over millions of years some of these terraces would have been transported from the sea and covered over with vast amounts of desert sand.

The first of several attempts to recover diamonds from the sea began in the early 1960s. In these treacherous waters, over the jagged submarine rocks, some ships were wrecked with tragic loss of life. But with large deposits known to exist at sea, what was once considered an 'immensely exciting mining frontier' has now become an established site of exploration and mining technology. State-of-the-art vessels, using crawler-based and rotating drill systems, operate at depths of up to 200 metres and remain almost unaffected by the conditions far out to sea. More than half of Namibia's total annual production now comes from the sea and it is widely accepted that the long-term future of diamond mining rests with its ocean reserves.

The austerity following the Second World War can have promised little reward for the diamond prospector. Not until 1961 did two partners, A. Fincham and W. Schwabel, find diamonds in their sieves in another parched region, 160 km north-west of Kimberley. Here they discovered a large pipe, later to be named Finsch mine, which, for more than 25 years, was to be South Africa's largest producer.

Four further major discoveries have been made in southern Africa since. Each has required substantial capital, human commitment and modern technology to bring into production. Three have been in Botswana, known as the Bechuanaland Protectorate prior to gaining its independence in

1966. Almost as if in celebration of the new republic, a cluster of kimberlite occurrences was delineated in 1967. The Orapa mine started in 1971 and two smaller pipes at nearby Letlhakane began operating as one mine six years later. Both have long been overshadowed by 'the most significant find to have been made since Kimberley' in terms of rough diamond size, colour and quality, and in the volume produced. Located 145 km west of the capital, Gaborone, the Jwaneng deposit was discovered under more than 30 metres of Kalahari sand and sediments. As a mine, it began production in 1982 and, together with Orapa and Letlhakane, has since made Botswana the richest diamond producer in the world.

The most recent major discovery was in South Africa's Northern Province, close to the Botswana and Zimbabwe borders. Officially opened in August 1992, the Venetia mine represents one of De Beers' largest single investments. To be mined as an 'open pit' from the surface for 20 years before going underground, this significant find has enabled the 'new' South Africa to retain a prominent position in today's much wider diamond world.

In 1906 a Belgian company began prospecting in the territory formerly known as the Belgian Congo, latterly Zaire, now the Democratic Republic of Congo. The following year a prospector identified a minute but bright pebble in gravels of the Tshimimina River. Two years later, others returned to collect 258 diamonds within a month along the Kasai and Kabambaie rivers. Since then, the country has been a major producer of industrial diamonds.

In 1912 diamonds were found in the north-east of neighbouring Angola. Although its large alluvial deposits are still being exploited, more of its primary sources have been located and one of these, Catoca, is in production. In 1919 the chain of discoveries was extended to west Africa when geologists identified diamonds near Abomuso on the Birim River in Ghana, formerly the Gold Coast. West Africa's rating as a leading producer was really

'Father of the Modern Diamond Trade': Sir Ernest Oppenheimer (1880–1957).

De Beers Archives.

Above right: contrasting diamond mining today with the past. Here, at Botswana's Jwaneng mine, massive hydraulic shovels load kimberlite ore into 117-ton dumper trucks in 24-hour mining operations.

Courtesy De Beers Centenary AG.

only established when diamonds were found in Sierra Leone during 1930. The initial discovery was made 225 km east of the capital, Freetown. The deposits are alluvial, but some small kimberlitic occurrences were identified. Marine surveys off the Sierra Leone coastline have shown mining to be uneconomic. The greater part of Sierra Leone's past production has consisted of gem quality stones, which have included some exceptional finds, as has Guinea's in recent years. The neighbouring Ivory Coast and Liberia are small producers of alluvial diamonds.

Finally in 1940 a Canadian geologist, Dr John Williamson, was behind the discovery of a diamond deposit in the Shinyanga district of Tanzania, then Tanganyika. This led to mining what was considered the largest pipe in the world. At the surface it measured 361 acres, almost eight times that of the Premier pipe. At a depth of 50 metres it had shrunk to 30 acres, reducing its diamond content accordingly. Diamonds of lesser significance have also been found in the Central African Republic, Lesotho, Swaziland and Zimbabwe.

Russia

Surprisingly, Russia is one of the older known sources of diamonds. Since 1829 alluvial deposits have been worked in the Ural mountains. Not long after the Second World War ended, the wife of the Soviet Foreign Minister, Madame Zshemchazhina Molotov, presented a ring set with a diamond mined and polished in the Urals to Mrs Winston Churchill. A note was attached to it for the wife of Britain's wartime Prime Minister which read: 'May relations between our two countries be as bright, pure, and lasting as this stone.' But Russia's position as one of the world's leading producers today is owing to more recent events. In 1937 a

geologist, Vladimir Sobolev, contended that there was a distinct similarity between the geology of the Siberian and the Kaapvaal cratons (the latter underpinning central and southern Africa).

Dr Sobolev believed that primary deposits would be identified in the vast area covering millions of square miles between Lake Baikhal and the Arctic Sea to the north, and the Zena and Yenisey Rivers to the west. Exploration was halted during the war, but the first alluvial deposits were located in 1949 on the Vilyuj River. Five years later, as the story goes, the first primary source was located by the female geologist, Larissa Popugayeva. Walking through the snow-covered forest, she caught sight of a red fox slipping between the pine trees and noticed that its chest and hindquarters were stained with a blue colour. She fired her rifle, not to kill the animal but to track it to its den. As first she had suspected, this had been dug in an underground hollow of kimberlite.

Zarnitsa ('Summer Lightning') had been identified but, while it may have covered 53 acres, it was poor in diamond content or of low grade. In June 1955, a group of geologists working not far from the fox's den radioed the now celebrated message, 'Have Started Smoking Pipe of Peace, Tobacco Good.' The discovery of this pipe, named Mir ('Peace'), was to mark a new era in the history of the world's diamond production. It was followed by, among others, Udachnaya ('Success') in the same year, by Aikhal ('Glory') in 1960, Internationalnaya in 1969, and Yubileynaya ('Jubilee') in 1975. Jubilee came late into production but is intended to replace Udachnaya as Sakha's major mine. The Botuobinskaya pipe, identified in 1994, is said to contain diamonds of 'unique content and high quality' and is ready for mining. The first ever commercial underground development in the CIS opened at the revived Internationalnaya mine in 1999. Besides Sakha, which currently produces 98 per cent of Russia's diamonds, the Archangel oblast on the Kola peninsula has been the subject of active diamond exploration and feasibility studies, with the biggest of the discoveries being the Lomonosov deposit, where six sizeable kimberlites have been identified.

Australia

Diamonds were first recorded in the Bathurst area of New South Wales in 1851. But not until the 1970s did interest begin to focus on the remote Kimberley region in the far north of Western Australia. Coincidentally this had been named after the same

Below: the open-pit at the Udachnaya mine in Yakutia, discovered in 1955. It is intended that Udachnaya (meaning 'Success') will soon be replaced by Yubileyna ('Jubilee') as Russia's major producer.

Courtesy Almazy Rossi-Sakha.

The Argyle diamond mine, currently the world's largest volume producer, situated in the isolated Kimberley region of Western Australia.

Courtesy Argyle Diamond Mines.

British Colonial Secretary who gave his name to the South African city and mine.

The first breakthrough came at Big Spring, near Fitzroy Crossing, in 1976, then the Ellendale fields, to be followed three years later by the identification of the 114-acre Argyle pipe. International geologists prospecting the area had expected to find indicator minerals associated with kimberlite, but it was the Australian field teams who enjoyed the achievement of locating the first viable lamproite pipe. With a grade ten times that of most mines, Argyle has been a prolific producer since coming on stream in 1985. In terms of volume, it has made Australia the world's largest producer, accounting for more than 30 per cent of global output. However, apart from its very rare pink and purplish diamonds, the gem content is small. Most are termed either 'near gem' or industrial.

New sources

Further primary and secondary deposits have been located over the past five years and it is Canada which has come most to the fore. Exploration there has been intense and the Ekati mine, owned by BHP/Diamet, at Lac de Gras, in the Northwest Territories, opened in 1998 – the first commercial diamond mine in Canada. The Riotinto/Aber Resources prospect at Diavik will follow during 2003–4 and a number of smaller deposits may also be mined. By the year 2005 Canada may produce up to 10 per cent by value of the world's gem diamonds. Diamond exploration continues across various parts of Canada, and also into Greenland.

Across the border in the USA, tourists have paid a small search fee at the Murfreesboro kimberlite deposit in Arkansas. Efforts to develop a small mine at Kelsey Lake on the border of Colorado and Wyoming were short-lived.

Elsewhere, diamond exploration continues in Australia, China, South America and Central and Southern Africa, but worth recalling is that of the 6,000 known 'pipes' in the world, only two per cent are known to be significantly diamondiferous. Fewer than one per cent have turned out to be significant producers. Proving a mine and bringing it into production is also an expensive business. In the case of the new Canadian mines, financial estimates place their start up costs at around US$1 billion each. Despite world diamond production more than trebling since 1980, the search for reliable sources of suitable rough diamonds, capable of yielding fine polished gems above 50 points (0.5 carats) is essential.

Sorting and selling

Considerable preparatory work is essential between the time diamonds leave their deposit and they reach the polisher or industrial user. Diamonds are unlike other mined products, which can be refined to a standard purity. Occurring in many thousands of forms, they cannot command a standard price and need to be handled individually. Each rough diamond has to be classified into a particular category and be given a specific value before it is sold.

When diamonds arrive in sorting offices they will have been cleaned, but are otherwise in the same condition as when they were extracted. The initial process is to remove those diamonds of evident industrial quality, which could not be set into jewellery, either in total or in part. No definite line of demarcation can be drawn between these 'cuttable' and industrial categories, as marginal goods do exist which may be used for either purpose, depending on the changing dictates of the market.

The cuttable diamonds are then classified according to their size, shape, quality (purity) and colour. Although the common 'habit' of a rough diamond may be octahedral, its shape can vary considerably. Within the trade, shape is often referred to as the 'model', which is sub-divided into six groups. Above one carat, these are termed: stones, shapes, cleavages, maccles, flats and cubes. Below this weight there are similar sub-divisions, with chips replacing cleavages to denote the smaller, broken or irregular-shaped crystals.

Evaluating diamonds for quality, or purity, is the most exacting task for the sorter and the one that takes longest. Only a minute proportion of diamonds is entirely free from inclusions, which would have occurred during their growth or in their transportation stages. Apart from the size of the inclusions – common are olivine and garnet –

consideration also has to be given to their positioning, as this will affect the polishing of the rough gem.

The colour grading of diamonds similarly calls for expert judgement, as refinements of colour, however slight, exert an influence upon ultimate value. Ideally a diamond should possess no colour at all, resembling a piece of ice. Unfortunately, the proverbial 'blue-white' – or 'gin and tonic' – is a rare object; most diamonds show a degree of colour, usually yellow or brown, which may extend from a slight tinge to a deeper shade. Some, but very few, are known as 'fancy coloured' diamonds, and possess a strong hue and saturation of colour, such as red, dark blue, pink, lilac-pink, purple, green, amber and canary yellow. These are extremely rare and command premium prices.

Today, around two thirds by value of the world's production of rough diamonds is distributed through the Diamond Trading Company, the selling arm of De Beers. Created by

Sir Ernest Oppenheimer, the chairman of De Beers, in the 1930s, this marketing channel has achieved on an international scale what Cecil Rhodes had accomplished in South Africa. Ever since, the DTC has been intent on maintaining the stability of the diamond trade and public confidence in diamonds as jewels of beauty and lasting value.

The diamond industry today

Over the years, the diamond industry has grown into an international and highly organized business. Although a quantity of rough gem diamonds are purchased outside the DTC, the majority are sold to its clients, known as 'sightholders', ten times a year. Some constitute the leading manufacturers, while others are dealers, who act as secondary distributors to the smaller concerns. Each

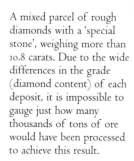

A mixed parcel of rough diamonds with a 'special stone', weighing more than 10.8 carats. Due to the wide differences in the grade (diamond content) of each deposit, it is impossible to gauge just how many thousands of tons of ore would have been processed to achieve this result.

Photo Donald Woodrow.
Courtesy De Beers

24

Highlighting some of the differences of colour in diamonds. Here, crystals of similar size and shape have been sorted into just eight of the many hundreds of colour classifications that exist today.

Courtesy De Beers Centenary AG.

manufacturer tends to specialize in a particular shape and size of stone, and this is recognized by the DTC in its 'allocations' to the various centres in Belgium, Israel, India, South Africa and the USA, although China, Thailand and some other Asian countries are now recognized as growing in stature.

Apart from India and these newer centres in the Far East, the trade and industry have witnessed Jewish domination. It dates back to the fifteenth century when the Inquisition in Spain and Portugal saw the expulsion of Jews, many of whom were occupied in trade. They settled in the Low Countries, where the diamond industry took root, first in Bruges, then Antwerp and, later, in Amsterdam, which became the most important centre, with the arrival of the new South African finds, until the period between the two World Wars. Then it was superseded by Antwerp and the nearby Kempen area where labour costs were lower. The

diamond trade established its roots in Hatton Garden, London, in the seventeenth century.

The advent of the Second World War and the events of 1940 led to many Jewish refugees fleeing from Belgium and the Netherlands to establish new operations in the USA, Great Britain and in what was then Palestine.

Much, of course, has changed since then. Larger diamonds are still crafted in New York; Antwerp remains the major trading centre and, despite its high labour costs, is intent on maintaining its specialist workforce; Israel has become a major player, both as an innovative, 'high-tech' manufacturer and a trader; but India, the first known source of diamonds, has proved most surprising of them all. Today it lays claim to process at least nine out of every ten polished diamonds on the market, handling more than 100 million carats of cuttable rough diamonds. In terms of value, rather than volume, its workforce of some

750,000 people could well have manufactured 50% of all the rough diamonds available in the course of a year. Its staggering growth, from almost nothing at the beginning of the 1960s, can be attributed to changes in the nature of diamond supply and to the increasing demand for diamond jewellery at prices new, international, consumers can afford.

Whatever else may have changed, the principle of 'diamond cut diamond' has altered little over the centuries. In ancient times the stones were left in their rough state because there were no known means of fashioning them. Even when a crude method was developed, it was used only to eliminate the more obvious inclusions, as Tavernier noted, leaving only an irregularly formed diamond.

Gradually, the shaping of the rough diamond became more elaborate and in the nineteenth century steam-driven machinery was invented to power and refine the operation. Diamond cuts also became more elaborate and stylized and one popular old-fashioned cut, often referred to in the text, is the rose. It is roughly hemispherical in shape, faceted on top and flat on the bottom, but it is only suitable for relatively small rough diamonds. Famous diamonds are almost invariably substantial, and to maximize their weight they have not always been polished to a standard shape. Special cuts were often devised for them, using extra facets to increase their brilliance, a recent example being the Centenary diamond.

A rough diamond is generally considered to be 'makeable' if it can be polished directly into one significant stone, without first requiring any other manufacturing process. A 'sawable' is a diamond that will yield more weight if it is divided into two. Like timber, diamonds have a grain; they may be cleaved or divided along the grain or sawn against it. In cleaving, an entry point or 'kerf' is scratched into the stone using another diamond, although today much of this time-consuming work is done by laser. Then the diamond is placed into a holder and a steel blade positioned on the 'kerf': one sharp blow is usually sufficient to split the stone cleanly in two.

Sawing makes use of a thin phosphor-bronze disc coated with oil and diamond powder, which revolves at high speed and cuts through the diamond. Depending on the various hardnesses it encounters, the disc may take several hours to saw through even the smallest diamond. The shape of the rough stone will dictate the cut of the polished gem and by far the greatest number of diamonds are fashioned into round brilliants. The so-called modern brilliant cut was introduced just after the First World War and has been refined since, but is essentially the same today. It has 58 facets, 33 above the girdle and 25 underneath, including the very tiny culet on the 'point', although some modern polishers will emphasize their skill by eliminating it altogether. The circular shape is achieved by 'bruting': the diamond is fixed in a lathe and held against another diamond as it revolves, thus rounding off the corners and edges.

The final process in preparing the finished gem is to polish the facets on to the diamond in three separate operations. Most cut diamonds – heart shape, marquise, oval, square and pear shape – are polished like brilliants, with their facets set at very precise angles to their neighbours. Others, such as the baguette, emerald, and square, have oblong facets and are called step-cut, but are polished along similar lines. The polishing instrument is a round wheel of porous cast iron with a steel spindle running through it. Its surface is coated with a binding agent and diamond powder, although this may not be impregnated. The wheel is spun at high speeds – about 2,800 revolutions per minute – as the diamond is fixed into a holder at the precise angle required to obtain a perfect facet. Regular inspection is necessary to ensure each facet is being correctly shaped.

The facets are polished on specially prepared parts of the wheel, both to eliminate tiny lines and irregularities and to impart a mirror-like surface to the gem. On completion of each facet, the polisher will turn the diamond to the position of the next and repeat the process until all the facets have been polished. Mathematical precision is required to achieve maximum brilliance.

Brilliance is a term commonly used with polished diamonds, and depends entirely on the diamond's 'life' and 'fire'. The essence of this 'life' is to return a maximum 83 per cent of light back to the eye of the viewer, without allowing it to escape through the diamond's back or sides. 'Fire' denotes the display of spectrum colours caused by white light reflecting internally before it is refracted back to the eye. It is those darting flashes of colour that are seen when either the diamond is moved or the viewer moves that constitute 'fire'. As more 'fire' is gained by more refraction, some light is lost, so that maximum 'life' and 'fire' cannot be achieved together at the same time.

Thus, during the course of the various processes employed in cutting a diamond, a very high degree of skill is called for, and modern technology now plays its part. Lasers, computer optics and graphics, micro-electronics and video cameras are being used to improve on the weight that can be retained from one of nature's most precious resources while helping to lessen some of the more labour intensive and costlier aspects of this remarkable craft. The purpose is to ensure the completion of a polished diamond that is appealing and has a brilliance unrivalled by any other gemstone, with a mystique and history to match.

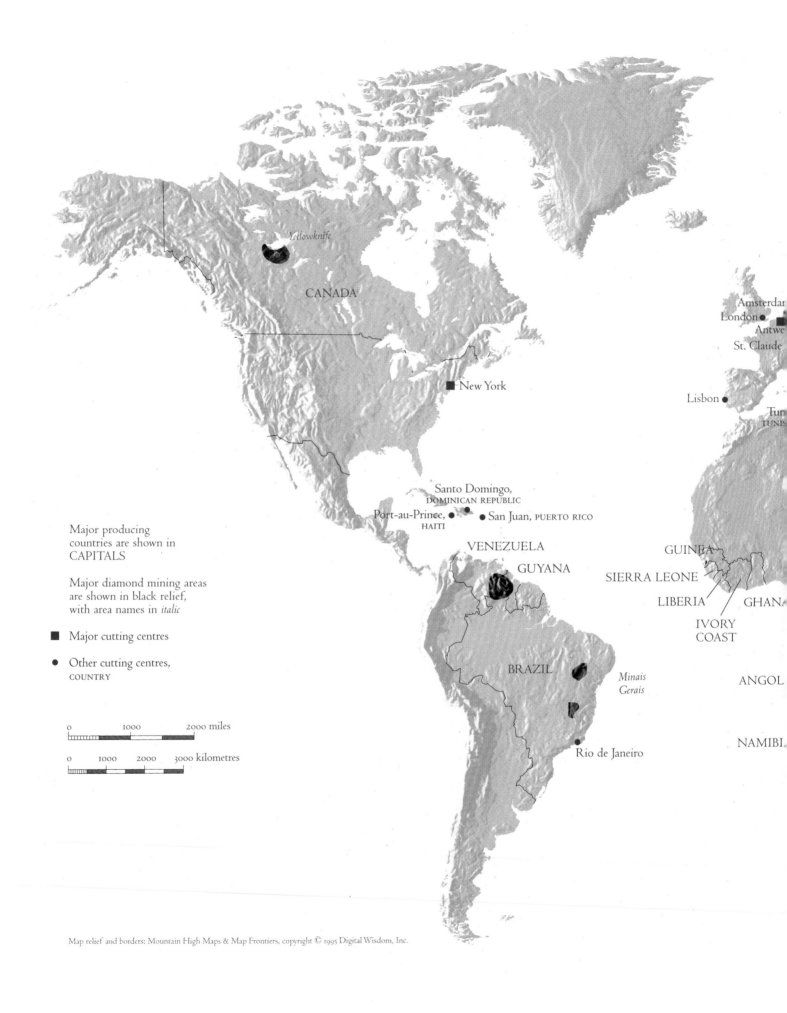

Yellowknife

CANADA

Amsterdar
London
Antwe
St. Claude

■ New York

Lisbon ●

Tun
TUNIS

Santo Domingo,
DOMINICAN REPUBLIC
Port-au-Prince, ● ● San Juan, PUERTO RICO
HAITI

VENEZUELA
GUYANA

GUINEA

SIERRA LEONE

LIBERIA   GHAN

IVORY
COAST

Major producing
countries are shown in
CAPITALS

Major diamond mining areas
are shown in black relief,
with area names in *italic*

■ Major cutting centres

● Other cutting centres,
COUNTRY

BRAZIL

*Minais
Gerais*

ANGOL

NAMIBI

Rio de Janeiro ●

0   1000   2000 miles

0   1000   2000   3000 kilometres

Archangel
RUSSIA
Sakha
Moscow

ar-Oberstein

Liaoning

etta, MALTA

Seoul
Tokyo
Tel Aviv
CHINA
Shanghai

Panna
T'ai-pei, TAIWAN
INDIA
Hong Kong
Surat
Mumbai
Viangchan, LAOS
Bangkok
Manila, PHILLIPPINES

Ho Chi Minh City

Colombo,
SRI LANKA
Sarawak, MALAYSIA
BORNEO
Kalimantan

NTRAL
RICAN
UBLIC
Jakarta
INDONESIA

MOCRATIC
EPUBLIC
OF
CONGO
TANZANIA
Aruska

Argyle

Zimbabwe
Port Louis,
MAURITIUS
andja
Serowe
Botswana
AUSTRALIA
Johannesburg
Swaziland
Lesotho

SOUTH
AFRICA
Perth

Agra

Recently recut, this light pink diamond was originally worn in his turban by the first Mogul emperor, Babur, after taking possession of the city of Agra in 1526.

No one should be surprised that an Indian diamond bears such an historic name. Agra is venerated as the site of the Taj Mahal, considered by generations of tourists and art critics alike to be the most sublime building in the world.

The city of Agra was founded by the Mogul Emperors who made it their capital for more than a hundred years in the sixteenth and seventeenth centuries until Aurangzeb, the sixth Emperor, transferred the seat of the monarchy to Delhi, in 1658. It was in Agra that Akbar received a letter from Queen Elizabeth I of England and Jahangir issued a charter to the British East India Company in 1612, granting it freedom to trade in India.

The legend of the Agra diamond begins in 1526 when Babur, the first Mogul Emperor (1483–1530), took possession of Agra after defeating the Rajah of Gwalior in battle. Born the son of Omar Sheik, King of Ferghana (Turkestan), Babur's real name was Zahir al-Din Muhammed, but he was given the sobriquet Babur, meaning the Tiger. He was both a brilliant soldier and a scholar, determined to become absolute ruler in India. After his success on the battlefield, Babur sent his son and successor, Humayun, to occupy Agra, a feat he duly accomplished, in the process capturing members of the family of the slain Rajah. Their lives were spared. It is said that as an expression of their gratitude they presented their captors with jewels and precious stones. Since it is recorded that Babur wore the Agra diamond in his turban, the stone was probably among those jewels.

It is likely that the Agra remained in the ownership of subsequent Mogul Emperors because Akbar (1556–1605), the third Emperor, was reputed to have worn the diamond in his headdress and Aurangzeb (1658–1707) had the stone lodged safely in his treasury. Later the Agra may have been among the loot captured by the Persian, Nadir Shah, when

he sacked Delhi in 1739. If that were so, then it must have been among the jewels recaptured when Nadir Shah encountered difficulties during the homeward journey because the gem returned to India.

The story of how a diamond of a pinkish hue, thought to have been the Agra, left India was told to Edwin Streeter, the famous London jeweller and author, by the 5th Marquess of Donegall in 1896. Lord Donegall stated that in 1857, the year of the Indian Mutiny, whilst he was serving in India, the diamond was taken from the ruler of Delhi. At the time he was engaged as secretary, and belonged to the same regiment as the young officer who had gained possession of the stone.

The officers decided to smuggle the diamond home to England rather than give it up, and to share the proceeds, but the question arose as to how to get it there. Nobody seemed able to suggest a method that would prove successful until the evening before the departure of the regiment. During the course of dinner the youngest subaltern suddenly jumped to his feet and said: 'I have it; we will conceal the diamond in a horse ball and make the horse swallow it.' The plan met with general approval. A ball was secured, the inside scooped out, the diamond inserted and the end stopped up. Finally the animal was made to swallow it. When the regiment reached the port of embarkation, the horse was – not surprisingly – taken ill and had to be shot. The diamond was then extracted from its stomach and taken to England.

There seems no reason to dispute the reality of these events, for what would be the purpose of inventing them? However, there is reason to cast doubt upon the date at which, it is said, they took place. We know that by 1844 the Agra was already in the possession of Charles, Duke of Brunswick, one of the nineteenth century's great collectors of jewels. The Duke of Brunswick paid 348,600 French

ازنخ وازسفیده وازسیاه وازرخت وازجنس ساحتها آوردۀ
فرمودم که درپیش من زیلوچه انداخشذارخ

30   Emperor Babur distributing
treasure at the city of Agra,
which he made the capital of
the Mogul Emperors during
the 16th century.

London, Victoria & Albert
Museum. Photo © V&A
Picture Library.

francs (£13,670), an enormous price, for the Agra on 22 November 1844 to Blogg, the name which appears in the 1860 catalogue of his jewels. Clearly this person must have been George Blogg, a partner in Blogg and Martin, a well known firm of diamond merchants in London. In addition the Duke bought three other diamonds from Blogg that same day and had previously bought four more from the same source on 8th November. A note in the catalogue specifically drew attention to the diamond having been taken by Babur in Agra in 1526 and to its position as being equal 14th in importance among the world's greatest diamonds.

In the normal course of events it would be unreasonable to expect a serving officer to possess a detailed knowledge of precious stones; on the other hand, accuracy would certainly be expected of the compiler of a catalogue such as that of the Duke of Brunswick's notable collection. One can only conclude, therefore, that the diamond devoured by the horse and subsequently smuggled to England was not the same stone as the one owned by the Duke of Brunswick, unless Lord Donegall's memory had played him false and the account he had related to Streeter referred to happenings before 1844. Possible confirmation of the existence of two separate diamonds is supplied by other writers who have stated that the smuggled stone weighed not 41 but 46 carats.

In due course the Agra was reduced in weight by recutting to $31^{13}/_{32}$ (32.24 metric carats). This was done so as to eliminate some black inclusions. The truth is even harder to come by as the result of a statement by an American visitor to Paris, the scene of the recutting, in 1899. He believed that the stone was the same one that he had owned for some time and which had formerly weighed 71 carats. Had the unfortunate horse then been forced to swallow an even greater caratage?

What is known for sure is that in 1891 Edwin Streeter purchased the Agra from Bram Hertz, one of the foremost diamond dealers in Paris and the man responsible for recutting the diamond. In exchange for the Agra, he gave Hertz a pearl necklace worth £14,000 and £1,000 in cash.

While Streeter was in possession of the Agra, in February 1895, it featured in a lawsuit that captured the attention of the public. One London newspaper hailed it as the 'Extraordinary Jewellery Case'. Certainly some of the allegations about the plaintiff, a young man named Joseph Charles Tasker, suggested that he was a true personage of the prevailing *fin de siècle* decadence. Indeed the ties between fact and fiction were further cemented because counsel for the defendants, Messrs Streeter and Co., was none other than Sir Edward Clarke who, less than two months later, was to appear for

Oscar Wilde at his famous trial. By the time he came to retire from the Bar, Sir Edward must have acquired a considerable degree of knowledge of historical diamonds because he also appeared for the owner of the Hope diamond in further litigation in July 1899.

In opening the case to the jury, Tasker's counsel, Mr Finlay, said that the action had been brought for the purpose of having certain alleged purchases made by his client declared invalid and set aside. The plaintiff was a gentleman aged 25 who, a few years earlier, had inherited a fortune of £700,000 from a relative. On 21st May 1894 Tasker, in company with his former tutor, Baron von Orsbach, went to Messrs Streeter's shop for the purpose of seeing a model of the Holy City set in jewels. While there he was introduced to a Mr Rogers who, in subsequent transactions, the jury would find acted as a canvasser for Streeter's. For the next three weeks Rogers seemed to have devoted himself to Tasker, lunching with him, dining with him and being constantly in his company. At that time the plaintiff was in feeble health owing to his intemperate habits, and was very often compelled to pass much of his time in bed.

Mr Finlay said that whenever Rogers saw Tasker he used to produce most costly gems which, it was alleged by the defendants, the plaintiff purchased. Within three weeks, goods worth £100,050 were alleged to have been bought. Furthermore Rogers produced the Agra diamond which the plaintiff was said to have bought while ill in bed for £15,000. Rogers also showed him a model of the Hope, saying that Streeter's would get it out of the Court of Chancery, where it then was, and sell it to him for £32,000. The plaintiff agreed to buy it at this price but, ultimately, the transaction came to nothing. Counsel then produced two 'experts' in Court to give their opinions concerning the value of the Agra. A Mr Jones, who said he was a dealer in precious stones, valued it at £8,000 while a Mr Spink valued it at £10,000. After the judge had overruled his submission that there was no case to go before the jury, Sir Edward Clarke addressed the jury.

Sir Edward said that when they considered the way in which this case had been launched and the way in which it had been conducted he did not doubt that they would think that no more unfair way of getting out of a bargain could be devised than that adopted by the plaintiff of traducing the tradesman with whom the bargain was entered into. This was a most serious attack on Mr Streeter and his employees. The case they had come to meet was that they had made a false representation, and by it the plaintiff was induced into these contracts. An attempt had been made to shirk the charge of misrepresentation, and to say now that the plaintiff was incapable of entering into any business transactions owing to his drunken habits. He was, however, surrounded by people who would have protected him if he was being attacked when in an unfit condition. Was it likely that Baron von Orsbach would have taken a man incapable through drink to Messrs Streeter's on the occasion of the exhibition of the Holy City?

Turning to the Agra, Clarke said that its purchase was not done in a single day. The bills in payment for it were brought ready drawn because the bargain had been made the day before. It was quite true that Mr Streeter, instead of giving actual money, had given jewellery worth £14,000 for the diamond, but having done this, he submitted that Mr Streeter was quite justified in saying that the diamond had cost him £14,000. That was not misrepresentation. The plaintiff had made this bargain and now wished to get out of it. It was arranged that he should pay the bills. When Mr Rowe and Mr Rogers, two employees of Streeter and Co., went to the hotel there was no secrecy or undue haste. The plaintiff's cousin looked at the bills before they were signed.

He submitted that there was no ground for saying that the defendants had taken advantage of the plaintiff or made any misrepresentations. Sir Edward then drew the jury's attention to the difference in the value of the jewels in dispute given by the two experts called in on behalf of the defendant, and said he would call others. Later during the proceedings they turned out to be a Mr Dodd, a diamond merchant, who stated that he had had thirty or forty years' experience in the trade. He considered that a stone of the size of the Agra was unique because of its rose-pink colour and that £15,000 was a fair price for a collector to pay. He was followed by a Mr James Amos Forster, of Holborn Viaduct, a wholesale diamond merchant with twenty-five years' experience. In his opinion the Agra was a pink-white stone of very unusual size; he had seen it seven years ago in Paris when the price asked was £20,000. It was a stone that would be saleable on the occasion of a Coronation or Royal Wedding. It would fetch anything from £14,000 to £20,000.

On the third day of the action Edwin Streeter gave evidence. After relating the circumstance of the purchase of the Agra from Hertz, Streeter said he had had plenty of experience of gems and that his book on diamonds was well known. When he wrote it there were not more than seventy diamonds above thirty carats known in the world. The rose-pink, the blue or the green varieties were rare. The Agra was thought cheap at £15,000. When cross-questioned about its so-called pedigree he said it had been written for him by a Colonel Birch, an Indian scholar, after the colonel had been to the India Office and obtained information. The pedigree spoke of the stone having been seen in the treasury of Aurungzebe [sic] in 1665 and previously it had been purchased by the Emperor Babur, the illustrious descendant of Timor, of Western Tartary, and founder of the Mogul Empire. It was also stated that Akbar had worn it in his headdress and that Nadir Shah had owned it. Under further cross-examination, Streeter said he knew nothing about the statements contained in the pedigree: he did not know that Babur died in 1530 and that Aurangzeb was not born until 1618 (inexplicable admissions by Streeter because he had narrated precisely the facts about the two rulers in his book *The Great Diamonds of the World*, published in 1882). Some comic relief was then supplied by the following exchange in Court:

Sir Edward Clarke: Is there only one Babur?
Mr Finlay: Only one Babur, founder of the Mogul Empire and only one Mr Streeter. (Loud laughter.)

Streeter then said he did not know who Aurangzeb was.

Mr Finlay: Was he a Frenchman?
Mr. Streeter: An Indian prince I should imagine from his name, but as I did not live in 1665 I cannot tell you. (Laughter.)
Mr Finlay: Did Hertz marry into the family of Nadir Shah?
Mr. Streeter: I do not know anything about Nadir Shah.
Mr Finlay: Is Mr Hertz a very old man? Because Nadir Shah died in 1747.
Mr. Streeter: He is about as old as myself.

Under further cross-examination, Streeter said that Hertz had told him the Agra had arrived in Europe and that he had it recut. He might, if he published a fresh edition, introduce a description of it in his book on the great diamonds of the world. He had never heard of the diamond until he bought it. He believed the stone was the only one of the kind in the world. He knew of no other Indian diamond of that colour.

On the fifth day, after the judge had summed up, the jury retired; four hours of deliberation resulted in a verdict for the plaintiff concerning certain items of jewellery and for the defendant concerning others. However, with regard to the Agra they found for the plaintiff, Tasker.

The year after this lawsuit, Lord Donegall related to Streeter his story of how a pink diamond, allegedly the Agra, had left India. Perhaps he had read of the court proceedings and wished to set the record straight, thereby in the process contradicting the researches of the Indian scholar, Colonel Birch – and the India Office too.

The Agra remained among Streeter's stock until he retired from business in 1904 when his successors, the Parisian firm of jewellers, La Cloche Frères, who had acquired the premises and stock through the United Investment Corporation, dispersed the contents. Many of the lower-priced items were bought by Debenham and Freebody. The remainder, comprising the more valuable items, were put up for sale in London by Christie's on 22nd February 1905. The Agra, as the highlight of the sale, was the final lot. It was described as 'a magnificent rose pink diamond of the highest quality, weight $31^{13}/_{32}$ carats'. Although no name was attached to the diamond, authorities considered it was the Agra. *The Times* reported that the sale attracted a large crowd of people, including a number of Indian collectors. The bidding opened at 1,000 guineas and, at 5,100 guineas, was knocked down to Mr Maz Meyer of Hatton Garden, with Mr S. Harris as the underbidder.

Four years later, on 24th June 1909, jewels belonging to the dealer Salomon Habib came up for auction in Paris. They comprised eight items: the fifth was the Idol's Eye and the eighth was the Hope. The sixth gem was a cushion-shaped rose-coloured diamond weighing $31^1/_2$ carats; it had a reserve price of 300,000 francs put on it but fetched only 82,000 francs. No name was attached to the stone although it is hard to believe that it can have been any diamond other than the Agra.

Shortly afterwards the gem was acquired by Mr Louis Winans. He had inherited a fortune from his father, William Walter Winans, an American railroad engineer from Baltimore, who built Russia's first commercial railway from St Petersburg to Moscow.

It was in 1843 that Tsar Nicholas I (1825–1855) invited George W. Whistler, half-brother of the artist, James McNeill Whistler, to be the consulting engineer on the proposed railway linking these cities. Whistler, in turn, asked Ross Winans, a leading engineer and inventor, to take charge of the mechanical department. However, Winans declined the invitation and sent his sons William and Thomas instead. The Winans brothers' contract was to equip the new Russian railway with locomotives and rolling stock and in so doing they established workshops in Alexandrovsky, near St Petersburg. When the railway was completed in 1851, Thomas Winans returned to Baltimore with his Russian wife, but William Winans stayed on until 1862 to complete existing contracts. In 1868 the Russian government took over the family's interests in return for the payment of a large bonus.

Louis Winans eventually settled at Brighton, in England, where he commissioned a local firm of jewellers, Lewis and Sons, to help form his remarkable collection of coloured diamonds. The Winans collection included some spectacular examples. Besides the Agra, which was the highlight, the Golden Drop, weighing 18.49 carats,

was one of the most intense and pure yellow diamonds of its size ever known.

The Agra and two other diamonds of this wonderful collection were put up for sale at Christie's in London on 20th June 1990, by the vendor who had inherited them in 1927. During the Second World War, she had commissioned her local blacksmith to make an iron casket and into this she placed the Agra along with all her jewels and coloured diamonds inherited from Louis Winans. This casket was buried in the garden and was still safely in place at the end of the war.

The Agra was certified by the Gemological Institute of America (GIA) as a fancy light pink natural colour, VSI2. It measured 21.10 by 19.94 by 11.59mm. It was expected to fetch £1,500,000 but, after fierce bidding, was sold for £4,070,000, thus making it the most expensive pink diamond in the world. The successful bid, made by telephone, came from the SIBA Corporation of Hong Kong. The total value of gems and jewellery sold in this record breaking auction reached £12,900,000. Since that appearance the Agra has been recut to a modified cushion shape, weighing 28.15 carats.

Edwin W. Streeter, the celebrated London jeweller whose 1895 evidence in court contradicted what he had written about the Agra in 1882.

Akbar Shah

The Mogul ruler Jahangir holding the portrait of his father Akbar, after whom this mysterious diamond was misnamed.

Early 17th century Indian miniature. Paris, Musée Guimet. Photo AKG London/ Erich Lessing.

This is one of the historic Indian diamonds which, before an act of vandalism, bore two inscriptions in Persian. In *The Great Diamonds of the World* Streeter incorrectly ascribed the first inscription to the reign of the third Mogul Emperor, Akbar (1556–1605) whereas the date gives the name of the diamond's first recorded owner as his son, Jahangir (1605–1627), whose Persian wife led him to encourage Persian culture in Mogul India.

The son of the Emperor responsible for the building of the great citadel of Fatehpur Sikri, Jahangir was the father of another great builder, Shah Jahan. He took the title of Jahangir, meaning 'World-Grasper', on ascending the throne, but he was for the most part content to let others perform the task of conquest. Jahangir's interests lay in other directions – principally in women and the culture of his court. He was also a lover of jewels, and his journal, the *Tuzuk-i-Jahangiri* or *Memoirs of Jahangir*, contains several references to diamonds and the methods of mining that are of especial interest.

The first inscription on the misnamed 'Akbar Shah' diamond denotes that it was officially entered into Jahangir's treasury between 10 March and 7 December 1619. It is possible that it may have been one of a group of diamonds which he acquired in September 1618 while he was in Gujarat. He recorded the occasion as follows:

On Friday the 5th [of the Persian month Mihr] Bahram, son of Jahangir Quli Khan, came from the province of Bihar, and had the good fortune to pay his respects. He laid before me some diamonds he had obtained from the mine at Kokhra.

There are three references to the diamond deposits situated within the province of Bihar whence Bahram had travelled westwards to Gujarat.

In the spring of 1616 the Emperor wrote:

The third piece of news was the conquest of the province of Khokara and the acquisition of the diamond mines, which

were taken by the excellent exertions of Ibrahim Khan. This province is one of the dependencies of the Subah of Bihar and Patna. There is a river there from which they procure diamonds. At the season when there is little water, there are pools and water-holes, and it has become known by experience to those who are employed in this work that above every water-hole in which there are diamonds, there are crowds of flying animals of the nature of gnats, and which in the language of India they call *ihinga*. Keeping the bed of the stream in sight as far as it is accessible, they make a collection of stones (*sanqchin*) round the water-holes. After this, they empty the water-holes with spades and shovels to the extent of a yard or 1½ yards [about 1 metre] and dig up the area. They find among the stones and sand large and small diamonds and bring them out. It occasionally happens that they find a piece of diamond worth 1,000,000 rupees … That province is now in the possession of the imperial servants of the State. They carry on the work in the bed of the stream, and bring to Court whatever diamonds are found. A large diamond, the value of which had been estimated at 50,000 rupees, has lately been brought from here. If a little pains are taken, it is probable that good diamonds will be found and placed in the jewel-room.

The Emperor's second reference to this particular source occurs in his account of the summer of 1618 after he has mentioned the existence of another mine in the province of Khandesh which, he considered, produced finer diamonds. It reads:

Of the second rank is the mine of Kokhra, which is on the borders of Bihar; but the diamonds of that place are not obtained from the mine, but from a river which in the rainy season comes down in flood from the hills. Before that they dam it up, and when the flood has passed over the dam and there is little water, a number of men who are skilled in this art go into the river bed and bring out the diamonds.

The third mention of diamonds from Bihar in Jahangir's journal occurs just after his account of receiving diamonds from Bahram in September 1618. He writes:

Some of the diamonds that Ibrahim Fathjang had sent to Court after the taking of the mine had been given to the Government lapidaries to cut. At this time Bahram suddenly

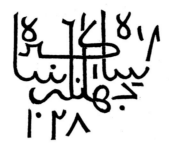

AKBAR SHAH

came to Agra and was going on to the Court (in Gujarat). Khwaja Jahan (the Governor of Agra) sent along with him some diamonds that were ready. One of them is of a violet colour and cannot be outwardly distinguished from a sapphire. Up to this time I had not seen a diamond of this colour. It weighed several *surkh*, and jewellers estimated its value at 3000 rupees, and represented that if it had been white (*safid*) and had had perfect marks, it would have been worth 20,000 rupees.

The mines which Jahangir refers to are situated at Khukra, about 64 km west of Ranchi in the Chota Nagpur district of the State of Bihar. Little is known about diamonds from this region; more often than not it is omitted from lists and maps of India's diamond-bearing areas. The methods employed to recover the stones do not appear to differ much from those in use in alluvial areas in other parts of the world more than three hundred and fifty years later. But what is of exceptional interest is the revelation of the discovery of a diamond of a violet colour, not outwardly distinguishable from a sapphire. This description, of course, fits the Hope diamond perfectly. It is not suggested that the original rough piece from which that famous gem was fashioned came from this region of Bihar – it is usually considered to have come from the Kollur deposits in Hyderabad – but it may possibly have been found there.

The second inscription that appeared on Jahangir's diamond recorded its ownership by his son and successor Shah Jahan (1628–58), who took the title Sahib-i Qiran-i Sani, meaning 'The Second Lord of the (Auspicious) Conjunction' in emulation of his ancestor Timur. The inscription denotes that the diamond came into his treasury some time between January and August 1629, although Shah Jahan would have inherited it on his accession in January of the preceding year.

Tradition has it that the Akbar Shah, which weighed 116 carats, was set as one of the eyes of the famous and fabulous Peacock Throne. On the other hand, as the largest of the three candidates (the others being the Shah and the Jahangir) it may have been the big diamond which Tavernier described as having been set as a pendant. Whatever its setting

may have been, the stone was lost sight of until it came to light in Constantinople in 1866. It is reasonable to assume that this was one of the diamonds carried off by Nadir Shah and the Persians when they sacked and pillaged Delhi in 1739. George Blogg, of the London firm of Blogg and Martin, purchased it in Turkey where it was known as the 'Shepherd's Stone' – could such a name have had any connection with Nadir Shah, who in his youth was a shepherd? Blogg brought the diamond to London where a cutter named Auerhaan recut it to a pear-shape of 71.70 (old) carats, equivalent to 73.60 metric carats. During the process of recutting the vandalic act of obliterating the ancient inscriptions on the diamond was perpetrated. In the following year Blogg sold the diamond to that famed collector Mulhar Rao, Gaekwar of Baroda, for £35,000. That is the last known fact in the history of the gem.

It is puzzling that Streeter should have headed his account of this diamond 'The Akbar Shah, or Jehan Ghir Shah' and one can only wonder whether he was aware of the existence of a separate diamond called the 'Jahangir' or whether he thought they were one and the same stone. The Jahangir, weighing approximately 83 metric carats, is another diamond bearing two inscriptions. The upper inscription is partly obscured by the hole that has been pierced through the stone but enough remains to show that it reads: 'Shah Jahangir-e (son) of Akbar Shah 1021' (AD 1612). The lower inscription reads: 'Shah Jahan (son) of Jahangir Shah 1042' (AD 1632). This diamond was formerly owned by the Maharajah of Burdwan who sold it in London in 1954, thereby contravening the (Indian) Antiquities Export Control Act. He and a Calcutta jeweller were fined £13,000, the amount it fetched at the sale, but the Indian government subsequently upheld the Maharajah's appeal against the fine on the grounds that it had failed to inform him that the gem was a historic one whose export was prohibited until after the sale had taken place. The buyer on that occasion was Mr Stavros Niarchos who, three years later, put it up for auction at Sotheby's in London where it was bought by an Indian businessman, Mr C. Patel.

Opposite: The Akbar Shah was said to have been set as one of the eyes of the famous Peacock throne under which Shah Jahan, son of Jahangir, is here seated.

London, Victoria & Albert Museum. Photo © V&A Picture Library.

Allnatt

The Allnatt diamond in its magnificent setting which Cartier designed in 1952 and the jeweller's original drawing (this page).

When Porter Rhodes travelled to the Isle of Wight in 1881 to show his fine white diamond to Queen Victoria and the Empress Eugénie of France, who was then residing nearby, he helped to destroy a myth: namely that South African diamonds were usually yellowish in colour and so less valuable. Both the Queen and, in particular, the Empress, who was knowledgeable about diamonds, believed this to be true and were, therefore, surprised to examine a fine white octahedron originating from the Cape. It was not until the Excelsior was found in 1893, the Jubilee in 1895 and, above all, the discovery of the Premier mine in 1902 that South Africa finally achieved recognition as the source of large white diamonds as well as yellow ones.

The early years of the South African diamond mining industry certainly witnessed the appearance, in unprecedented numbers, of large yellow stones, many of them octahedral in shape. The reigning Shah of Persia, Nasir ud-Din Shah (1848–1860) was among the first to appreciate them because he added numerous yellow diamonds to the Crown Jewels of Iran. A few, including the Tiffany, came from the Kimberley mine but by far the greatest number originated in the De Beers mine, which is the likely source of the Allnatt.

This 102.07-carat cushion cut, the colour of which has been certified by the GIA as Fancy Intense Yellow, is named after its former owner, Alfred Ernest Allnatt. He was a soldier, a sportsman, an active patron of the arts and a noted benefactor in many spheres. He paid a world record price for the *Adoration of the Magi* by Rubens which he then presented to King's College, Cambridge, as an altarpiece for its famous chapel. He also had a passion for the Turf and bought eleven yearlings formerly owned by the late Sir Sultan Mohammed Aga Khan; he commented at the time, 'All I know

about horses is that they are nice things to amble about on.' The Aga Khan also owned several exceptional diamonds, among them the 33.13-carat pear shape Aga Khan III, which came up for sale by Christie's in Geneva in May 1988.

Major Allnatt did not buy any of the Aga Khan's diamonds to add to his yearlings, but he did purchase this very fine diamond, and in the early fifties he commissioned Cartier to design a setting. It was auctioned by Christie's, again in Geneva, in May 1996. On that occasion it realized the extraordinary sum of $3,043,496.

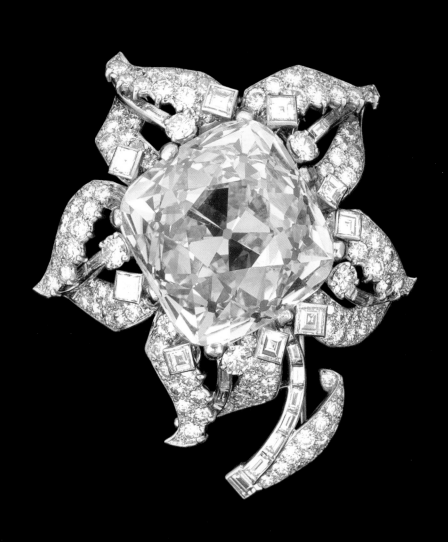

ARCHDUKE JOSEPH

Archduke Joseph

This 78.54-carat diamond takes it name from a previous owner, the Archduke Joseph August (1872–1962), a prince of the Hungarian line of the Habsburg dynasty. The Archduke was a descendant of the Emperor Leopold II, son of the Empress Maria Theresa who owned the famous Florentine diamond, one of the great gems of history and for many years an heirloom of the Habsburgs. But whereas the Florentine was, unusually for a large Indian diamond, light yellow in colour, the Archduke Joseph is a colourless gem; it possesses the most notable characteristic of the finest Golconda diamonds, namely an internal limpidity. Hence its 'D' colour certification. It is cut as a somewhat old-fashioned cushion shape, perhaps a style of cutting that is not wholly incongruous with its Indian provenance. Is it entirely fanciful to suggest that improvements in the techniques of cutting diamonds, during this century, are more suited to diamonds found principally in Africa?

The Archduke Joseph – better known as Joseph of Alcsut – was the eldest son of Duke Joseph Carl Ludwig and Princess Clothilde of Saxe-Coburg. In 1893 he married Augusta, daughter of Prince Leopold of Bavaria and Duchess Gisela, and a grand-daughter of the Emperor Franz Joseph. He began his distinguished military career in 1902 when he enlisted in the Hungarian territorial reserve, simultaneously studying law at Budapest University. On the death of the Emperor Franz Joseph he became Commander of the Hungarian front-line forces during the First World War, reconquering the eastern section of Siebenburgen and initiating the negotiations for a cease-fire. In October 1918 he was named Regent of Hungary by the Emperor Charles I, but his efforts to form a government were overturned by the onset of the 31 October Revolution, whereupon he retired to his Alcsut estate.

During the so-called 'Traitor Republic', on account of his great popularity, Archduke Joseph was put under surveillance whilst remaining at Alcsut. In August 1919 he did succeed in becoming Regent of Hungary but was compelled to resign within two months because the Allies would not allow a Habsburg to hold a commanding position in Hungary. At the end of 1944 he emigrated to the United States and later returned to Europe to live with his sister, Princess Margaret von Thurn und Taxis, and published several reminiscences and historical studies. He died in 1962, not completely retired from politics, having become a member of the Upper House soon after its restoration.

It is believed that at some point he gave the diamond to his son, Joseph Francis (1895–1957). Minutes taken on 1 June 1933 record that the diamond, then the property of Archduke Joseph, was at the time deposited with the Hungarian General Credit Bank in the presence of a State Counsellor. Three years later the diamond was sold to a European banker who kept it in a safe deposit box in France during the war where it fortunately escaped the attention of the Nazis.

The whereabouts of the stone remained a mystery until it came up for auction in London in June 1961. At the time it was believed to be the largest unmounted fine quality diamond ever to have been auctioned in Great Britain, but it was withdrawn from sale when the bidding stopped at £145,000. Subsequently it was reported that a syndicate of Hatton Garden buyers had made an unsuccessful bid for the gem. It came up for sale again at Christie's in Geneva in November 1993, when it was sold for $6,487,945.

A cushion-shaped diamond with all the prerequisites of the finest Golconda diamonds: an internal limpidity with 'D' colour certification.

Arcots

Mohammad Ali Khan, the Nawab of Arcot, who gave seven diamonds to Queen Charlotte in 1777.

Portrait by Tilly Kettle, Madras, 1770.

Opposite page: the Arcot I set as a pendant in a necklace designed by Van Cleef & Arpels, after it had been recut by Harry Winston in order to obtain greater brilliance and clarity.

De Beers Archives.

The Hanoverian rulers of Great Britain accumulated a large collection of personal jewellery and Queen Charlotte, the consort of King George III, was certainly no exception. She received many jewels, the most notable being the diamonds she accepted from the Nawab of Arcot. These included five brilliants, the largest of which weighed 38.6 carats, was oval-shaped and was subsequently set in a necklace with the two smallest stones. The other two diamonds were pear-shaped and were set as earrings; one weighed 33.70 carats and the other 23.65 carats. These two have become known as the Arcot diamonds.

Arcot, a town near Madras, became famous for its capture and defence by Clive in 1751, during the war between the rival claimants to the throne of the Carnatic. It passed into British hands in 1801 following the resignation of the government of Nawab Azim-ud-daula, who had given the diamonds to Queen Charlotte in 1777.

The Queen died in 1818 and under the terms of her will the Arcots were ordered to be sold to Rundell & Bridge, who in 1804 had been appointed jewellers and silversmiths to the Crown by George III. The clause about her 'Personals' read:

... of chief value being the jewels. First those which the King bought for £50,000 and gave to me. Secondly those presented to me by the Nawab of Arcot... I give and bequeath the jewels received from the Nawab of Arcot to my four remaining daughters, or to the survivors or survivor in case they or any of them should die before me, and I direct that these jewels should be sold and that the produce... shall be divided among them, my said remaining daughters or their survivors, share and share alike.

However, a delay ensued in implementing the Queen's will. This was the result of the attitude taken by her eldest son, George IV, who, upon the death of his father in 1820, decided that the whole of his father's property devolved upon himself, not upon the Crown. Consequently he appropriated the

money and the jewels and acted in a similar manner with regard to his mother's jewellery. The Arcots were, therefore, set in the crown made for George IV and later in the crown made for Queen Adelaide, the consort of his successor, William IV.

The terms of Queen Charlotte's will concerning the items of jewellery were thus not executed until many years after she had died. In 1834, John Bridge of Rundell & Bridge died; the firm was sold and his executors ordered the sale of the Arcots together with the round brilliant which may have been the Hastings diamond and which had also been set in the crown made for George IV. The historic sale took place in London at Willis's Rooms in St James's on 20 July 1837. The first Marquess of

44

ARCOTS

Westminster bought the Arcots for £11,000 as part of a birthday present for his wife; he also bought the round brilliant and the Nassak diamond.

The Arcots and the other diamonds remained in the possession of the Grosvenor family for many years. In 1930 the Parisian jeweller Lacloche mounted the Arcots in the Westminster Tiara, of bandeau form, together with the round brilliant and no less than 1421 smaller diamonds. The tiara was pierced to form a design of pavé-set scrolls with arcading, and with clusters of navette-shaped diamonds between the sections, tapering slightly at the sides, with baguette diamond banding framing the large centre stone and with diamond baguettes dispersed singly throughout the ornament. In her memoirs, Loelia, Duchess of Westminster, third wife of the second Duke, wrote of the Arcots, 'fixed by themselves on the safety-pin they looked extremely bogus, so that a friend who saw me that evening remarked, "What on earth does Loelia think she's doing, pinning those two lumps of glass on herself?"'

In June 1959 the third Duke of Westminster sold the Westminster tiara to help meet the cost of heavy death-duties. Harry Winston paid £110,000 for it at an auction – then a world record price for a piece of jewellery. Mr Winston had the two Arcots recut to obtain greater clarity and brilliance, the larger to 30.99 metric carats and the smaller to 18.85 metric carats. Each was remounted as a ring and sold to American clients in 1959 and 1960 respectively. Arcot I was then set as the pendant to a diamond necklace by Van Cleef & Arpels and was later auctioned at Christie's in Geneva in November 1993 when it was bought by Sheik Ahmed Hassan Fitaihi, the Saudi Arabian dealer.

Queen Charlotte, consort of King George III and an avid diamond collector, portrayed by Allan Ramsay.

45

The Royal Collection
© Her Majesty the Queen.

Opposite page: the Duchess of Westminster wearing the Westminster tiara in which the Arcots were mounted. The diamonds could be extracted from the tiara and worn separately as earrings.
Photograph by Cecil Beaton.

© *Vogue*, August 15, 1931.
Courtesy *Vogue*. Copyright © 1931 (renewed 1959, 1987) by the Condé Nast Publications Inc.

Banjarmasin

The formation in the mid-1980s of a consortium, comprising an Australian public company, a British private concern and a firm representing the Indonesian government, to search for and to mine diamonds in the Banjarmasin/Martapura area of Kalimantan will have done much to revive interest in Bornean diamonds. The northern part of the island, now part of Malaysia, has been opened to tourism but the central and southern parts, known as Kalimantan and ruled by Indonesia, have remainded relatively unknown to the outside world. Far removed from international airports, Kalimantan is a remote region and an adventurous challenge.

At the same time we should be grateful to the Dutch historian, René Brus, known for his research into the Dutch regalia and Crown Jewels, for acquainting us with much of the recent history of an important Bornean diamond.

In 1836 an expedition of Dutch scientists travelled to Borneo and after months of travel arrived at Banjarmasin, in the south of Kalimantan. One member of the party, Salomon Muller, published an account of the visit in 1857. According to him the visitors were received by the Sultan, Panenlaka Adam, in a palace described as rather a ramshackle affair which had clearly seen better days. However, in the midst of the abject poverty the travellers noticed the extremes of wealth evinced by the Sultan who wore a brocade robe and was dressed from head to foot in silks with gold and diamonds scattered around his person. His jewels included both diamond rings and earrings. The largest and most valuable stone was, according to Muller's reckoning, a diamond of 77 carats set in a gold pendant. It was an uncut octahedron and hung from a simple piece of string round the Sultan's neck. This stone and a gold medallion, surrounded by precious gems and inscribed in both Dutch and Malay, were the most valuable possessions of the Sultan. In general, diamonds accounted for the greatest part of the wealth of the Sultan and his immediate family. This particular ruler is said to have been of a very benign disposition, not imbued with intelligence and totally ruled by Njai Komala, his eldest and tight-fisted wife. The Dutch visitors were told that this woman owned wine bottles full of diamonds as well as money, all this wealth being buried in the ground beneath her chambers in the palace.

The Banjarmasin region then had a population of 100,000 and was governed by the Sultan without recourse to a written constitution. He received a monthly income from the Dutch government of 1,000 guilders which, he complained, was quite insufficient for his needs since he was a great admirer of female beauty and, apart from his four wives, had at least 60 young concubines in his harem. The philosophy of life of this easy-going ruler was 'Gentlemen are not suited to work: They must be amused.' Apparently his entire family was happy to accept and to enact this philosophy.

There are no records to indicate when the 77-carat diamond entered the Banjarmasin treasury. It may have come into Sultan Adam's possession after his accession in 1825. But the stone was destined not to remain much longer in Borneo because following the Sultan's death civil war engulfed his realm and the Dutch colonial authorities decided to dissolve the sultanate. On 25 June 1859, the centuries-old Banjarmasin sultanate ceased to exist; the regalia and other valuable possessions of the late ruler passed into the hands of the Dutch. Amongst this haul was the 77-carat diamond which arrived at Rotterdam on 24 April 1862. From that moment the diamond became known as the 'Banjarmasin'. When it was weighed it was found to be 70 carats.

The fame of the Banjarmasin became so widespread following its arrival in Europe that King

William III of the Netherlands (1849–1890) expressed a wish to inspect the stone before it was sent to the Museum of Natural History in Leiden. But the stone never got as far as the museum because the board of directors decided not to accept this specimen for the museum's collection. Since no other Dutch museum wanted the Banjarmasin the Minister for the Colonies decided to sell it. Government officials and so-called experts expected the diamond to fetch around 300,000 guilders; but no buyer appeared, even after the firm E. and J. Vital Israels of Amsterdam had cut it into a white, rather square-cut gem, weighing approximately 40 carats.

From this point onwards the history of the Banjarmasin is a testimony to the oafish stupidity of bureaucracy. After the diamond had been cut the Dutch ministers were undecided about what to do with it. They finally decided to place the gem among the collections of the Rijksmuseum as a 'historical memento'. But eleven years were to elapse before the necessary papers were written and signed, and a safe showcase had been constructed to house this important acquisition. Then on 20 December 1897, the government changed its mind, deciding that the Banjarmasin had neither artistic value nor historical significance because the rough crystal was no longer in existence – this despite the unrivalled reputation of its fellow countrymen as connoisseurs of all aspects of the diamond. It seems that none of the responsible authorities was aware that in neighbouring countries such as France and England important historical diamonds had changed through the years due to cutting or recutting, and were nonetheless regarded as valuable objects to be treasured and protected with care as well as displayed publicly.

Once more E. and J. Vital Israels were called upon, on this occasion to handle the sale of the Banjarmasin, but they were unable to obtain a price acceptable to the government, and the gem was returned to the dreaded ministerial hands in 1902. It was then decided that the right moment had come to send the diamond again to the Rijksmuseum: the museum would not own it but simply display it, on loan from the Kingdom of the Netherlands, which remained the gem's sole owner. The Banjarmasin was exhibited in the museum together with the jewellery of the Rajah of Lombok, which had been taken as booty by the Dutch forces in the Dutch East Indies. Lombok had suffered a fate similar to that of Banjarmasin: at the end of the nineteenth century the kingdom ceased to exist and the ruler's treasury had subsequently changed hands.

The authorities again sought the assistance of E. and J. Vital Israels when the firm was requested to appraise the Lombok treasure, in particular the precious stones. This led to the sale of some unset stones, the remaining items being dispatched to the Rijksmuseum. At first the curators intended to place all this hoard of treasure, including the Banjarmasin diamond, on display for just two months, but because of the great stream of visitors it was prolonged for a month. Before the exhibition closed nearly 23,000 people had seen the display. Any hopes that such precious objects, which were state property, might be put on permanent display were not fulfilled; by now the interest of the authorities had waned to such an extent that they did not even bother to make a detailed inventory.

With the establishment of the Republic of Indonesia after the conclusion of the Second World War, the Dutch authorities were obliged to take a renewed interest in the diamonds and other gems. After years of discussions between the Dutch and Indonesian governments some form of agreeement was finally reached in 1977 whereby 250 pieces of jewellery were returned to Indonesia. The Banjarmasin, however, was not among these items and the gem remains to this day the property of the Kingdom of the Netherlands, sadly reposing in a dark vault, hidden from view.

Strangely deprived its just recognition the 40-carat Banjarmasin has remained hidden from public view in a Dutch vault for over twenty years.
Courtesy René Brus.

Beau Sancy

The Beau Sancy diamond.

Courtesy Prince Hohenzollern.

Nicholas Harlay de Sancy, diplomat, financier and ardent monarchist, is remembered as the owner of the 55.23-carat pear-shaped diamond, the Sancy, one of the most celebrated gems of history. Sancy also owned another sizeable and beautiful diamond whose existence was documented on 31 January 1589 as follows:

A great flawless diamond, facet cut, weight 37 to 38 carats or thereabouts, set in a golden frame at the end of which hangs a great round pearl, flawless and perfect, of about 20 carats; also a great heart-shaped ruby set in gold at the base of which hangs a great pear-shaped pearl, for the price of 20,000 ecus. The large jewels were pledged and put into the hands of the said Sieur de Sancy that he might pawn them in Switzerland, Germany or elsewhere with the charge that if they were pledged for less than 24,000 ecus. His Majesty will only pay to the said Sancy the price for which they were pledged.

This diamond came to be known as the 'Beau Sancy' or 'Little Sancy' and was destined to pursue a different course of history from Sancy's larger diamond. The Beau Sancy is a colourless, rounded pear shape, cut with a total of 108 facets, plus the table and culet.

Both of Nicholas de Sancy's diamonds came to be the subject of protracted negotiations with parties in Constantinople and the Duke of Mantua, a connoisseur and avid collector of fine gems. On 10 October 1589, Sancy wrote to M. de la Brosse, who was acting on behalf of the Duke:

One of my diamonds weighs 60 [old] carats, the other 34 [old] carats. I want nothing less than 80,000 ecus for the big diamond and 60,000 for the smaller. If it pleases His Highness to take one or both of them, I will sell them to him, but I wish ready money, or most of it guaranteed, for the rest, in Venice or in France, and wish no delay which for the most shall exceed three years.

The negotiations with the Duke of Mantua continued well into 1604 and ultimately came to nothing. Instead, Sancy sold the larger diamond to King James I of England. There remained the Beau Sancy which, in 1604, was bought for merely 25,000 ecus by Marie de Médicis, the consort of King Henry IV of France. In *The French Crown Jewels*, Bernard Morel suggests that it is a strong bet that the King himself paid for the diamond in order to assuage the feelings of indignation aroused in the Queen when she learned that Sancy had sold his bigger diamond to the King of England. The Beau Sancy was set in the top of the crown which Marie de Médicis wore at her Coronation in 1610.

After the murder of Henry IV in the same year, the Queen became Regent and devoted herself to affairs of state; she developed a passion for power which led to civil unrest in France and estrangement from her son, King Louis XIII. Marie de Médicis was exiled in disgrace to Compiègne, escaped to Brussels in 1631 and died at Cologne in 1642, having intrigued in vain against Cardinal Richelieu, the statesman who is acknowledged as the architect of France's greatness in the seventeenth century. She died in straitened financial circumstances which led to the sale of her possessions to pay her debts. The Beau Sancy was sold to Frederick Henry, Prince of Orange, for 80,000 florins. It is said that history never repeats itself but does sometimes produce curious parallels: in 1644, two years after the death of Marie de Médicis, her daughter, Queen Henrietta Maria, the wife of Charles I, King of England, was forced to pawn Sancy's larger diamond so as to raise funds to support the Royalist cause in the Civil War in England.

Prince Frederick Henry (1584–1647), the son of William the Silent, the principal leader of the Dutch struggle for independence from Spain, achieved fame as a general and a politician. He was the first of this line to assume, as leader of the United Provinces of Holland, a semi-monarchical status and to determine both domestic and foreign policies. Until the age of 41 it was said of him that he was 'too fond of women to tie himself permanently to one of them'. He did eventually succumb, to Amalia van Solms, a lady-in-waiting to the exiled Queen of Bohemia. The Princess of Holland thereupon endeavoured to endow the Hague in the seventeenth century with some semblance of baroque court life.

It was a grandson of Prince Frederick Henry who, in 1689, ascended the throne of England as William III. He inherited the Beau Sancy and gave it to his consort, Queen Mary II, as a wedding gift. The couple were childless so the diamond came into the possession of another grandson of the Prince of Orange, Frederick III, Elector Prince of Brandenburg, who, in 1701, became King of Prussia under the name of Frederick I. Valued at 300,000 Reichstalers, the Beau Sancy became the most important stone in the Crown Jewels of Prussia and was set in the royal crown. In an inventory of the jewels made in 1913 the diamond featured as the pendant to a necklace of 22 diamonds, part of a diamond suite which also included a large breast ornament, a pair of earrings and a fan.

The Beau Sancy is now in the possession of the head of the house of Hohenzollern, Prince Louis-Ferdinand of Prussia, grandson of William II, the last Emperor of Germany.

Marie de Médicis, Queen of France, bought the Beau Sancy in 1604. Set in the top of a crown, it was worn at her coronation as Regent of France in 1610.

Portrait by Frans Pourbus, 1609. Paris, Musée du Louvre. Photo AKG London/Erich Lessing.

49

BEAU SANCY

Blue Heart

Of a rare dark blue, the Blue Heart diamond remains a favourite among specialists today, although its origins remain a mystery.

Courtesy Smithsonian Institution.

Some accounts refer to this rare diamond as the 'Eugénie Blue' although it is now recognized that there is no evidence of its having been owned by the Empress. Had she owned it, might the Empress Eugénie not have chosen to flee with this valuable gem rather than the diamond which is named after her? However, a French connection does exist because the cutting firm of Atanik Eknayan of Neuilly, Paris, cut this heart shape, weighing 30.82 metric carats and of a rare dark blue colour, in 1909 and 1910. This date raises the question whether the rough stone came from India or Africa.

In 1910 Cartier's purchased the diamond and sold it to an Argentinian woman named Mrs Unzue. At the time, it was set in a lily-of-the-valley corsage and remained so until Van Cleef & Arpels acquired the gem in 1953. They exhibited it as the pendant to a necklace valued at $300,000 and sold the jewel to a European titled family. In 1959 Harry Winston acquired the diamond, selling it five years later, mounted in a ring, to Marjorie Merriweather Post. Finally Mrs Merriweather Post donated the Blue Heart to the Smithsonian Institution in Washington where it remains on display today.

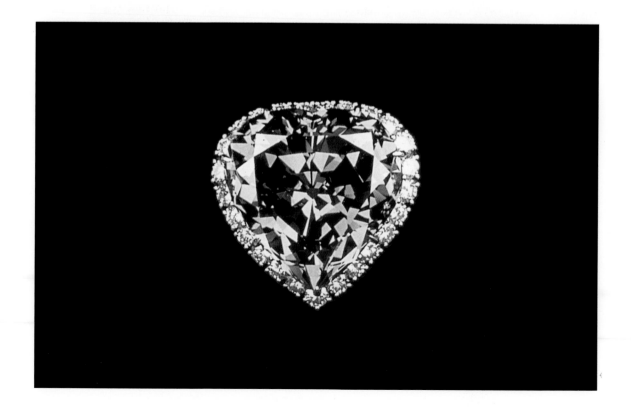

Braganza

Confusion, conjecture and considerable doubt about its authenticity as a diamond surround the Braganza – or 'King of Portugal' as it is sometimes called. The gem is said to have been the size of a goose's egg and to have weighed no less than 1,680 carats in the rough; such a weight would have meant that in the event of it having been a diamond, it would have exceeded all known gem-quality diamonds before the discovery of the Cullinan. However, there have always been suggestions that the Braganza was not a diamond but some other species of gemstone, most likely a white topaz. The earliest and most detailed version of the stone's discovery appeared in John Mawe's *Travels in Brazil*, published in 1812:

A few leagues to the north of the Rio Plata is the rivulet named Abaité, celebrated for having produced the largest diamond in the Prince's [King of Portugal's] possession, which was found about twelve years ago... Three men having been found guilty of high crimes were banished into the interior, and ordered not to approach any of the capital towns, or to remain in civilized society on pain of perpetual imprisonment. Driven by this hard sentence into the most unfrequented part of the country, they endeavoured to explore new mines or new productions, in the hope that, sooner or later, they might have the good fortune to make some important discovery, which would obtain a reversal of their sentence, and enable them to regain their stations in society. They wandered about in this neighbourhood... for more than six years, during which time they were exposed to a double risk, being continually liable to become the prey of the Anthropophagi, and in no less danger of being seized by the soldiers of the Government. At length they by hazard made some trials in the river Abaité, at a time when its waters were so low, in consequence of a long season of drought, that a part of its bed was left exposed. Here... they had the good fortune to find a diamond nearly an ounce [28g] in weight. Elated by this providential discovery, ... yet hesitating between a dread of the rigorous laws relating to the diamonds and a hope of regaining their liberty, they consulted a clergyman who accompanied them to the Villa-Rica, where he procured them access to the Governor. They threw themselves at his feet, and delivered to him the invaluable gem on which their hopes rested, relating all the circumstances connected with it. The Governor, astonished at its magnitude,

could not trust the evidence of his senses, but called the officers of the establishment to decide whether it was a diamond, who set the matter beyond all doubt. Being thus by the most strange and unforeseen accident put in the possession of the largest diamond ever found in America, he thought proper to suspend the sentence of the men as a reward for their having delivered it to him. The gem was sent to Rio de Janeiro, from where a frigate was despatched with it to Lisbon. The sovereign confirmed the pardon of the delinquents and bestowed some preferment on the holy father.

It is interesting to note that Mawe states that the weight of the diamond was about one ounce (144 old carats); moreover he repeated this figure in his *A Treatise on Diamonds and Precious Stones* published in 1823. Later authorities who have written about the Braganza have incorrectly attributed the weight of 1,680 carats to Mawe, a figure subsequently repeated in most accounts of the stone's history. If the Braganza had weighed as much, Mawe would certainly not have referred to it as having been merely the largest diamond found in America, but the largest ever found anywhere.

There is on record the discovery of a diamond in 1791 which weighed 144 carats in the rough and was almost an octahedron in shape. Since it too is said to have been found by three criminals who, with the assistance of a priest, subsequently gained their freedom, it is clear that this must be the same gem which Mawe refers to as the Braganza. In this connection, Brazilian mineralogists have said that this gem was found in an area where only diamonds, not topaz, are found.

Nevertheless, there are indications that an immense gem was in the possession of the Portuguese Royal Treasury. It was reported that the Regent John, who assumed this position in 1792 when his mother lost her reason and who reigned as John VI from 1816 to 1826, owned a huge gem in which holes had been drilled and which he wore suspended around his neck on gala days. Successive

Jean-Andoche Junot, Duke of Abrantès, sent as Ambassador to Lisbon by Napoleon Bonaparte in 1805, was rumoured to have possessed the great diamond of Portugal.

Lithograph by Delpech, 1832. Coll. Archiv für Kunst & Geschichte, Berlin. Photo AKG London.

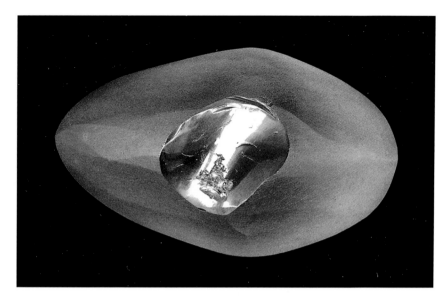

A model of the Braganza in its rough state. The existence of the diamond has never been confirmed and remains a mystery to all.

De Beers Archives.

Portuguese governments were always reluctant to give information about this gem: they may have considered it politic to preserve the legend of the Braganza by saying nothing to dispel the illusion surrounding their great national possession. Certainly a king with a topaz around his neck would compare poorly, if not ridiculously, with one of the Mogul emperors who had similarly worn an Indian diamond.

In answer to a request for information concerning the Braganza, officials of the mining company, Companhia de Diamantes de Angola, in more recent times have drawn attention to the activities of Andoche Junot, Duc D'Abrantès (1771–1813), French general and Napoleon Bonaparte's first aide-de-camp. In 1805, Napoleon sent him as Ambassador to Lisbon. Two years later he returned to Portugal in a military capacity but in this respect his career was chequered: in 1808 he was defeated at the battle of Vimeiro by Wellington during the Peninsular War. His wife was the author of some celebrated memoirs; while in Portugal she entertained on a lavish scale, deeming it her duty to give a high opinion of French women. Napoleon's opinion of her was, however, somewhat low – he called her 'la petite peste' and ordered her banishment from Paris upon her return to France.

When the Duc D'Abrantès was obliged to retreat from Portugal into France, he sent to his wife a case containing 40,000 Portuguese gold coins. On arrival at his house, the case fell and burst open, displaying these coins to the eyes of his family, servants and bystanders who were both astonished and envious of so much money. For several days afterwards the rain of Junot's gold was the principal topic of conversation. In addition, it was rumoured that he had possessed himself of the great diamond of Portugal, 'the largest of all known and much finer than that of the Great Mogul'. The Duchesse

referred to the diamond in her memoirs, saying it was in Portugal in 1805. An imitation of the stone, in crystal, having the identical shape and dimensions, was, she said, to be seen in the Lisbon Natural History Museum.

The Duchesse D'Abrantès affirmed that the Regent John and his suite, when they fled from Portugal, took with them all the Crown diamonds, both cut and rough, and even the imitation of the great diamond which they had seen three years before in the Natural History Museum. What became of that gem and whether in fact it was a diamond is unlikely ever to be known.

An added complication in the saga of the Braganza is provided by the reported existence of another diamond called the 'Regent of Portugal'. Its rough weight does not appear to be known, but is said to have been cut into a round gem of 215 carats. There are two points of interest to note concerning this diamond. First, its name obviously suggests that it was discovered sometime during the Regency of the future King John VI; no other regents ruled Portugal. Secondly, if the weight of the gem was 215 carats it would have surpassed any other cut diamond known at the time; indeed, only a few gems would surpass it today. Such a gem would certainly have merited the description of the 'Great Portuguese Diamond'. It clearly would not have had a hole drilled in it if it were round in shape, but would have been worn in a more traditional ornament.

We are thus left with several possibilities: that the Braganza was not a diamond but a huge specimen of some other kind of gemstone; that it was a diamond but one weighing considerably less than 1,680 carats – possibly 144 carats – in the rough; that it might have been known alternatively as the 'Regent of Portugal', not the 'King of Portugal'. We will probably never know the truth but can only speculate.

Finally, Lord Twining, a distinguished colonial administrator and the author of the monumental study *A History of the Crown Jewels of Europe*, has drawn attention to the fact that among the Portuguese Crown Jewels which have survived the vicissitudes of the country's history and which are kept in the National Palace of Ajuda at Lisbon, there is a large, rough uncut aquamarine, the weight of which is given as 1,750 carats. He has noted the fact that the putative weight of this gem is sufficiently close to the weight of the Braganza to make it possible for the two stones to be identical. Could this, after all, be the solution to the mystery of the Braganza?

Brunswick Blue

The mysterious affair of the Brunswick Blue diamond has long continued to interest gem historians. It suggests the title of a work of fiction and, indeed, the central character in the chain of events appears to a considerable extent more fictitious than real. The diamond's eponymous owner, Charles II, Duke of Brunswick, was an unpopular ruler who, after an unfortunate reign, was driven from his land by a popular rising in 1830. He was also an ardent collector of jewels – and an eccentric. He owned a collection said to have been valued at £500,000, a princely sum indeed for that time, which he kept in his house in Paris. Such was his passion for his prized jewels that he would not spend a single night away from his residence, which had been built more from the point of view of security than of comfort. It was surrounded by a high thick wall on top of which was a 'chevaux-de-frise', so arranged that when a hand was laid upon one of the spikes, a bell immediately rang.

The diamonds were kept in a safe let into the wall and the Duke's bed was situated in front of it. If an attempt had been made to force open the safe, four guns would have been discharged, thereby killing the burglar on the spot, and connected with the discharge of the guns was a mechanism which would ring alarm bells in every room of the house to arouse the household.

The bedroom had only one small window; the bolt and lock of the door were made of the stoutest iron and could only be opened by someone who knew the secret. Finally, a case containing twelve loaded revolvers stood by the side of the bed.

It is reassuring to know that diamonds were as highly prized in the last century as they are today, but doubtless the Duke had in mind the events surrounding the theft of the French Crown Jewels from the Garde Meuble in September 1792.

After the Duke of Brunswick's death in 1873 some of his jewels were put up for sale in Geneva the following year. One of them, the 30-carat Brunswick Yellow diamond, was bought by Tiffany's. Among the other gems was at least one diamond of a rare dark blue colour, the weight of which remains uncertain to this day.

Unwittingly, the noted London jeweller and gemmologist, Edwin Streeter, is partly to blame for this uncertainty, for in his two books he wrote contradictory accounts of the diamond's weight. When he examined the stone he concluded that it must have been cut from the French Blue diamond, weighing 67½ (old) carats, which had been among the Crown Jewels since the time of Louis XIV. Until recently, it has always been assumed that the Hope diamond, weighing 45.52 metric carats (equivalent to 44.34 old carats), constitutes the major portion of this legendary stone and that some time after its theft from the Garde Meuble it had been recut to avoid detection. In the 1882 edition of his celebrated work *The Great Diamonds of the World*, Streeter suggested that after it had been cleaved the largest piece became the Hope, while an irregular triangular-shaped piece would have remained. (If the French Blue had been fashioned to produce the Hope diamond around the year 1800 it would, for technical reasons, have been cleaved, not sawn.)

Streeter thought that if a drop-shape of the same colour as the Hope, weighing from 12 to 13 (old) carats with its base corresponding to the straight side of the Hope, were to be found then there was enough presumptive evidence to suggest that it must have formed part of the French Blue diamond. He wrote as follows:

Such a stone did actually come into the market in April 1874. It was purchased in Geneva at the sale of the late Duke of Brunswick's jewels. The purchaser put the stone for a short time into my hands and I examined it in juxtaposition with the

Charles II, the eccentric Duke of Brunswick, who prized his collection of diamonds so highly that he transformed his house into an armed fortress.

Courtesy Duc Souverain de Brunswick-Luneburg. *Le duc de Brunswick: sa vie et ses mœurs*, 1875.

Hope diamond. It is identical in colour and quality.

I do not know how to avoid the conclusion that the Duke of Brunswick's Blue Drop diamond once formed the triangular salient gibbosity which formerly appears to have characterized the stone now known as the Hope brilliant. Besides the Hope and Brunswick diamonds, there are only three diamonds known in Europe that can justly be termed 'blue', and these all differ from the Hope and from each other in colour.

Yet in the sixth edition of *Precious Stones and Gems* published in 1898 Streeter's account differed considerably. Here he stated that the original French Blue had been cut into three, not two, pieces. The Hope diamond remained the larger portion while the weight of the Duke of Brunswick's diamond was reduced to an estimated weight of between 6 and 7 (old) carats, to allow for the existence of a third piece. Streeter stated that he bought this third diamond, known as the Pirie, for £300 in Paris; it weighed 1 (old) carat and was identical in colour to the Hope.

It is somewhat perplexing that such an expert could have written two such varying accounts of these stones. However, the earlier theory concerning the weight of the Duke of Brunswick's diamond has been clearly disproved by Albert Monnickendam in his book *The Magic of Diamonds*. Mr Monnickendam considers that it would have been technically impossible to have cut a drop shape weighing from 12 to 13 carats if the principal piece – i.e. the Hope, cut from the French Blue – weighed as much as 44 or 45 carats. In his opinion, the pear-shaped diamond could not have weighed more than 10 carats.

But recent research by officials of the Smithsonian Institution in Washington has shown that no other diamond besides the Hope was fashioned from the former French Crown Jewel (see page 126). If there is a link between the Duke of Brunswick's pear shape, the Pirie and the Hope then it would date from 1673 when the French Blue, weighing about 110 carats, was cut into the Blue Diamond of the Crown, weighing just over 69 metric carats. The substantial loss of weight, equivalent to 40 per cent, that resulted from this recutting could have led to the cutting of a number of smaller gems.

We are left, therefore, with Streeter's second account stating that the Brunswick Blue diamond weighed between 6 and 7 carats. If such a stone comes to light then the owner will possess not only a gem of a colour still rare today, in spite of further discoveries in southern Africa, but one of exceptional historical interest. Ultimately, scientific advances in gemmology may be able to provide the answer by matching the physical properties of polished diamonds and determining whether, in fact, they were cut from the same rough gem.

54 The French Blue (top) with three of the gems which, according to Edwin Streeter, may have been cut from it: the Pirie (second), the Brunswick Blue (third) and the Hope (bottom).

De Beers Archives.

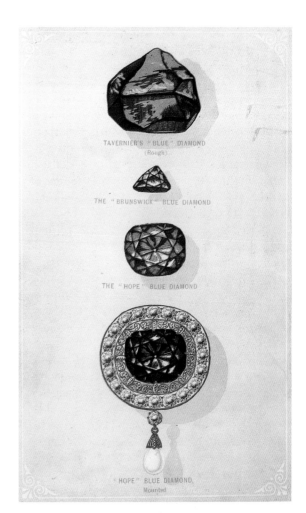

TAVERNIER'S "BLUE" DIAMOND
(Rough)

THE "BRUNSWICK" BLUE DIAMOND

THE "HOPE" BLUE DIAMOND

"HOPE" BLUE DIAMOND,
Mounted

Centenary

The diamond Jubilee of De Beers Consolidated Mines passed off quietly in 1948; the phenomenal post-war growth and expansion of the diamond industry had barely begun, while several important sources of diamonds, including the Premier mine, were still closed, others remaining to be discovered. Forty years later the annual output of diamonds exceeded 100 million carats and sales of rough diamonds reached some five billion dollars.

On 11 March 1988, the centenary celebrations of De Beers took place in Kimberley and a banquet was held close to the Kimberley mine (the 'Big Hole'). An audience of four hundred, comprising representatives of several governments of diamond-producing countries and dignitaries from various sections of the industry, listened to the welcoming speech of the chairman, Julian Ogilvie Thompson, totally unprepared for his final sentence: 'We have recovered at the Premier mine a diamond of 599 carats which is perfect in colour – indeed, it is one of the largest top colour diamonds ever found. Naturally it will be called the Centenary diamond.'

No more appropriate way of celebrating one hundred years of achievement by De Beers could have been devised than the discovery of such a diamond and nowhere was it more likely to have been recovered than at the Premier mine. Over the years this remarkable mine has yielded several outstanding diamonds of the most superb colour, which have been cut into famous gems: in 1905, the Cullinan; in 1954, the Niarchos; in 1966, the Taylor-Burton and in 1978, the Premier Rose. Now that the second millennium has come to its close it is salutary to reflect that only nineteen rough gem quality diamonds larger than the Centenary have come to light during its course. The Premier mine has produced nearly three hundred stones weighing more than 100 carats and a quarter of all the world's diamonds larger than 400 carats.

The Centenary diamond was found on 17 July 1986 by the electronic X-ray recovery system at Premier mine. Only a handful of people knew about it and all were sworn to secrecy. In its rough form it resembled an irregular matchbox, with angular planes, a prominent, elongated 'horn' jutting out at one corner and a deep concave on the largest flat surface. The shape of the stone implied difficulties in polishing with no obvious solution.

The man chosen to appraise the Centenary was Gabi Tolkowsky, renowned in the diamond industry as one of the most accomplished cutters in the world. His family had long been in the trade and it was his great-uncle, Marcel Tolkowsky, diamond expert and mathematician, who in 1919 published a book, *Diamond Design*, which for the first time set out the exact methods of producing the modern brilliant cut. Gabi Tolkowsky himself was the inventor of five new diamond cuts, unveiled in 1988, which concentrate on maximizing brilliance, colour or yield – or a combination of all three – from off-colour rough diamonds previously considered difficult to manufacture profitably into conventional round or fancy shapes. Named after flowers, the cuts are largely based on non-conventional angle dimensions. The overall proportions, as well as the use of more facets round the culet, increase brilliance and improve visual impact when viewed face-up.

When he first saw the Centenary Tolkowsky was astounded by its exceptional top colour. 'Usually you have to look into a diamond to appreciate its colour, but this just expressed itself from its surface. That is very rare.' He knew that the protruding 'horn' would have to be removed as well as other 'asperities', as he termed them, which interfered with the stone's basic shape. At the same time, Tolkowsky realised that the diamond would be difficult to polish because its shape did not offer an obvious approach. Generally

a diamond will suggest two or three shapes to its cutter but the Centenary was more generous – if more perplexing – by providing several possibilities. In the end Tolkowsky submitted his appraisal, saying that the diamond must be kept whole to produce one single, large modern-cut diamond.

He was then asked to cut the Centenary, and late in 1988 Tolkowsky, two expert polishers – Geoff Woollett and Jim Nash – together with a hand-picked team of engineers, electricians and security guards, set to work in a specially designed underground room in the De Beers Diamond Research Laboratory in Johannesburg. It was essential that the room, like the special tools needed for the cutting, should be stable and strong; nothing must rattle, everything must be tight, there should be no mechanical vibration or variation in temperature around the polishing table.

For one whole year, while the right tools and technical conditions were created, the Centenary remained untouched. Tolkowsky examined the stone until he came to know every cranny and crevice. Using the most sophisticated electronic instruments he gazed deep within the crystalline structure. 'From the moment I knew I was going to cut it,' he said, 'I became another man, a strange man. I was looking at the stone in the day, and the stone was looking at me at night.'

The first step, before the diamond could be polished, was the elimination of large cracks from the edge of the stone running a considerable depth within it. He decided neither to saw nor to employ a laser as both methods would have entailed heat or vibration passing through the diamond. Instead, he resorted to the time-honoured method of kerfing by hand. It took Tolkowsky 154 days to remove about 50 carats which otherwise would have been polished to dust. At the end was a roughly-hewn rounded crystal, about the size of a bantam's egg,

weighing about 520 carats. There followed an endless process of sketching and measuring as possible shapes began to emerge. In all, thirteen different shapes were presented to the De Beers board, with the strong recommendation they should choose a modified heart shape. Once this recommendation had been accepted, the final process of polishing the Centenary began in March 1990. By January 1991 it was nearing completion.

When the polishing was completed the Centenary weighed 273.85 carats and possessed 247 facets, 164 on the stone and 83 on the girdle. Never before had so many facets been polished onto a diamond. In addition, two flawless pear shapes weighing 1.47 and 1.14 carats were cut. Among top-colour diamonds the Centenary is surpassed only by the First Star of Africa and the Second Star of Africa, which were cut from the Cullinan before modern symmetrical cuts were fully developed in the 1920s, making the Centenary the largest modern-cut diamond in the world and the only one to combine the oldest methods – such as kerfing – with the most sophisticated modern technology. This marvellous gem, which has become the ultimate revelation of those qualities for which the diamond is esteemed – 'fire' and 'brilliance' – was shown to the world for the first time in May 1991. Mr Nicholas Oppenheimer, then Deputy Chairman of De Beers, rightly declared, 'Who can put a price on such a stone?' confirming that it was insured for more than $100 million.

Whether the Centenary has since been sold is unknown. The De Beers Group's policy is not to disclose such information so that the anonymity of its clients is preserved. Thus it is unlikely that we shall ever know the whereabouts of the world's largest 'D' colour, internally flawless diamond, unless its puchasers or their descendants wish to reveal the fact for themselves.

The Centenary in the rough (above) and its completed form (opposite) – the world's largest modern cut, top colour, 'D' internally flawless diamond – took over a year to cut and polish.

De Beers Archives.

Cleveland

President Grover Cleveland, after whom the diamond was named but who never received it, refusing to accept gifts whilst in office.

De Beers Archives.

This diamond is associated with the firm of Maurice S. Dessau Co., Inc., which is believed to be the oldest diamond tool manufacturing company in the United States. It has passed its 150th anniversary, one of only 36 American companies with such a long history.

The origins of the firm are unusual. In 1844 the lawyer David S. Dessau of New York somewhat reluctantly accepted, as a legal fee, a bag containing pebble-like objects. They were, in fact, diamonds of industrial quality. Dessau examined them with a despairing curiosity. He scraped the window pane in his office with one of the stones and found that it scratched the glass with ease. This simple experiment may well have been the first application of industrial diamonds in the United States. At any rate, it led David Dessau to investigate the capabilities of industrial diamonds. Shortly afterwards, he abandoned his law practice and began manufacturing diamond cutting tools for the glass industry and other trades, so putting to practical use his newly-earned industrial diamonds.

Not surprisingly, such an old company has more than its share of colourful experiences, traditions and memories. In the industrial field, it won the gold medal award in 1880 at the Millers International Exhibition in Cincinnati, Ohio: the best barrel of flour had been ground from stones dressed with Dessau diamonds. Both David Dessau and his son, Simon, were trained in the art of diamond cutting and were the first in the United States to cut a large diamond. In the summer of 1884 they purchased a diamond that had been found ten years before in Kimberley – possibly in the Kimberley mine itself. It was then smuggled to London where it was purchased and held by a syndicate for eight years until being sold to the Dessaus.

The stone, which weighed more than 100 old carats, was cut into a gem which a leading magazine then described as 'white, without a flaw or fault of any kind... in all respects an absolutely perfect stone. It is cut in the cushion shape, having 64 facets upon the upper and an equal number on the lower surface.' Its weight of 50 carats meant that it was the largest diamond to have been cut in the United States at the time. Its value was in excess of $50,000 – at a time when a dollar bought more than two packs of cigarettes. The gem was exhibited at the New Orleans Exhibition where it attracted considerable attention. It was eventually named after Grover Cleveland who had just been elected the twenty-second President of the United States.

During the Presidential election the Messrs Dessau, father and son, favouring rival candidates, agreed that the successful one should enjoy the distinction of christening the gem: the result was seen in the choice of Mr Dessau, Sr. Some of the President-elect's friends proposed a popular subscription with which to procure and present the stone to him, but it was not certain at the time whether such a gift would have proved acceptable to the official who publicly stated his determination not to accept presents. So despite giving his name to the diamond, President Cleveland was not its recipient.

Instead, the Cleveland diamond was given to Minnie Palmer, a musical comedy star of the time whom a newspaper described as a 'pretty, pert, petulant, pouting bit of humanity with the step of a fairy, the carol of a bird and the exuberance of a schoolgirl'. Nobody is certain who gave Miss Palmer the diamond, but it may have been Simon Dessau himself – then a 42-year-old widower who dabbled in the theatre and was known to have been infatuated with the star. Others contend that it was the gift of her agent, John R. Rogers, to whom Minnie was married for some years. Mr Rogers had other claims to fame: he had crossed the Atlantic one hundred and eleven times and, in 92 years, had never drunk one single drop of water. Rogers also had a temper. While Minnie and he were engaged, he became so annoyed with persistent suitors that he had an advertisement inserted in a newspaper warning of dire consequences if she were not left alone. But it had little effect: Minnie continued to receive presents – £6,000-worth while on a tour of Great Britain, and enough to bank £20,000 during the tour. Newspapers headlined their accounts with 'Hearts at Minnie's Feet' and 'An American Girl who Befuddled English Lords'.

Like the Hope diamond, the Cleveland came to be associated with misfortune. Most of Simon Dessau's many business enterprises came to grief in the panic of 1907, while Minnie herself fell on hard times. She died in 1936, in a home on Long Island, aged 71 or 76 depending on the accounts given.

In 1966 Dessau's grandson Stephen announced that he wanted to buy back the Cleveland diamond so that he could present it to the Smithsonian Institution. However, what befell the diamond is unknown; the last time it was seen, Minnie Palmer was wearing it.

The Kimberley mine, where the Cleveland diamond was thought to have been found in 1874, before being smuggled to London.

De Beers Archives.

Colenso

John William Colenso, Bishop of Natal, after whom John Ruskin named the diamond in honour of his loyalty and friendship.

De Beers Archives.

The story of this diamond unites the careers of two remarkable and controversial men towards the end of the nineteenth century. The gem itself is a pale-yellow octahedron with rounded edges – longest edge 2.5 cm , major axis 3.2 cm – and triangular markings on its faces. It weighs 133.14 metric carats.

The Colenso is one of the earliest notable diamonds to have come from the diggings in South Africa and was found at a time when complete records of important discoveries were not kept. Some doubt has consequently arisen as to its exact source. The General Manager of De Beers Consolidated Mines Limited, Alpheus Williams, listed the Colenso as a discovery in the famous old Kimberley mine, in 1883; however, his contemporary, Arend Brink, Chief Valuator to De Beers, considered that, judging from its character, the diamond had come from one of the upper levels of the De Beers mine.

A comparison of the output of large diamonds from the five principal mines in the Kimberley area between 1880 and 1912 may provide the answer. (Wesselton, originally named Premier in honour of Cecil Rhodes but renamed when the existing Premier mine was discovered, was found some years after the other mines and was transferred to the control of De Beers in 1891.)

	Bultfontein	De Beers	Dutoitspan	Kimberley	Wesselton
500 + carats	—	1	—	—	—
4–500 carats	—	2	—	—	—
3–400 carats	—	7	1	—	—
2–300 carats	—	48	10	4	—
1–200 carats	4	523	134	158	—

A considerable difference in the number of large stones yielded by each of the mines is thus apparent. But even greater interest lies in the difference between the *types* of diamonds, especially in the case of the diamonds produced by the

adjacent properties, Bultfontein and Dutoitspan, where gems of the greatest dissimilarity are found. The main output from the Kimberley mine consisted of substantial quantities of boart and shot boart; occasionally large yellowish diamonds were found, the most famous specimen being the Tiffany. But the De Beers mine abounded in large stones, many of which were yellow octahedrons, making it the more likely source of the Colenso.

According to an article in the *Strand Magazine* on 6 April 1896, the diamond came to light in the following circumstances. A storekeeper at the Cape left his shop and went up country to try his luck at prospecting for diamonds. He invested £2000 in a claim in which he had two partners. After some time, when the claim appeared to be valueless, the storekeeper and another of the partners decided to give up, leaving the third to go on alone. The workings fell in on this unfortunate man – by no means an uncommon occurrence in the early days of open-pit working on the diggings – and the other two, in fear of being accused of murder, went home. After some months had elapsed the former storekeeper returned to give the body a decent burial and found interred with it several loose diamonds, of which the largest was the one now known as the Colenso. He brought it to England and sold it to R. C. Nockold of Soho, well known as a dealer in precious stones.

Here the diamond was seen by John Ruskin (1819–1900), the author, art critic and social reformer, who did more than anyone else to influence the taste of Victorian England, although he outraged the opinions of many during his lifetime. His views on social welfare and the need for reforms caused a furore in the somewhat cosy *laissez-faire* atmosphere that prevailed in England during the later years of Queen Victoria's reign. He is probably best remembered today for his views on painting, which tended to veer between extreme praise and vilification. Ruskin also displayed an interest in geology throughout his life and read this subject while an undergraduate at Oxford. As a frequent visitor to Nockold's shop he was, therefore, instantly appraised of the arrival of the yellow diamond from South Africa. He apparently received it on approval and sent the following letter to the Nockolds:

'Brantwood'
Coniston,
Lancashire

My Dear Couple, — I had nearly congealed into a diamond myself with fright when I opened the box. I thought in your first letter that 130 (it was written like that) meant 13 1/2 carats, or I never would have asked for the loan! I'm most thankful to have it, for it is safe here and is invaluable to me just now; but what on earth is the value of it? I don't tell anybody I've got such a thing in the house.

Ever gratefully and affectionately yours,
J. Ruskin

Later he asks:

And now, please will Mr Nockold and you advise me whether to buy this diamond for Sheffield Museum or not?

Ruskin eventually bought it for £1,000 and he and his secretary, W.G. Collingwood, spent weeks studying the diamond: many sketches were made of it but unfortunately their present whereabouts is unknown. He was the founder of the Guild of St George, which was largely financed by him, and it was his original intention to present the diamond to its museum. It was at this stage called the 'Guild' or 'St George's' diamond. However, he was on very friendly terms with Sir Lazarus Fletcher, Keeper of Minerals in the British Museum (Natural History), and suggested that the museum might like to have the diamond on loan. Ruskin was asked if he would like it to be called the 'Ruskin' diamond, to which he replied:

The diamond is not to be called the Ruskin, nor the Catskin, nor the Yellowskin diamond. (It is not worth a name at all, for it may be beaten any minute by a lucky Cape digger.)

In February 1884 the diamond was deposited in the museum and exhibited at Professor Ruskin's own risk. In January 1887 he decided to present it to the museum on condition that it should always be exhibited with the following description:

The Colenso Diamond, presented in 1887 by John Ruskin, in Honour of his Friend the loyal and patiently adamantine First Bishop of Natal.

Ruskin also stipulated that the diamond should never be cut; this was in accordance with the views propounded in his book *Deucalion and other studies in rocks and stones*, in which he wrote:

For literal truth of your jewels themselves absolutely search out and cast away all manner of false, or dyed, or altered stones. And at present to make quite sure, wear your jewels uncut; they will be twenty times more interesting to you so. The ruby in the British Crown is uncut; and is, as far as my knowledge extends — I have not had it to look at close —, the loveliest precious stone in the world. And as a piece of true gentlewoman's and true lady's knowledge learn to know these stones when you see them uncut. So much of mineralogy the abundance of modern science may, I think, spare, as a piece of required education for the upper classes.

Then when you know them and their shapes, get your highest artists to design the setting of them.

Doubtless Ruskin was sincere in promulgating such a view of gemstones, although somewhat naive, or simply uninformed, if he truly imagined every diamond to be as perfectly shaped as the beautiful specimen which he had presented to the British Museum. Certainly a fine octahedral diamond is as mouthwatering an object of mineralogy as one could wish for, but if one begins to reflect upon all

John Ruskin in 1856: the notorious Victorian critic and social reformer who somewhat naively advised people always to wear their jewels uncut.

Photo AKG London.

61

A roadway through the Kimberley diamond diggings in the 1870s. These roads frequently collapsed due to chaotic conditions in the early days of mining.

De Beers Archives.

the other extraordinary shapes found in diamond, it soon becomes apparent that it would require a most oddly shaped human figure to wear them!

No less controversial a figure is the friend of Ruskin after whom the diamond is named.

John William Colenso (1814–83) was both a notable mathematician and the first Anglican Bishop of Natal. Born in Cornwall, he was chosen for the newly created diocese of Natal and consecrated in 1853. Colenso became a pioneer of written Zulu, translating both the scriptures and the Prayer Book as well as compiling a Zulu–English dictionary containing more than 10,000 entries. The Bishop's enlightened views on African customs that were publicized in his *Letter to the Archbishop of Canterbury on Polygamy* (1861) infuriated the orthodox missionaries. But it was on purely theological matters that Colenso was destined to offend the susceptibilities and beliefs of so many Christians.

In 1862 he published a six-volume work entitled *The Pentateuch and the Book of Joshua Critically Examined*. This work, together with an earlier one, caused a sensation and upset the Church. For a bishop to participate in a reinterpretation of the scriptures and of the Church's dogma in the light of new knowledge, profoundly disturbed the Anglican

hierarchy, who promptly demanded his resignation. But Colenso refused to resign, an act which led to his subsequent excommunication and deprivation at Cape Town by the nominal bishop. The sentence, however, was nullified on appeal by the Judicial Committee of the Privy Council in 1865. Colenso retained his position as Bishop of the Church of England in Natal, but remained cut off from the main body of the church.

During the last ten years of his life Colenso proved a stalwart champion of Zulu interests and became known by his Zulu name of Sobantu, meaning 'the father of his people'. The British statesman Benjamin Disraeli clearly had Colenso in mind when he commented, 'A remarkable people the Zulus, they convert our bishops, they defeat our generals and they alter the history of Europe' (the last referring to the death in action of the young Prince Imperial of France).

The final episode in the history of the diamond, however, is a melancholy one. After gracing the display of gems at the Natural History Museum in London for so long and surviving two World Wars, the Colenso diamond fell victim to a thief one night in April 1965. It has never been recovered and, merely for the sake of its donor, one must hope that it has not been cut and polished.

Condé

Known as the 'Condé' or the 'Great Condé', this is a pink pear-shaped diamond of 9.01 carats. If its weight is small in comparison with that of most historical diamonds, nonetheless the gem deserves to be labelled 'great' on account of the career of the man after whom it is named.

The Princes of Condé were the heads of an important French branch of the House of Bourbon. Their most illustrious representative was the fourth Prince, Louis II, Prince de Condé (1621–1686), called 'Le Grand Condé'. By the age of seventeen he was already Governor of Burgundy. Then he began to assume a major role in the Thirty Years War which culminated in the battle of Rocroi against Spain in 1643. This was the greatest French victory for a century and beyond question was due to Condé's personal efforts. In 1645 came another victory at Nördlingen, against the Bavarians. By 1648 Cardinal Mazarin was obliged to give Condé the Flanders command and in August of that year he crushed the Spanish forces at the battle of Lens and secured the signing of the peace at Munster.

Recognizing Condé as a growing rival, Mazarin had him arrested in January 1650 while they were both attending Court, and imprisoned him for thirteen months. Condé rebelled in 1651 and entered into the service of the Spanish, undertaking various campaigns. After he had been pardoned in 1660 he returned to his seat at Chantilly, north of Paris, which became a centre for the arts and was visited by the most brilliant men in Europe. The Prince was an ardent patron as well as being an ardent womaniser – although one of his admirers remarked that his achievements on the battlefield were not matched by those in the bedroom.

Louis XIII, King of France, gave the diamond to Condé, probably after the battle of Rocroi, which took place shortly before Louis XIII's death, in

appreciation of the great service which he had rendered to his country. It remained in the ownership of the Condé family until 1886 when a descendant, the Duc d'Aumale, bequeathed it, together with the Château de Chantilly, to the Institut de France. According to the terms of the Duc d'Aumale's will it must always remain in Chantilly.

The sole occasion on which the diamond has left Chantilly was on the night of 11 October 1926, when it was stolen by two thieves from Alsace. It was recovered a few days later when found in an apple which the thieves had left in a Paris hotel room.

Above: Louis II, Prince of Condé, known as 'Le Grand Condé', who was a brilliant ruler and an ardent patron of the arts. Engraving by Nicolas Poilly, 1660.

Photo AKG London.

Below: the diamond given by Louis XIII, shortly before his death, in recognition of services Condé had rendered to France.

Chantilly, Musée Condé. Photo Giraudon, Paris.

63

Cullinan

The Premier mine in its early days – where the Cullinan was discovered in January 1905.

De Beers Archives.

On 26 January 1905, one of the most momentous events in the entire history of gemstones took place when the Cullinan, the mightiest and most magnificent of all diamonds, was found in the Premier mine in South Africa.

The diamond was named after Thomas (later Sir Thomas) Cullinan, born in South Africa in 1862 of Irish descent. His grandfather, James Cullinan, who came from Co. Donegal, had originally decided to emigrate to America and in 1836, accompanied by his wife, crossed the Irish sea to England where he intended joining one of the emigrant ships sailing for New York. His plans were wrecked by his over-enthusiastic celebration of his pending departure; not only did he contrive to miss the ship but also to lose nearly all his spare cash. Stranded in England almost penniless he could afford to travel neither to

New York nor to Donegal. He solved this problem by joining the British Army. In due course his regiment was sent to South Africa for garrison duties on the borders of the old Cape Colony.

James Cullinan's grandson, Thomas, who was to make the family name famous throughout the world, became a successful building contractor on the Witwatersrand where he resided for nine years. But his main interest lay in prospecting and he was obsessed with the idea that one day he would discover a diamond mine. Cullinan was especially interested in the fact that diamonds were turning up in increasing quantities on farms outside Pretoria, a district easily accessible from his home in Johannesburg. While prospecting on a farm called Franspoort he found some alluvial stones washed down into the valleys and the spruits by storm

water; but his main concern was to discover the exact origin of these diamonds. The most likely explanation for their presence in the area was that they had been thrust to the surface in a volcanic 'pipe' and it was this pipe which Cullinan hoped to find. This theory was derided by knowledgeable prospectors in the district who maintained that the geology of the Pretoria area differed completely from that of Kimberley.

Yet there were others at work prospecting in the region which was interesting Cullinan: according to some old-timers, the first man on the scene was Perceval White Tracey, who had worked a claim on the original De Beers mine in Kimberley and been well known to Cecil Rhodes. When gold was discovered on the Witwatersrand, Tracey moved northwards to Johannesburg, becoming connected with one of the gold mines there. At the same time, he started prospecting for diamonds and came upon very definite signs of a diamond pipe not far from Pretoria.

On one of his expeditions Tracey was confronted by the irate owner of the farm on which he had begun to dig. He could not have encountered a more dangerous adversary than Willem Petrus Prinsloo, a man with a strong personality, imbued with a deep distrust of all who dared to approach his property to prospect for minerals. Twice previously Prinsloo had been persuaded to sell for handsome sums properties on which he had settled. The first farm had proved to be the birthplace of the East Rand gold mines while the second, the farm Kaalfontein, in the Orange Free State, had been the site where the Kaalfontein Diamond Mining Company was subsequently established. In his third attempt to secure privacy, Prinsloo retired beyond the expected reach of prospectors to the farm Elandsfontein, situated about 38 km east of Pretoria. Every day he would load his rifle, sit on the stoep of his farm house and scan the horizon for any sign of interlopers. It was in these circumstances that Tracey first came face to face with the farmer and it is not to be wondered at that he withdrew, deciding that discretion was the better part of valour.

Thomas Cullinan also displayed interest in visiting Elandsfontein, particularly after he had been shown a fine blue-white diamond that had been found there. He joined forces with Tracey and according to one story they presented themselves as cattle inspectors on the lookout for anthrax in the district; at the same time they succeeded in confirming the existence of diamonds on Prinsloo's property. The outbreak of war in South Africa put an end to all mining operations in the Transvaal (now Gauteng). But the war was also disastrous for the Prinsloo family, who were reduced to a state of

near poverty, so that after hostilities had ceased they were obliged to listen to offers which the newly-formed Premier Syndicate Limited, led by Cullinan, made to them. The particular part of the Elandsfontein farm which the Syndicate wished to purchase was then owned by Maria Elisabeth Prinsloo, the daughter of old Prinsloo, who had died in 1898. Eventually after protracted negotiations the Syndicate purchased this portion for £52,000 and a new company, Premier (Transvaal) Diamond Mining Company Limited, was formed in 1903 to raise the capital. Thomas Cullinan was appointed Chairman. The new company was named 'Premier' in honour of Rhodes, the Premier of the Cape government, who had died the previous year. (The mine also known as 'Premier', situated at Kimberley, was later renamed Wesselton.)

Thomas Cullinan and his colleagues proved to be correct in their supposition that Prinsloo's farm indicated the presence of a sizeable diamond deposit. Operations were to show the existence of a pipe, roughly oval in shape, about 0.8 km long by 0.4 km wide. Open-pit mining began in April 1903, the diamondiferous ground being raised by endless rope haulage. Washing pans were used to separate the diamonds from the sludge. In the following year a pulsator plant was built to speed up operations.

Not long after mining had begun at Premier, Sir Alfred Beit, one of the original directors and life governors of De Beers, visited the scene. Both the size of the pipe and the scale of mining greatly impressed Sir Alfred; at the same time there has been much controversy over the precise effect which it had over him physically. According to one writer, the sight of such a rival to De Beers' own operations gave him such a shock that he 'dropped down in a fit of apoplexy, never fully recovered and died a few years afterwards'. But another individual asserted that Beit had informed him that the cause of the slight stroke which he suffered had been the exertion entailed in walking all over the property on

William McHardy, first General Manager of the Premier mine, holding the Cullinan diamond, with Thomas Cullinan (left) and Fred Wells (right).

De Beers Archives.

a very hot day after a heavy meal. Sir Alfred Beit died in England three years later from another stroke which doctors at the time said 'was not connected with the first'.

The most dramatic moment in the history of the Premier mine occurred early in its life.

It was late afternoon on Thursday 26 January 1905 and the men were going off shift when a mineworker came running up, breathless with excitement, to F. G. S. Wells, the mine's Surface Manager; he wanted to draw his attention to a shiny object in the side wall of the open mine that was reflecting the rays of the setting sun. The sparkling came from a point high up in the earth wall of the nine-metre-deep crater, near enough for Wells to clamber down for a closer inspection. He climbed down to the place (the exact spot is situated in the western half of the mine today) and with his pocket-knife he finally succeeded in prizing out a diamond of colossal proportions. According to a bystander Wells' only coherent statement was 'Cor, Mr Cullinan will be pleased when he sees this!'

Scarcely able to accept the evidence of his own eyes, Wells rushed to the mine office to have the stone weighed. When he arrived there he was kept waiting because the Manager was busy. Members of the staff wanted to know what he had come about so Wells showed them the diamond, whereupon someone exclaimed, 'This is no diamond,' and slung it out of the window.

Wells quietly went out and retrieved the diamond. Eventually, when they condescended to weigh it, the stone tipped the scales at 3,025¾ carats, equivalent to 3,106 metric carats or almost 1⅓ lb avoirdupois. The same evening Cullinan was entertaining friends to dinner when a telegram bringing news of the discovery was handed to him. He was not impressed and as he handed the message round the table he remarked casually, 'I expect they are wrong. It is probably a large crystal.'

When the stone was confirmed as a diamond Cullinan, as a first celebration, promptly had twelve replicas made of glass, one for himself and the others for his eleven dinner guests. Mr Wells was given a bonus of £2000 and the mineworker also suitably rewarded. Both Cullinan and Wells may be forgiven if they thought that a practical joker had embedded a piece of glass in the mine instead of a diamond because up to that time the largest authenticated diamond had been the Excelsior, found in Jagersfontein mine in 1893, which weighed a mere 995.2 metric carats. In addition to its remarkable size – it was 101 mm long, 63.5mm high, and 50.8mm broad – the Cullinan was notable for its marvellous blue-white colour and exceptional purity. Intriguingly, the stone also possessed a cleavage face on one side, which was so smooth as to

General Louis Botha who introduced a motion authorizing the purchase of the Cullinan by the government of Transvaal in 1904.

suggest the possibility of its having once formed part of a much larger crystal. On this much discussed and debated topic, Dr Molengraaf, a former State Geologist of South Africa, to whom the directors of the Premier Mining Company had given the opportunity of examining the stone, wrote as follows:

This big diamond is a portion of a much larger stone, the original form of which can only be roughly guessed at. Four pieces of this original stone have been broken off along cleavage-planes, which we know to have the position of octahedral planes.

Each of these pieces has been a considerable size. Consequently the stone itself shows only a portion of its original natural surface (called 'nyf' in the diamond cutter's jargon) the greater portion being formed by these four flat cleavage-planes. The remaining part of the surface shows one octahedral face and a curved irregular surface roughly corresponding to six faces of the dodecahedron, while one very irregular face of the hexahedron is indicated by quadrilateral impressions which are characteristic of these faces in minerals which possess the octahedral mode of formation.

The stone is a single crystal, no twinning planes or twinning lamellae being present. The stone is quite colourless, its perfect transparency being best compared to that of fine ice or of the variety of siliac known as 'hyalite'.

There are a few grains (inclusions) and also some flaws or internal cleavage-planes – 'glessen' as the diamond cutters call them – in it, but their position is such that they do not detract from the value of the stone as a gem. It is certainly the purest of all the very big stones known.

The question is whether there is any likelihood of finding other parts which have been detached from this stone by cleavage. It is, of course, possible, but nobody can say whether or where they will be found in the mine. Diamonds are formed at very great depths from carbon dissolved in the molten basic igneous rock (blue ground), from which, under the conditions of enormous pressure and very high temperature which prevail at these depths, the carbon crystallizes out in the form of diamond. During the period of eruption the diamonds were carried to the surface with great force and the extensive friction which must have existed in the magma during the ejection through the water pipe caused the fragments to be cleaved from the original stone. They may have been blown out during the eruption, or they may still be in the volcanic chimney (diamond pipe) and may be unearthed some other day in the long and promising life of this big mine.

Sir William Crookes, the President of the Royal Society from 1913 to 1915 and recognized as one of the greatest physicists and chemists of the day, concurred with this view, believing that the Cullinan constituted only the smaller part of an octahedron broken by natural process at its cleavage-planes. On the other hand, Dr J. R. Sutton, the author of *Diamond. A Descriptive Treatise*, agreed with the opinion voiced by Mr R. Weatherby, the valuator of the Diamond Corporation, that the Cullinan 'was a whole stone as nature made it, saving minor accidents'.

Dr Sutton was writing at the time of the discovery of the Jonker diamond, just one of several large diamonds found in the region, whose discovery has served to keep alive the question of the missing half of the Cullinan. First came a fine stone of 334 carats found shortly after the Cullinan and near the spot where it was unearthed; next came a large diamond, estimated to have weighed 1500 carats, that was found in 1919 but unfortunately disintegrated, a victim of the mine's crushing gear. Most recently have been the discovery of the 353.9-carat Premier Rose in 1978, the 755.50-carat Golden Jubilee and the 599-carat Centenary in 1986.

The news of the discovery of the Cullinan not unnaturally created great interest in the outside world and caused an appreciable rise in the price of Premier shares overnight. It is difficult to be impressed by certain comments in the British press which accompanied reports of the great discovery; they tended to vary from the malicious to the mendacious. For instance the *Morning Post* stated:

Yesterday the 5/– preference shares of the company rose ⅛ to £9.5.0; the 2/6 deferred shares rose 2¼ to £18. Thus the £80,000 capital of the company is now valued in the market at £7,240,000. There may be other and more imposing stones of the same kind in the Premier Mine. By the way, at the last meeting of the poor little De Beers company whose deferred shares yesterday fell 1/8, the Chairman stated that 'not withstanding the fact that prospecting was carried on everywhere De Beers has yet found no formidable rival'.

The *Daily Express* added the following to its report of the discovery:

According to diamond merchants in Hatton Garden, the immense gem was the one theme of discussion. The opinion was freely expressed that the Premier Mine is destined to become the greatest of the world's diamond producers. Until now, the De Beers group has ruled the diamond market of the world and by automatically restricting the supply of diamonds has succeeded in keeping up the price of the precious stones. But now, unless the two great competitors decide to come together, a trial of strength may ensue. Such an event would mean an increase in the quantity of diamonds and a consequent fall in price.

At the same time the directors of the mining company were taking a somewhat different view of the situation, since there seemed little prospect of finding a buyer for such a diamond. Their dilemma is apparent in an extract from the Third Annual Meeting and Directors Report for the year ended 31 October 1905, which stated:

This stone is the world's record, both as regards size and colour. Your Directors have not finally decided what course to adopt regarding the eventual disposal of this enormous asset but they hope to arrive at a decision during the Financial Year. It will be noted that your Directors have included this stone in the item 'Diamonds on Hand' at the purely nominal figure of £3,290: 4s. 7d., thus forming a very strong inner reserve.

The Premier directors also considered that if more such stones were unearthed, the value of diamonds, especially large ones, might be considerably diminished. At the time their fears seemed well-founded because between September 1903 and June 1905, no fewer than twenty-two diamonds weighing

more than 100 carats had been found at Premier; four of them exceeded 300 carats while sixteen weighed between 100 and 200 carats.

After being put on display at the offices of the Standard Bank in Johannesburg where it could be viewed by the public, it was decided to send the Cullinan to London. Not surprisingly the transport of such a valuable gem posed problems throughout the journey. It reached Cape Town safely after being hidden in the hatbox of the wife of an employee of the South African postal service. When it came to the sea voyage it was heavily insured before being despatched in February 1905 by ordinary parcel post, with a purely nominal recovery value. As a blind, a dummy stone in a carefully sealed package was placed in the captain's safe on board a mail ship and assiduously guarded by detectives throughout

Members of the Asscher family about to cleave the Cullinan in February 1908.

De Beers Archives.

the voyage to Britain. Both stones reached their destination safely, the genuine one being deposited in a bank vault. Shortly after its arrival, it was taken to Buckingham Palace for inspection by King Edward VII before being returned to the vault.

For the next two years the Cullinan remained a public wonder, no one being prepared to pay the asking price. The diamond was shown to many prospective customers and whenever it was removed from the bank it was insured by a 'floater' policy of £500,000 even though it was, at all times, guarded by a squad of detectives. A suggestion appeared in the *Transvaal Leader* that the gem be purchased by public subscription and presented to the King, but nothing came of it. However, in the end a solution to the problem was found through the imagination of a man who may claim to be considered as one of the most magnanimous soldiers and statesmen this century has witnessed.

General Louis Botha (1862–1919) had not long before been a leader of the Boer Commandoes during the South African war and had strenuously opposed the British by force of arms. He had also

been one of those who had negotiated the Treaty of Vereeniging in 1902 which put an end to the hostilities. On 6 December 1906, the British government had issued letters patent granting self-government to the Transvaal and, in the ensuing elections, General Botha's party gained a majority in the Legislative Assembly. On becoming Prime Minister of the Transvaal in 1907, Botha introduced a motion authorizing the government to acquire the Cullinan and present it to the King 'in token of the loyalty of the Transvaal people and in commemoration of the grant of responsible government'. However, there was considerable opposition to the proposal, as is recorded by *The Times* correspondent in Johannesburg, whose despatch dated 19 August 1907 read as follows:

The situation created by General Botha's motion for the purchase of the Cullinan diamond is not rendered any less delicate by the circumstance that the motion was forced through the House of Assembly after a division. Whatever the advantages or disadvantages of the original proposal may have been, there is no question that the Progressives represent a very large body of a public opinion in holding that such a gift, made at a moment of appalling poverty and distress, is inopportune and unjustifiable. As Sir George Farrar said 'We are faced with the fact that owing to the financial position of the Colony and the acute depression which consequently exists large numbers of his Majesty's subjects, very many of whom proved their loyalty most unmistakably during the late war, are, through no fault of their own, daily losing their employment owing to retrenchment and in many cases are without certain means of livelihood, while large numbers are unemployed and do not know where tomorrow's meal is to come from. We cannot help thinking that it would be a source of greater satisfaction to his Majesty, to know that such people were duly provided for.' Moreover, the motion was deliberately brought in in the face of Sir George Farrar's solemn warning to General Botha and to Lord Selbourne [High Commissioner for South Africa], that his party would feel it their unwelcome duty to oppose it. In these circumstances even those who feel the glamour of the gift most strongly regret that the Government should have disregarded Sir George Farrar's appeal for postponement and so laid themselves open to the charge of making party capital out of a motion which under happier conditions would have been endorsed spontaneously by the whole colony.

Strong stuff. Nevertheless General Botha continued to plead for unanimity in order to make the gift a national one. He said he did not contemplate fresh taxation: the Premier Company had been unable to sell the diamond and were content to accept payment over some years. Jan Smuts, the Colonial Secretary, added his opinion by stigmatizing the action of the opposition as churlish and unworthy. The government, he said, had been accused of sliminess but their motives were of the highest. Moreover, not long since the opposition had been anxious to present the Imperial government with a £30,000,000 loan towards the expenses of the war. They had been magnanimous; now they were most

scrupulous. In the end General Botha's motion was carried by forty-two votes to nineteen in the Legislative Assembly, the Labour Party voting with the government.

Since the proposal to present the diamond to the King had not been unanimous and opposition to it had emanated from the Progressives, who were predominantly of British stock, the government in Britain began to feel somewhat unenthusiastic about the King's acceptance of the Cullinan. When the question came before the Liberal Cabinet of the day, the Prime Minister, Sir Henry Campbell-Bannerman, wrote to the King declaring that 'they did not really want to shirk the responsibility' – which is precisely what they did – and suggesting that 'in matters of this sort his judgement was so good that the decision might safely be left in his

hands'. But young Winston Churchill, the Colonial Under-Secretary, who had been General Botha's prisoner in the Boer War, chided the Cabinet for taking a very unimaginative view. Both he and the High Commissioner for South Africa urged that the King should accept the gift while the Prince of Wales, later George V, wrote to his father, who was then abroad, telling him that he had heard from General Botha how disappointed the Dutch would be if the offer was refused. In due course, the Cabinet reached a unanimous decision that refusal would be difficult and the King telegraphed from Biarritz that he would accept the gem as soon as it was officially or formally offered by General Botha.

The offer of the diamond was formally conveyed by the Transvaal government in a telegram sent by the Deputy-Governor of the colony to the Colonial

Office on 19 October 1907. It read:

My ministers request you to approach His Majesty The King and enquire if he would be pleased to accept on his Birthday the gift of the Cullinan diamond as a token of the loyalty and attachment of the people of the Transvaal to His Majesty's person and Throne, together with their hearty congratulations on his birthday and best wishes for a long, happy and peaceful reign.

On behalf of the King, Lord Elgin, the Secretary of State for the Colonies, replied on 9 November:

The King commands me to desire you to inform your Ministers that he has read with the greatest pleasure the communication received from them, and that he acknowledges with much satisfaction the cordial congratulations and good wishes which it conveys. His Majesty accepts for himself and his successors the valuable gift of the Cullinan diamond as being, in the words of your Ministers, a token of the loyalty and attachment of the people of the Transvaal to his Majesty's throne and person and he will cause this great and unique diamond to be kept and preserved among the historic jewels which form the heirlooms of the Crown. The King also wishes me to express his warm desire for the welfare and prosperity of the people of the Transvaal.

Accordingly Sir Richard Solomon, the Agent-General of the Transvaal in London, and Sir Francis Hopwood, the Under-Secretary of State for the Colonies, to whom had been entrusted the duty of presenting the diamond to the King, travelled by train in a reserved first class compartment to Wolferton Station in Norfolk, the nearest to Sandringham House where the Royal Family and guests had assembled to celebrate the King's sixty-sixth birthday. They were accompanied by a Chief Inspector and Police Inspector of Scotland Yard who had actual custody of the diamond.

In both its rough and polished state the Cullinan made several excursions, but it is doubtful whether it ever enjoyed such protection as it did during its brief sojourn in Norfolk. One wonders whether it was solely due to the pomp and circumstance surrounding the occasion or whether there had been a tip-off that someone was planning 'something big' because the safety precautions taken in this rather remote part of rural England certainly were extraordinary. It was reported that:

The police force in the vicinity of Wolferton and Sandringham was considerably strengthened. A large number of detectives were assembled on the platform of the station, a considerable body of country policemen in plain clothes guarded the outside of the station, and along the whole route to Sandringham House, uniformed constables were stationed at short intervals.

On their arrival at Wolferton the party

… was met by an Inspector, Chief of His Majesty's private detective force as they entered a closed carriage, and policemen on bicycles rode on either side: behind it in a wagonette were other plain-clothes Superintendents of the Norfolk Constabulary: other detectives followed also driving.

The same precautions were taken on the return journey.

The Transvaal government paid £150,000 for the Cullinan; as it exacted a tax of 60 per cent upon all diamonds mined within its jurisdiction, the actual

outlay was only 40 per cent of that amount. The gift did not include the cost of cutting it. After consultation with Mr Arthur Levy, the senior partner of the firm of diamond dealers M. J. Levy and Nephews, of Holborn Viaduct, it was decided to entrust the task of cutting to the celebrated firm, I. J. Asscher of Amsterdam. They had been the cutters of the Excelsior diamond in 1903. So three members of the Asscher family travelled to London and the diamond was handed over to them at the Colonial Office on 23 January 1908. The three men decided to return by train from Calais to Amsterdam, choosing to cross from Dover to Calais because it was the shortest route, thereby reducing the perils of the sea to the minimum. Unfortunately for them their train was delayed by fog and they missed their connection at Brussels and were obliged to spend a night in the city before continuing their journey the following morning.

The task of cutting such a huge stone presented difficulties at each stage of the operation. So large a crystal could not be cut into a single gem: it would, therefore, have to be cleaved or sawn. For some time before it arrived in Amsterdam experts at Asschers had been considering how this could best be done so as to avoid the imperfections which existed inside the stone and obtain the largest gems possible. After the diamond had come into their hands they continued to study it closely for about a fortnight and to practise with oversize tools on glass and waxed models before coming to a final decision.

It was thought inadvisable to employ the saw for splitting the Cullinan because there was always the risk that the sawing disc, having penetrated some distance into the stone, might bend and so cause the cut to deviate from the desired line. Therefore, it was decided to cleave the stone. The making of the groove into which the steel cleaving knife is inserted proved a laborious process with the Cullinan because it had to be made about 6.5 mm deep – around three times deeper than usual. The work was begun on 6 February 1908, and by the afternoon of 10 February the stone was ready to be split.[1]

Joseph Asscher, who was recognized as the most skilful cleaver in the firm, clamped the diamond in a specially made holder and inserted his cleavage knife in the groove which he had ground into its surface. Then, as his assistants watched with excitement, he struck the blade with a heavy steel rod. At the first blow the knife broke and the diamond remained intact. With beads of sweat on his face, in tense silence, stretched almost to breaking point, Asscher fitted a second cleavage knife and tapped it sharply. On this occasion the diamond split into two pieces, weighing 1,977½ and 1,040½ (old) carats, with a few splinters. The story that Joseph Asscher collapsed in a dead faint is

70

apocryphal; as his nephew, Louis Asscher, remarked, 'No Asscher would faint on an operation over a diamond. He's much more likely to open a bottle of champagne!'

On 14 February the task of dividing the larger of the two pieces was taken in hand. This operation proved even more anxious than the cleaving of the original stone. Its shape at the point where the split had to be made was such that, had an attempt been made to carry it out in the usual manner, the fingers of the craftsman's left hand, with which he held the knife in position, would have been liable to be hit with the rod. Nervousness induced by this possibility might have been sufficient to have spoiled the blow with the probable result of damage to the stone. It was, therefore, decided after much consultation and with the approval of all the experts concerned to make an innovation in the accustomed methods of diamond splitting by employing a knife with two handles, which was held in the groove, not by the cleaver, but by two assistants. The results completely justified the experiment – for experiment it was, though one which, in the opinion of those best qualified to judge, was unavoidable – and all the subsequent splittings required for the stone were performed likewise. Curiously enough the same two-handled knife broke just as the last one of them was completed.

The next process, of grinding and polishing the various parts into which the diamond had been divided, was started on 2 March. Work was begun on the largest piece while the second largest piece was held in reserve. No decision had yet been taken about what should be done with the latter and it was considered advisable to have it available for the production of a large gem lest any mishap occur in dealing with the largest piece. In the end, the King, who followed the process of cutting the Cullinan with much interest, wished it to be cut into a second large gem (Cullinan II), and the cutting was begun on 29 May. For the polishing of all the gems a special room was constructed on the third floor of the factory that could be overlooked from the windows of the private office of the heads of the firm. All the subsequent operations were carried out here under the supervision of Henri Koe, a polisher of exceptional ability who had been twenty years with Asschers. Mr Koe was a Londoner by birth though his parents were Dutch. Owing to the size of the stones, special appliances had to be provided for the task and special precautions taken to protect them from accidental damage – for instance the floor of the room was thickly carpeted to minimize the risk of them being chipped if dropped. When it came to the polishing of the Cullinan gems specially large tools were again necessary. The diameter of the scaife was increased from the customary size of about 240 mm to double that size, while it was thought prudent to reduce the normal speed of 2400 revolutions a minute to 2000. The dop made for the Cullinan measured about 140 mm in diameter and weighed over 8 kg. In addition the weights placed upon the dop as a means of forcing it down against the scaife weighed as much as 20.5 to 25 kg. It was realized that if the diamond were brought suddenly or roughly into contact with the cutting disc it would run the risk of being damaged or even shattered, so Henri Koe fitted up a device whereby whenever the dop was raised a thick pad of felt was automatically interposed between it and the disc, thus ensuring that if the diamond slipped from his hand it would fall on a soft surface.

The most thorough precautions were taken to ensure the safety of the Cullinan. Nobody was permitted to leave or enter the cutting room unaccompanied by a member of the firm. At night the diamond was kept in a strongroom guarded by four policemen and every half hour a night-watchman made a certain mark at the strongroom to show everything was properly guarded. The walls of the strongroom, of iron and cement, were 68.5 cm thick and the door was opened by a combination known only to the three heads of the firm. Within the room, the safe was hidden behind a mahogany cupboard with two handles but no locks visible. There were nine locks, however, behind a sliding panel, and two safes in one of which was the diamond, and the door of the safe was made of 200 mm steel.

The task of faceting and polishing the gems cut from the Cullinan began on 3 March 1908 and took three polishers, working fourteen hours a day, eight months to complete. If Joseph Asscher did not faint, Henri Koe suffered a nervous breakdown as a result of the strain imposed on him and was sent to South Africa to recover. The work on the greatest of all diamonds was finished on 12 September and the resulting gems were brought to London by members of the Asscher family and deposited in a bank.

On 21 November the two largest gems were formally presented to King Edward VII at Windsor. The total weight of the gems cut from the Cullinan amounted to 1,055.90 carats, representing a loss in weight in cutting of 65.25 per cent. The nine principal diamonds are:

Cullinan Number	carats (metric)	Shape
I	530.20	Pear shape
II	317.40	Cushion shape
III	94.40	Pear shape
IV	63.60	Cushion shape
V	18.80	Heart shape
VI	11.50	Marquise
VII	8.80	Marquise
VIII	6.80	Oblong-shape brilliant
IX	4.40	Pear shape

Until the 545.67-carat Golden Jubilee was recently cut, the magnificent Cullinan I, which measures 58.9 mm by 45.4 mm, was by far the largest cut diamond in the world; because of this the number of facets was increased to 74. King Edward decided to call it the 'Great Star of Africa' and ordered it to be set in the British Royal Sceptre where it has remained ever since. The Crown Jewellers had to re-design the sceptre to accommodate the great diamond and they successfully achieved this without upsetting the Sceptre's magnificent and traditional style.

Cullinan II, which measures 44.9 by 40.4 mm and is cut with 64 facets, is set in the brow of the British Imperial State Crown.

Two days after they had been presented to the King, these two great diamonds were placed among the Crown Jewels in the Tower of London for inspection by the public. However, it would appear that the authorities there were hardly adept at displaying the King's 'historic jewels which form the heirlooms of the Crown' because, incredibly, in its issue of 25 November, *The Times* reported that:

Their magnificent fire and brilliance are scarcely, however, exhibited to full advantage, since those responsible for putting them in position have not remembered that a brilliant is meant to be looked at with its table facing the observer, and placed them so that their tables are turned downwards, and consequently only their collets and the portions below their girdles are presented to view. It is to be hoped that this mistake will be promptly rectified and the public given the opportunity of seeing the faces of the stones, instead of merely their backs.

Fortunately that mistake has been rectified and the two diamonds are today on permanent display in the Crown Jewel House at Waterloo Barracks within the Tower which were moved there in 1994.

King Edward VII expressed a wish to see the actual implements with which the cleavage of the Cullinan had been performed. So Messrs Asscher presented him with the knife and hammer which were also for a time exhibited at the Tower. In the edge of the knife, which bears the inscription 'Cullinan Gekloofd' and the date, may be noticed a nick where a portion of the steel broke away as the stone split into two pieces. Nowadays they are on permanent display in the Asscher offices.

The Great Star of Africa and Cullinan II are Crown Jewels. By arrangement, the 'chippings' from the Cullinan were retained by Messrs Asscher in remuneration for their services, and a small part presented to Mr (later Sir) Arthur Levy and Mr Alexander Levy, who had acted as expert supervisors of the operation in Amsterdam. The 'chippings' constituted the whole product of the Cullinan except for the two principal stones. The King immediately bought Cullinan VI as a present for Queen Alexandra; it is now a drop pendant in an emerald and diamond necklace owned by

Queen Elizabeth II. The other six large gems, 96 small brilliants and a quantity of unpolished fragments weighing about 19.5 carats were bought by the Transvaal government in 1910, again on the insistence of General Botha and on the suggestion of Messrs Levy and Nephews, who feared that they might pass into private ownership. It was their intention that they should be presented to the Princess of Wales (later Queen Mary) on the occasion of her proposed visit to South Africa with her husband for the purpose of opening the first Parliament of the Union of South Africa. The visit had to be cancelled because of the death of King Edward VII in 1910: instead the diamonds were presented to Queen Mary at Marlborough House by the High Commissioner for the Union of South Africa, on behalf of the Government and people of South Africa.

Replicas of the nine principal gems cut from the Cullinan together with a model of the original rough.

De Beers Archives.

Together with Cullinan II, the third and fourth gems have become known as the 'Lesser Stars of Africa'. Cullinan III and Cullinan IV were originally set in the new crown made for Queen Mary on the occasion of the Coronation of King George in 1911 but in such a way that they could be detached for personal wear. Queen Elizabeth II inherited these two gems from her grandmother: they have become affectionately known as 'Granny's Chips' and are now set in a brooch. When the Queen paid a state visit to the Netherlands in March 1958 she wore this brooch during a tour of the Asscher factory; this was the first time the diamonds had returned to Holland for half a

century. Her Majesty wears the heart shape Cullinan V in a brooch; Cullinan VII and Cullinan VIII are together in another brooch, while Cullinan IX is mounted in a ring. These smaller gems frequently travel with the Queen.

One of the 96 small brilliants cut from the Cullinan was exhibited in London in June 1932. It was named the 'Romyn' after Jacob Romijn (later Romyn) who had worked in Amsterdam, first as a cleaver then as a diamond broker: in the latter capacity, he came into contact with many of the leading firms including Messrs I. J. Asscher. Jacob Romijn was one of the joint founders of the first trade union in the diamond industry. Subsequently, he became involved in the diamond industry in South Africa as well as in that country's political situation in which he had dealings with General Louis Botha.

Later two others, a marquise weighing 2.5 carats and a brilliant weighing 1.5 carats, were displayed at the exhibition 'The Jewel Box 1966' arranged in Johannesburg by De Beers to commemorate the centenary of the discovery of diamonds in South Africa. They had been a gift to General Botha. Presumably the General must also have received a third gem because in April 1977 a marquise weighing 1.58 carats, mounted in a plain gold ring, which he had presented to his daughter Helena, the late Mrs de Waal, on her seventeenth birthday, was auctioned in Johannesburg. Known as the De Waal diamond, it was bought by a Johannesburg jeweller for 25,000 rand – more than three times the estimated price. An official of the De Beers diamond laboratory was able to examine the stone and described it as being 'without a shadow of doubt the purest form of diamond I have ever encountered'.

Unlike so many historic diamonds, the Cullinan has enjoyed a peaceful existence; the only cloud on its horizon was caused by the controversy surrounding its presentation to King Edward VII by the Transvaal government, but even that gesture served to bring about a degree of reconciliation between previously warring factions. However, one strange episode deserves to be recounted.

In 1907, within two years of the discovery of the great stone, a Black South African named Johannes Paulus, said to have worked at one time in the Premier mine, indicated that he had an enormous diamond in his possession for which he was asking £1,000 in gold. Paulus said that it was larger than the great diamond which had recently been given to the King. A farmer – and apparently a notorious criminal – Johannes Fourie heard of Paulus's diamond and decided to contact him. Accordingly, a meeting was arranged between the two men at dead of night on the lonely veldt between Premier and Pretoria. Fourie produced a bag and opened it

to reveal a handful of sovereigns but Paulus, already suspicious, plunged his hand deep in the bag and found under the sovereigns only some metal washers. He fled and was not seen again. But also present at the mysterious meeting was a Detective-Superintendent of the Police who, together with a doctor, had accompanied Fourie to the rendezvous. This man declared that in the dim light of the lamp he saw what appeared to be a huge diamond 'one side flat and smooth, the other obviously broke from a much larger stone.'

Fourie did not give up hope in his search for the diamond and later he learned that a tribal chief, Amos Mathibe, living in the vicinity of Pretoria, had obtained a very large diamond. He became involved in the intrigues surrounding the chief and after the latter's death was sentenced to death as one of his murderers by poison. Before he was hanged Fourie said:

I alone know the man who has the other half of the great diamond. He is a man of Mathibe's tribe. Had it not been for the diamond I should never have got into this trouble, for while searching for it I got to know this business of the tribe.

In 1920, after the First World War, there was a further report of the existence of this diamond, still believed to be the missing part of the Cullinan. A German woman, owner of a boarding-house in a small town in the Northern Transvaal, had among her lodgers a prospector who is alleged to have given her a present of a large piece of diamond, struck off a monster stone by means of a chisel. Apparently the woman returned to Germany taking the diamond with her.

Finally, in 1923 it was rumoured that the huge diamond had turned up in the possession of a Black South African living in a kraal near Krugersdorp, a few miles west of Johannesburg. He was said to have asked £1,000 for the stone. Some citizens of Krugersdorp and the neighbourhood organized an expedition to the kraal to do business with the owner, but on their arrival he was stated to be unwell and in no condition to transact any business. Since then there has only been silence and the mystery remains unexplained.

The Imperial State Crown of Great Britain, in which Cullinan II, known as the Second Star of Africa, is set in the brow.

1. In maintaining the precedent set in 1852 with the re-cutting of the Koh-i-noor, King Edward VII requested that notarized deeds should be kept throughout the cutting and polishing of the Cullinan diamond. Extracts of these records appear pp.310-14.

Cumberland

More questions are posed than answers supplied by the Cumberland. The Duke of Cumberland after whom the diamond, which weighs 32.82 metric carats, is named, is always considered to have been William Augustus, the second surviving son of George II. He pursued a military career, becoming a Field Marshal and Commander-in-Chief. After he had joined his father in Hanover, he took part in the battle of Dettingen in 1743: this was the last such engagement in which a British sovereign actually participated. Cumberland fought bravely and sustained injuries. Two years later he commanded the army at the battle of Fontenoy where he was defeated by the French. Then a need arose to reinforce the English forces in Scotland who were fighting those of Prince Charles Edward, the 'Young Pretender', the grandson of James II and the Stuart claimant to the throne.

There followed the events for which Cumberland was to become famous – or rather, infamous. The Battle of Culloden, east of Inverness, was decided within less than half an hour; the Highlanders fought bravely but stood little chance against the superior arms and greater numbers of Cumberland's forces. Cumberland was held responsible for the terrible atrocities that followed Culloden and many stories came to be collected of his own personal brutality.

In the southern part of the kingdom, however, Cumberland was regarded as a hero. At the time of Culloden, Parliament was sitting and both Houses conferred upon him the annual sum of £25,000 in augmentation of the £15,000 that had earlier been settled on him by an Act of Parliament passed in 1739. It is recorded that:

A run of addresses, like the waves of the sea jostling out each other, crowded out upon the throne from every quarter; the pulpits and theatres sounded with the praises of our Deliverer; the streets rang with his eulogium, the presses teemed with the recital of his virtues, and the newspapers were filled with his applause; the sons of genius vied in his enconium.

Cumberland received the freedom of York on 23 July 1746, and the freedom of the City of London on 6 August 1746. It has often been stated that on the latter occasion Cumberland was presented with a diamond for which the City of London had paid £10,000. Authors have justifiably remarked that to have been worth such an amount, the diamond must have been an exceptional stone.

However, there is no official record of the City of London ever having made such a presentation. The records of the City of London reveal that at the Common Council held in the Guildhall on Thursday 23 January 1746:

A Motion was made and Question put that the Freedom of this City be presented in a Gold Box to his Royal Highness William Duke of Cumberland for his magnanimous behaviour against the Rebels and for his vigilant care in protecting this City in a late time of imminent danger. The same was resolved in the Affirmative and ordered accordingly.

The City's cash accounts for the year ending at Michaelmas (29 September) 1746 record, amongst the foreign charges, the bill for the gold box: £144 10 s. At a meeting of the Common Council on 3 December 1745 the Council paid £1,000 into the subscription fund which had been opened in the Chamberlain's Office towards the relief of soldiers of His Majesty's Forces during the winter season in the suppression of the 'present unnatural rebellion'. Perhaps this sum was mistakenly increased tenfold by an earlier writer. Similarly there is no record of the presentation of a diamond by the Mercers' Company who admitted Cumberland to its freedom.

After the general adulation he had received at first, there was a gradual shift in the feelings of the populace towards Cumberland, largely due to the machinations of his elder brother, Frederick, Prince of Wales, who had become jealous of his younger brother's popularity. This prince, though generally held to have been amiable, had an unfortunate knack of putting his foot in it on almost every occasion that presented itself. His epitaph is contained in the well-known lines:

> Here lies Fred
> Who was alive and is dead;
> There's no more to be said.

The Prince of Wales was so successful in his intrigues that a stream of satire and invective emanated from his supporters. It did its work by fastening upon Cumberland the nickname of 'Butcher'. One contemporary has stated that when a proposal was made to elect him a freeman of a City company – in addition to the Mercers' – one alderman was heard to shout: 'Ay, then let it be the Butchers.'

Cumberland died unmarried in 1765. Along with military affairs, his interests centred on women, gaming, breeding horses and racing – he was responsible for the construction of the course at Ascot and the founding of the Royal Meeting. Cumberland professed to despise money but his style of living certainly necessitated it: his expenditure was put at £40,000 per annum. However, he did possess jewels which may have formerly belonged to Queen Caroline of whom he was the favourite son. In addition, under the terms of the will of George III, dated 11 April 1751, Cumberland was left 'all my jewels except those already disposed by my former will (April 3rd) or belonging to the Crown and what at my demise may be in my Scritoires or strong boxes'. Lady Suffolk described the jewels as comprising sixteen pieces, valued at £53,930, including a stomacher of £25,900. On 9 April 1761, George III instructed the Lord Chamberlain, the Duke of Devonshire, to purchase his uncle's jewels at a valuation; subsequently he gave them to his bride, Princess Charlotte of Mecklenburg-Strelitz, as a wedding present. It is more than likely that the jewels included the diamond which became known as the Cumberland, but the question as to whether it was George II or Queen Caroline who had bequeathed it to the Duke of Cumberland must remain a matter for conjecture.

Queen Charlotte kept the jewels she received from the King apart from those which she had received from other sources and ordered Rundell & Co., the Crown Jewellers, to fit the cases with small brass plates engraved with an inscription relating their origin. In her will she bequeathed them to her descendants according to the laws of the House of Hanover. When her eldest son, the Prince Regent, succeeded as King George IV in 1820, he appropriated all these jewels, believing them to be his own private property. However, they did pass to his brother, the Duke of Clarence, who succeeded him as William IV in 1830, and it was in a reference to the jewels worn by that king's consort, Queen Adelaide, that the name of a diamond called the 'Cumberland' appears for the first time.

When the whole question of the ownership of the Hanoverian Crown Jewels came to be considered in 1843, Sir Frederick Pollock, who was the Attorney General from 1841 to 1846, wrote to the Prince Consort a report on the Royal Collection as it was on the death of King William IV in 1837. He had examined the jewellery together with Mr Bridge of Rundell & Bridge. In this report item no. 24 is given as 'The Stomacher of the late Queen [Charlotte]' and, according to this report, 'on the

Coronation of King William the Fourth, most of the diamonds of the stomacher were used to form a crown for Queen Adelaide, which crown was subsequently broken up and the diamonds composing it now form what is called the "Grand Diadem".' The diamonds of the stomacher included a large stone 'bought for £18,000, and a second for £5,800...' In a list dated April 1853, headed 'An Account of Diamonds broken out of the Grand Tiara as worn by Queen Adelaide' the first item is referred to as '1 Large Centre Brilliant (the Cumberland) 32 cts'.

The dispute concerning the ownership of the Hanoverian Crown Jewels – which has a vital bearing on the history of the Cumberland diamond – revolved round Prince Ernest Augustus,

78

CUMBERLAND

the fifth son of King George III. Of all that monarch's sons, Prince Ernest Augustus is deemed to have had the strongest will, the finest intellect and most courage. Early on in his life he realized his ambition of taking up a military career and distinguished himself in numerous campaigns. As a result of a scar and an eyeless socket – injuries sustained in battle – he became known as the 'ugly' son of George III. Then in 1810 he sustained a terrible head wound which would have been fatal had the assassin's weapon not struck against his sword. In the next room his valet lay with his throat cut. The Prince was completely absolved of any crime by a jury of 17, summoned to inquire into the matter, but his political enemies, the Whigs, lost no opportunity of casting aspersion upon the conduct of the Prince or the verdict of the inquiry.

In 1799 George III created his four younger sons peers of the realm: Prince Ernest Augustus became Duke of Cumberland and Teviotdale. In 1837, under the regulations of the salic law, he succeeded his brother, William IV, as King of Hanover, while his niece, Victoria, ascended the throne of England. A dispute concerning the Hanoverian Crown Jewels soon arose between the two Courts. Since William IV had not been particularly meticulous in such matters, it was not clear which of the Hanoverian possessions and heirlooms had belonged to the family as such and, therefore, ought to return to Hanover, and which had belonged to the sovereign of England. The Whigs were again presented with an opportunity of getting their own back on the King of Hanover who, when he had spoken in the House of Lords, had proved to be a formidable opponent. The Whig Attorney General and the law officers advised Queen Victoria to claim these heirlooms for the British Crown, in the process advancing claims which seemed absurd, even to a layman.

On the recommendation of his friend and confidant, Lord Strangford, the King of Hanover submitted a legal claim for the jewels. Endless arguments then ensued among the legal profession and, as no agreement could be reached, the British government set up a commission of three High Court judges to investigate the matter. Considerable delays in dealing with the case followed and on the very day that the commission was due to have met to pronounce a decision, one of the three members died. Since the remaining two members could not agree, no award could be given; the Lord Chancellor refused to renew the commission so the dispute between the two Crowns continued.

In 1843 King Ernest Augustus visited England but his stay was thoroughly soured by the argument with the Court. He pressed upon Queen Victoria

the necessity of bringing about a settlement concerning the Crown Jewels of Hanover. The Whigs were no longer in power and Lord Aberdeen, the head of the new administration, proved more reasonable so that it was resolved to settle the matter by arbitration, as the king himself had suggested six months before. He had only to wait for the appointment of the commissioners from the Government side, then he would name his own and leave. Writing to his son, the Crown Prince of Hanover, he declared, 'Thus stands the business now and more plague I never had in my life, and had I not taken it in hand myself, I doubt its ever coming to a close.'

But the affair dragged on. In June 1851, the King wrote to Strangford: 'I hear that the tomfool Ball was rather a failure, as no one was pleased, and the little Queen herself in a very bad humour, but that she was loaded with my diamonds, which made a very fine show.' He died in November of that year and it was not until 1857 that the British government established a commission to decide the destiny of the Hanoverian Crown Jewels. When it eventually pronounced a decision, it was unhesitatingly in favour of the late King. According to one of its members, they 'had ample evidence and they were all quite satisfied upon this point'. Not surprisingly Queen Victoria was annoyed. In 1853 she had ordered from Garrards, the Crown Jewellers, a splendid regal tiara in which the Cumberland was set.

On 28 January 1858, the jewels were officially handed over to the Hanoverian Ambassador in London, Count Kielmansegge, on behalf of King George V of Hanover, who had professed his satisfaction with the outcome of this protracted business. The Schedule of Jewels included: '2. A large brilliant stomacher.'

It may be supposed that this was the jewel in which the Cumberland had been set before its transfer to the tiara in 1853. There was no specific reference to the handing over of the diamond to Hanover in 1858 and several writers have given 1866 as the date when it was most likely returned. This was the year when King George V of Hanover, Queen Victoria's first cousin, was forced by Bismarck to abdicate, with the result that Hanover became a province of Prussia. One fact is certain: the Cumberland ceased to be part of the British Crown Jewels, because more than three quarters of a century later it was to appear on the international market.

Regarding the handing back of the Cumberland to Hanover, Lord Twining has considered that it would have been returned as an heirloom of the Dukes of Cumberland, not as a Hanoverian jewel. Surely not. Each successive dukedom of Cumberland had been a newly created, not an

Queen Victoria wearing the tiara in which the large round gem at the centre is thought to have been the Cumberland.

Detail of an engraving by H. Cousins after G. Hayter. By courtesy of the National Portrait Gallery, London.

Opposite: Adelaide Amelia Louisa Theresa Caroline of Saxe-Coburg Meiningen, consort of William IV. The Cumberland is believed to have been used in her Grand Tiara, worn at the King's coronation.

Portrait by Sir William Beechey, 1831. By courtesy of the National Portrait Gallery, London.

inherited peerage, so that it would not have entailed the passing down of possessions and heirlooms from one holder of the dukedom to the next. Throughout the correspondence of King Ernest Augustus there is not a single mention of a diamond known as the Cumberland; indeed it is possible that he was aware neither of the existence nor the appellation of the stone. If he had been, there is every reason to suppose that the King would have doubled his efforts to claim the diamond, both as an heirloom of the Dukes of Cumberland and a Crown Jewel of Hanover. In addition it must be remembered that between 'Butcher' Cumberland and the King of Hanover there was another Duke of Cumberland, one who, in his straitened financial circumstances, would assuredly have been glad to have owned the gem. One year after 'Butcher' Cumberland died, his nephew, Henry Frederick, fourth son of Frederick, Prince of Wales, and a younger brother of George III, attained his majority and was created Duke of Cumberland. Educated by his mother who allowed him to mix with no society other than his own dependants, he became notorious for his excesses once released from her control. In 1770 his brothers had to help him find £10,000 which Earl Grosvenor recovered against him for 'having criminal conversation' with the Countess. After leading a controversial life Cumberland died without issue in 1790.

Following the annexation of Hanover in 1866, the Prussian invaders endeavoured to secure the Crown Jewels, but they were thwarted by a series of mainly nocturnal ruses engineered by members of the royal household to safeguard them. In due course many items were smuggled into England. The next mention of the Cumberland does not occur until 1935 when Cartier's were offered it, but declined to buy it on account of its 'banal colour and shape'. However, the fact that they were willing to act on behalf of the owner is evinced by Hans Nadelhoffer's fascinating book entitled *Cartier, Jewellers Extraordinary*, wherein he relates how another Royal Family was offered the chance of buying the diamond. In 1938 representatives of Cartier travelled to Albania where the marriage of King Zog to Queen Geraldine was being celebrated. The Queen chose a few items of jewellery while the King 'appraised the "Cumberland" diamond and waved a magnifying-glass about, but bought nothing'. However, the diamond, weighing 32.82 carats, was sold by Cartier later in the year to an undisclosed buyer.

Of the diamond, Lord Twining wrote:

The diamond must have been an unusually fine one because

Lord Twining suggested that the triangular shaped diamond sold by Christie's London in 1953 (opposite) may have been the Cumberland but this has never been confirmed. The brooch sold for only £1,700 because the diamond was not brilliant cut.

the purchase cost the City of London Corporation £10,000. According to Streeter, it is not known what happened to this stone, though he states that it is understood to have been restored to Hanover by Queen Victoria in 1866. If this was so, it would not have been restored as a Hanoverian crown jewel as such, but as an heirloom of the Duke of Cumberland. It is possible that this stone is identical with one which was sold at Christie's on 16th December 1953. It is described as 'an important diamond brooch composed of a large triangular-shaped diamond in a diamond border of hexagonal form supported by a single diamond in a lozenge-shaped collet, a pear-shaped diamond'. The description in the catalogue adds that the above triangular-shaped diamond is reputed to have belonged to the crown jewels of Hanover. The sale was on behalf of Lord Grantley and the brooch was purchased by P. Lindsay for £1,700. The reduction in value would be explained by the fact that it was not brilliant cut and the value of stones not so cut has depreciated considerably in modern times.

The present location of the diamond is unknown.

Darya-i Nur

All who write about the history of diamonds must forever remain grateful to Jean Baptiste Tavernier, the eminent seventeenth-century French traveller. His descriptions of the alluvial mining in India, the methods of valuing stones and, perhaps above all, some of the great diamonds which he was able to examine there and elsewhere constitute a valuable source of information to later writers.

In Chapter XIX of Part II of his *Les Six Voyages*, published in 1676, Tavernier made eight drawings in which he illustrated six stones, two of them twice. This chapter is headed 'Observations upon the fairest and largest diamonds and rubies which the author has seen in Europe and Asia…; as also upon those which the author sold to the King upon his last return from the Indies: with the figure of a large Topaz and the fairest Pearls in the World'. The king to whom Tavernier referred was Louis XIV of France (1643–1715). Tavernier's comments upon these drawings were as follows:

Number 1
This Diamond belongs to the Great Mogul, being cut into the same form; and it weighs 319 Ratis and an half, which makes 279 carats and nine 16th of our Carats: when it was rough, it weigh'd 907 Ratis, which make 793 Carats.
Number 2
Is the figure of a diamond belonging to the Great Duke of Tuscany. It weighs 139 carats and an half: the fault of it is, that the water enclines somewhat to a Citron-colour.
Number 3.
Is a stone that weighs 176 and one 8th Mangelins, which makes 242 Carats and five 16th. A Mangelin coming to one and three 8ths of our Carats. Being at Golconda I saw this Stone; and it was the biggest that I ever saw in my life in a Merchant's hands. It was valu'd at 500000 Roupies, or 750000 Livres of our Money: I offer'd 400000 Roupies but could not have it.
Number 4.
Is the figure of a Diamond which I bought at Amadabat; and it weigh'd 178 Ratis, or 157 Carats and a quarter.
Number 5.
The fore-mentioned Diamond after it was cut.
Number 6.
Another Diamond I bought. It weighs 63 carats and three 8ths.

Number 7 and Number 8
Two pieces of Stone that was cut in two, which being entire weigh'd 104 Carats. Though of good water it seemed foul in the middle. A Hollander bought it and cutting it in two found in the middle of it 8 Carats of filth like a rotton weed. The small piece happened to be clean but for the other wherein there are so many cross flaws there was no way but to make seven or eight pieces of it.

The drawing under Number 1 refers to the legendary Great Mogul diamond whose present whereabouts are not known for certain; however, it has been identified with several famous stones, the most likely being the Orlov now displayed in the Kremlin in Moscow. The second diamond depicted by Tavernier is the Florentine which has not been seen since shortly after the First World War.

It is the table-cut stone under Number 3 which interests us here. Tavernier saw it at Golconda in 1642 and it has come to be known as the Great Table diamond. The owner of this extraordinary stone allowed Tavernier to make a casting of it which he sent to two of his friends in Surat, drawing their attention to its great beauty as well as its price.

It would be surprising if all trace had been lost of such an exceptional diamond, the more so in the case of the Great Table because in Tavernier's time it was, so to speak, on the market instead of being hidden away in some potentate's collection of jewels or a sacred place of pilgrimage. In *The Great Diamonds of the World*, published in 1882, Edwin Streeter considered that the unusual shape and size of the stone would allow it to be easily recognizable should it ever come to light again, but he suggested that it was more likely that it had been broken up by being cleaved into two or more stones. Streeter suggested that the so-called Russian Table diamond, whose weight he recorded as 68 carats, might possibly be one of the fragments. Nothing is known for sure of such a stone today, although among the contents of the Kremlin Diamond Fund there is a thin, flat,

82

DARYA-I NUR

irregular pear-shape, known as the Russian Table Portrait diamond. But this stone, which weighs 25 carats, cannot have any connection with the Great Table diamond for a reason which will become apparent later in this account. Streeter also wrote of the Great Table diamond that '... since the time of Tavernier it has not been seen by any European expert'. As we shall see, he was totally, but intriguingly, wrong on this point.

In the meantime another theory concerning the Great Table was put forward by the late Professor Samuel Tolansky, a physicist from London University, who was one of the first group of scientists chosen to examine dust brought to earth by the crews of the Apollo moon missions. In a pamphlet entitled 'The Great Table Diamond' which he published in 1962, Professor Tolansky drew attention to Tavernier's precise differentation between 'diamond' and 'stone' in the captions to his illustrations. Tolansky put forward the suggestion that Tavernier's Great Table was not a diamond but a ruby.

To support this theory Tolansky pointed out that the shape of the stone was completely anomalous as a diamond and that nothing resembling it had appeared before or since. He concluded by stating that Tavernier never said explicitly that Number 3 was a diamond: instead he referred to it as a stone whilst using the word diamond for other gems. The mystery of the disappearance of Tavernier's great diamond had, therefore, been solved – it was never a diamond in the first place.

Four years later Professor Tolansky's theory about the Great Table was refuted as the result of one of the most painstaking pieces of detection in the field of gemmology for many a year. This arose from a grant from the Birks Family Foundation which enabled three officials from the Royal Ontario Museum in Toronto, Dr V. B. Meen, Dr A. D. Tushingham and Mr G. G. Waite, to study and to authenticate the Crown Jewels of Iran. Their researches led to the publication in 1968 of a book, *Crown Jewels of Iran*, which is the most exhaustive and valuable record ever to have been published on this legendary collection of jewels. It remains indispensable to anyone writing upon the subject of historical diamonds and is all the more valuable in the light of the events in Iran in the late 1970s.

Since the Persian invaders under Nadir Shah sacked and pillaged Delhi in 1739, carrying off hoards of booty, it had been taken for granted that the treasury in Teheran contained several famous diamonds. Indeed if certain accounts were to be relied upon, it would appear that the belligerent Nadir Shah should be held responsible for the disappearance of the majority of the celebrated diamonds of Indian origin! In the event, research revealed that the Iranian Crown Jewels contained

two famous historical diamonds, the Darya-i Nur and the Taj-i Mah, both weighing over 100 old carats, as well as a number of lesser Golconda stones. In addition there were several large cape-coloured diamonds, clearly of South African origin, which had probably been purchased during the visit of Shah Nasir ud-Din to Europe in 1889.

The Taj-i Mah, meaning 'Crown of the Moon', is a fine unmounted oval Mogul-cut diamond weighing 115.06 metric carats. But it is surpassed by the Darya-i Nur, or 'Sea of Light', which is the principal gem in the collection and one of the great diamonds of history. It proved impossible to ascertain the exact weight of the Darya-i Nur because it was mounted in a setting containing many smaller Indian diamonds. It is estimated to weigh between 175 and 195 metric carats, a figure which accords with the weight of 186 old carats (190.9 metric carats) given by Sir John Malcolm (1769–1833), an administrator and diplomat, in his book *Sketches of Persia*, which he published in 1827. Malcolm visited Teheran early in the nineteenth century and was permitted by the Shah to inspect the Persian regalia. He noted that the Darya-i Nur and the Taj-i Mah were set as the principal gems in a pair of bracelets, valued at nearly one million pounds.

The Darya-i Nur almost certainly came from the alluvial diamond fields in the vicinity of Golconda. It is a rectangular, step-cut tablet with a crown so shallow as to be almost negligible. It measures 41.4 mm long by 29.5 mm broad (at the centre) by 12.15 mm thick. The pavilion consists of a few large step-facets which terminate in a culet about 20 to 25 mm square and considerably off-centre, an additional shallow step-facet having been added to the pavilion on the narrow end. The finish on the table is superb. On one of the pavilion facets is a Persian inscription: 'The Sultan, Sahib Qiram, Fath Ali Shah, Qajar 1250' (AD 1834 – the year of his death). The Darya-i Nur is pale pink, flawless and possesses that exceptional limpidity so characteristic of the finest Indian diamonds. Its weight makes it by far the largest pink diamond in existence and leads one to speculate whether Edwin Streeter was aware of its true colour when he wrote, 'the "Darya-i Nur" which in imagination might seem to flash blood red rays'.

It was the colour of the Darya-i Nur which led to the detection of the diamond's true identity by the Canadian gemmologists. Their conclusion was that the Darya-i Nur constitutes the major portion of Tavernier's Great Table diamond.

The clue was found in the introduction to *The Dynasty of the Kajars* by Sir Harford Jones Brydges (1764–1847), a diplomat and author who, after entering the service of the East India Company, was later appointed envoy extraordinary and plenipotentiary to the Court of Persia from 1807 to

Jean Baptiste Tavernier, the eminent seventeenth century traveller, who visited and described the Indian mines, elaborating on their customs and trade. In his writings he added drawings of remarkable diamonds, some of which have been preserved in their original form.

Portrait by Nicolas de Lagillière (1656–1746). Photo B. P. Keiser. Herzog Anton Ulrich Museum, Braunschweig.

1811. In 1791 Harford Jones, as he then was, visited Luft-Ali Khan, the last of the Zend dynasty which then ruled Persia. This ruler wished him to act as agent in the sale of the Darya-i Nur and other gems in order to raise funds to pursue his war against the Qajar chief, Aga Mohammed Khan. Harford Jones had visited Persia before and had become a trusted and respected visitor to the country with the additional attraction to Luft-Ali Khan of a knowledge of gems.

As a result of this invitation from the Persian ruler Harford Jones was able to handle and examine his collection of jewels. He described the Darya-i Nur as a 'table diamond', its colour 'a slight tinge of a palish pink' and its 'water... perfect and brilliant'. Furthermore, he stated that 'the shape and size of the gem perfectly agreed with the size of the drawing given in Tavernier'. This is Number 3 of Tavernier's drawings in his book, a copy of which Harford Jones had with him at the time. The one discrepancy which apparently caused him some concern lay in the question of the precise weight of the diamond, which was reported to him as being '176 carats and a small fraction', whereas Tavernier had stated the stone he had seen at Golconda had 242 carats. Dr Meen and his colleagues suggested that the weight that was reported to Harford Jones should have been '176 mangelins and a small fraction' not '176 carats and a small fraction'. Such an error could have arisen either through a slip of the tongue by the jeweller in reporting the weight to him, through a fault in his inspection or an error in recording. In any event all are agreed upon the validity today as much as then of Harford Jones' statement that 'it was not likely that there should be two stones in the world of such magnitude without it being known in whose possession they were'.

However, if it is agreed that the diamond known as the Darya-i Nur is identical to the Great Table stone of Tavernier, it will become apparent that there is a difference between the Darya-i Nur which Harford Jones saw in 1791 and the diamond of the same name in existence today. The existing Darya-i Nur is considerably shorter than Tavernier's Great Table and a comparison also indicates that the breadths are similar and that both taper towards one end. The diamond known to us today has a few facets cut round the girdle and on the pavilion. In addition, the diamond which Harford Jones saw apparently bore no inscription whereas the present-day gem now bears the name of Fath Ali Shah and a date equivalent to 1834.

The Darya-i Nur may now possess a greater symmetry to Western eyes but this would appear insufficient reason to have persuaded an oriental potentate to reduce so drastically the size of the gem. One recalls that in the East a gem's size rather than its symmetry or brilliance has always been appreciated as its most prized asset. This fact suggested to the Canadian experts that at some stage in its history the Darya-i Nur had suffered some accident, most likely around the year 1834, which is the date inscribed on the pavilion facet.

If, therefore, the Darya-i Nur comprises the major part of Tavernier's Great Table, what then became of the rest of the diamond? This question was answered by the discovery of another pink diamond among the Iranian Crown Jewels. This is the Nur ul-Ain or 'Light of the Eye', a slightly drop-shaped oval brilliant-cut measuring 30 by 26 by 11 mm, of a pink colour and limpidity that matches perfectly those qualities of the Darya-i Nur. The Nur ul-Ain is the central stone in a tiara created by Harry Winston for the Empress Farah at the time of her wedding, and is estimated to weigh approximately 60 metric carats.

So as to test the possibility of the Nur ul-Ain having been cut from the remaining part of the Great Table, Mr Waite made precise models of that stone, assuming that its thickness was identical to that of the Darya-i Nur as we know it today, the Darya-i Nur itself and the cleavage piece which would have remained. From the latter, after much experimenting, he fashioned a model of the pink brilliant which corresponded with its dimensions. Indeed, Mr Waite discovered that the very shape of the fragment dictated the cutting of the pink brilliant as a shallow stone with the slight drop-shape and asymmetric shoulders which it actually possesses.

Because the Great Table is said to have been flawless, some concern was caused by the presence of a slight flaw in the Nur ul-Ain. However, far from being an obstacle to the theory, the existence of such a flaw was considered to have provided further confirmation of its validity. Examination showed the flaw to be incipient cleavages. Consideration of the orientation of these cleavages led to the conclusion that when the crystallographic orientation of the Nur ul-Ain was matched to that of the Darya-i Nur, the former lay in the position it must have occupied to have been cut from the cleavage fragment. Furthermore it was clear that the flaw lay on the surface which had been adjacent to the existing Darya-i Nur: this fact, in turn, suggested the reason for the large asymmetrically placed pavilion facet on the Darya-i Nur.

In the accident which befell the diamond which Harford Jones had seen, incipient cleavage was formed in both pieces. When the larger piece of the Great Table was cut into the existing Darya-i Nur it was returned to its flawless condition by grinding away the incipient cleavage, thus forming the asymmetrically placed facet. The inscription bearing the name of the ruler at the time together with the date 1834 strongly suggest that the accident to the Great Table had occurred shortly before.

The date of the recutting of the smaller piece into the Nur ul-Ain is unknown but it is thought most likely to have taken place during the long reign of Nasir ud-Din (1848–96). Not only was this monarch apparently responsible for the recutting of some of his predecessors' acquisitions but it was almost certainly during his reign that a number of very large South African stones were purchased, following the opening up of the diamond deposits in that country in the 1870s and 1880s. The Golestan Palace in Teheran contained workshops where diamond cutting was carried out. Concerning the Nur ul-Ain it is fortunate that the oriental preference for size rather than brilliance manifested itself and that the cutter did not remove the flaw in the gem because it served as a vital clue linking it to the Darya-i Nur and, in turn, identifying both diamonds with the legendary Great Table.

There remained one discrepancy in the theory advanced by Dr Meen and his colleagues for linking these three diamonds, and it is still unresolved. The weight of the Darya-i Nur together with that of the Nur ul-Ain exceeds the weight of the Great Table as reported by Tavernier; furthermore it does not allow anything for loss in cutting. But experiments made with the models clearly demonstrated that originally the Great Table must have weighed over 300 old carats and that its weight, recorded by Tavernier as 242 carats, is incorrect. In any event it is important to remember the remark of Sir Harford Jones Brydges that it was unlikely there would be two stones of such size in existence without their ownership being known. Two hundred years on, the validity of his observation remains indisputable.

Since the publication of the book *Crown Jewels of Iran* momentous events have taken place within the country. The overthrow of the Pahlevi dynasty in 1979 has led to the rule of the Ayatollahs. The fate of the Crown Jewels during this turbulent period is not known. It was rumoured that the late Shah had succeeded in removing most of them with him and

his entourage – surely an unlikely event for several reasons, not least the size of the collection – but this has always been denied by the Empress. Then in 1982 it was reported that the Iranian authorities planned to sell some major pieces, including the Darya-i Nur, to help finance the war with Iraq then taking place. Dealers from the USA, Japan and elsewhere were supposedly to be sent invitations to visit Teheran and inspect 'several hundred pieces' offered for sale. But the invitations never arrived, so presumably the matter was dropped. However, it is rumoured that the Iranian government paid for arms for this war direct in diamonds.

Then in August 1984 four Afghan smugglers were apprehended by the Pakistani police in a village near the border with Iran, apparently trying to get away with a loot of jewels and art treasures said on first sight to be worth several million dollars and to include 'a diamond as big as an apricot'. Iran had formally requested the return of these goods but no news of this happening emerged, nor of their identification. In the circumstances one can only hope that one of the world's truly historic diamonds has suffered no further damage and remains intact.

One fact which the Canadian scholars were able to ascertain during their researches was that the Darya-i Nur had never at any time left the treasure vaults of the Central Bank of Iran in Teheran. This confirms, therefore, that it was not the same diamond as the one entitled the Derrea-i-noor or 'Sea of Light' which the East India Company showed at the Great Exhibition held in Hyde Park in 1851. It was reported that this stone weighed 66 carats and was valued at £34,848 and that, compared with the Koh-i-noor, universally adjudged the lion of the exhibition, it was 'much more brilliant and effective from the large surface it exposes, although comparatively insignificant in point of value'.

At the conclusion of the 1851 Exhibition the Nawab of Dacca is said to have bought this diamond. Eventually it was set in a gold bracelet and in this same setting the family of the Nawab offered it for sale in 1955 and again in 1959.

Tavernier's drawing of the Great Table. Recent research has disclosed that the Darya-i Nur constituted the major part of the diamond.

Not long after the incorporation of De Beers Consolidated Mines Limited, in March 1888, a huge, light-yellow octahedron was found in the De Beers mine. The stone weighed 428½ (old) carats – equivalent to 439.86 metric carats – and measured 47.6 mm through its longest axis and 38.1 mm square. Excluding the Victoria or Great White, the source of which remains doubtful, the De Beers was the largest diamond to have been recovered from the four mines at Kimberley at the time.

The Annual Report and Accounts of De Beers for the year ending 31 March 1890 recorded that:

A 428½ carat rough, 1⅞ inches long, was found in the De Beers mine by a native whose 'brother' gave information which led to its recovery while being taken from the mine. It was cut and exhibited at the Paris Exhibition of 1889. Its weight after cutting was 228.5 carats, having lost 200 carats in the cutting.

Expressed in metric carats – i.e. 234.65 – the weight of the De Beers places it as the seventh largest polished diamond in the world, if one excludes the Nizam which is reputed to be only partially cut. It is not known where the De Beers was cut into its shape as a cushion cut, but because of its pre-eminence as a cutting centre at the time it may be assumed that the work was carried out in Amsterdam.

Following its display in Paris the Maharajah of Patiala bought the De Beers: in 1928 Cartier Paris set it as the centrepiece of a ceremonial necklace. Some time during the 1930s the diamond was acquired by its present owners who loaned it in 1973 for an exhibition staged in Israel.

On 6 May 1982, the De Beers came up for auction by Sotheby's in Geneva. It was generally thought that bidding might reach as much as 4.5 million dollars. In the event the stone was bought in when the highest bid of 3.16 million dollars (£1,750,000) remained below its undisclosed reserve.

In his book *Precious Stones and Gems*, Edwin Streeter has unwittingly been the cause of some confusion concerning this diamond. He declared that it was shown at the Paris Exhibition as the 'Victoria'; this has led to the listing in some publications of a diamond called the Victoria I, weighing 228½ old carats, also found in 1888 and afterwards sold to an Indian prince. A mathematical calculation will show that this is precisely the same stone as the De Beers and not to be confused with the even larger diamond variously referred to as the 'Imperial', 'Great White' or 'Victoria' which had been found in somewhat mysterious circumstances four years before.

The De Beers, which weighs 234.65 metric carats, is the seventh largest cut diamond in the world.

De Beers Archives.

87

Dresden Green

The Dresden Green, mounted in an epaulette.

Courtesy of the Staatliche Kunstsammlungen, Dresden. Photograph by Jürgen Karpinski.

In the rough, greenish diamonds tend to occur as one of three types: a stone, often a crystal, possessing a light tinge rather like the colour of water in a swimming pool; a stone with a dark green skin not dissimilar to the colour of a well-known brand of gin bottle; a yellowish-green stone characterized by a degree of lubricity. After they have been cut and polished, diamonds of the first and second types usually lose their greenish tinge to become fine blue-white gems or, alternatively, become yellower, as silvery capes. The few green polished diamonds, therefore, originate from the third type. The famous collection of De Beers 'fancies', which has been displayed throughout the world, includes some beautiful examples.

Since this is an account of a truly unique gem, a scientific explanation for the phenomenon of green diamonds is called for. The green colour is usually caused by the crystal's coming into contact with a radioactive source at some moment during its lifetime, and, in geological terms, this is measured in millions of years. The most common form of irradiation encountered by diamonds is through bombardment by alpha particles which are present in uranium compounds or percolating groundwater. Long exposure to these particles forms a green spot on the surface of the diamond, or sometimes produces a thin green coating which is only skin deep and can easily be removed by polishing the stone on a scaife. But bombardment by beta and gamma rays as well as neutrons will discolour the stone to a greater depth and in some cases turn the whole of the stone's interior green.

Heating the stone may sometimes improve its colour but care must be taken to keep the temperature below 600°C, because at this critical temperature the green colour is liable to turn to a light yellow or brown. The change in colour is due to the change in the crystal's lattice structure. Before bombardment by radioactive particles the crystal's lattice was stable but the initial radioactive shock was sufficient to disturb the equilibrium and produce a green discoloration. Annealing will distort the lattice further and produce another change of colour. This phenomenon is analogous to a piece of elastic that has been overstretched; it will come back so far, but never returns to its original length. Similarly, after treatment the diamond's lattice remains permanently distorted.

Research has disclosed that green or irradiated diamonds are more common from alluvial deposits, although they are found in primary sources, usually in the upper part of the pipe. But green stones of any size are rare. The Dresden Green, which probably weighed over 100 (old) carats in the rough, is unique among world famous gems. Originally, it was probably an elongated unbroken piece since greenish diamonds seldom occur as cleavages.

The Dresden Green derives its name from the capital of Saxony where it has been on display for more than two hundred years. The earliest known reference to its existence occurs in *The Post Boy*, a London news-sheet of the eighteenth century. The issue dated 25–27 October 1722 included this item:

On Tuesday last, in the afternoon, one Mr Marcus Moses, lately arrived from India, had the Honour to wait on his Majesty [King George I (ruled 1714–27)] with his large diamond, which is of a fine Emerald Colour, and was with his Majesty near an hour. His Majesty was very much pleased with the Sight thereof. It is said there never was seen the like in Europe before, it being free from any Defect in the world; and he has shown his Majesty several other fine large Diamonds, the like of which, 'tis said were never brought from India before. He was also, the 25th, to wait on their Royal Highnesses with his large Diamond; and they were surprized to see one of such Largeness, and of such a fine Emerald Colour, without the help of a Foil under it. We hear the said Gentleman values it at 10,000£.

Marcus Moses was an important diamond merchant in London during the first part of the eighteenth century: he had once been involved with the Regent diamond.

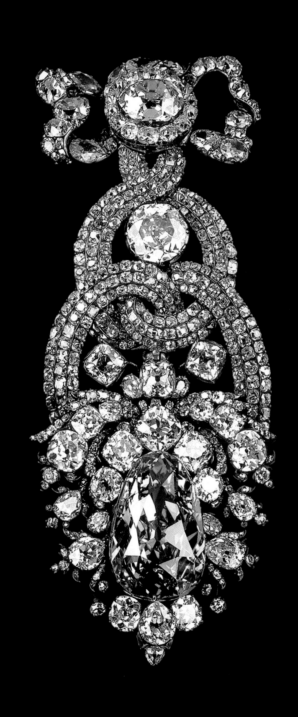

Another early reference to the Dresden Green is found in a letter, dated 1726, from Baron Gautier, the 'assessor' at the Geheimes Rath's Collegium in Dresden, to the Polish ambassador in London, which speaks of the green diamond being offered to Frederick Augustus I (1694–1753) by a London merchant for £30,000. This ruler, known as Augustus the Strong, was responsible for the erection of some outstanding buildings in Dresden, which he duly filled with great collections of rare and costly treasures – sculptures, paintings and *objets d'art*. He amassed a collection of crown jewels as the ruler of Saxony, and when he was elected to the throne of Poland in 1697 he commanded new regalia to be made for his coronation. Frederick Augustus set aside a series of rooms in Dresden Castle to house his collection of jewels and other treasures, named the Green Vault, their interior decoration being entrusted to Parisian designers. The final result was considered to be one of the finest examples of the Baroque. Nowadays, the contents of the Green Vault are housed in a contemporary museum, the Albertinium, built on the site of the original castle, destroyed during the last war.

A model of the green diamond was owned by the eminent physicist Sir Hans Sloane (1660–1753), whose collection of books, manuscripts and curiosities formed the basis of the British Museum. When Sloane retired from active work in 1741 his library and cabinet of curiosities had grown to be of unique value and, on his death, he bequeathed his collection to the nation, on condition that Parliament pay his executors £20,000. The bequest was accepted, and went to form the collection opened to the public as the British Museum in 1759.

Neither George I nor Frederick Augustus I purchased the green diamond; instead it was the latter's son, Frederick Augustus II (1733–1763) who became its first royal owner. He bought the 'Dresden Green' from a Dutch merchant, named Delles, at the Leipzig Fair in 1741. Various figures have been quoted for the purchase price but the most interesting is found in a letter of Frederick the Great, King of Prussia (1712–1786), which states that 'For the seige of Brünn the King of Poland was asked for heavy artillery. He refused due to the scarcity of money; he had just spent 400,000 thaler for a large green diamond.' On the orders of Frederick Augustus II, the court jeweller, Dinglinger, set the diamond in the Decoration of the Golden Fleece, but this setting lasted only four years as it was broken up in 1746. The King then commissioned the goldsmith Pallard, in Vienna, to design another Golden Fleece incorporating both the Dresden Green and the Dresden White, a cushion-shaped diamond of 49.71 carats.

From 1756 to 1763, during the continued hostilities of the Seven Years War, the contents of the Green Vault were removed for safety to the fortress of Königstein, situated south-east of Dresden by the river Elbe. Several years after the war, which saw the defeat of Saxony, Pallard's Golden Fleece was also broken up. In 1768 another jeweller, Diessbach, worked the green diamond into a hat clasp along with two other white brilliants, weighing almost 40 carats, and a number of smaller diamonds. The Dresden Green survives in Diessbach's ornament today.

In 1806 Saxony became a kingdom and the royal line continued until 1918 when the last king abdicated. The contents of the Green Vault remained on display to the public until the beginning of the Second World War. In 1942 they were removed again to Königstein, thus escaping the shattering air raid by the Allies on the night of 13 February 1945 which devastated Dresden. Later the same year, the Soviet Trophies Commission, which had made its headquarters in Pillnitz castle near the centre of the ruined city, took the contents of the Green Vault to Moscow, the Crown Jewels being amongst the first items to travel there. They were returned in 1958.

The gemmological examination of the Dresden Green undertaken by two senior members of the staff of the GIA in November 1988 revealed that the weight of the diamond is approximately 41 carats; it is a modified pear-shaped brilliant cut with 58 facets and 'fancy green' in colour. The diamond measures 29.75 by 19.88 by 10.29 mm. The experts were impressed by the exceptional transparency of the Dresden Green, reminiscent of that observed in colourless diamonds from Golconda. Most interestingly, it was found to be a very rare Type IIa.

90

The Dresden Green, here out of its setting, is unique for its exceptional transparency.

Photograph Shane F. McClure. Courstesy of the Gemological Institute of America.

Emperor Maximilian

At a time of linguistic over-emphasis and exaggeration, both conversationally and on the printed page, some words, notably certain adjectives and adverbs, have come to be used so often as to have lost much of their true meaning. One such word is 'tragic' which people nowadays tend to apply to comparatively minor misfortunes. But it remains the most appropriate epithet to describe the fate which befell the unfortunate Maximilian, Emperor of Mexico (1832–67) during the last century.

The Archduke Maximilian was the younger brother of Francis Joseph I, the Habsburg Emperor of Austria, whose own life was marked by a series of personal tragedies: his wife, only son and his heir-presumptive nephew all met sudden death by violence. In 1859 some Mexican exiles whose property had been confiscated by the Liberals under Benito Juarez approached Maximilian with the suggestion that he assume the throne of Mexico. The country was then in a state of anarchy, and Maximilian, though he was tempted by the challenge, turned their proposal down. He did, however, decide to visit the New World. The Archduke displayed a keen interest in the sciences, particularly botany, and in 1860 he travelled to Brazil on a botanical expedition.

While he was in Brazil, Maximilian acquired two diamonds which have been named after him. The smaller of the two was a cushion-cut with a greenish-yellow tint weighing 33 carats. It became known as the 'Maximilian' diamond. Maximilian gave it to his wife, the former Princess Charlotte (known as Carlotta), daughter of King Leopold I of Belgium, who wore it as a pendant. The larger diamond, which has the more resounding name of 'Emperor Maximilian', weighs 41.94 carats and is also cushion-shaped. It is not known where either diamond was cut but it is possible that they were

cut in Brazil, which has long possessed a diamond cutting industry, albeit on a smaller scale than in some other countries.

Having failed with their initial proposition to Maximilian, the Mexican exiles then approached the Emperor Napoleon III of France. They succeeded in convincing him that with the assistance of the French army he could obtain glory by regenerating Mexico with a Catholic prince. Consequently Napoleon III urged Maximilian to accept the throne of Mexico, although the Emperor of Austria endeavoured to dissuade his brother from taking such a step. In the end Maximilian accepted the crown, whereupon he and his wife set sail, arriving in Mexico in May 1864.

The venture was an ill-fated one from the start. Neither Maximilian nor Carlotta was acquainted with the country and its problems and it was not long before it became clear to Napoleon III that the

Above: the unusual Emperor Maximilian diamond, possessing very strong blue fluorescence.

Top: Maximilian I, the ill-fated Emperor, whose reign lasted barely two years.

Courtesy Christie's/The New York Historical Society, New York City. Photo Malcolm Varon.

The Execution of Maximilian, Edouard Manet, 1868–9. The Emperor was believed to have worn the diamond around his neck at his execution.

Copenhagen, Ny Carlsberg Glyptothek. Photo AKG London.

Archduke Maximilian was temperamentally unsuitable as a ruler. The reigning government lacked popular appeal and relied solely on French military support, while a series of bad decisions and reports of extravagance came to alienate the people. In addition, Benito Juarez, a native Mexican and the Republican leader, constantly opposed Maximilian and the French.

By the spring of 1865 Napoleon III realized that the Mexican venture was a failure, and that he could not continue with it on account of growing opposition within France itself. Then the United States government refused to accord recognition to the Mexican Empire and urged the withdrawal of the French forces. In the following year the French agreed to retire within eighteen months and in October 1866 Maximilian drafted an abdication proclamation. However, he allowed himself to be persuaded to remain in Mexico, and determined not to desert his supporters. Meanwhile the

Empress Carlotta returned to Europe to seek aid for her husband.

As a result of the treachery of one of his officers, Maximilian was captured on the night of 14 May 1867. Some foreign governments petitioned to have the Emperor sent back to Europe, but in vain. On 19 June 1867, Maximilian was court-martialled and shot at Querétaro with two of his generals.

It is reported that the Emperor walked to the spot which had been assigned him and then asked for the men who were going to shoot him and gave each of them one ounce of gold. It has also been stated that on this dreadful day he wore the Emperor Maximilian diamond in a small satchel tied around his neck when he faced the firing squad.

After this infamous deed, which did little credit to the parties concerned, the Maximilian diamond disappeared. It came to light in 1901 when two Mexicans were apprehended trying to smuggle it into the United States. The customs officials seized the diamond, which later that year was auctioned by the United States government; it was bought for $120,000 by a Congressman named Levy. In the following year Levy sold it to William R. Phelps, a jeweller of New York's Maiden Lane, the precursor of 47th Street. In 1946, another jeweller from New York, Morris S. Nelkin, bought the Maximilian and he kept it until one fateful day fifteen years later when a member of his family, suspecting that a burglar was in the house, hid the stone with other valuables in the rubbish bin. Subsequently the rubbish was collected and despite an intensive search of the municipal dump the diamond was never recovered.

Fortunately the Emperor Maximilian has survived. After the Emperor's execution the diamond was returned to his widow who, as the result of these events, was to remain mentally deranged until her death near Brussels in 1927. The gem was sold in order to help pay her medical expenses. In 1919 a Chicago diamond dealer named Ferdinand Hotz acquired the Emperor Maximilian, and displayed it at the 'Century of Progress' exhibition held in that city in 1934. Despite several offers to buy it, one of which came from Lord Anglesey, Hotz refused to sell the stone and he kept it until he died in 1946, when it was sold to a private collector in New York.

The name of this purchaser has never been revealed and the diamond remained in her possession, mounted in a ring by Cartier, until Christie's auctioned it in New York on 20 July 1982. On this occasion the sale catalogue stated that the diamond was the property of a lady, sold by order of the Trustees. It was expected that the diamond would fetch $330,000 (£194,110) but in the event it was sold for $726,000 (£427,050). The sale of the Emperor Maximilian attracted worldwide interest from collectors and journalists alike; during the sale the bidding was so keen that by the time the auctioneer had reached $500,000 no less than ten hands still remained in the air.

The purchaser of the Emperor Maximilian diamond was Laurence Graff, the London jeweller, who has since added the purchases of other notable diamonds to this particular one. Mr Graff had been prepared to go up to $1,000,000, having gone to New York specially to bid for it. He remarked:

It is a wonderful stone, cut like a modern one, and to do anything to it is unnecessary and would be a shame. I've never seen such a stone – the way it shines with a purple glow in the sunlight is extraordinary – with such a high fluorescence. Several offers have already been made to me for it.

In January 1983 Mr Graff sold the Emperor Maximilian, together with the Idol's Eye and the Sultan Abd al-Hamid II, in a single transaction to the same buyer.

93

The Empress Carlotta, c.1864, to whom the diamond was returned following her husband's execution.

Photo AKG London.

EMPEROR MAXIMILIAN

Eugénie

Catherine the Great of Russia, the first of the two Empresses to own the Eugénie, gave the diamond to one of her lovers and political allies, Potemkin.

Portrait by Vigilius Erichsen, 1770. Chartres, Musée des Beaux-Arts. Photo AKG London

The contrasting fortunes of two Empresses are linked by the history of this diamond.

The first was the formidable Catherine the Great of Russia. Born in 1729, the daughter of an obscure German Prince, at the tender age of fourteen she was chosen to be the bride of the Duke of Holstein-Gottorp, the grandson of Peter the Great, who, as the Grand Duke Peter, was heir to the throne of Russia. She arrived in that country in 1744, and married the following year. At that time Peter the Great's daughter, the Empress Elizabeth, ruled Russia, her twenty-year reign doing much to stabilize the monarchy. She was devoted to luxury and pleasure and longed to impart to her Court the brilliancy which characterized so many others in Europe, and to that extent she paved the way for Catherine.

The marriage between the Grand Duke Peter and his young bride proved to be a complete failure. Catherine, who was a woman of charm, possessed both a lively intelligence and great energy; she was not only bored with and constantly humiliated by her husband, but, because of her serious and studious disposition, was regarded with suspicion by many at the Russian Court. Following the death of the Empress Elizabeth in 1762, it was not long before the new Emperor Peter III discredited himself by numerous foolish actions, principally of a political nature, and prepared to rid himself of Catherine. But she enjoyed the support of both the Imperial Guard and the more enlightened elements of the nobility. In July 1762 she led the regiments that had rallied to her cause into St Petersburg and had herself proclaimed Empress. Peter III abdicated and eight days later was assassinated. On 9 July the Empress was crowned with great ceremony in Moscow as Catherine II, beginning a reign which was to last for thirty-four years.

With the Russian Court's traditional love of

opulence and splendour, it was not surprising that Catherine showed a fondness for jewels. She was able to secure the services of some highly skilled jewellers such as Posier and Duval so that there was a continuous stream of items of jewellery through the Treasury for remodelling and of rose-cut diamonds for recutting as brilliants. Among the diamonds which the Empress came to own was a pear-shaped oval brilliant, which was set as the centre stone of a hair ornament; it weighed 54.12 metric carats, measured 20.505 mm wide, 24.2 mm long and 11.255 mm deep, and had 120 facets.

At the time nothing seems to have been known about this diamond, so where might it have come from? It is, of course, quite natural to assume that the stone came from India. However, it does not appear to be so in this instance because the most detailed account of the important Brazilian diamonds, *Os Grandes Diamantes Brasileiros*, written by Esmeraldino Reis and published under governmental auspices in 1959, includes this diamond. Under the name of the 'Empress Eugénie', it is stated to have weighed more than 100 carats in the rough and to have been found about 1760 in the region of Chapada Diamantina, an area in the province of Minas Gerais which had yielded several other notable stones. Afterwards the Empress Eugénie is said to have been cut in Holland – more than likely since many of the biggest Brazilian diamonds were then being exported to Lisbon before being sent on to Amsterdam for cutting. At that time the Dutch capital flourished as both a trading and cutting centre for diamonds; a few years later it was to be the location for the purchase of the Orlov, the most celebrated of all the diamonds that ended up in Russia.

Among the Catherine the Great's supporters in the coup of July 1762 was Grigori Aleksandrovich Potemkin (1739–1791). He distinguished himself in the war between Russia and Turkey which began in 1768 and was not resolved until six years later. The year 1774 marked a watershed in Potemkin's career: he became the lover of the Empress and the most powerful man in Russia. Potemkin was the only one of Catherine's lovers to play an extensive political role in the running of the country. Generally the Empress refrained from mixing business with pleasure – doubtless an admirable precept, increasingly disregarded in recent times – and chose her ministers for their abilities. Potemkin's liaison with Catherine lasted for only two years but he was always treated as an equal by her and was the only one of her favourites to whom she referred as 'my husband'.

The Empress bestowed upon Potemkin the surname of Tavrichesky (a name taken from the Khersonesus Taurica or Crimea, an area added by Potemkin to the Russian Empire); a magnificent palace called the Tauride, later the seat of the Imperial Duma (Parliament); and the 51-carat brilliant which for a time became known as the Potemkin diamond. The gem was just one of the objects in the vast personal wealth which Potemkin amassed; he revelled in ostentation and on one occasion is said to have given a banquet which cost more than 20,000 roubles. After his death he bequeathed his large collection of jewellery to his favourite niece, Countess Branitsky, who, in turn, left it to her daughter, Princess Coloredo.

The second of the two Empresses to have owned the diamond now appears on the scene. Eugenia Maria de Montijo de Guzmán was born in 1826, the daughter of a Spanish nobleman who had fought on the French side during Napoleon's Peninsular War in Spain. Eugenia travelled to Paris when Louis Napoleon became President of the Second Republic in December 1848. Unlike Catherine the Great, Eugenia was a great physical beauty so that she soon attracted the attention of the President. After he had been proclaimed Emperor, Napoleon III married Eugenia (who became the Empress Eugénie) on 29 January 1853. He bought Potemkin's diamond from Princess Coloredo as a wedding present for his young bride. Henceforth the diamond became known as the 'Eugénie' and was set as the centre stone in a fine diamond necklace.

The Empress became known as a leader of fashion, so that jewels were constantly being added to her collection, but the diamond named after her always remained her favourite gem. At the same time it also became apparent that her influence upon her husband's policies, both domestic and foreign, was bad. She encouraged extravagance at Court; is credited with having had a preponderant voice in the disastrous decision to create a French-sponsored

The Eugénie diamond, now privately owned. 95

Photograph Donald Woodrow. De Beers Archives.

kingdom in Mexico; and urged Napoleon III to fight Prussia. This last step led to the calamitous defeat of France in the Franco-Prussian War of 1870 and the collapse of the Second Empire.

The Empress escaped to England (where she was befriended by Queen Victoria) with a few of her jewels, including the Eugénie diamond, which were placed in the custody of the Bank of England for safe-keeping. It is believed that they had been smuggled out of the Tuileries in Paris wrapped in newspapers. In 1872 Christie's auctioned some of these jewels in London but the sale did not include the Eugénie diamond. This was bought privately for £15,000 by that celebrated collector of diamonds, Mulhar Rao, the Gaekwar of Baroda. After his deposition in 1875 the Eugénie disappeared but

eventually resurfaced in the ownership of Mrs N.J. Dady of Bombay. The diamond was shown in public for the first time in November 1998, when it featured in an exhibition in Paris entitled 'Treasures of the Tsars'. The author expresses his warm appreciation to the present owners, not only for providing the photograph, but also for giving their permission to reproduce its likeness here.

On coming to England, the Empress Eugénie settled first at Chislehurst in Kent, before moving to Farnborough in Hampshire. After the death of her husband in 1873 she continued to play a dominant role in Bonapartist political activities. Her only child, the Prince Imperial, was killed while fighting with the British forces in the Zulu war of 1879. The Empress herself died while on a visit to Madrid in 1920.

96 The Empress Eugénie, known for her great beauty, received the diamond as a wedding gift from her husband, Napoleon III.

Portrait by Winterhalter, 1855. Arenenberg, Napoleon Museum. Photo AKG London

EUGÉNIE

Eureka

In the middle of the last century, southern Africa was a pastoral land. The economy of the oldest and most populous of the colonies, Cape Colony, was both backward and poor, with wool the most important export. There was little in this part of the globe to attract the steady stream of European emigration that was making its way to Australia, New Zealand and the Americas.

So the discovery of diamonds in South Africa in the 1860s and the subsequent opening up of the diamond fields not only marked the beginning of a new era in southern Africa but ultimately led to the transformation of large areas of the continent of Africa.

Before telling the story of the discovery of what came to be recognized as Africa's first diamond, the Eureka, it would be as well to remember that it is possible earlier finds may have preceded it. There are stories that the Bushmen knew about diamonds and found some use for them. Moreover it is of interest to relate the facts concerning two diamonds which found their way into European hands before the Eureka was discovered.

In February 1852 the British troopship, HMS *Birkenhead*, was wrecked off the Cape of Good Hope with the loss of 445 lives. The disaster spawned the saying 'women and children first' as the troops and seamen aboard were ordered to stand fast on the deck while eight women and thirteen children were taken off by lifeboat. One of the officers who had been aboard was Captain McGeough-Bond-Shelton of the 12th Royal Lancers. He had previously bought a rough diamond in Cape Town which he hid for safe-keeping by sewing it into the waistband of his trousers. When HMS *Birkenhead* foundered he was thrown into the shark-infested waters and while he struggled to stay alive, a shark snapped at him. Fortunately it only caught the torn cloth of his trouser leg, ripping it off just below the

diamond in his belt. Eventually, after being rescued, he arrived in London where he had the diamond cut into a gem of 18 carats. In 1873 he returned to his family seat in Co. Tyrone, Ireland, and when he was married he gave his bride a pendant in which the diamond was set.

In 1858 a diamond passed into the hands of Captain E. S. Hanger, of the Bloemfontein Rangers, who had fought in the Basuto War of that year. The gem, which had been found in clay, was said to have been a fine yellowish octahedron; such an item is of course a characteristic South African diamond and one scarcely common in the diamond fields of either India or Brazil, till then the only known sources of diamonds. Captain Hanger sent the diamond to Amsterdam where it is said to have been polished into a fine rose-cut gem. The Countess of Charlemont, who also happened to live in Co. Tyrone, bought Captain Hanger's diamond for £300, depositing it in a bank in the hope that the gem, which she could not then afford to have made up, might in due course become very valuable.

Now Lord Charlemont was at one time the Lord Lieutenant of Co. Tyrone; it is, therefore, likely that he was aware of the existence of Captain McGeough-Bond-Shelton and more than probable that he knew him personally. Could the realization that South Africa was a diamondiferous country have thus spread further afield?

In September 1866, a sale of leases of Crown Lands took place at Hopetown, situated in the most northerly part of Cape Colony, about 800 km north-east of Cape Town. Included among the advertisements of farms for sale were notices concerning the neighbouring farms of De Kalk and Holpan. The former was owned jointly by Schalk Jacobus van Niekerk and his stepfather Siewert Christiaan Wiid, while the same van Niekerk and his brother Hendrik Jacobus were the owners of

Holpan. In November of that year Schalk van Niekerk agreed to sell his share of De Kalk to Daniel Johannes Jacobus Jacobs for £1,125. This sale is of interest because, probably in December 1866, the Eureka diamond was found there.

Recent investigation has suggested that the Eureka was picked up in a hole probably made by a Bushman digging for roots, somewhere within 180 to 360 metres of an old dam wall on the western side of the Orange River, on the De Kalk farm. It has always been thought that the finder of the diamond was Erasmus Jacobs, the fifteen-year-old son of the farmer, and many years later when he was an old man he maintained that this was so in an affidavit. However, it is of interest to note that *The Times* of London, in a report dated 30 September 1867, by which time a degree of excitement about the Cape discoveries had ensued, stated that 'the first diamond was picked up by a little girl at Hopetown'. Further suggestion that it was the daughter, not the son, of Johannes Jacobus Jacobs who found the Eureka is provided by Marian Robertson, the South African writer and broadcaster, in her book *Diamond Fever, South African Diamond History 1866–69 from Primary Sources*. Mrs Robertson discovered the primary sources among the Cape Archives: consequently she has written by far the most compelling and comprehensive accounts of these momentous years in African history. All later writers owe her an incalculable debt. Whether it was the boy or girl who found the Eureka Mrs Robertson thinks it likely that both were present at the historic moment and that a quarrel took place, probably during a game of Five Stones. (This resembles the Roman game whereby the pebbles are placed on the knuckles of a clenched fist: then they are thrown up and attempts are made to catch them all in the hand.)

Early in 1867 the Eureka passed through the hands of several individuals. The first was Schalk van Niekerk, whose involvement in the story of the diamond is best summarized in a long letter which William Buchanan Chalmers, then Civil Commissioner and Resident Magistrate at Hopetown, wrote to the *Grahamstown Journal*. Mrs Robertson's opinion is that of all the personalities who came to be involved with the diamond's discovery, it was Chalmers who provided the most reliable account of the facts therein. Chalmers wrote as follows:

> ...The first diamond was discovered by pure accident. It was used for a long time by the children of a Dutch farmer called Jacobs, as a plaything. These people are very ignorant... This diamond might have been lost or thrown away... but fortunately another Dutch farmer, a Mr Schalk van Niekerk, a very observant man, and one more intelligent than the rest of his countrymen in this district, happened to visit Jacobs' place. Seeing the children playing with some nice stones he had a look at them, and at once took notice of the gem. He had no idea that it was a diamond, but thought it was a rare-looking stone, very different from the others. He took it up, feeling it heavier than the weight of an ordinary pebble of such a size, his enquiring mind thought he would try to find out what sort of stone it was. He offered to purchase it from Mrs Jacobs, but she laughed at the idea of selling a stone, and told him that if he took a fancy to the stone he could have it for nothing. Niekerk then took it to O'Reilly, and asked him to find out what sort of stone it was...

Interestingly, another much earlier writer on the diamond fields, George Beet, tells of a story about the van Niekerk family to the effect that a government surveyor named von Ludwig had told Schalk van Niekerk that the country appeared to be of a diamondiferous nature. Von Ludwig is said to have given van Niekerk a book on precious stones and told him to keep his eyes open. Examination of the folio of Hopetown farms in the Cape Town Registry of Deeds has revealed that W. F. J. von Ludwig was involved in surveying Crown Lands along the Orange River during 1859. Among the farms which von Ludwig surveyed was De Kalk together with others upon which diamonds were subsequently found.

The next person to figure prominently in the history of the Eureka was the O'Reilly mentioned in Chalmers' account. John Robert O'Reilly, son of the former Civil Commissioner of Somerset East, Cape Province, was a hunter and trader. He happened to be returning from an expedition in the interior when van Niekerk showed him the stone and asked him to find out what it was. According to Chalmers, van Niekerk mentioned to O'Reilly his suspicions that it was a diamond because of its hardness, its weight and the fact that it cut glass so easily and well. However, O'Reilly always maintained that he was the first person to have recognized it as a diamond. He travelled to Hopetown where he showed it to everyone, saying so, but because they laughed at him he nearly threw the object away. He persevered, however, and went on to Colesberg where apparently one half believed his theory and the others scoffed at it.

Whatever the truth may be, O'Reilly never stopped trying to get full credit for the discovery of the Eureka as a diamond. On 27 July 1869 he petitioned Parliament; the petition read 'Mr John Robert O'Reilly of Colesberg, praying the House that as it was through his instrumentality the valuable discovery of diamonds in South Africa was made public, he may be awarded a Grant of Land or a Sum of Money in recognition of his Services.' The Speaker ruled that the petition could not be received by the House as it was contrary to the Standing Rules. Three years later O'Reilly petitioned again and once more he was unsuccessful. Although presented for the 'favourable consideration of the House' it was withdrawn after discussion. In 1894 he petitioned for the third time and it was referred to the Select

Traditional belief has attributed the discovery of the Eureka in 1866, on the banks of the Orange River, to Erasmus Jacobs, then aged fifteen.

Committee on Pensions, Grants and Gratuities but the petition was not recommended for any recognition, pension or reward. In addition O'Reilly wrote to Cecil Rhodes in his capacity as a Director of the British South Africa Company requesting his influence with the company to give him a farm in Matabeleland. The Secretary of the British South Africa Company also forwarded a copy of O'Reilly's letter for consideration by the Board of Directors of De Beers Consolidated Mines Limited.

Whether or not O'Reilly has been treated unfairly concerning the part which he claimed to have played in the discovery of the Eureka, he can at least derive some posthumous satisfaction in knowing that the stone is still today often referred to as the O'Reilly diamond.

To return to Colesberg, O'Reilly's son stated in an interview that when his father visited the place some men grabbed hold of the diamond, threw it out of the window and poured scorn on his father's opinion. Next morning he was obliged to hunt for hours before he found the precious stone. Fortunately O'Reilly acted upon the suggestion of Chalmers and sent the stone to the man who proved to be the first person to authenticate the Eureka as a diamond.

By 1867 Dr William Guybon Atherstone, of Grahamstown, already had a notable career behind him. He had the distinction of being the first doctor in South Africa and the first person outside Europe and America to use an anaesthetic for an operation. Atherstone had also become a Fellow of the Royal Geographical Society, a distinction that reflected his lifelong preoccupation with geology, mineralogy and botany. His fame as an amateur geologist was widespread so that it was not surprising that Chalmers should have suggested the stone be sent to him for examination.

After receiving O'Reilly's stone by post, Atherstone submitted it to the necessary tests: he pronounced it to be a veritable diamond weighing 21¼ carats, worth £800. In his letter of confirmation to Richard Southey, the Colonial Secretary, Cape Colony, Atherstone, as befits a man of many parts, only mentioned this fact in the third paragraph of his letter. However, from the same communication we can see that it was Atherstone who inspired the idea of sending the diamond for display in the Cape Colony's stand in the forthcoming Paris Exhibition. Atherstone wrote similarly to Lorenzo Boyes, Clerk to the Civil Commissioner and Clerk of the Peace, Colesberg, with the result that the latter's local paper, the *Colesberg Advertiser*, lost no time in printing the following piece:

The Wonderful South African Diamond.
There is a story this morning afoot in the village. It has just been told us by a lady, and we give it just as we have heard it. A Mr. John O'Reilly, a hunter, explorer, &c., something of the Dr. Livingstone stamp, though not yet quite so well known, in his travels in the North Country – somewhere about the Orange River, picked up a stone two or three months since, which he thought had something remarkable about it, and brought it down with him. It was shown to several persons here, and was at length sent down to Dr. Atherstone of Grahamstown to be examined, and as the lady told us, a letter has come by this morning's post from the Doctor, saying that it is a Diamond and worth £800. Now we quite expect that the 'Great Eastern' will have a grand laugh at us about the South African Diamond, as he did some time ago about the Orange River Serpent – but we have stated the report just as we have heard it. – Stranger things, however, have come to pass in the world than the discovery of diamonds in South Africa.

The Colonial Secretary acknowledged Atherstone's letter and suggested he send the diamond to him at Cape Town to be forwarded to the Crown Agents in London for examination and, if it should prove to be a genuine diamond, for exhibition afterwards. On 18 April Southey wrote:

I have had it examined by such persons as I could find competent to judge – among others, one Louis Hond, a Hollander, and a professional Diamond Polisher of 22 years standing; and another Hollander, a Diamond Cutter; both of whom pronounce it to be a genuine Diamond, of good quality equal to the Bahia diamonds. Also, Mons. Héritte, the French Consul, who knows a good deal about these matters; and he concurs. Hond weighed the stone and found it, according to his scales 21 3/16 carats and his estimate of value is £500 in the rough and £800 after being cut and polished which he thinks would reduce its weight to between 12 and 15 carats. This morning he offered me £400 for it. Of course I cannot sell; and, as it may be worth much more, it is better to let is be sold in England for account of O'Reilly.

There is evidence to show that Hond, the experienced Dutch diamond cutter, was a somewhat shifty character. Moreover, it is interesting to speculate upon the reason for him leaving his home country and settling in Cape. Could it have been that while he was working in Holland he came to learn of the presence of diamonds in South Africa as the result of the cutting in Amsterdam of Captain Hanger's diamond?

At any rate Hond, who was soon to move to Hopetown and set up a business there, tried to obtain his cut out of his visit to the Colonial Secretary's office, sending in an account for the part he played in the valuation of the diamond.

On the other hand it is clear that Southey was more than justified in seeking the opinion of M. Héritte, the French Consul at the Cape since August 1864. In a letter to Southey, dated 18 June 1867, Héritte clearly showed a considerable knowledge not only of the diamond itself but of the workings of the diamond trade as it existed at the time. A century later he would certainly not have been out of his depth in the contemporary diamond industry! But somewhere along the line, dismissal of his knowledge, professional jealousy or probably suspicion regarding his nationality must have wounded the susceptibilities of the Consul because earlier the following letter to Southey had

99

appeared in the columns of the *Cape Argus*:

Cape Town, April 26, 1867

Monsieur The Colonial Secretary — The Advertiser and Mail having published an article doubting the statement which I made respecting the Stone which was shown to me at the Colonial office, and which at the distance of six paces I declared to be a real diamond — not, as the Argus stated, because I am a Frenchman, and that all Frenchmen have knowledge of diamonds, which is a great mistake, but because I have a knowledge of mineralogy, especially of precious stones — I am ready now to purchase the stone in its present rough state for £500. The stone is worth more, but as there are risks attending its internal organism and the cutting on that account I reduce my offer to £500. Should my offer be accepted by the Government at once, I will pay the £500 so soon as the stone shall be received by me, and I am ready to give in writing an undertaking to that effect.

Receive, Monsieur the Colonial Secretary the assurance of my deepest respect.

Héritte, Consul of France.

The interest — indeed almost excitement — in some quarters in the Cape died down as the Eureka was despatched to England in the Union Company's steamship *Celt* which, after a voyage of thirty-two days, arrived at Plymouth on 21 May 1867. *The Times* of London drew its readers' attention to the fact that the ship had brought two unusual items of cargo, two live koodoos, the first of this species of antelope to be brought to England, and a specimen of some stones found in the Orange River and pronounced by the Colony to be diamonds.

The agent for the Cape Colony in London, Penrose G. Julyan, lost no time in collecting the diamond from the Colonial Office and submitting it to the Crown Jewellers, Garrard & Co. On 8 June they wrote to Julyan informing him that the stone submitted for valuation was a diamond of good quality, slightly coloured, having one or two small defects, weighing 21⅞ carats, and worth about £500. Southey, in due course, received the following letter from Julyan which he must have been keenly awaiting:

The gem which you sent me by that last Mail proved to be a veritable Diamond, the estimated value of which is about £500 in its present state.

Seeing the possibility of some unfair play being practised upon me if I submitted the Stone direct to the diamond dealers who are the only reliable judges as to quality and value, I thought it best to place the matter in the hands of Garrard and Co who are from time to time entrusted with the Crown Jewels and who have large dealings in Diamonds. They at once pronounced it a real stone, but before sending me the letter of which a copy is enclosed, they submitted it to a Mr Costa who is considered a great authority on diamonds, and their note may be considered as expressing his opinion as well as their own. The far famed 'Kohi-nor' [sic] was cut by Mr Costa on the premises of Messrs. Garrard, indeed he is probably more extensively engaged in cutting diamonds than any man in Europe.

I shall wait for the arrival of the next Mail before I take any steps to exhibit it in Paris, as there will be considerable risk and expense attending such a step, and if it is to be sold I think I may possibly make it a condition with the purchaser that he is to exhibit it there, as 'The Cape Diamond' — or failing that, to Exhibit a model instead of the real thing. Mr Currey strongly advocates the latter course, as he does not relish the responsibility attending its custody. If this should lead to the discovery of a Diamond field equal to that found at Pasaquassu, in Brazil, in the year 1845, it will be a fine thing for the Colony.

Messrs. Garrard would I think be glad to buy any number of such gems as you could produce at the market price of the day.

The diamond was taken to Windsor for

inspection by Queen Victoria. Doubtless much to the relief of J. B. Currey, the man entrusted with the management of the Cape Colony's stand at the Paris Exhibition, it was not exhibited there; instead, Currey's suggestion was adopted and a replica in crystal of what the Eureka would look like after cutting was sent. Although neatly arranged, this Exhibition attracted little notice among the profusion of magnificent objects on display and added only slight interest to the Colony's stand. However, the tone of another letter which Julyan wrote at this time to Lorenzo Boyes indicates that doubts still existed in London about the Eureka: not so much about the genuineness of the stone as a diamond but whether some kind of hoax had been perpetrated and it had not come from Africa at all. Meanwhile the diamond remained in the safe of the Crown Agents until after it had been purchased.

Its purchaser was none other than Sir Philip Wodehouse, the Governor of the Cape Colony and High Commissioner during the period of the Eureka's discovery. By then Sir Philip had already purchased for £200 the second diamond to have been found in South Africa; however, his desire to purchase the Eureka was to involve numerous individuals in voluminous correspondence for the rest of the year 1867. Some of this was caused by the claim of Wiid, the stepfather of van Niekerk, that he was the owner of the De Kalk farm and was, therefore, entitled to the proceeds from the sale of the diamond.

The Governor considered that this particular matter was no concern of the government at the Cape as he had understood that in sending it to England for examination the Colonial Secretary, Richard Southey, had acted only as a personal friend. Eventually Wiid was obliged to waive his claim to any of the proceeds. It was John O'Reilly who received the £500 which the Governor paid for the diamond. According to the promise which he had made to van Niekerk, O'Reilly gave half the amount to him and told him to give the little boy, Erasmus Jacobs, something; it is possible that van Niekerk, as one of the vendors of De Kalk to the Jacobs family, may have taken the share of proceeds of the Eureka off the price of the farm. However in 1932, by which time he was over eighty years of age, Jacobs recorded that neither he nor any of his family had ever received any money from their neighbour or O'Reilly for the original diamond, or from the South African government in recognition of the fact that they had made the discovery which had brought so much prosperity to the Cape. Sadly, Jacobs spent the last years of his life in extreme poverty.

Sir Philip Wodehouse is known to have purchased

100   Opposite: The Eureka — this first African diamond to have gained authenticity, remains historically important, despite its yellow colour and inclusions.

De Beers Archives.

EUREKA

five diamonds that passed through the hands of the Colonial Secretary in addition to the Eureka. Following his relinquishment of the office of Governor of Cape Colony and his return to England in 1870, he had all his diamonds cut and subsequently sold. Towards the end of the century the third Marquess of Bute bought the Eureka. His biographer has written that he purchased some jewellery for Lady Bute in the 1870s at the time of the birth of his son and heir so that it is possible that the Eureka was among the items. Lady Bute survived her husband by some thirty years during which time her youngest son, Lord Colum Crichton-Stuart, continued to live with her. At some time in this period Lord Colum received the diamond as a present from his mother for it was he who sold it at Christie's after the Second World War. On 17 April 1946, *The Times* reported that on the previous day £5,700 had been given for a diamond bangle, the entire circumference mounted with twenty large stones graduating from the centre – the centre oval diamond being the Eureka, the first diamond discovered in South Africa. The bangle was listed in the catalogue of sale as the 'property of a nobleman'.

Mr Peter Locan was the buyer on this occasion; he lent the bangle for display at the splendid exhibition entitled 'The Ageless Diamond' that was staged on the premises of Christie's in 1959. Eight years later, and exactly one hundred years after it had been found, the Eureka returned to South Africa. In April 1967 De Beers bought the diamond and presented it to the Speaker of the House of Assembly as a gift to the people of South Africa. Finally, in October 1983 De Beers announced that the Eureka was coming home. The South African government had decided that Kimberley would be the most fitting place for its display. So it is now on permanent loan to the Mine Museum, situated near the old Kimberley mine, or 'Big Hole' as it is familiarly known to many.

If the Eureka were to be displayed alongside many of the most celebrated diamonds it would probably attract comparatively little attention from an aesthetic point of view. It weighs merely 10.73 metric carats, is off-colour, possesses numerous internal imperfections and has not even been well cut – it has a flattish appearance which imparts little of the brilliance one normally expects from such a gem. Historically, however, its importance cannot be over-emphasized, for as the first African diamond to have been authenticated and to have been the harbinger of such momentous events, it illustrates to perfection the truth of lines written by an eighteenth-century English poet:

> Large streams from little fountains flow,
> Tall oaks from little acorns grow.

On 28 May 1971, a sad but inevitable event in mining history occurred: operations finally ceased at Jagersfontein. Not long before, the mine had celebrated its centenary, the first diamond having been picked up in the valley of Jagersfontein in the then Orange Free State in August 1870. Although Jagersfontein was the first of the South African 'pipe' or 'dry diggings' to have been established, its fame was always overshadowed by that of the mines in the Kimberley district, some 130 km north-west. Yet the output of the mine was sufficient to give rise to the use of the term 'Jagers' to denote a diamond of a beautiful faint bluish tint. In addition Jagersfontein was the source of two of the largest and finest diamonds ever to have come to light.

The earlier of these discoveries provided the most dramatic moment in the mine's history. On the evening of 30 June 1893, an African picked up an immense diamond in a shovelful of gravel which he was loading into a truck; he hid it from his overseer and delivered it directly into the hands of the Mine Manager. As a reward he received £500 and a horse equipped with saddle and bridle.

The diamond weighed 971 old carats, equivalent to 995.2 metric carats. It did indeed possess that marvellous blue-white colour characteristic of the finest Jagersfontein diamonds, especially cleavages, and was of very fine quality, although there were numerous internal black spots, another Jagersfontein characteristic. In shape the stone was flat on one side and rose to a peak on the other, rather like a loaf of rye bread. Apparently it was this fact which caused the diamond to be given the name of 'Excelsior', meaning higher.

The Excelsior may justly claim to be the Great Unknown of famous diamonds. As will be explained later on, there is no single 'Excelsior' gem of exceptional size which would have helped to keep its name in the public eye. In addition, except

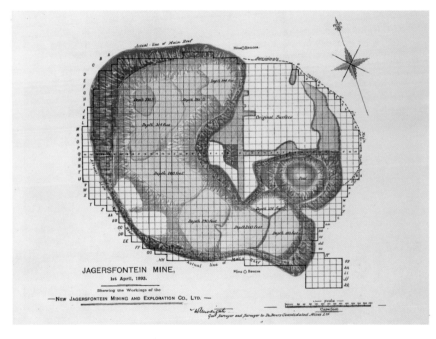

JAGERSFONTEIN MINE,
1st April, 1893.
Shewing the Workings of the
— NEW JAGERSFONTEIN MINING AND EXPLORATION CO., LTD. —

Plan of the Jagersfontein mine, one of the first South African 'dry diggings' to be discovered, which yielded two of the largest and finest diamonds in the world.

Courtesy Phillips/De Beers.

for having stimulated some interest among local diggers, the finding of such a mighty stone seems to have made singularly little impact. No account of the discovery appeared in the more authoritative and prestigious British newspapers which often reported lesser discoveries at the time. Perhaps if the diamond had originally been given a rather less prosaic name its fame might have spread further afield. Yet consider the facts. Prior to the discovery of the Excelsior the only rival to the stone was the legendary Great Mogul of Indian origin, generally thought to have weighed 787½ old carats. The so-called 'Braganza', which was found in Brazil in the eighteenth century and according to some sources weighed 1,680 carats, was considered to have been a white sapphire, topaz or aquamarine, certainly not a diamond. So the Excelsior still rates as the second largest rough diamond of gem quality ever to have been found, being surpassed only by the Cullinan.

After various vicissitudes the Jagersfontein mine eventually became the sole property of the New Jagersfontein Mining and Exploration Company Limited, formed in April 1887. It so happened that on the very day that the Excelsior was found the contract between the mining company and the syndicate of London firms which purchased the mine's output expired. Had the diamond been found a few hours earlier it would have made a substantial difference in profit to the parties concerned. However, the Excelsior was shipped to the London offices, located at 29 and 30 Holborn Viaduct, of Messrs Wernher, Beit & Co., the largest of the ten firms that comprised the London Syndicate. Wernher, Beit & Co. endeavoured to insure the diamond for £40,000 but at first could only effect insurance to the extent of £16,250.

In the Directors' Report for the year ended 31 March 1894, the Chairman of the New Jagersfontein Mining and Exploration Company stated:

In addition to the foregoing the Company still retains an undivided one-half share in the 'Excelsior' diamond weighing 971 carats, found on 30 June 1893, which (although it is impossible at the present moment to place any exact value upon, and has therefore not been stocked at all) will ultimately prove a very valuable asset of the Company.

The valuable asset remained in London where it was joined in 1895 by the second of the two great diamonds to have originated in Jagersfontein. This weighed 634 carats, equivalent to 650.8 metric carats, and was first named the 'Reitz' after F.W. Reitz, then President of the Orange Free State. It was renamed the 'Jubilee' when it was cut in 1897, the year which marked Queen Victoria's Diamond Jubilee. Accordingly the Chairman of the Mining Company, at the Annual General Meeting held in Kimberley 28 May 1896, stated:

Since the last meeting a large and very fine diamond of 634 carats, named the Reitz Diamond, has been found, and although neither the 'Excelsior' nor this recent acquisition has yet been disposed of, your Directors have deemed it advisable, in the interests of present shareholders, to stock the Company's one half interest in both diamonds, but the actual figure, as will be obvious to all, it is most injudicious to state publicly.

The very next day after his meeting, the minutes of a Company Board meeting recorded the receipt of the following letter to the Secretary, New Jagersfontein Mining and Exploration Co. Limited, Kimberley:

Dear Sir, I beg to inform you that Messrs Wernher, Beit & Co, Barnato Bros & Mosenthal Sons & Co have accepted your offer to buy your Company's half interest in the two Stones called the 'Excelsior' and 'Reitz' Diamonds weighing 971 and 634 carats respectively for the sum of £25,000 (twenty five thousand pounds) cash.

It is specially agreed upon that the price paid above is not to be disclosed outside the Diamond committee or your Board of Directors.

I should thank you to confirm the terms of this letter and shall on receipt of your reply pay your Company the stipulated £25,000 on behalf of the above-named firms.

I am, Dear Sir, Yours faithfully, Herrman Hirsche

The minutes continue: 'Resolved that the above offer be accepted and the Secretary was instructed to confirm the same.'

Thus was concluded what can only be described as one of the most profitable transactions – from the purchaser's point of view – ever to have been made in the diamond trade. As a result of the sale the Jubilee diamond was cut in the following year into two gems. The larger of the two was a cushion shape weighing 245.35 carats, which would rank as the sixth largest polished diamond in the world. But no buyer appeared on the scene for the Excelsior and eventually, in 1903, it was despatched to I.J. Asscher of Amsterdam. This famous firm, destined to cut the Cullinan diamond, had been founded by Mr. J.J. Asscher (1843–1902).

Yet again misfortune dogged the Excelsior, since it was destined not to be one of those diamonds which yields a single magnificent gem; instead, it was cut into several smaller ones. There were suggestions that no prospective buyer could be found owing to the diamond's exceptional size. In his book *Some Dreams Come True*, Alpheus F. Williams, who succeeded his father as General Manager of De Beers, entertained no doubts about the matter, considering the decision to cleave the diamond into several smaller fragments as the greatest tragedy of modern times in the history of famous diamonds. He wrote:

It was unpardonable that this exquisite diamond was so cleaved that the largest stone cut from it weighed only 70 metric carats. The intrinsic value meant more to its owners than its historical importance, so different from the spirit of the owners of the Cullinan diamond who, in deciding to have the diamond cleaved into nine pieces, insisted that one of the pieces so cleaved should be, when cut, the largest diamond in the world.

On the other hand two points should be borne in mind when considering this extract from Mr Williams's book. First, it will be recalled that the owners of the Excelsior had also been the owners of the Jubilee; no accusation, therefore, could be levelled at them of necessarily wanting to place value before historical importance since the Jubilee had been fashioned so as to yield one truly exceptional gem. Secondly, a comparison between the Cullinan and Excelsior diamonds is meaningless. Whereas the Cullinan had only one large imperfection in the heart, the Excelsior possessed numerous dark inclusions. Dutch cutters, the world's best, decided this meant considerable loss of weight.

After prolonged study it was, therefore, decided first to cleave the diamond into ten pieces: this

The Excelsior I, cut from the second largest rough diamond of gem quality ever found, possesses the rare blue-white colour characteristic of the finest Jagersfontein diamonds.

Courtesy Phillips.

operation, which was performed by Mr A. Asscher, resulted in the three largest pieces weighing 158, 147 and 130 carats. The polishing was supervised by Henri Koe and yielded 21 gems, ranging from 70 carats to less than 1 carat. They totalled 373.75 carats which represented a loss in weight of almost 63 per cent. The final result, however, was considered to have been better than anyone had dared to forecast. The details of the larger gems cut from the Excelsior are as follows:

Excelsior I	69.68 metric cts	Pear-shape
Excelsior II	47.03 metric cts	Pear-shape
Excelsior III	46.90 metric cts	Pear-shape
Excelsior IV	40.23 metric cts	Marquise
Excelsior V	34.91 metric cts	Pear-shape
Excelsior VI	28.61 metric cts	Marquise
Excelsior VII	26.30 metric cts	Marquise
Excelsior VIII	24.31 metric cts	Pear-shape
Excelsior IX	16.78 metric cts	Pear-shape
Excelsior X	13.86 metric cts	Pear-shape
Excelsior XI	9.82 metric cts	Pear-shape

The Excelsior gems were sold separately, three of them being bought by Tiffany & Co., in their old store in Union Square in New York City. The names of the other buyers have not been disclosed but it is known that De Beers displayed one of the marquises at the New York World Fair in 1939.

In January 1984 Graff Diamonds Limited, of London, announced the acquisition and subsequent sale of five exceptional diamonds among a series of transactions to clients. The most historic stone was the Excelsior I which, according to Laurence Graff, had remained in the possession of the same family in the United States until his firm's purchase of it. The gem reappeared for sale in May 1991, when the GIA certified it as 'G' colour (rare white), and again in May 1996, when it was bought by Robert Mouawad for $2,642,800.

It is possible that two more of the larger gems cut from 'The Great Unknown' diamond may have come to light within recent years. At an exhibition called 'The Court of Jewels', presented by Harry Winston, Inc., in San Antonio, Texas, in 1949, there was a 40-carat marquise, measuring 25.4 by 19 mm. Little appears to have been known about this diamond before its purchase by Mr Winston from a prominent American family. Could it have been Excelsior IV? On 23 January 1957, a diamond necklace with a pendant, owned by Mrs John E. Rovensky, came up for auction at the Parke-Bernet Galleries. The pendant was a pear-shaped diamond weighing approximately 46.50 carats. Since it had originally been acquired from Tiffany's, is there not a distinct possibility that this gem was none other than Excelsior III?

The history of this, one of the most famous of all diamonds and variously known as the 'Florentine', 'Tuscan', 'Grand Duke of Tuscany' or the 'Austrian Yellow', has over the centuries become very confused.

In 1880 the Austrian authorities issued a publication entitled *Catalogue of the objects contained in the Treasury of the Imperial Royal House of Austria* which only served to add to the confusion. The account of the 'Florentine' contained therein stated that the diamond had once been in the ownership of Charles the Bold, Duke of Burgundy (1433–77). The name of this mediaeval warrior, who devoted a large part of his energies to establishing Burgundy as a powerful and independent kingdom, often crops up in diamond literature. It has been stated that in 1476 the Duke of Burgundy handed over three diamonds for cutting to the celebrated cutter Lodewyk van Bercken, who is credited with having been the first to conceive the idea of cutting diamonds to a deliberate geometrical design, thereby releasing their brilliance and 'fire' to an unprecedented degree. According to Lodewyk's descendant, Robert de Berquen, the Duke of Burgundy gave away two of these diamonds: a triangular-shaped stone that was presented to Louis XI of France, with whom he had allied himself, and a thinly cut stone that was presented to Pope Sixtus IV.

Charles the Bold retained the third diamond, a thickly cut stone set in a ring, which at the time was described as 'one of the largest diamonds in Christendom'. It was of a pyramidal shape, 15.8 mm square at the base, with the apex cut into a four-rayed star coinciding with the middle of each face of the pyramid. It is often alleged, as in the above-mentioned catalogue, that this diamond is the Florentine.

Other accounts have identified it with other famous diamonds, while it has further been stated that, according to the custom of the day, the Duke of Burgundy always went forth into battle with his jewels, first to keep them under observation, secondly on account of the mysterious powers attributed to precious stones. However, if one were to believe the various accounts of the exploits of Charles the Bold it would almost seem as if he went into battle with a portmanteau marked 'Famous Diamonds' and that he lost all his possessions on a variety of battlefields. Two facts are beyond doubt: first, that his pyramidal-shaped diamond is a different gem from the Florentine, and secondly that he was defeated and killed by the Swiss at the Battle of Nancy in 1477.

The authentic history of the Florentine begins with its ownership by the Medicis, one of the most famous and powerful families in Europe, whose name appears in Florentine chronicles as early as the 12th century. The Medicis started as rich merchants in Florence, became rulers of the city during the Renaissance and, in due course, Grand Dukes of Tuscany in the sixteenth, seventeenth and eighteenth centuries. That indefatigable traveller and collector of gems, Jean Baptiste Tavernier, visited the Court of the reigning Duke of Tuscany, Ferdinand II (1610–70), in 1657 and he was able to examine and weigh the Florentine, which had probably reached Italy via one of the customary trade routes from the East. In his celebrated work *Six Voyages of John Baptiste Tavernier* (an English edition was published in London in 1678) he wrote as follows:

The Great Duke of Tuscany's Diamond weighs 139 carats, clean and well-shaped cut in facets every way: but in regard the water inclines somewhat toward the colour of Citron; I do not value the first carat above 135 livres; so that by the rule the Diamond ought to be worth 2608336 livres.

Five pages further on in his book, Tavernier drew the diamond and wrote:

Number 2: Is the figure of a Diamond belonging to the Great Duke of Tuscany. It weighs 139 carats and a half: the fault of it is that the water inclines somewhat to a Citron colour.

The illustrious Florentine diamond, destined to pass through the hands of numerous rulers, disappeared with the last Austrian Emperor and has since remained a mystery.

De Beers Archives.

According to the current system of weights, the Florentine would weigh 137.27 metric carats. When Tavernier saw the diamond it was the largest known in Europe. If the measurements of the Duke of Burgundy's diamond have been correctly reported, such a gem would not have approximated the weight of the Florentine. The great diamond was cut as a double rose, with 126 facets and an irregular nonagonal outline, giving it the appearance of a nine-rayed star. This style of cutting was recognized as being typically Indian which renders it even more unlikely that it was one of the diamonds which van Bercken cut for the Duke of Burgundy.

When it became evident that the Medici family was nearing the end of its long and illustrious reign, the European powers made arrangements in 1735 whereby Tuscany would come under the rule of the Dukes of Lorraine. Following the death of the last male Medici, Gian Gastone (1671–1737), this plan was put into effect, but not without considerable resistance from Gian Gastone's sister, Anna Maria Medici. It was due to her efforts that a considerable part of the treasures amassed by the Medicis was preserved for the city of Florence and its citizens. The Florentine diamond, however, did leave the home of the Medicis in 1743 to become part of the Crown Jewels of Austria when that country's ruler, the Empress Maria Theresa, was betrothed to Francis Stephen, Duke of Lorraine, who had earlier inherited the dukedom of Tuscany. At his coronation as the Emperor Francis I, he wore the Florentine diamond set in a crown. Subsequently, the gem was set in a hat surrounded by other diamonds.

After the collapse of the Habsburg Empire in 1918, the Crown Jewels, including the Florentine which was then set in a brooch, accompanied the royal family into exile in Switzerland. Since then, nothing definite has been known of the whereabouts of this famous gem. According to a spokesman for the Empress, it may have been among the jewels which a member of the royal family's entourage, who proved less than honest, suggested selling in South America. The Crown Jewels in exile had many adventures, including a lawsuit after they had been put up for sale in Lucerne.

At the conclusion of the Second World War there came a report that the Florentine had been returned to Vienna. Previously Hitler had seized what remained of the Austrian Crown Jewels and, for safety's sake, ordered them to be buried in a salt mine near Salzburg. This area of Austria came into the American zone of occupation at the end of the war and General Mark Clark had all the loot restored to Vienna in a public ceremony. Amid much rejoicing, someone reported that the Florentine had returned to its former home. Alas, the report proved false. Officials of the Treasure Room in the Museum of Art confirmed that the gem had left with the last Emperor and had never since been seen in Vienna.

The question of the whereabouts of the Florentine has continued to arouse the interest of gemmologists and historians alike and there has been considerable speculation on the subject.

In 1923 a large yellow diamond, weighing 99.52 carats, appeared in the United States. Significantly, this diamond, known as the Shah of Persia, showed evidence of having been recut and there were veiled suggestions that it may have been the missing Florentine. It was claimed that the Shah of Persia had a history of its own: that it had been brought to America by General V. D. Starosselky, a Russian military expert, who had been loaned to the Persians by the Czar and subsequently rewarded with the diamond by the Persian government in appreciation of his excellent command of its army.

Several facts about the history claimed for the Shah of Persia are, to say the least, puzzling. Considering the prevailing political situation at the time, it would appear strange that the last Czar would have done anything at all to assist the Persians. Furthermore, there is no mention of a General Starosselky in any one of the standard encyclopaedias, works of reference or historical studies on either side of the Atlantic devoted to this period of history. One should surely have expected even a slight reference to someone of this importance. Who was General V. D. Starosselky? He sounds like the invention of one of the French naturalist school of authors – a White Russian who had strayed into the red-light quarter of some city. Lastly, recent research on the Crown Jewels of Iran has disclosed that the country's rulers were by nature rather more apt to acquire jewels than to give them away.

However, the Shah of Persia is cushion-shaped and it is, therefore, debatable whether a diamond of this particular cut, with a weight of almost 100 carats, could have been fashioned from the Florentine. The only way to resolve the question of the identity of the Shah of Persia vis-à-vis the Florentine would be to submit the former to a thorough examination. If it originally came from South Africa, the source of so many large Cape-coloured diamonds, its 'water' would differ considerably from that of an Indian gem.

It is more than probable that if the Florentine had been recut so as to escape detection, it would have been as a brilliant, both for technical and commercial reasons, and in this connection it is interesting to note the research which the American gem historian, Jim Becker, has recently carried out. He has pointed out that only three large round, yellow diamonds are known to exist. The largest is the Moon diamond, a light-yellow brilliant cut, which can be discounted because its weight, 183 carats, exceeds that of the original Florentine. The second, the Stern's Star, weighing 85.93 carats, must be eliminated since the rough stone was only found in South Africa in 1972. It is the third diamond which is of special interest. This is a brilliant weighing 81.56 carats, then set as the pendant to a diamond necklace, which was put up for sale in Geneva in November 1981; its colour is said to have been identical to that of the Florentine. Further investigation undertaken by Mr Becker has revealed that this brilliant showed definite signs of having been recut from a larger stone and that its former owner, a member of a royal family, remembered her father-in-law saying that the gem originally possessed a very old-fashioned cut.

One must hope that this diamond will not be lost sight of and can be examined to determine whether it represents the reincarnation of a historic jewel.

Emperor Francis I of Austria, who wore the Florentine set in his crown at his coronation, was himself a keen mineralogist.

Portrait by Franz Messmer, 1773. Vienna, Natural History Museum. Photo AKG London.

Golden Jubilee

Previously known as the Unnamed Brown, the Golden Jubilee – the world's largest diamond – was renamed in celebration of the 50th anniversary of the reign of King Bhumibol of Thailand.

De Beers Archives.

In 1986 a 755.50-carat rough diamond was found in the Premier mine in South Africa. It was of a beautiful, golden yellow colour with a bright reddish hue at its centre, and measured 53.65 mm in width, 49.20 mm in length, and 34.23 mm in depth. The appearance of this huge diamond could not have come at a better time as much of the advanced technology, which was shortly to be successfully employed in the cutting and polishing of the Centenary, was first practised upon it.

When Gabi Tolkowsky – who was responsible for the cutting of the Centenary – first set eyes on the big brown diamond, he commented that 'within its heart lay a wonderfully mysterious shine, that gave to the diamond a character unlike any other'. But it also provided him with a formidable challenge. The stone possessed a large surface with deep cracks extruding from its interior and it contained several inclusions which could have caused serious problems at any time during the cutting and polishing process.

Before work on the diamond could be started, an underground room had to be constructed in an area totally free of vibration. Work began on 24 May 1988, and by the end of June the stone's weight had been reduced to 716.84 carats. Then it was realized that the equipment would have to be redesigned so that it was not until the end of May in the following year that the weight of the stone was further reduced to 700.70 carats.

By May 1990 the stone was finished; the result was a magnificent golden-yellow gem, weighing 545.65 carats, whose cut was described by Gabi Tolkowsky as 'Fire-Rose cushion-shape'. It was given a total of 148 perfectly symmetrical facets, 55 above the girdle, 69 below and 24 on the girdle itself – the 'circle of light' said Tolkowsky, speaking of the diamond's girdle a few years later. The gem measures 51.08 mm by 47.26 mm by 33.50mm.

The Unnamed Brown, as it was then called, became the largest polished diamond ever, surpassing the weight of Cullinan I by more than 15 carats, although it cannot be compared in either colour or quality with that great diamond. The GIA Gem Trade Laboratory described the brown diamond thus: 'according to the records of the GIA Trade Laboratory, the 545.65 carat modified cushion brilliant cut described in Identification and Origin of Color Report 8424655, dated February 4, 1994, is the largest diamond which we have reported on as of the date of this letter and the report issued.'

The Golden Jubilee was graciously received by the King's daughter, Princess Matia Chari Sirindhom, on his behalf in 2000, and the stone is now on display at the Royal Museum at Pimammek Golden Temple Throne Hall in Bangkok. officials estimating that between 350,000 and 450,000 people had gazed at the showcase.

King Bhumibol and Queen Sirakit visited the fair and showed great interest in the brown diamond, which was removed from the case for them to handle. It was then realized that the acquisition of the gem would be a most appropriate way to celebrate the 50th anniversary of the King's ascent to the throne. Accordingly, a group of Thai businessmen arranged for the diamond to be given to the King as a gift from the people of Thailand. Once the arrangements had been concluded, and with the consent of the King, the diamond was named the Golden Jubilee, in honour of the occasion.

The Golden Jubilee was graciously received by the King's daughter, Princess Matia Chari Sirindhom, on his behalf in 2000, and the stone is now on display at the Royal Museum at Pimammek Golden Temple Throne Hall in Bangkok.

Great Mogul

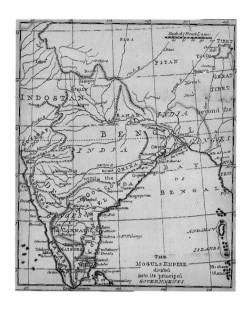

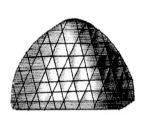

Tavernier's drawing of the the Great Mogul to which he referred to three times in his book *The Six Voyages of Jean Baptiste Tavernier.*

Above right: original map of India depicting the extent of the Mogul Empire in the 17th century.

Courtesy Eric Bruton.

Opposite page: the Mogul Emperor Aurangzeb enthroned, who showed the jewels to Tavernier when the latter visited his court in 1665.

Indian 17th century miniature. By permission of the British Library.

he legendary Great Mogul is the largest diamond yet recorded to have been found in India – that is according to the accepted accounts of its mysterious history. However, even though it may be heretical to do so, one must query its original weight, stated to have been 787 ½ carats.

The diamond is believed to have been unearthed in the Kollur diggings in the vicinity of Golconda around 1650, thus placing its discovery during the reign of the fifth Mogul Emperor, Shah Jahan. But it was that ruler's son and successor, Aurangzeb, who was responsible for having the diamond shown to Jean Baptiste Tavernier. Tavernier referred to the gem three times in his *Six Voyages*. The first reference is in Volume II, where he writes:

On November 1st, 1665, I was at the palace to take leave of the King. But he sent word to say that he did not wish me to leave without seeing his jewels, since I had seen the splendour of his fête. Early next day there came five or six officers from the Nabob Jafer Khan to summon me to the King's presence. On my arrival at the Court the two keepers of the royal jewels, of which I have elsewhere spoken, accompanied me to his Majesty, and after the customary salutations they brought me to a small room at one end of the hall where the King was seated on his throne, and whence he could see us. In this room I found Akel Khan, chief keeper of the State jewels, who on seeing us ordered four of the King's eunuchs to fetch the jewels which were brought on two large trays, lacquered with gold leaf, and covered with small cloths, made on purpose, one of red velvet, the other of embroidered green velvet. After uncovering and counting over the pieces there several times, an inventory of the same was drawn up by three scribes present on the occasion. For the Indians do everything with great care and composure and when they see anyone acting in a hurry or irritated they stare at him in silence and laugh at him for a fool.

The first piece that Akel Khan placed in my hands was the great diamond which is rose cut, round and very high on one side. On the lower edge there is a slight crack, and a little flaw in it. Its water is fine, and weighs 319½ ratis, which makes 280 of our carats, the rati being ⅞ of a carat. When Mirgimola [Mir Jumla], who betrayed his master, the King of Golconda, presented this stone to Shah Jahan, to whom he withdrew, it was in the rough state (brut), and at that time weighed 900 ratis, which makes 787½ carats, and there were several flaws in

it. Had this stone been in Europe it would have been treated differently: for some fine pieces would have been taken from it, and it would have remained heavier than it now is, instead of which it has been quite ground down. It was Hortensio Borgio who cut it, for which he was also badly paid. When it was cut he was reproached for having spoilt the stone which might have remained heavier, and, instead of rewarding him for his work, the King fined him 10,000 rupees, and would have taken more if he had possessed more. If Hortensio knew his business well, he would have taken from this large stone some fine pieces without wronging the King, and without having so much trouble to grind it down. But he was not a very skilful diamond cutter.

Fifty pages later is Tavernier's second reference:

A number of stones are now found here from 10 to 40 carats, and even occasionally of much larger size. But amongst others, the great diamond which weighed 900 carats before being cut, and which Mirgimola presented to Aurangzeb, as I have elsewhere said, had been taken from this mine.

The third reference occurs when Tavernier gives details of all the large gems which he had encountered during his travels, illustrating his accounts with drawings. Tavernier describes the stone as follows:

This diamond belongs to the Great Mogul, who did me the honour of showing it to me with all his other jewels. The form is shown in which it remained after being cut, and having been permitted to weigh it, I found that it weighs 319½ ratis, which make 279⁹/₁₆ of our carats. In the rough state it weighed… 907 ratis which make 793 carats. This stone presents the form of an egg cut in half.

Tavernier was surprised at the heaviness of the diamond when he weighed it, but was assured that it was the same stone which had originally come from the Kollur diamond field. His surprise was justified because, although the rough stone had possessed numerous flaws, the loss of weight incurred in the grinding down operation amounted to more than 64 per cent. He would also have been aware of the oriental preference for size above all qualities, a consideration that ought too to have been uppermost in the mind of the cutter. Furthermore the process of

reducing the stone's weight to 280 carats or
thereabouts must have occupied weeks, months –
even a year or two – so that it is likely that the
Emperor would have been kept informed of the
progress of the work that was being laboriously
carried out on a unique diamond whose weight
apparently greatly exceeded that of any diamond
hitherto found in India.

The account of the recutting of the Great Mogul, as it
has come down to us, is baffling. It comes as no
surprise that the unsatisfactory results of the work of
the Venetian cutter Hortensio Borgio should have led
to him being heavily fined. However, the Indian author
N. B. Sen, in his book *Glorious History of Koh-i-Noor*,
considers the whole story of the diamond's cutting,
including the involvement of Borgio, to be unbelievable.
He has observed that there is no support for it in
contemporary Indian chronicles which contain
authentic and accurate accounts of the period, some
of which are directly connected with the diamond. In
his view, if a European cutter had ruined the stone
such an event would not have gone unrecorded in the
history of Shah Jahan.

Mr Sen gave another reason for suggesting that
the story of the Venetian's handling of the Great
Mogul ought not to be regarded as historically
correct. Far from Indian cutters of the time being
looked upon as inferior practitioners of their craft,
it was the Europeans who were so regarded; the
local cutters possessed greater experience and were
considered more skilful. In particular, while not
denying the presence of Borgio on the scene at the
time, he was known to have been bad at his trade so
that it is inconceivable that the Mogul Emperor
would have chosen him to cut the stone.

In Mr Sen's opinion the whole story of the
cutting of the Great Mogul is incorrect. On the
other hand, Tavernier's account explicitly refers to
the Venetian – although he misspells his name –
and to the earliest history of the stone: but it was
not what he himself witnessed but what he was told
by others. So his surprise at the huge reduction in
the weight of the diamond may suggest that the
Great Mogul weighed less in its rough state than
787½ carats and that the cutting had not in fact
been such a lamentable operation.

We can be certain of one fact: Tavernier saw the
diamond and remarked that its shape was like half
an egg. This observation is important when
considering the complicated question of the
subsequent history of the Great Mogul which is
discussed elsewhere, under the Koh-i-noor and the
Orlov. Let it suffice here to suggest that Edwin
Streeter erred when he wrote that in his opinion the
Great Mogul had ceased to exist as such, and to
assert that this legendary diamond is none other
than the Orlov.

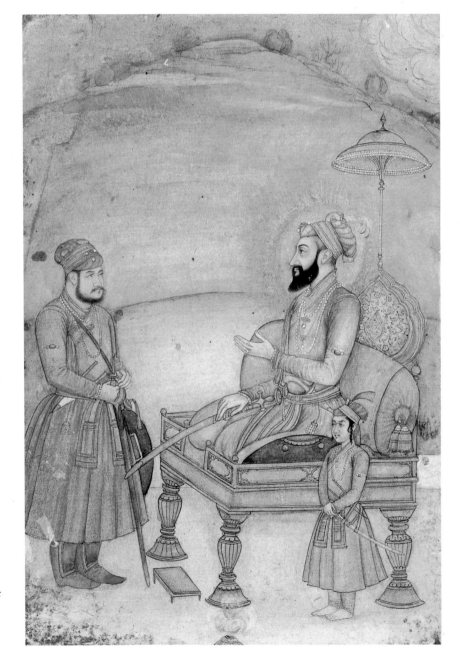

GREAT MOGUL

Hancock Red

The Hancock, life-size.

Photo © Tino Hammid,
Los Angeles.

Red is one of the rarest colours in which diamonds may be found. A list of red diamonds reported in gemmological literature, published in 1993, contains fewer than thirty specimens during the past one hundred and fifty years. These include red stones which are variously described as Blood Red, Brownish Red, Chinese Red, Deep Red, Port Wine Red, Ruby Red, Purplish Red and Rose Red. These diamonds are said to have come from different sources: Borneo, Brazil, India and South Africa.

An addition to the list is a cushion cut brilliant the colour of which has been described as 'blood red' or 'fancy brownish orange-red'. Named the Raj Red, this gem, weighing 2.23 carats, came to light in 1988. It was valued at 42 million dollars and acquired from India by Mr Ronald Winston who, at the time of its purchase, commented: 'I think it is one of the rarest objects on earth. My father never saw a red diamond and he'd seen everything.'

Another rare gem is the red-brown brilliant-cut, weighing 5.03 carats which was given to the Smithsonian Institution in 1987 as a bequest from the estate of the late S. Sydney De Young, a prominent Boston gem dealer. Unfortunately, little is known about the De Young Red, which is thought to have come from India and then been locked in a vault for some fifty years.

But the diamond which has caused the greatest interest in both the auction rooms and the field of gemmology is a brilliant cut, weighing 0.95 carats and described by the GIA as 'purplish-red' in colour, which appeared in 1987.

This unique diamond is named after Warren Hancock, the founder of Hancock Enterprises, a Montana-based oil exploration company. Hancock was a connoisseur of rare fancy-coloured diamonds, collecting them from the early 1950s until his death in 1981 at the age of 65. According to

Arnold Baron, a retired dealer in coloured stones who operated a jewellery store in Billings, Montana from 1948 to 1977, Warren Hancock became hooked on coloured diamonds the first time he entered his store and noticed a fancy-blue diamond, just under two carats, in a showcase. Arnold Baron told Hancock that Lazar E. Kaplan Inc., a long-established client of De Beers, had received a small quantity of blue stones in his 'sight' and for a considerable period had been unsure about what to do with the cut stones. At that time coloured diamonds were looked upon as curiosities by many, but Kaplan sent one to each customer with whom he was friendly to see if they could sell them. Hancock was so taken with Baron's blue diamond that he bought it at once for $5,550.

This transaction marked the beginning of a lasting business relationship between William Hancock and Arnold Baron which led to Hancock on one occasion providing Baron with the financial backing to buy a massive collection of coloured diamonds when it quietly came on the market in 1956. This collection had formerly been left to the son of a Brazilian diamond cutter who for decades used to buy rough from a fellow prospector in Brazil, keeping the fancy-coloured stones for himself. Baron recalled: 'I wanted that collection in the worst way. Fortunately, the son loved wine, women and song. Sooner or later, I was told, he would get thirsty enough to sell it.'

When Baron was finally able to buy the gems, he found that three of them were red or on the cusp of being so. The reddest and the largest of the three weighed 95 points. Baron sold this stone together with a pinker one, weighing 59 points, to Hancock, charging him $13,500 for the larger one. Baron admitted that he lost a few nights' sleep worrying if the price had been too high, but in the light of what was to happen three decades later when the diamond was sold at auction, he added that he should have had no qualms.

After Warren Hancock's death, his family was faced with an enormous tax bill for his estate which compelled his heirs to make a choice. His son, William Hancock, said, 'Either we sell the stones or the oil business. We chose to sell some of the stones.' Knowing that the 95-point, purplish-red diamond represented the highlight of the collection, the family consented to its being displayed in Antwerp. This resulted in a flurry of enquiries, and it was finally decided to sell the gem, along with others including the 59-point pink, at Christie's.

The atmosphere at Christie's in New York, on April 28 1987, was highly charged. In the afternoon session, first the New York dealer, William Goldberg, paid $148,000 (equivalent to $251,000 per carat) for the 59-point diamond. When François Curiel banged his gavel to close the bidding, the capacity crowd broke into boisterous applause. This constituted a new record – but in less than one hour it was to be superseded. The auction of the 95-point Hancock Red gave rise to one of the most breathtaking bidding battles witnessed in auction history. The bidding opened at $250,000, a new record high of $263,000 per carat: within minutes it had reached $500,000. By that stage the field had narrowed to two contenders: Lisa Moussaieff from London and the late Theodore Horovitz from Geneva. When Mr Horovitz finally bought the diamond for $880,000, he received a standing ovation. It was assumed that he was acting on behalf of the Sultan of Brunei, whose known interest in coloured diamonds has been responsible for many of the very high prices paid for such gems in recent years, but Mr Horovitz denied that he had been an intermediary, adding that he had since sold the Hancock Red to a private collector. When he was asked whether he was willing to go higher, Mr Horovitz said he was prepared to pay $1 million for the diamond. He added that he had only seen one other diamond that was comparable.

It is astounding to see that the highest price ever paid at auction, equivalent to $926,316 per carat, was obtained for the smallest of notable diamonds.

This small 95-point purplish-red Hancock diamond, took the auction world by surprise in April 1987, when it sold for $880,000. This equated to a record per-carat price of $926,000.

Photo © Tino Hammid, Los Angeles.

HANCOCK RED

Hastings

Below: the execution of Marie Antoinette in October 1793, following a scandal involving her purchase of a necklace containing diamonds said to be worth 1,800,000 francs.

'ODiamond! Diamond! Thou little knowest the mischief done!' was a rebuke administered by Isaac Newton to his dog of that name after it had knocked over a candle, thereby causing the destruction of papers containing some valuable work of the great scientist. Newton's words addressed to the gem rather than to a dog might well serve to express the feelings of several individuals whose fortunes suffered as a result of their involvement with diamonds.

Events in France during the early 1980s provide a perfect illustration. It will be recalled that during the last years of his tenure of office, the former French President, Valery Giscard d'Estaing, became embroiled in the so-called 'Bokassa diamonds' scandal. Giscard had received a present of diamonds from the self-styled Emperor Bokassa of the Central African Republic, which he put to his own account rather than that of the State. Allegations filled the air, books were said to have been written on the subject, while inevitably the gossip columns of the press had a field day. Subsequently, Giscard stated that 'the accusations had become so far-flung, so preposterous, there was no answering them'. Nevertheless, the taint of scandal undoubtedly helped to undermine his campaign for the Presidency, leading ultimately to his defeat at the polls on 10 May 1981.

The principal participants in an earlier French scandal, the celebrated affair of the 'Queen's Necklace' which took place towards the end of the

eighteenth century, were treated rather more harshly. Four years before the onset of the French Revolution, a necklace said to have contained diamonds worth 1,800,000 francs was secretly purchased from the court jeweller, presumably for Queen Marie Antoinette and on her own instructions. The necklace – not yet paid for – was delivered into the hands of no less a personage than Cardinal Prince de Rohan, first prelate of the French Church. He, in turn, gave it to the *femme fatale* of the whole affair, the notorious Comtesse de la Motte-Valois, who claimed she was acting on behalf of the Queen. It was then handed to a messenger, supposedly from the Queen, before vanishing without trace, never to be seen again. The arrest of the Cardinal and his subsequent trial on charges of theft and *lèse-majesté* set off a scandal which became just one in the chain of events leading up to the Revolution. The reputation of the unfortunate Queen, who to the end denied that she had had anything to do with the necklace, suffered most and she paid the full penalty. She was guillotined on 16 October 1793.

At about the same time as these momentous events were taking place in France, a lesser scandal involving a diamond was occupying the stage in English affairs. It centred on the figure of Warren Hastings (1732–1818), the first and most famous of the Governors-General of India and without doubt one of the great men of Britain's imperial past. The first stage of Hastings' rule lasted for two and a half years, and was the most placid and constructive. The second phase began with the arrival in India of three councillors appointed under the Regulating Act passed by Parliament in 1773. The previous year, the East India Company had been driven to ask the British government for a loan of one million pounds to avert bankruptcy. One of the three councillors who were appointed was Philip Francis, who hoped to succeed Hastings as Governor-General. In Macaulay's words, Francis was 'a man prone to the error of mistaking his malevolence for public virtue', and was mainly responsible for initiating the contest which was to colour the whole of Hastings' life.

During the years 1780–84, England suffered several reverses in the western part of the world, notably during the American War of Independence. Hastings succeeded in avoiding similar disasters to British interests in the East. However, the tenseness of the situation and the dire peril of the East India Company's position in India probably accounted for some of his high-handed actions which were later to be bitterly attacked by his enemies.

Following the passing of the India Act in 1784 by the administration of William Pitt the Younger, Hastings became convinced that there was no future for him in the East and he returned to England the following year. At first, Pitt was friendly to Hastings but then gradually turned against him, being unable to support him on one particular issue. Spurred on by the ever-malicious Francis, now a Member of Parliament and keen to continue his vendetta against the former Governor-General, the Whigs – led by Edmund Burke – succeeded in having charges brought against Hastings.

It was precisely at a time when Hastings needed all the support he could possibly muster that a diamond, weighing 101 carats, appeared on the scene as a source of embarrassment to himself and of delight to his opponents.

The diamond had been sent as a gift to King George III by Nizam Ali Cawn, the most important and influential of the Indian princes. At a levee held in St James's Palace, the Secretary of State for the Home Department, Lord Sydney (after whom the Australian city is named), formally presented the diamond together with a rich purse containing a letter from the Nizam to his Sovereign. Unfortunately for himself, Hastings was present on this occasion, a circumstance quickly seized upon by his enemies. They lost no time in spreading a story to the effect that in order to obtain the support of the King, Hastings had offered him a bribe in the form of a valuable diamond. It was certainly not considered difficult to gain the support of Queen Charlotte by these means since she enjoyed the reputation of being very avaricious where jewellery was concerned.

It was not long before caricatures and scurrilous writings began to circulate in London. One particular poster that appeared under the heading 'The Great Stone Eater' and advertised a juggler who claimed he could eat and digest stones like an ostrich provided a heaven-sent opportunity for the satirists. They substituted the King for the juggler and depicted him as 'The Greatest Stone Eater' with a diamond in his mouth and a pile of others ready for consumption. Among the numerous street ballads that appeared was the following, reprinted with some slight but necessary modifications by Thomas Wright in his *Caricature History of the Georges*:

A FULL AND TRUE ACCOUNT OF
THE WONDERFUL DIAMOND PRESENTED TO
THE KING'S MAJESTY BY WARREN HASTINGS, ESQ.,
ON WEDNESDAY, THE 14TH OF JUNE, 1786

I'll sing you a song of a diamond so fine,
That soon in the Crown of our Monarch will shine;
Of its size and its value the whole country rings,
By Hastings bestowed on the best of all kings.
    Derry down, &c.

From India this jewel was lately brought o'er,
Though sunk in the sea, it was found on the shore,
And just in the nick to St James's it got,
Conveyed in a bag by the brave Major Scott,
    Derry down, &c.

Lord Sydney stepped forth when the tidings were known,
It's his office to carry such news to the throne,
Though quite out of breath to the closet he ran,
And stammered with joy, 'ere his tale he began.
    Derry down, &c.

"Here's a jewel, my liege, there's none such in the land,
Major Scott with three bows, put it into my hand,
And he swore, when he gave it, the wise ones were bit,
For it never was shown to Dundas or to Pitt."
    Derry down, &c.

"For Dundas," cried our Sovereign, "unpolished and rough
Give him a Scotch pebble – 'tis more than enough –
And jewels to Pitt, Hastings justly refuses,
For he has already more gifts than he uses."
    Derry down, &c.

"But run, Jenky, run!" adds the king in delight,
"Bring the queen and the princesses here for a sight;
They never would pardon the negligence shown,
If we kept from their knowledge so glorious a stone."
    Derry down, &c.

"But guard the door, Jenky! No credit we'll win
If the prince, in a frolic, should chance to step in;
The boy to such secrets of State we'll ne'er call,
Let him wait till he gets our crown, jewels, and all!"
    Derry down, &c.

In the princesses run, and surprised, cry "O, la!
'Tis as big as the egg of a pigeon, papa!"
"And a pigeon of plumage worth plucking is he,"
Replies our good monarch, "who sent it to me!"
    Derry down, &c.

Madam Schwellenberg peer'd thro' the door at a chink,
And tipped on the diamond a sly German wink,
As much as to say, "Can we ever be cruel
To him who has sent us so glorious a jewel?"
    Derry down, &c.

Now God save the Queen! while the people I teach,
How the king may grow rich, while the Commons impeach,
Then let nabobs go plunder, and rob as they will,
And throw in their diamonds as grist to his mill.
    Derry down, &c.

Warren Hastings, the first Governor-General of India, accused by his rivals of bribing King George III with the diamond in order to obtain his support.

National Portrait Gallery, London.

When reference was made in the House of Commons to the scandal surrounding the diamond, Major Scott, a personal friend and prominent champion of Warren Hastings, supplied the House with the full facts about the stone. During the Commons debate on the East India Company's Relief Bill on 26 June 1786, Scott referred to the affair of the diamond. His speech was reported as follows:

... he [Major Scott] would, with the permission of the House, say a very few words relative to the diamond that had lately made so much noise in town: and he trusted the House would permit him to do this, because he had been calumniated very much for a few days past, in consequence of what an hon. gentleman [Mr Sheridan] had dropped a few evenings ago, without any serious design, he believed: but what appeared then so farcical, was now become very serious; and he wished to retrieve his character from the imputation under which it laid.

George IV, who was said to have had the Hastings set at the centre of the crown worn for his coronation in 1821.

Portrait by Sir Thomas Lawrence. Courtesy of the Wallace Collection, London.

118

The Major said that, on 2 June, when he was in the House of Commons, a Member of Parliament whose name he could not recollect, delivered to him the following letter:

2 June, 4 o'clock

My dear Scott, I have just received a packet, of such apparent importance as alarms me for the consequences of keeping it in my possession, and I therefore give you this unseasonable trouble, to request that you will take the earliest possible means to communicate this information to Lord Sydney, with the following circumstances relating to it, which are all I yet know concerning it. The packet was delivered to me by Mr Blair, brother-in-law to Mr Richard Johnson, and I have given him my receipt for it. It was directed to me: I opened it and found it to contain an English endorsed paper, sealed, which I have not opened, a letter from the Nabob Nizam Ali Cawn to the King, a letter from the same Nabob to myself, damaged, and scarce legible...; and a small bulse [pouch] sealed with three (or I believe four) seals bearing the Nabob's principal title. These are all much soiled with the sea water, having been originally sent on board the Hinchinbrooke, and recovered from the wreck. Besides the above, there were a letter of a more recent date, from the same Nabob to me, and other English papers. — I guess the purport of the effaced letter to be a commission to me to deliver a letter to the King and most probably the bulse with it, the contents of which I have not a clue to conjecture. Supposing that it may contain something of value, and in that case of no small value, I think it neither consistent with my interest or credit to keep it an hour longer in my custody than absolute necessity may require, and therefore request that I may be relieved from the charge; and that for that purpose you will be so good as to endeavour to obtain Lord Sydney's permission so that you may deliver the packet with all its contents to him; concluding that, while the present inquiry lasts, his lordship would prefer that mode to my own personal attendance.

Your affectionate, Warren Hastings

The central part of Major Scott's speech in the House of Commons then consisted of a long account of the delay on his part in meeting Lord Sydney and acquainting him with the facts concerning the packet containing the diamond. Eventually, the report of his speech concludes:

Having thus stated all the circumstances of an affair which has been grossly misrepresented, he [Scott] begged leave to say, that if there was a blamable delay in delivering this packet to Lord Sydney, it rested solely with him — that he delivered it publicly, not as a matter of secrecy, or to be concealed; for he did conceive it to be of infinite importance to the prosperity of this country, as connected with India, that Nizam Ali Cawn, the first prince in part of family in Hindostan, and of great power and weight, who had formerly been so hostile to our nation, and so connected with France, should, for the first time, seek a connexion with us, and that he should have addressed a letter to the Sovereign. With regard to the mode of doing it, it was highly respectful on the part of Nizam Ali Cawn, being the invariable mode in which an inferior addresses a superior — nor could there be a man acquainted with the established customs of Hindostan, who would have supposed he could have commenced a correspondence in any other manner.

Scott declared that he was utterly ignorant of the contents of the bulse, but he was convinced it had never been opened after it left Hyderabad, as it was sealed with the Nizam's seal when he delivered it to Lord Sydney.

Major Scott's explanation of the circumstances surrounding the diamond was received with incredulity by the hostile faction. Events took their course, however, and two years later Hastings was formally impeached. Amid great excitement, proceedings began in Westminster Hall in February 1788; they were to drag on for seven years and three months. The trial stands unique in British history both on account of its length and the eloquence of the opposing counsel. In the end, it resulted in the acquittal of Hastings on all accounts in April 1795. Though acquitted, he was financially ruined and denied further office, but in 1813 when he appeared before the House of Commons to give evidence on Indian affairs, the whole House rose in his honour. In the following year he was appointed a Privy Councillor.

Since the presentation of the Hastings diamond to George III nothing more appears to have been heard of it.

Now a polished diamond weighing more than 100 carats is a rare object at any time but even more so in the eighteenth century when the total world output constituted a fraction of what it is today. (It is assumed that the diamond which the Indian Prince gave to the King was a cut gem: the gift of an uncut stone would have been a poor reflection on the ability of Indian cutters.) It is, therefore, somewhat strange that all trace appears to have been lost of such an outstanding diamond. The King would surely not have refused such a gift from the most important and influential of the Indian princes; refusal would not only have been insulting to its donor but also politically damaging to British interests in India. Furthermore, the Queen would never have pardoned negligence on the part of anyone who had failed to show her such a diamond. Doubtless she would have been more than pleased to have added it to her collection of jewels, of which the most notable items were the two fine pear-shaped diamonds given to her by the Nawab of Arcot. Thus on all accounts it is reasonable to suppose that Hastings' diamond found its way into the Crown Jewels.

Assuming this is to be so, is there a diamond formerly among the British Crown Jewels which may at some period be identified as the Hastings? The answer is yes.

George III died in 1820 and was succeeded by his eldest son, formerly the Prince Regent who, as George IV, was crowned on 19 July 1821. In the chapter devoted to England in his monumental work *A History of the Crown Jewels of Europe*, Lord Twining relates some interesting information about the regalia, in connection with the coronation of the new king, that derives from an account of Rundell & Bridge, the noted firm of jewellers who had been appointed Jewellers and Silversmiths to

the Crown by George III. The author of the account, George Fox, wrote as follows:

The crown made for this occasion was really a magnificent one, very many remarkable fine ornaments were introduced into it, the principal one being a very fine round stone of the diameter of a shilling weighing... It was cut in the truest style and its proportions being mathematically correct. This stone was valued at the sum of £12,000 but on being sold in the year 1837 when many other large and fine diamonds belonging to Rundell & Bridge came to be auctioned by Messrs Sharp of Winchester Street at Willis's Rooms, King Street, St James's, it was knocked down to Emmanuel Brothers for... These gentlemen bought it with other fine jewels at that sale for the Marquis of Westminster, in whose possession the whole of the diamonds thus bought still remain.

The figures showing the weight of the diamond and the amount it fetched at the sale were left blank in Fox's original manuscript. However, the weight of the diamond is recorded elsewhere as 125½ grains, equivalent to 32.20 metric carats.

It is immediately apparent that there is a big discrepancy between the weight of this brilliant and that of the stone which was presented to George III by Nizam Ali Cawn. There are two possible explanations for this: either the diamond was at some stage recut or, more likely, the original weight was wrongly recorded. Nothing appears to be known about the origin of this 32.20 carat diamond or how it came to be included among the Crown Jewels. John Mawe, in the second edition (1823) of his *A Treatise on Diamonds and Other Precious Stones*, wrote of the Hastings diamond that 'it made a most perfect brilliant'. It would seem, therefore, not unreasonable to assume that this clearly exceptional gem in the crown may have been the same diamond which had caused so much trouble to the former Governor-General of India.

The Marquis of Westminster paid £3,500 for the circular diamond as a birthday present for his wife. At the same sale, he bought the Arcot pear shapes and the Nassak, which had originally been brought to London by the East India Company before being sold to Messrs Rundell & Bridge.

The round brilliant and the Arcot pear shapes were subsequently set in the Westminster Tiara, the former being contained in the centre section. It was detachable and could be worn as a corsage ornament for which two additional diamond sections with fittings were supplied. Harry Winston purchased the tiara at an auction held in London by Sotheby's on 25 June 1959. He had the circular diamond removed from its setting and, to improve its brilliance, recut to 26.77 carats. Set as a ring, it was sold to an American client later in the same year. Finally it came up for auction in New York on 9 December 1970.

Holland

Historical engraving depicting Goa, an important Portuguese diamond trading centre for many centuries.

Several authors have considered the possibility of the Holland being the same diamond as the Bantam, which Tavernier saw during his visit to Java in 1648. In view of the long-standing connection between the Netherlands and the East Indies, the diamond known today as the Holland may have come originally from that part of the world but recent research by the Dutch historian, René Brus, has revealed that it is not the same stone as the one seen by Tavernier.

Queen Wilhelmina, the grandmother of Queen Beatrix, who ruled the Netherlands upon reaching the age of eighteen in 1898 until 1948, always showed great interest in the history of her illustrious ancestors; she did not refer to the diamond as the 'Holland' but the 'Stuart', after its former owner, Queen Mary II of England, wife of the Dutch Stadholder, Willem III of Orange.

After the coronation, in 1689, of Queen Mary and her husband, who ascended the throne of England as William III, a large uncut diamond was offered for £30,000 to the Queen. The Dutchman, Hans Willem Bentick, who accompanied his royal

master to England and was created Earl of Portland in 1689, negotiated on her behalf. As soon as the buyer and seller came to an agreement that the cutting of the stone was the risk of the buyer, Lord Portland made a down-payment of £4,000. The contract specifically mentioned that if Queen Mary wished to have one large, single stone fashioned from the rough, this would accordingly be undertaken. At the same time the seller pointed out that the rough piece could also be cleaved, thereby resulting in the cutting of two pear-shaped gems. Finally, when both parties had reached agreement concerning the sale and the cutting, Sir William Langhorn Barre & Company received a total of £12,228 which represented the expenditure costs plus interest.

In due course a rose-cut diamond was produced: it is not known where the cutting took place but it is thought that Amsterdam was the likely location.

After Queen Mary died at the end of 1694, a member of the Royal Household, Lady Derby, made an inventory of her jewels: one item was described as 'a large diamond and large facet-stones

and 12 others.' The unnamed large diamond is specifically mentioned, thus indicating that it was one of the late Queen's most important possessions. In the Dutch translation of the inventory no shape or position of the diamond is given but the original document, in English, describes the brooch as 'A great jewel of diamonds to be worn with a large heart diamond in the middle thereof.'

Many items of the jewellery of Queen Mary were heirlooms of the House of Orange of which the jeweller Walchart, of the Hague, had made an inventory before she became Queen of England. Papers, dated 13 June 1668, showed that the jewellery was valued at 217,705 guilders. William and Mary were childless so following the death of the King in 1702, a chest containing their jewellery was opened in the great Treves Hall at the Binnenhof of the Hague on 6 July of that year; among the items was the brooch containing 26 diamonds including the large rose cut which was set in the centre. In her lifetime Queen Mary had bequeathed her jewels to her husband and had stipulated that thereafter they should return to her husband's family where they rightfully belonged.

The existence of Queen Mary's jewellery was known to her sister, Anne, who succeeded her brother-in-law on the throne of England. Through a lawsuit, begun in 1706 at the Court of Holland, Queen Anne laid claim to those items which had been acquired by the late royal couple after they had jointly been crowned as rulers of England. At first her claim was found to be partly acceptable but the Dutch heir of William III, Stadholder Prince Johan Willem Friso, contested it and appealed against the decision. In 1709 Queen Anne was requested to present new facts: unable to do so, she subsequently received none of the jewels which by then were already in the possession of the House of Orange.

The second half of the eighteenth century was a turbulent period of European history. In 1782 the Dutch Stadholder, Willem V, decided to make a family contract or Erbverein which would make it almost impossible for himself or any of his successors as the head of the family to sell any property belonging to the House of Orange without the permission of all the members of the family. Two years later this Prince and his Prussian born Princess, Wilhelmina, decided to make an inventory of the family diamonds and pearls which had to become inalienable or 'onvereemdbare' gems and remain forever in the possession of the head of the family. The rose-cut diamond of Queen Mary was recorded as being surrounded by 22 brilliants and weighing 158 grains; its value was estimated at 120,00 guilders.

Correspondence between Willem V and his eldest son showed that this valuable piece, as well as the other diamonds and pearls, had become a burden to him. When, in 1795, French armies invaded the Netherlands and the princely Dutch family decided to go into exile in England, financial problems became so great that the English royal family more or less supported the exiles. In a letter, dated 26 July 1796, Willem V told his son that he looked upon himself merely as the custodian of the gems 'just like the dog in the fable whose only duty was to guard a treasure and who finally died of starvation'.

Since fashion, in addition to warfare, played an important part in life at the beginning of the nineteenth century, Queen Charlotte, the consort of George III, introduced Princess Wilhelmina to the Crown Jeweller, Rundell & Bridge. On 18 January 1801, the firm delivered to the Dutch Princess various items of jewellery which they had reset: they included the diamond of Queen Mary II which was hung on an impressive necklace. The

Above: the Holland diamond, reset as the centre-piece of a tiara for the formal inauguration of the young Queen Wilhelmina of the Netherlands, 1898, remains the property of the Duch Royal Family.

Courtesy René Brus.

122

HOLLAND

stone's weight was recorded as 39.75 carats or 159 grains. At a birthday party of Queen Charlotte, Princess Wilhelmina appeared wearing her diamonds and in a letter to her daughter, Princess Louise, dated 20 January 1801, she described the scene as follows:

... a necklace newly mounted with large stones without surround and on a large pendant. The earrings were in the same fashion [i.e. pendant]. On my head a superb tiara in the latest style, I also wore a belt and bracelets at the tops of my arms, some pulled up, some set straight, which were also of the latest fashion.

Everything was really of the best possible taste. Furthermore it brought the admiration of everyone. However, without the kindness of the Queen and the princess, who find great amusement in organising my dress, I would never have been so successful in these important arrangements.

The exiled Dutch Prince requested Rundell & Bridge to make yet another inventory of his and his wife's jewels. The author, John Murray, who obtained much information from the Crown Jewellers and published his book *A Memoir on the Diamond* in 1831, wrote of the principal diamond: 'the stone was valued at 10,368 pounds and we believe that the stone is conical in shape. This notable diamond had the size of around 30 x 25mm, was rose-cut and covered with 24 triangular shaped facets.' In the course of the first half of the nineteenth century this stone was named the Holland, although it is not known by whom. Reference was made to the gem at the time of the Great Exhibition of 1851 in London wherein it was stated that 'The King of the Netherlands is in possession of only one diamond called the Cone. It is of unfortunate form in proportion to its weight: it, however, is of the purest water. It weighs 36 carats, and is valued at £10,368.'

After the defeat of Napoleon Bonaparte the Dutch Prince and Princess returned home, finally becoming sovereign rulers of the Kingdom of the Netherlands. Queen Mary's diamond was made detachable and in later years was worn in an agraffe; at the end of the nineteenth century the Frankfurt jeweller Schurmann was commissioned to mount the gem as the centre-piece of a tiara. The reason for resetting some of the diamonds of the House of Orange was the formal inauguration of the young Queen Wilhelmina, who succeeded to the throne on the death of her father, Willem III, in 1890. On 6 September 1898, the young monarch stood in the New Church in Amsterdam and raised her right hand, her regal appearance enhanced by the enormous diamond-studded tiara with the historic Stuart or Holland diamond in its centre.

Opposite: the diamond was originally named the 'Stuart' after Queen Mary II to whom it was given following her coronation as Queen of England in 1689.

Portrait by William Wissing, 1685. By courtesy of the National Portrait Gallery, London.

123

Hope

And the Curse shall be on thee
For ever and ever.

In the eyes of many people these words by the English poet, Southey, could serve as the motto of this most celebrated gem, probably the best known diamond after the Koh-i-noor.

The Hope is well known for its rare colour, a sapphire-like dark blue, but above all it has acquired a reputation as the bringer of misfortune, so that mention of it invariably leads to such questions as 'Does it really bring bad luck?' or 'Have all its owners died suddenly or violently?' It may, therefore, come as something of a disappointment to learn that the Hope has not always brought misfortune to its owners, nor has it been the cause of their early demise; in fact many who have owned the so-called 'Diamond of Disaster' lived to a ripe old age. Most of the myths which have become attached to the gem, some of them invented for a deliberate purpose, are examined and summarily dismissed in a book entitled *Blue Mystery, The Story of the Hope Diamond*, written by Susanne Steinem Patch and published in 1976 by the Smithsonian Institution Press. It is the Smithsonian Institution in Washington DC that owns the Hope today.

The earliest known facts about the blue diamond which is generally recognized as the precursor of the Hope date from the middle of the seventeenth century. The Kollur mine in the vicinity of Golconda is said to have been its source. According to some accounts the blue diamond is yet another of these old Indian stones that were set as eyes in a sacred idol before being stolen. Suffice it to say that there is no evidence to support this and that to judge by drawings of the diamond which have come down to us, the shape of the idol's eyes would have had to be somewhat unusual to have accommodated this particular stone. In addition, since dark blue diamonds are extremely rare, the idol would almost

certainly either have been heterochromous or possessed just one eye.

What is known for sure is that the indefatigable Jean Baptiste Tavernier bought a dark blue diamond which he sold to Louis XIV of France early in 1668, not long after he had returned from his sixth and final voyage to the Orient. According to some authorities Tavernier had purchased the diamond as early as 1642, yet it is difficult to believe that he would have kept such a rare gem for more than a quarter of a century before showing it to his sovereign, whose penchant for jewels, diamonds in particular, was widely known and who would certainly have soon come to learn of its existence. Therefore, the suggestion made by others that Tavernier did not acquire the blue diamond in India but instead bought it later in some other trading centre, possibly Venice, whence it had travelled from the East, appears to be not unreasonable.

The diamond which first became known as the Tavernier Blue appears as No. 1 in drawings of the twenty finest diamonds which Tavernier sold to Louis XIV. Its shape corresponds to that of a typical Indian gem, transformed from the rough with only minimal loss of weight. In a lecture entitled 'The "Hope" Diamond and its Lineage', which he presented at the 15th International Gemological Conference held in the Smithsonian Institution in October 1975, Herbert Tillander argued that the weight of the diamond, recorded as 112$\frac{3}{16}$ carats, was probably measured in Florentine carats and that since the Florentine carat was equivalent to 197.2 milligrams, the original weight of the Tavernier Blue must have been about 110.50 metric carats.

A contemporary of Louis XIV, writing about the diamonds which Tavernier had brought back with him from his travels to the East, stated that 'their brilliance seemed even more resplendent owing to their distant and somewhat mysterious origin'. The King was enthralled by the diamonds Tavernier showed him and ordered Colbert to buy a number of them; ultimately he purchased 44 large diamonds in addition to the blue stone and no less than 1,122 smaller ones. The total price amounted to 897,731 livres. When the purchases which the Sun King made from other sources are added to those which he made from Tavernier it is not surprising that the Crown Jewels of France became the finest collection of gems amassed in Europe and probably in the world at that time.

Jean Baptiste Colbert (1619–83), the statesman and Minister of Finance, has been described as the most remarkable minister in the history of France. Colbert revolutionized his country's finances and established them on a sound foundation; it is tempting to consider that his acquiescence in his master's multitudinous purchases of diamonds displayed not only an appreciation of their intrinsic beauty but also their commercial value.

Although Tavernier was a Protestant, Louis XIV rewarded him for his services by granting him certain letters which conferred upon him a title of nobility. Therefore, Tavernier bought the Barony of Aubonne in Switzerland which he later sold to Duquesne, the great navigator. Tavernier was one of the owners of the blue diamond who certainly did not labour under any curse bestowed by the stone; he died in Russia at the age of eighty-four and was buried in the Protestant cemetery near Moscow. The extraordinary myth that he was 'torn apart by wild dogs' was apparently perpetrated by an individual who will figure later in this account.

Louis XIV retained the Tavernier Blue in its existing shape for four years until 1673 when he ordered his goldsmith Pitau to recut it, thereby sacrificing the oriental preference for the size of a gem to the occidental liking for brilliance. The blue diamond became a heart shape weighing 67⅛ carats, equivalent to 69.03 metric carats. The King appropriated the gem together with the other Crown Jewels of France for his own use. The blue diamond, which now assumed the name 'Blue Diamond of the Crown', was employed in various ways. It is recorded that not long before his death, Louis XIV received the Persian Ambassador at his court in February 1715, and that on that occasion he wore a large blue diamond suspended from a ribbon around his neck in addition to jewels estimated to have been worth 12,000,000 livres. It is perhaps doubtful whether any other historical personage has ever equalled the caratage of jewels that were worn on such occasions by the Sun King.

Louis XIV incorporated jewels in the insignia of orders of chivalry, a custom which his great-grandson and successor Louis XV maintained. In 1749 Louis XV ordered Jacquemin, the Crown Jeweller, to mount both the blue diamond and the spinel known as the 'Côte de Bretagne' in the decoration of the Golden Fleece. The insignia which resulted from this was considered to have been a masterpiece of the jeweller's art as well as an object of exceptional value. This same ornament was worn by the next King of France, Louis XVI, who succeeded his grandfather in 1774.

After the splendour of the French court during the two previous reigns, a less lavish epoch set in with the accession of Louis XVI. His consort, Marie Antoinette, was a lover of jewellery but she preferred light settings in which stones were set for design purposes rather than ornaments designed specifically to show off the qualities of a great gem. It has often been asserted that Marie Antoinette was

Louis XV wearing the decoration of the Golden Fleece in which the 'Blue Diamond of the Crown' was set on a ribbon around his neck.

Pastel by Maurice Quentin de La Tour. Paris, Musée du Louvre. Photo AKG London.

125

one of those cursed by ownership of the blue diamond; however, there is no record of her having worn it nor is it likely that she did so because it remained in its setting in the Golden Fleece, an exclusively male ornament. Nor was the blue diamond one of the diamonds which were despatched to Amsterdam and Antwerp for recutting, thereby upsetting French jewellers and craftsmen.

The start of the reign of Louis XVI coincided with the first stirrings of unrest within the country. The King's main interest was hunting and he showed such scant interest in the affairs of state that on the day the Bastille fell (14 July 1789), the sole entry in his diary was 'nothing'. However, events moved quickly – albeit too quickly – for the monarchy: the attempted flight of the King and Queen in June 1791 was followed by the storming of the Tuileries, the imprisonment of the royal couple, their trials and subsequent executions in 1793.

Two years before, the ruling Constituent Assembly had ordered an inventory to be made of the Crown Jewels; the Blue Diamond of the Crown was valued at 3,000,000 francs. During this period of upheaval in France the jewels were removed to the Garde Meuble, part a museum, part a furniture store, situated then in the Place de la Concorde. On certain days members of the public were permitted to view the treasures – a singularly rash decision which doubtless greatly assisted the eventual robbers, who comprised vagrants and petty thieves. The robbery lasted for almost a week, with the thieves operating at night; it culminated, on the night of 16th to 17th September 1792, with the breaking of the seals that had been placed on the display cabinets and the removal of their priceless contents. Thereafter, each political faction was only too ready to blame another.

Among the depositions subsequently taken from some of the fifty thieves who had participated in the robbery, one significant fact was recorded: within three months of the theft the Blue Diamond of the Crown had been carried off to England. According to the French historian Bernard Morel, it was the leader of a gang from Rouen, named Cadet Guillot, who was responsible for carrying off the Golden Fleece in which the blue diamond was set. After ridding himself of his companions, he left for Nantes and made his way to Le Havre where he boarded a ship for London, taking up residence there.

We are indebted to John Sampson White, a former official of the Smithsonian Institution, Washington DC, and Mary T. Winters, for their astute detective work which led to the publication in 1991 of the most plausible account of the blue diamond's history in the years following the 1792 robbery.

Early in the nineteenth century a lapidary named John Françillon of 26 Norfolk Street, London, reproduced a sketch to which a note was appended:

The above drawing is the exact size and shape of a very curious superfine deep blue diamond. Brilliant cut, and equal to a fine deep blue sapphire. It is beauty full and all perfection without specks or flaws, and the colour even and perfect all over the diamond.
I traced it round the diamond with a pencil by leave of Mr Daniel Eliason and it is as finely cut as I have ever seen a diamond.
The colour of the drawing is as near the colour of the diamond as possible.
Dated: 19th Sept 1812.

Now the date of this note, September 19th, 1812 – is precisely twenty years and two days after the theft of the French Crown Jewels and its significance was grasped by Winters and White. In 1804 the French

Assembly had passed an amnesty law under which all crimes committed in times of war were forgiven after a period of twenty years. The twenty years from 1792 to 1812 have always been considered the most mysterious in the history of the blue diamond. Can it, therefore, be doubted that after the adoption of the amnesty law the diamond was deliberately held in secrecy until, the legal interval having passed, any liability for its theft would have been excused? From being an item of property stolen from the French government in 1792, the status of the diamond had changed to that of an openly marketable asset owned by a dealer in England.

The circumstances of the recutting of the blue diamond have not been fully ascertained but it is likely that both Françillon and Eliason, named in Françillon's note as the owner of the gem, were involved. Daniel Eliason was a London diamond merchant who had marital ties with a family of diamond dealers; furthermore he had a brother living in Amsterdam, then the principal centre of diamond cutting in Europe. It is not known whether the blue diamond was cut in that city or in London which, as well as being a cutting centre, was then beginning to act as a focal point for trading in polished diamonds in the aftermath of an influx of refugees and jewellery from France. However, it has been proved that the shape of the recut gem can be traced back to the former French Crown Jewel.

In 1985 a leading polished dealer, the late Theodore Horovitz of Geneva, visited the Smithsonian Institution, bringing with him the original design drawings for the Golden Fleece in which the blue diamond had been set in 1749. These drawings, made by Jacquemin, the Crown Jeweller, of the former French Crown Jewel, were compared with the Hope diamond. Four conclusions were drawn from this comparison. First, the changes in shape and weight are the result of recutting or reshaping rather than cleaving the Blue Diamond of the Crown into two or more pieces. Secondly, the depth or thickness and the flat side are common to both stones. Thirdly, none of the existing facets on the Hope correspond precisely to any of those of the French Blue diamond except in part for the culet. Fourthly, no satellite stones could have resulted from the recutting operation. This last conclusion, therefore, demolishes the theory held by some that the dark blue pear shape, between 6 and 13 carats, once owned by the Duke of Brunswick and sold at Geneva in 1874, the Pirie diamond weighing one carat, and the dark blue diamond set in a pin among the former Russian Crown Jewels, may have once formed part of the French Blue diamond (see pages 53, 131).

Besides the aforementioned Françillon and Eliason, the Americans consider it likely that a third

Opposite: Francesco de Goya's painting, *The Family of Charles IV*, 1800. Queen Maria Luisa (centre) is depicted wearing a large dark blue gem which may have been the Hope.

Madrid, Museo del Prado. Photo AKG London.

person was involved with the blue diamond at this stage of its history. This was John Mawe, a leading authority on diamonds and a gem historian who published *A Treatise on Diamonds and Precious Stones* in 1813. A footnote to Chapter 3 reads: 'There is at this time a superlatively fine blue diamond, of above 44 carats, in the possession of an individual in London, which may be considered as matchless, and of course of arbitrary value.' Yet in the text of Chapter 6, entitled 'Notice of some particular diamonds', Mawe wrote: 'Perhaps one of the largest and most beautiful coloured diamonds is a rich sky-blue brilliant, belonging to the Crown Jewels of France: it weighs 67 3/16 carats, and is estimated at three millions of livres.' Did Mawe genuinely believe that there were two stones or was he, by referring to both of them, endeavouring to lay a

smokescreen so as to facilitate the eventual sale of the 44-carat gem? Whatever the reason for the two references in 1813, by the time of the second edition, in 1823, he was more specific. He wrote: 'A superlatively fine blue diamond weighing 44 carats, and valued at £30,000, formerly the property of Mr Eliason, an eminent Diamond Merchant is now said to be in the possession of our most gracious sovereign.'

The acquisition of the blue diamond by George IV would have been wholly in accordance with his character; he may have been one of the more cultured English monarchs but there was no limit to his extravagance and his liking for jewels in particular. It will be recalled how, following the death of George III, the new King lost no time in appropriating his father's jewels and money and all

his mother's jewellery. But no evidence has been forthcoming to suggest that George IV ever owned the diamond; Morel states that Mawe was mistaken in claiming that the King had bought the blue diamond and that his error arose from the fact that Eliason had presented it on several occasions to the sovereign. (Recent research has disclosed that the blue stone in the portrait of the King, painted by Sir Thomas Lawrence, in 1822, and housed in the Wallace Collection, in London, today, is a sapphire.)

No more of the blue diamond was heard until 1839 when its ownership by Henry Philip Hope became known.

Henry Philip Hope and his elder brother, Thomas Hope, were members of the banking family, Hope & Co., established at Amsterdam. Hope & Co., formed in 1762, became a firm with an

Mlle Ladre, an actress at the Folies Bergères who allegedly was lent the Hope by her lover, Prince Kanitowsky. Either he or another lover shot at her across the footlights as she wore the diamond. He was later killed in the Russian Revolution.

Hulton Getty Picture Collection.

bank, Baring Bros. & Co. Ltd, crashed so spectacularly in 1995.

Nothing is known of the circumstances of Henry Philip's purchase of the blue diamond; it is possible that he bought it from Eliason or his heirs at around the time of the latter's death at the end of 1824. What is known for sure is that Henry Thomas Hope, the eldest son of Thomas Hope, had served, as a young man, as Groom of the Bedchamber to George IV and his successor, William IV; therefore, he would have been in a position to know what 'went on' at Court, including the repeated efforts of Eliason to interest the King in the blue diamond. Probably he alerted his uncle, already known as a keen collector of diamonds – in particular 'fancy colours' – to the existence of such a rare gem.

Hope requested Bram Hertz, himself an expert

international reputation, making loans to many countries: one of them was Russia whose ruler at the time, Catherine the Great, had so esteemed Henry Hope, the uncle of Henry Philip Hope, that she offered to ennoble him, an honour which he declined. Henry Philip Hope and his brother belonged to a branch of the family that had emigrated to London in 1794 to escape the dangers of the French Revolution. After 1808 the fortunes of Hope & Co. waned, so that by 1813 the house was a shadow of its former self: its assets, together with those of Henry Hope & Co., of London, were purchased for £250,521 by Alexander Baring, a member of the merchant banking family whose

on gems and a collector, to catalogue his collection, said to have been worth £150,000. The resulting *Catalogue of the Collection of Pearls and Precious Stones formed by Henry Philip Hope, Esq.*, was published in 1839 and consisted of two parts: the first comprised descriptions of the jewels and the second showed line drawings of them.

The catalogue of Hope's jewels contained descriptions of fifty diamonds, nine of which were coloured stones of the highest quality weighing from 23 to 3.70 carats. The Hope diamond figures as No. 1 in the collection, under the heading 'Polished Diamonds', and merited the following description:

A most magnificent and rare brilliant of a deep sapphire blue, of the greatest purity, and most beautifully cut; it is of true proportions, not too thick, nor too spread. This matchless gem combines the beautiful colour of the sapphire with the prismatic fire and brilliancy of the diamond, and, on account of its extraordinary colour, great size and other fine qualities, it certainly may be called unique; as we may presume that there exists no cabinet, not any collection of crown jewels in the world, which can boast of the possession of so curious and fine a gem as the one we are now describing; and we may expect to be borne out in our opinion by our readers, since there are extant and historical records and treatises on the precious gems, which give us descriptions of all the extraordinary diamonds in the possession of all the crowned heads of Europe as well as the Princes of Eastern countries. But in vain do we search for any record of a gem which can in point of curiosity, beauty, and perfection, be compared with this blue brilliant.

Diamonds are found of almost every colour which is proved by the great variety of coloured diamonds in this collection; but the blue colour is the most rare and most valuable, since there has very seldom been found a diamond of any size of a fine deep sapphire blue, those which are termed blue diamonds being generally of a very light or of a steel-blue colour; it would, therefore, be a difficult task to form a just estimate of the value of this unrivalled gem, there being no precedent, the value cannot be established by comparison. The price which was once asked for this diamond was 30,000 livres... but we must confess, for the above-stated reasons, that it might have been estimated even at a higher sum. To convey to the reader by a description a just conception of the beauty and splendour of this unique production of nature would be a vain attempt.

This beautiful gem is most tastefully mounted as a medallion with a border en arabesque of small rose diamonds, surrounded by 20 brilliants of equal size, shape and cutting, and of the finest water, and averaging four grains each. Its weight is 177 grains. This gem, particularly on account of its mounting, could not be placed in the drawer with the diamonds, but is left in Drawer 16 together with the other extraordinary specimens of this collection.

As well as indulging in his liking for collecting diamonds and other precious stones, Henry Philip Hope also bought paintings which he added to a collection begun earlier by his eldest brother. Hope himself never married and when he died in 1839 he left large fortunes to each of his three nephews. The eldest, Henry Thomas Hope, who had inherited from his father the family residence in London and the mansion at Deepdene, in Surrey, bought the Hope diamond from his uncle's estate. He displayed the gem at the Crystal Palace Exhibition, held in Hyde Park in London in 1851, and at the Paris World Exhibition in 1855; on the latter occasion the Emperor, Napoleon III, ordered a model to be made of it.

Henry Thomas Hope's period of ownership of the diamond marked a quiet phase in its history, but those who are always ready to attribute sinister qualities to it may point out that Hope died at the comparatively early age of fifty-four. His widow and his daughter, Henrietta Adela, were his heirs: the latter married Henry Pelham-Clinton, who was destined soon to succeed his father as the sixth

Duke of Newcastle. Mrs Hope retained the gem and in 1887 bequeathed it to her younger grandson on condition that he added the name 'Hope' to his patronymic of Pelham-Clinton. He accepted the terms of the will and thus became Lord Henry Francis Hope Pelham-Clinton-Hope, although during the ensuing bout of litigation he was always referred to simply as Lord Francis Hope. If he were to die without issue his eldest sister stood to inherit the life interest and if she died thus, the second sister would inherit the life interest and so on through the family.

In 1893, six years after receiving his inheritance, Lord Francis Hope was in financial difficulties that were caused principally, it appears, by his fondness for gambling. He petitioned the Court for permission to sell some of the Dutch and Flemish paintings which his grandmother had left him, but his brother and three sisters opposed the sale so the petition was withdrawn. In the following year Hope was secretly married to an American actress named Mary Yohé. According to her, her husband gave her 'a string of gorgeous pear-shaped pearls' for which he paid a substantial sum despite his financial situation. In 1895 Hope was declared bankrupt, but next year was discharged from bankruptcy. His wife enjoyed some success on the English stage and contributed to their support.

However, in May 1899 Lord Francis Hope was in court again, on this occasion asking for an order approving a provisional contract drawn up in December 1898 between himself and L. M. Lowenstein & Co. for the sale of the Hope diamond. The sum mentioned as the price for the diamond was not stated in court but was understood to approximate to £18,115. This was the value estimated by Mr Edwin Streeter, the jeweller of Bond Street, on behalf of the appellant.

In an affidavit Streeter said that when arriving at his estimate of the diamond and the surrounding brilliants he had taken into consideration its historical interest. However, he had valued it at less than he would have a short time before because a large blue diamond (double the size of the Hope diamond in the rough) had recently come on to the market, and had been cut into a fine lozenge-shaped diamond and a fine drop, weighing in the aggregate 34 carats. He added that the Hope diamond had previously been considered the only blue diamond of any importance known, but the advent of the two diamonds mentioned above naturally reduced its value. In addition to this opinion of Streeter, Lord Francis produced other expert evidence in support of the diamond not being worth more than the contract price.

Counsel on behalf of Hope's eldest sister said that she would be desirous of wearing the diamond in the event of her surviving Lord Francis and that she and her elder brother, the Duke of Newcastle, were united in their wish that the diamond should not be sold. Evidence was produced on their behalf that the diamond was worth far more than the contract price; furthermore it was stated that one of the counsel in court had been instructed by an intending purchaser to make a higher offer than the price stated in the contract.

In his submission, Hope's counsel referred to the jewel as being absolutely useless to the tenant for life and a 'Damnosa Hereditas'; it was a mere curio – its future value was problematical, and as an heirloom it had no real ancestral association, being a comparatively recent purchase. To this submission counsel for the other members of the family rejoined by saying that the diamond was in fact a unique possession, highly regarded by the family as such. The judge said that he could not sanction the contract under any circumstances because the evidence that had been before him showed such a wide discrepancy between the experts that he could not say that he was satisfied a fair market price was going to be given for it; furthermore every member of the family was opposed to the sale. Not unexpectedly the judge refused the application for approval of the contract.

In July of the same year the appeal of Lord Francis was heard in the Court of Appeal; on this occasion his counsel was that eminent lawyer, Sir Edward Clarke, QC, who four years earlier had appeared for Oscar Wilde at his famous trial. The Duke of Newcastle was again represented by a Mr Benn. The Master of the Rolls, who heard the appeal, said that this was not a case in which they ought to differ from the learned judge in the court below. He did not wish to say anything unkind or unpleasant about Lord Francis Hope but it was obvious that he had brought himself into difficulties by his own fault. It was impossible to say that the proposed sale was for anybody's benefit except his: the sole object of it was to increase his income. Not only did nobody want the sale to go through, but everyone objected to it. He could not ignore the fact that this was a unique diamond of a colour the like of which had not been seen till quite recently and he was satisfied that there was no reasonable probability of the value of the diamond becoming diminished. The appeal failed.

In 1901 Lord Francis succeeded in securing permission to dispose of the Hope diamond; it was sold by order of a Master in Chancery. The vendor's solicitors announced on 13 November that Hope had sold the diamond to Adolf Weil of 25 Hatton Garden. They added that it was understood that a major New York diamond merchant was also interested in the purchase and that the diamond's destination was America.

So the blue diamond finally passed out of the hands of the family which had bestowed upon it the name by which it is still known today. According to the ninth Duke of Newcastle, who was the son of Lord Francis Hope's second marriage (he divorced his first wife in 1902) his father, who succeeded to the dukedom in 1928, would never talk about the Hope diamond. He died at seventy-five and would surely have disapproved of his obituary notice in *The Times* of 22 April 1941, which was headed 'The Duke of Newcastle, Former owner of the Hope Blue Diamond'. The notice went on to say that the diamond 'has provided romancers with many a tale and novelists with many a plot. It is a stone of 44½ carats and was probably a part of the Regent diamond, a blue brilliant of 67 3/16 carats which was brought to Europe early in the 18th century and was for a time the property of the Duc d'Orleans, Regent of France.' On this occasion the diamond provided the obituary writer with total confusion rather than romance: he was guilty of mixing details of the Hope with those of that famous stone, the Regent. But in mitigation it is only fair to recall that at that time most people were preoccupied with rather more serious matters than the histories of gemstones.

Among all the legal proceedings that surrounded the wish of Lord Francis Hope to sell the diamond the most puzzling part is the contents of the affidavit which Edwin Streeter supplied to the court. It will be recalled that Streeter valued the Hope diamond at less than he had previously owing to the recent appearance of two stones weighing a total of 34 carats; up to that time the Hope had been considered the only dark blue diamond of any importance to have been discovered. Now Edwin Streeter was much respected both as a jeweller and a chronicler of the history of gems, having published two books, *The Great Diamonds of the World* and *Precious Stones and Gems.* In both the author had carefully examined the question of the recutting of the former Blue Diamond of the Crown and had concluded that the Hope constituted the major portion of it; because this diamond was straighter on one side than on the other it strengthened his argument that the stone had been cleaved. He then went on to state that the dark blue pear-shape, weighing between 12 and 13 carats, included in the sale of the jewels belonging to the late Charles, Duke of Brunswick, held at Geneva in 1874, probably formed the other part of the famous French crown jewel. In later editions of *Precious Stones and Gems* Streeter suggested that a third diamond, the Pirie weighing one carat, which was in his possession, might also have been cut from the Blue

Diamond of the Crown. But, as the comparison of the drawings of the Golden Fleece in which it had been set in 1749 with the Hope diamond as it exists today has demonstrated, no smaller gems could have been cut from the former French crown jewel.

In the nineteenth century (and even today) a dark blue diamond is a rarity, all the more so if its weight is between 12 and 13 carats. It is strange then that when he stated in his affidavit that the Hope diamond was considered the only dark blue diamond to have been found Streeter appears to have overlooked the existence of the Duke of Brunswick's diamond – or did he, perhaps, consider it to be of little significance?

Recently two other dark blue diamonds have come to claim our attention. The first is an octagonal brilliant and weighs around 2¼ carats. It is mounted in a gold ring surrounded by twelve small white brilliants with a further three set as a triangle on each shoulder. The ring has formed part of the collection of the Victoria and Albert Museum in London since 1869. Along with six other coloured diamonds (three green – including an octahedral crystal, one pink, one yellow and a black) and a large collection of other gemstones, it was bequeathed to the museum by the Reverend Chauncey Townsend (1789–1868). All seven coloured diamonds earlier formed part of the collection of Henry Philip Hope.

The second is a lozenge shape, weighing 7.6 carats, which once belonged to the Empress Maria Feodorovna, daughter-in-law of Catherine the Great, who had it set as a ring. In her will of 1827 she bequeathed it to her own daughter-in-law who subsequently had the stone, which is surrounded by small white diamonds in a yellow-gold setting, made into a stickpin. She gave it to the Russian state in 1860.

Following the collapse of the Soviet Union, a senior consultant to the directors of the Hermitage Museum, Lili Konstantinovna Kuznetsova, has studied a mass of documents that had been turned over to the State Diamond Fund. The Russian authorities claim that the Empress Maria Feodorovna's gem may have been cut from the same stone as the Hope; but if either this diamond or the one in the Townsend Bequest does have a link with the Hope, then it can only date from the time when the Tavernier Blue was fashioned from its weight of 110 carats, or thereabouts, into the heart shape which became known as the Blue Diamond of the Crown, weighing 69.03 carats. The large loss of weight – 40 per cent – that occurred in this recutting could have resulted in a number of satellite stones. Likewise one writer has propounded the same theory with regard to the Brunswick Blue and the Pirie: namely that if, as Streeter asserted, they were identical in

colour to the Hope, it is more probable that all three diamonds had been cut from the same original piece, or pieces, of rough diamond found in the Kollur mine. In this connection it is of interest to note that whenever the very rare Type IIb diamonds running from a steely blue to the darker shades of blue are found, they are almost always cleavages in the rough.

Gemmologists, however, remain divided about whether sufficient test methods exist to determine, categorically, that any of these diamonds could be matched with the Hope diamond – that is, of course, provided permission were granted to remove them from their historic, antique settings.

The New York diamond merchant previously mentioned as being interested in acquiring the Hope diamond was Simon Frankel of Joseph Frankel's Sons. The sum which he is stated to have paid for the gem was £33,000. There follows another series of lurid and bizarre events which are alleged to have befallen the diamond. First, a French broker named Jacques Colot (or Colet) is stated to have bought it before becoming insane and committing suicide; a Prince Ivan Kanitowsky, variously described as a Russian or Eastern European prince, either gave or loaned the diamond to a Folies Bergères actress who was shot across the footlights next day by her lover or by the prince as she wore the stone; the Prince was later stabbed to death by revolutionaries; a certain Simon Montharides, a Greek jeweller, after selling the diamond to the Sultan of Turkey, was thrown over a precipice while riding in a car with his wife and child. However, there is no evidence to substantiate any of this except for the fact that there was a record of a jeweller by the name of Colot and the Sultan of Turkey, Abd al-Hamid II (1842–1918), certainly existed.

In 1908, Frankel sold the Hope to the dealer Salomon Habib for two million francs, but a year later Habib found himself in financial difficulties and was obliged to put his collection up for auction in Paris, in June 1909. The reserve price of the Hope was placed at 1,500,000 francs but the highest bid received was 400,000 francs. Immediately after the auction Habib was able to sell the stone to the Paris dealer, Rosenau, who, in turn, sold it to Pierre Cartier.

The part which Cartier played in the history of the diamond is threefold; first, according to Tillander, it was Cartier who had the Hope removed from its setting and its girdle faceted; secondly it was he who sold it to Mrs Evalyn Walsh McLean, the lady whose name was to be bracketed with the Hope for the next thirty years or so; thirdly it appears that he was the person who put about the story that the diamond brought misfortune not only on its owners but also on those who had even

The Hope set in as a pendant to the necklace which Evalyn Walsh McLean wore.

Photo © Tino Hammid. Los Angeles.

touched it. No doubt his powers of inventiveness were stimulated by the fact that Mrs McLean had informed him that objects of ill-luck actually produced the opposite effect upon her.

Mrs McLean was the daughter of Thomas F. Walsh; her early childhood was spent in a succession of mining camps in Colorado and South Dakota. Her father 'struck it rich' and with the fortune which he amassed in gold mining he had his daughter educated in style in Washington DC and in Europe. In 1908 she married Edward Beale McLean, whose father John R. McLean was the owner of two newspapers, the *Cincinnati Enquirer* and the *Washington Post*. While on their honeymoon trip the newly-weds walked into Cartier's store in the Rue de la Paix in Paris to look for the wedding present which Walsh had promised his daughter. Mrs McLean said that the salesman on this occasion 'hypnotized me by showing me an ornament that made bright spots before my eyes'. The ornament was a necklace of square links of platinum set with diamonds from which hung three loops of diamonds. Attached to the bottom loop was a pearl of 21¼ grains, the size of a little finger tip; suspended below it was a six-sided emerald weighing 32¼ carats, and hanging below that was the 'Star of the East', a pear-shaped diamond weighing 94.80 carats. This gem had formerly been owned by the Sultan Abd al-Hamid II.

On their next visit to Paris, in 1910, not long after the birth of the McLeans' first child and the death of Mrs McLean's father, Pierre Cartier came to call on them at their hotel with the Hope diamond. He reminded Mrs McLean of an earlier conversation during which she had said to him that when they were visiting Turkey on their honeymoon she had seen one of the members of the Sultan's harem wearing a great blue stone around her throat (possible evidence that the Sultan had indeed once owned the Hope). At this meeting Mrs McLean did not apparently contradict Cartier's assertion, but in her autobiography, published in 1936, she wrote that she did not, in fact, recall seeing the Hope although she had seen other jewels that 'made my finger itch'. On this occasion no deal was done, Mrs McLean informing her husband that she did not like the setting.

Cartier, however, was nothing if not persistent and in October of the same year he travelled to New York with the diamond. In the meantime he had had the girdle faceted and the gem set in a magnificent new necklace. The Cartier establishment in Fifth Avenue informed Mrs McLean that M. Pierre Cartier had arrived from Paris with documents – presumably the aforementioned concocted history – concerning the Hope diamond which he wished to show Mrs McLean. However, it transpired that not only did Cartier want her to study the documents

but the diamond too, requesting her to keep it over the weekend. The strategy worked: in the course of the weekend Mrs McLean decided that she wanted the diamond.

The deal hung in the air for several months before a final selling price of $180,000 was decided. Mrs McLean agreed to pay $40,000 at once, and, within three years, $114,000. As part of the price Cartier accepted an emerald and pearl pendant with a diamond necklace, probably the one that had supported the Star of the East.

Mrs McLean loved diamonds and was financially always in a position to add to her collection. She remained a customer of Cartier's and there is a story of an occasion when salesmen from the firm called on her. Trying on a pair of earrings with pendants of diamonds she suggested that one more diamond be added to each pendant. The designer suggested discreetly and politely, 'My dear madam, no lady would possibly wear earrings with more than these,' to which Mrs McLean replied, 'Dammit, I'm no lady, put on some more diamonds.' The salesman promptly obeyed.

Soon after she had bought the Hope, Mrs McLean took it to a priest to have it blessed; from then on she became inseparable from the diamond, wearing it as a charm. As a leading figure in the social life of Washington, she entertained lavishly and was invariably photographed wearing the blue diamond, often along with her other jewels. There is a photograph taken of her wearing three necklaces, the Hope on its diamond-studded chain, the Star of the East on another necklace, and a third necklace of diamond-studded links, plus diamond earrings, a pair of diamond clips and a wristful of bracelets. (Such caratage would appear to surpass even that of Louis XIV!) Once when asked why she wore so much jewellery, Mrs McLean replied, 'If I take out one or two pieces to put on when I dress up I might as well put it all on and then I know where it is.' At the same time as entertaining the social and government elite of Washington, Mrs McLean was a warm-hearted and generous person who during the Second World War entertained many servicemen recuperating in local hospitals. Often she would allow some of her women guests to wear her diamonds for the evening and on one occasion she allowed a bride to wear the Hope at her wedding.

Although Evalyn Walsh McLean refused to believe the legendary curse that has come to be associated with the Hope her life was marked by a series of personal tragedies. Following the early death of her brother, her eldest son was run over and killed by a car when he was nine years old; she divorced her husband who drank heavily and eventually died in a mental institution; while the crowning blow was the death of her only daughter

The Hope diamond is a fine example of the rare Type IIb, characterized by its colour and the fact that it is a semi-conductor of electricity. It owes its distinctive electrical properties and colour to the boron element.

Smithsonian Institution. Photo © Tino Hammid, Los Angeles.

HOPE

from an overdose at the age of twenty-five in 1946. Mrs McLean never recovered from the last of these tragedies and died from pneumonia at the age of sixty in the following year. Even after her death tragedy continued to haunt her family, for her grand-daughter Evalyn McLean died at Dallas in 1967, also at the age of twenty-five.

The day of Mrs McLean's death, 26 April 1947, was a Saturday, a fact which was to cause problems for her executors. After they had spent some time in collecting the jewellery – bracelets, brooches, necklaces etc. had apparently been scattered around the house in numerous locations, while the Hope reposed in the back of a table-top radio – they were confronted by the problem of where to put it for safe-keeping. Since it was a Saturday evening all the banks were closed and they were unable to find a bank manager who was willing to take charge of it. Finally they appealed to J. Edgar Hoover, who gave permission for the jewellery to be placed in one of the FBI's secure safes.

In her will Mrs McLean requested that her jewellery be held in trust until the youngest of her grandchildren at the time when the will was drawn up had attained the age of twenty-five. It was then to be divided equally between those and any future grandchildren. This would have meant that the jewellery could not be distributed until 1968. However, two years after Mrs McLean's death the court granted a petition of the executors, trustees and members of the family to sell the jewels so as to pay debts and claims against the estate. In the official appraisal the Hope was valued at $176,920 and the Star of the East at $185,000. There were seventy-two other pieces of jewellery.

When the jewels became available for purchase there was no lack of prospective buyers for the Hope: an individual from Ohio disclosed how keen he was to obtain it while it was reported that the Soviet government sought to purchase it in an effort to reassemble Catherine the Great's collection of jewellery. However, in April 1949 Harry Winston bought Mrs McLean's entire collection of jewellery for an undisclosed sum believed to have been between $1,250,000 and $1,500,000.

Mr Winston displayed little concern about the so-called curse attached to the Hope and carried it across the Atlantic on several occasions. He especially enjoyed telling the following story concerning it:

A few years ago I travelled to Lisbon with my wife. Since our two sons were quite young at the time we decided to return home on separate planes, as people with children often do. It was arranged that my wife would leave Lisbon for New York on the Friday evening and that I would take a plane on the following day. My wife's plane took off on schedule and landed at Santa Maria (in the Azores) for the usual refuelling.

There some slight engine trouble caused a delay of two or three hours. While waiting for repairs to be done, the passengers chatted among themselves, and the fact that Mrs Harry Winston was on the plane was soon known to all. One man went as far as to refuse to continue the journey and asked to be booked on the next plane.

On the way to the airport the next day I was handed a cablegram from my wife announcing her safe arrival. I hastily crammed it into my pocket with other papers. Climbing aboard the plane, I took a sedative and settled down, glad to notice that the adjacent seat was vacant and I could sleep in peace. I awoke from a pleasant nap when we touched down at Santa Maria to refuel and got out to stretch my legs for a while.

When we reboarded the plane to take off for New York I found that the seat that had been vacant was now occupied. Its occupant was bubbling over with a story about his escape from travelling on the same plane as the wife of the owner of the Hope diamond. 'I'm not superstitious,' he said 'but why should I tempt fate? I decided then and there to change planes and here I am, safe and sound!' He talked animatedly for some time, but eventually grew quiet enough for me to drop off to sleep again. Then his voice broke in on my slumber: 'I wonder if that plane arrived safely?' I couldn't resist it. I fished the cablegram from my pocket and handed it to him, saying nothing. He gazed dumbly at me, and didn't open his mouth again that night.

On 10 November 1958 Mr Winston presented the Hope to the Smithsonian Institution, saying that he hoped that this would be the beginning of a national collection which in time would rival that in the Tower of London. He had long wished to start such an undertaking and was glad that he was in a position to afford it. During the nine years in which he had owned it, the Hope had travelled many thousands of kilometres, being insured for $1,000,000 while in transit, and had raised millions of dollars for charity. Within the first three days of its display at the Smithsonian, attendance rose sharply – 9,504 compared to 5,519 in the same period the week before. In September 1997 the Hope was for the first time displayed in a specially designed vault within the new hall that permits a complete walk-around view of the diamond necklace in which it is set. The necklace slowly rotates and is lit with state-of-the-art fibre optic lighting, while the case has water-clear glass to provide the best possible viewing.

Since its presentation the Hope has left the Smithsonian on four occasion, the first being in 1962 when it was taken to Paris for the exhibition in the Louvre entitled 'Ten Centuries of French Jewellery'. At first the authorities of the Smithsonian refused the request to lend the diamond to the Louvre, being reluctant to deprive visitors of a chance to view the diamond for a month during the spring, always a busy time, and concerned for the safety of the diamond. It was ultimately through the intervention of the wife of President Kennedy, who had been appealed to by M. André Malraux, the French Minister of Culture, that the Smithsonian agreed to despatch the diamond. (Subsequently there was a gracious and civilized response when the

Louvre permitted Leonardo da Vinci's *Mona Lisa* to be exhibited in Washington's National Gallery of Art.) While the Hope was on exhibition in the Louvre it met up with two of its former companions among the French Crown Jewels, the Regent and the Sancy. The last occasion on which they had been housed under the same roof was the fateful night of 16–17 September 1792.

In 1965 the Smithsonian lent the Hope for exhibition at the Rand Easter Show in Johannesburg. On that occasion senior officials from the De Beers Research Laboratory were able to examine the diamond scientifically.

Like other natural blue diamonds, ranging in colour from a light metallic blue to a fancy dark blue, the Hope was found to belong to the rare Type IIb variety. This is characterized by its blue colour, indeterminate crystal shape in the rough and, in particular, by the fact that it is a semi-conductor of electricity. These properties are a consequence of the inclusion of boron atoms in substitutional positions in the diamond lattice, i.e. some carbon atoms have been replaced by boron atoms. These boron atoms, at a concentration of a few parts per million only, contain one electron fewer than their surrounding carbon neighbours. This leads to an interchange of electrons and a state whereby the diamond is rendered semi-conductive. Some absorption of light in the red part of the spectrum also occurs, resulting in the diamond appearing blue.

The fact that the Hope is a diamond of such a rare category did not surprise the officials: what intrigued them was that up to that time Type IIb diamonds had been known to have come from only one source – the Premier mine. The Kollur mine, then, appears to be the only other known source of Type IIb diamonds.

The dimensions of this 45.52-carat historic gem are as follows: depth 12.00 mm, length 25.6 mm, width 21.76 mm. Its proportions are a depth of 55.1%, a table of 53%, with a very thin to slightly thick girdle and a very large culet. It is a cushion brilliant, with a fair symmetry and a good polish.

The GIA has graded the Hope as VS1 for clarity, due to whitish graining. Its colour is fancy deep grayish blue, of natural origin with even distribution and no fluorescence.

135

The Hope diamond possesses extraordinary luminescent properties, glowing like a hot coal for several minutes after exposure to ultraviolet light.

Photo © John Hatleberg, New York.

HOPE

Hortensia

Hortense de Beauharnais, Queen of Holland, and stepdaughter of Napoleon Bonaparte, after whom the diamond was named.

Portrait by Felix Cottrau, 1834. Arenenberg, Napoleon Museum. Photo AKG London/Erich Lessing.

Opposite: the Hortensia, bought by Louis XIV, currently displayed in the Galerie d'Apollon at the Musée du Louvre, Paris.

Photo © RMN, Paris.

King Louis XIV was responsible for the addition of this pale pink diamond to the Crown Jewels of France. However, the Hortensia was not one of the diamonds which the King had purchased from Tavernier, because the largest stone of this particular colour which he brought back from India weighed only 14⅞ carats. The Hortensia was the foremost diamond in the third of the 19 florets of buttonholes listed in the inventory of the Crown Jewels of France, made in 1691.

The diamond, which weighs 20 carats (20.53 metric carats) is pale pink, rather flat and rectangular in shape and is cut on five sides. In the 1791 inventory of the Crown Jewels it was valued at no more than 48,000 livres on account of a crack extending from the edge of the girdle to the culet. It takes its name from Hortense de Beauharnais, Queen of Holland, doubtless because she wore it. Hortense was the daughter of the Empress Josephine, the step-daughter of Napoleon Bonaparte, and the mother of Napoleon III.

The Hortensia was among the jewels stolen from the Garde Meuble in September 1792. One year later it was recovered from an old house in the Halles district of Paris. As he was on the point of being executed, a man named Depeyron disclosed that he had hidden it in a bag containing gold and other diamonds, including the Regent, in a garret.

During the First Empire the Hortensia was mounted on the fastening of Napoleon's epaulette braid. Later it was set in the centre of the head-band of the great diamond-encrusted comb made by the Court Jeweller, Bapst, for the Empress Eugénie in 1856. In between, in 1830, the diamond was stolen again, on this occasion from the Ministry of the Marine, but it was quickly recovered.

When the French Crown Jewels were sold in 1887 the Hortensia was one of the items excluded, because of their historic or artistic interest.

HORTENSIA

Idol's Eye

Abd al-Hamid II, Sultan of
Turkey, said to have owned
the diamond until his
deposition and exile in 1909.

Photo © Hulton Getty Picture
Collection.

The various published accounts of the early
history of the Idol's Eye are worthy of being
included in *A Thousand and One Nights*; unfortunately,
for the most part they must be considered to be
entirely spurious. The diamond may have been
found at Golconda around 1600, but seven years
later it was certainly not seized from the Persian
Prince Rahab by the East India Company as
payment for a debt. No such person is recorded in
the history of Persia, while the East India Company
did not start to trade in that country until several
years later.

The first authenticated fact in the diamond's
history was its appearance at a Christie's sale in
London on 14 July 1865, when it was described as
'a splendid large diamond known as the Idol's Eye
set round with 18 smaller brilliants and frame-work
of small brilliants'. It was knocked down to a
mysterious buyer designated simply as 'B.B.'. Later
it is stated that the 34th Ottoman Sultan,
Abd al-Hamid II (1842–1918), owned the Idol's Eye.
However the Idol's Eye would never, as has often
been asserted, have been set in the eye of a temple in
Benghazi because there are neither temples nor
idols in that city, Benghazi having been Muslim
since the eighth century AD.

When consideration is given to the shape of the
Idol's Eye – something between a cushion and a
pear – it is not difficult to envisage its setting
elsewhere as an eye. Indeed the stone compares
favourably with others deemed to have been set in
this manner which suggest that certain idols found
in sacred buildings in the East have had very oddly-
shaped ocular orifices. The Idol's Eye weighs 70.21
metric carats and is clearly a Golconda stone,
possessing that slight bluish tinge so characteristic
of many diamonds from that source.

Abd al-Hamid II presided over the most
autocratic regime that the Ottoman Empire had

experienced since the eighteenth century. He was
eventually defeated by the internal opposition
which coalesced as the Young Turks. After his
deposition in 1909 he lived in exile, first in Salonika,
then in Istanbul where he died in 1918. It is said that
the Sultan, sensing in which direction the political
wind of his country was blowing, made provisions
for his coming enforced retirement, which included
the despatch of his jewels to a place of safety.
Unfortunately the servant entrusted with them
turned traitor and sold them in Paris. Whether or
not this is the true version of events, it is known
that the Idol's Eye was one of several large
diamonds belonging to the dealer Salomon Habib
that came up for auction in Paris on 24 June 1909.
Subsequently a Spanish nobleman bought the
diamond which he kept in a London bank for some
years.

After the end of the Second World War the
Idol's Eye re-emerged when it was acquired by a
Dutch dealer, from whom Harry Winston bought
it in 1946. In the following year Mr Winston
sold it to Mrs May Bonfils Stanton, daughter
of Frederick G. Bonfils, the publisher and
co-founder of the *Denver Post*. If many of the earlier
characters associated with the diamond's history
have proved to be fictitious, Mrs Stanton goes some
way to make up for them. Once a great beauty, she
became a legendary figure in American life. From
her early girlhood she displayed an interest in jewels
and began to assemble a famous collection. In
addition to the Idol's Eye it was to include the
Liberator diamond and a diamond necklace
studded with twelve emeralds weighing 107 carats,
once owned by the Maharajah of Indore. She lived
in splendid isolation in a palatial mansion copied
from the Petit Trianon in Versailles, and was said to
have worn the Idol's Eye at her solitary breakfast
every morning. The gem was set as the pendant to a

diamond necklace containing 41 brilliants, weighing about 22.50 carats, and 45 baguettes weighing about 12 carats. Mrs Stanton was also a supporter of numerous philanthropic causes in her native state of Colorado. After her death, in her eighties, in March 1962, her jewels were auctioned in November by Parke-Bernet Galleries Inc. of New York; in accordance with the directions contained in her will the proceeds were distributed among various charities.

The Chicago jeweller Harry Levinson bought the Idol's Eye for $375,000. In 1967 he loaned it to De Beers for exhibition at the Diamond Pavilion in Johannesburg. Six years later Mr Levinson put the diamond up for sale in New York but subsequently withdrew it when the bidding failed to reach his minimum of $1,000,000. In 1979 Laurence Graff of London purchased the Idol's Eye. Harry Levinson loaned the diamond, before it was sold to Laurence Graff, for display at the Metropolitan Museum of Art in New York, at a 1982 reception celebrating the fiftieth anniversary of Harry Winston Inc. In the following January, Mr Graff sold the Idol's Eye together with the Emperor Maximilian and a 70.54-carat, fancy yellow diamond, named the Sultan Abd al-Hamid II and thought to have once been part of that ruler's jewellery collection. The sale of these three diamonds to the same buyer is considered to have been one of the highest priced transactions ever known.

The Idol's Eye, set as a pendant in a necklace containing 41 brilliants, was auctioned after Mrs Stanton's death. It now forms part of a private collection.

De Beers Archives.

Incomparable

'A diamond as big as the Ritz' – at one time it was thought possible that one worthy of Scott Fitzgerald's title might ensue from the cutting of this 890-carat stone, the fifth largest flawless diamond ever discovered, which was found in the town of Mbuji Mayi in the Democratic Republic of Congo (formerly Zaïre) in the 1980s. It was discovered by a young girl playing in a pile of building rubble outside her uncle's house. This rubble had been legitimately collected from old mine dumps from the nearby MIBA diamond mine, having been rejected during the recovery process as being too bulky to be worth screening for diamonds. The young girl gave the diamond to her uncle, who sold it to some local African dealers, who in turn sold it to a group of Lebanese buyers operating out of Kinshasa.

It was later purchased in Antwerp by the senior De Beers buyer. Subsequently, Sir Philip Oppenheimer, then president of the Central Selling Organisation and a De Beers director, sold it to Donald Zale, chairman of the board of the Zale Corporation, the Dallas-based jewellery retailer. He bought the diamond in partnership with Marvin Samuels, of Premier Gems Corp., and Louis Glick, both leading figures in the New York diamond industry. The huge stone was unveiled to the world in November 1984, which coincided with the Zale Corporation's diamond anniversary year. Shortly afterwards it was put on display at the National Museum of Natural History in the Smithsonian Institution, Washington.

The task of overseeing the cutting was entrusted to Mr Samuels, renowned for his experience and expertise in the manufacture of large diamonds. This diamond certainly presented its fair share of problems. Its basic shape was extremely irregular: it was thicker at one end, narrower at the other; sunken and pitted on one side, ridged on the other. The surface was very rough, pitted with various protuberances, cavities and cracks. At least it came as something of a relief that, after a part of the surface had been initially polished and the interior opened up for inspection, it was free of inclusions.

Four years were spent studying and cutting the stone. Its owners were faced with a dilemma: should they go for a gem the weight of which would exceed that of the largest diamond hitherto cut, namely Cullinan I (530.20 carats), or fashion a smaller, flawless gem, by removing the internal inclusions. 'Never forget it – 531 carats. That indelible, non-negotiable 531, and only one chance to get it,' Samuels reflected. However, during the course of the second year's work on the stone, Mr Samuels and the cutters came to realize that it would be necessary to give up any thought of surpassing the weight of Cullinan I, despite the reluctance of some who continued to argue for size as opposed to perfection.

Before polishing of the biggest piece began, work was started on the 14 fragments that had been sawn from the rough stone. Mr John Sampson White, then Curator in Charge of the Division of Mineralogy at the Smithsonian, examined these 'leftovers' and he made an interesting discovery; the first thing that caught his eye was their variation in colour. He had handled the 890-carat uncut stone many times before but he had never noticed any differences of colour within. Some of the fragments were a rich yellow with a slight brownish cast, like a smoky amber; others were pale yellow, and the rest virtually colourless. Those with the brownish cast had come from the darkest zone of the crystal, but making up just a part of the crystal's surface, most of this dark material had been removed. With this removal, the final body colour of the diamond turned out to be mostly an intermediate yellow, or champagne, colour.

Mr Sampson White's examination caused him to realize that the rough stone had not been uniformly

Cut from an 890-carat stone, the unusually shaped Incomparable reached the highest price ever bid at auction for a single stone.

Photo © Tino Hammid, Los Angeles.

141

coloured, but rather prominently colour-zoned. That is, the crystal had been composed of sharply defined areas of differing colours, each colour representing some change in the environment that must have occurred as the crystal was growing. At one stage, the crystal had been colourless; then nature had added a certain thickness of pale yellow diamond, followed by a 'skin' of smoky amber-coloured diamond. From the fragments, fourteen satellite gems were cut, the largest being a kite shape of 15.66 carats; the others, of varying shapes, weighed 6.01, 5.28, 4.33, 3.45, 3.32, 3.31, two of 2.74, 1.99, 1.74, 1.63, 1.52 and 1.33 carats.

The biggest piece of the rough gem ultimately yielded a gem weighing 407.48 carats; it is the third largest ever cut, surpassed only by the Golden Jubilee and Cullinan I. Measuring 53.90 x 35.19 x 28.18 mm,

it has been graded by the Gem Trade Laboratory, Inc., as a shield-shape step cut, internally flawless and fancy brownish-yellow in colour. Its unusual triangular shape elicited a new and imaginative term from Marvin Samuels – a 'triolette'.

Prior to its appearance at auction in New York, on 19 October 1988, the diamond was shown at Christie's in London where it was called 'The Golden Giant'. However, when the gem came up for auction again it had been renamed 'The Incomparable', the largest diamond ever offered to the public for sale. It was hoped that the diamond would fetch $20 million but it was withdrawn from sale when bidding failed to reach the seller's reserve price. Nonetheless, history had been made: the late Theodore Horovitz, of Geneva, placed a bid of $12 million, the highest price ever bid at auction for a single stone at that time.

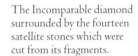

142   The Incomparable diamond surrounded by the fourteen satellite stones which were cut from its fragments.

Photo © Tino Hammid, Los Angeles.

INCOMPARABLE

Indore Pears

These two diamonds are linked to the 'Malabar Hill Murder': one evening in January 1925 at an hour when the hanging gardens of Malabar Hill, one of the most salubrious parts of Bombay, were crowded with people, an official of the Bombay Corporation was driving along its ridge , accompanied by a friend and a Muslim woman. Suddenly their car was attacked by armed men. The official was murdered and the two others badly injured. Four British officers passing by went to their aid, and managed to detain one of the assailants. The press reported that the evidence indicated that robbery was not the motive for the crime, but rather revenge or an attempt at abduction. *The Times* stated that the Bombay police were offering a reward of 10,000 rupees for information, but added that 'it is feared however that the organization behind the gang is so powerful, wealthy and unscrupulous, that it would offer even greater inducements to remain silent'.

During an earlier case before the Bombay High Court it was revealed that the Muslim woman, Mumtaz Begum, had been a dancing girl at the Court of Tukoji Rao III, Maharajah of Indore, one of the three great Maratha states in central India. She had been one of the many concubines of the Prince, who was captivated by her, but she did not return his feelings. While the entourage of the Maharajah was travelling, the girl had jumped off his private train, escaping to Amritsar, thence to Bombay where she came under the protection of a rich merchant. It was agreed that the crime on Malabar Hill could not be ignored: Mumtaz Begum had recognized her assailants as an aide-de-camp of the Maharajah and members of the Indore army and mounted police. The Maharajah's involvement in the crime was never made public but he was asked either to appear at the subsequent official inquiry or abdicate in favour of his son. In the following year he chose the latter course.

While travelling in Switzerland after his abdication, he met Nancy Ann Miller, a rich young American. Amid much publicity the couple married in 1928. The bride embraced the Hindu religion and subsequently became known as the Maharanee Shamista Davi Holkar. In 1946 Harry Winston bought the two pear-shaped diamonds, weighing 46.95 and 46.70 carats, which the Maharanee had worn on many occasions. Mr Winston had the gems recut to 46.39 and 44.14 carats and shown in his famous exhibition called 'The Court of Jewels'. In 1953 he sold them to a client from Philadelphia, repurchasing them five years later and selling them to another client in New York. In 1976 Mr Winston bought the Indore Pears yet again before selling them to a member of a royal family. Finally Christie's auctioned them in Geneva, in November 1980, and again in November 1987. Mr Robert Mouawad is the present owner of the diamonds.

Jonker

The Jonker I, considered to be one of the most perfectly polished diamonds in the world.

De Beers Archives.

The career of a diamond digger is very different from that of a diamond miner. Whereas the latter may be exposed to a greater degree of physical risk – although the safety record of diamond mines is second to none – he will also enjoy all the benefits that a large corporate concern can confer upon him both during his active working life and his retirement.

On the other hand diamond digging is generally a very precarious occupation and even the most experienced diggers barely make enough money to keep body and soul together. However, hope springs eternal in the human breast and this faith alone is enough, it would seem, to spur diggers on to continue to work their claims, in spite of the tremendous odds stacked against them.

Occasionally a lucky digger has struck it rich and made an exceptional discovery. One such person was 62-year-old Johannes Jacobus Jonker who for 18 years had been trying his luck at various claims throughout the country. At the time of his momentous find he was working a claim at Elandsfontein, just 4.8 km from the Premier mine and about 40 km east of Pretoria, South Africa's administrative capital. It was said of of him that he was always on the brink of fortune but always poor – and he had seven children.

January 17 1934 dawned a raw, windy day. After the lashing rain had ploughed up the earth, Jonker decided to stay at home as he had been out of luck and was feeling discouraged. Instead, he sent his son Gert, along with two of his black employees, to direct operations on the claim. One of them, Johannes Makani, was washing a bucketful of gravel when suddenly he stopped dead in his tracks and picked up something. Without saying a word he walked to the cleaning camp and scrubbed the object which he had found. Then he threw his hat in the air and shouted, 'Oh God, I have found it.'

He rushed across to Gert Jonker who at first thought he was looking at a piece of glass, but when he realized it was a real diamond he rushed to tell his father. When he found him, all he received was a paternal rebuke for riding recklessly. However, when Jacobus Jonker too realized it was a diamond he went down on his knees and thanked God.

The object did indeed turn out to be a diamond: an oblong-shaped piece measuring about 63.5 by 31.75 mm, of superb ice-white colour, weighing 726 carats. At the time of its discovery the Jonker was the fourth largest gem quality stone ever to have been found; it was relegated to fifth place four years later when the President Vargas, weighing 0.6 carat more, was unearthed.

Naturally no one in the Jonker household had ever set eyes upon a diamond about the size of a hen's egg and some still doubted whether it could be a diamond. Mrs Jonker, however, was taking no chances; she plunged it down a stocking and tied the stocking round her neck. She went to bed but did not sleep while men kept guard at the door of the poor hut with loaded revolvers.

The story of the Jonker diamond brings together the names of several men prominent in the annals of the diamond industry. One of them was Joseph Bastiaenen who had started his career in the London offices of the Diamond Syndicate, the precursor of the modern Diamond Trading Company, after the First World War. Ten years later he was sent by Sir Ernest Oppenheimer as head sorter to the Diamond Corporation's office in Kimberley; then he was appointed a buyer for the Diamond Corporation on the alluvial fields and it was in that capacity that he bought the Jonker against severe competition from buyers representing famous diamond firms from all parts of the world.

About a week after the purchase of the Jonker Mr Bastiaenen brought the diamond into the Kimberley office where his colleagues proceeded to bombard him with questions, many of which were pertinent to the parlous state of the diamond trade at the time and the vast amount of money that the stone had cost the company. In the midst of these deliberations the great diamond fell off the sorting table and rolled onto the floor and in a light-hearted moment one or two more boisterous members of the staff started kicking it around the office, much to the consternation of the man who had so recently paid a king's ransom for it.

Reports of the exact amount paid for the Jonker varied between £61,000 and £75,000. The transaction actually involved another large stone weighing 287 carats, which had been found within 100 metres of the Jonker a few days earlier. This was the Pohl, named after another digger, J. M. Pohl. However, although of an extremely fine colour, it contained several imperfections. Soon after the sale of the Jonker to the Diamond Corporation, the South African government was quickly on the scene demanding more than one-third of the stone's value – the equivalent of six years' work – in income tax, super-tax and provincial tax. The Minister of Mines agreed that certain sums of money spent in the discovery of the stone should be deducted from the purchase price and exempted from taxation. Accordingly the Jonkers claimed:

£14,755:	cost of digging operations for 18 years
£3,600:	'donations'
£1,000:	preliminary expenses
£1,000:	costs of negotiating the sale
£755:	donations to churches
£200:	travelling expenses

The Receiver of Revenue disallowed all items except for the first and the last. He cut the allowance for digging operations from £14,755 to £2,000 and reduced the travelling expenses from £200 to £100. Thus faced with a reduction of the exemption from £21,310 to a mere £2,100, the Jonkers petitioned the House of Assembly to grant them the exemption they claimed – but in vain. Truly the good Jonker must have thought himself a citizen of the Holy Roman Empire rather than of the Union of South Africa and recalled in his Bible, St Luke Chapter 2, verse 1: 'And it came to pass in those days, that there went out a decree from Caesar Augustus, that all the world should be taxed.'

This misfortune proved only the first for Jonker. His diamond may have brought him riches but it totally destroyed his peace of mind. For years he had led the life of an indigent digger, wandering from one diamond field to another with never a fixed abode – when his famous gem was found he was living in poverty in a prospector's shack.

The child film-star, Shirley Temple, holding the Jonker diamond in the rough.

Courtesy of Harry Winston Inc., New York.

With the money he received for the diamond he bought a farm, some cattle and a grand limousine, but he remained at heart a simple countryman and was never able to cope with the realities of the commercial world into which his great discovery had pitch-forked him. This had a disastrous effect on his capital and within a few years all he had left were his good name and his memories; fame and fortune had forsaken him.

The discovery of the Jonker in diggings a mere 5 km from the Premier mine and the superb colour and quality of the stone inevitably led to speculation as to whether it had once been part of the Cullinan. It will be recalled that this mighty gem, which had been found in the Premier mine twenty-nine years before, possessed a cleavage face on one side so smooth as to suggest it may have previously formed part of a much larger crystal. Indeed the 'missing half of the Cullinan' has remained to this day a topic for debate amongst specialists. Among those who examined the question was Dr J. R. Sutton, author of *Diamond, A Descriptive Treatise*. who wrote the following letter to a gemmological publication 20 March 1934:

Dear Sir,
I have delayed answering your letter until I could see the newly found Jonker diamond. This I have seen and compared it with the fine glass model of the Cullinan. Also I have discussed the matter of the latter stone with Mr E. Weatherby, Valuator of the Diamond Corporation, who had examined it carefully after it was found.

The resemblance between the Cullinan and the Jonker stones is remarkable. In fact, if the latter were four times its actual size the two would almost be twin brothers. Each stone has the same broad base (Cleavage plane). Each has suffered damage by splintery fracture; and what is significant, the base on each is surrounded by a small rounded bevel mainly conforming to the dodecahedral plane both about $^1/_{10}$ of an inch [2.5mm] across. The chief difference is that whereas the base on the Cullinan is not exactly plane, though smooth, the base of the Jonker is not smooth and carries some small projections.

Mr Weatherby is emphatic that the Cullinan is not a cleavage piece in the mineralogical sense. He never had any doubts that it was a whole stone as Nature made it, saving minor accidents. All this confirms me in my opinion.

Of the authors you quote is there one who can be regarded as an expert in the study of the natural diamond, especially diamond and cleavage? Is there one whose knowledge is equal to, say, a week's work in a big diamond office? They have all been in museums and elsewhere, and Crookes experimented somewhat on the stone. But their united testimony only comes to this: that one copies what the other has said, all taking Corstorphine's 'technical description' as gospel!

I have seen an unbroken diamond fresh from the mine which I would wager diamond to paste that every one of the same authors would have said had been roughly shaped by a cutter ... My definition of cleavage would be 'the opened face of a split diamond'. Cleavage as a trade term includes both broken diamonds and unbroken misshapen lumps.

Both the Cullinan and the Jonker would be trade cleavages.

I left Corstorphine's technical description behind in South Africa; but speaking from memory there was no suggestion in it of a proper examination of the 'cleavage faces'. With few exceptions octahedral faces of the diamond crystals carry triangular indentations. But on 'occasional so-called glassies' one may look in vain for these markings: the surface being as mirror-like as a cleavage face...All things considered it seems to me that those who claim the Cullinan as a piece of a much bigger stone have a stiff proposition to prove.

P.S. The Jonker and Cullinan clearly grew under identical conditions. Therefore, the Jonker not being a portion of a much bigger stone it is a fair argument that the Cullinan is also not a fragment.

As well as being an event in itself, the discovery of the Jonker recorded several firsts in diamond lore. The stone became the first large one to be sold through the De Beers Central Selling Organisation which, under the guidance of Sir Ernest Oppenheimer, had superseded the old syndicate of diamond buying firms. The Jonker was shipped by ordinary registered post to the group's London offices in Charterhouse Street.

Simultaneously Harry Winston became interested in acquiring the diamond. In 1935 he contacted Hugo Prins who, in turn, referred him to his brother George Prins, then senior partner of the firm of I. Hennig & Co., who were already brokers to a number of important firms in the diamond cutting industry. Ultimately these contacts led to Mr Winston's purchase of the Jonker and marked the first of many successful important purchases of large diamonds which the firm of Harry Winston Inc. was to make over the years from the Central Selling Organisation. In the case of the Jonker the negotiations lasted several weeks, with Hennig's acting on behalf of Mr Winston. It was believed that the Jonker was sold for a figure in excess of £150,000 with the Pohl diamond once again included in the transaction.

The year 1935 marked the Royal Silver Jubilee celebrations and in order to accommodate the many prominent persons who had come to London for the event and who wished to inspect the Jonker, Mr Winston consented to its being left in London for a while. The decision to let the gem remain there was also influenced by the suggestion emanating from several influential quarters that the Jonker would make an appropriate Jubilee gift to King George V and Queen Mary, both of whom had viewed the diamond. It was believed that a popular subscription with this objective in view was considered but in the end nothing came of it and the Jonker duly made the trans-Atlantic trip to Mr Winston's offices in New York.

When the Jonker reached New York Harry Winston received numerous requests throughout the United States to place it on exhibition, so he consented to its display at the Natural History Museum. But there was the more immediate and important problem of cutting the diamond. No diamond of comparable size or value had been cut in the United States. Mr Winston's choice of cutter fell on Lazare Kaplan, who was descended from three generations of jewellers and had learned the craft of diamond cutting in Belgium. Mr Kaplan had established a reputation as an outstanding cleaver and cutter, known especially for his insistence on obtaining the maximum fire and brilliance in a gem even if this resulted in a slightly greater loss of weight. In 1914 Mr Kaplan transferred his business to the American continent

	Estimated			Actual Finished	
Rough Wt (ct)	Dimensions (mm)	Approx. Wt (ct)	Dimensions (mm)	Weight (ct)	
35.82	30 × 12	17	29.5 × 12.2	1 Mq – 15.77	VIII
79.65	23 × 17	42	23.2 × 18.3	1 Ec – 41.29	II
43.30	17 × 14	20	17.3 × 14.6	1 Ec – 19.76	VII
54.19	21 × 16	30	21.7 × 16.2	1 Ec – 25.78	V
52.77	22 × 16	35	22.8 × 16.3	1 Ec – 30.71	IV
65.28	24 × 15	35	24.8 × 16.5	1 Ec – 35.45	III
13.57	16 × 7.5	6	15.5 × 8.8	1 Ec – 5.70	XI
53.95	20 × 15	25	20.3 × 15.2	1 Ec – 24.91	VI
10.98	10.5 × 10	5	10.8 × 10.3	1 Ec – 5.30	XII
220.00	33 × 31	150	33.7 × 30.8	1 Ec – 142.90	I
29.46	15.25 × 12.25	14	15.3 × 12.2	1 Ec – 11.43	X
27.85	16.5 × 12.5	14	16.5 × 12.3	1 Ec – 13.55	IX
8.28	Baguette	4	12.3 × 7.2	1 Ec – 3.53	XIII
695.10	Total				
10.74	Rough and miscellaneous fancies returned to Harry Winston Inc.				
5.37	Cleaving loss				
13.22	Sawing loss				
1.57	Opening loss				
726.0	carats				

Abbreviations: Mq = Marquise, Ec = Emerald Cut, Wt = weight, ct = carat

and he was the pioneer in establishing the diamond cutting industry in Puerto Rico.

An additional reason for choosing Lazare Kaplan to cut the Jonker was the fact that, not long before, he had successfully cut its constant companion, the Pohl. The yield had been fifteen gems, all flawless except for one, which nonetheless sold for $50,000. The largest diamond, an emerald cut of 38.10 metric carats, has retained the name Pohl and was once owned by Bernice Chrysler Garbish, daughter of the founder of the Chrysler Motor Corporation.

But the task of cutting the Jonker confronted Mr Kaplan with a far greater challenge – the biggest he had ever met. Only two diamonds comparable to this stone had previously been found – the 3,106-carat Cullinan and the 995.2-carat Excelsior – and of the two only the former had been cleaved. The task of cutting the Jonker was not made easier by the fact that it possessed a degree of frostiness on its surface, thereby rendering its cutting and polishing an even more hazardous operation. In addition, the insurers refused to cover the cutting of the diamond – even though they had been prepared to let it travel to New York by ordinary registered mail!

Lazare Kaplan studied the Jonker for months: he made many models of it, precisely reconstructing the crystallization of the diamond. At the time it was said that he lived, ate and breathed the stone. His minute examination of the Jonker paid off, for he noticed a small ledge on the stone – a fact which opened his eyes to the mistake that those European experts who had studied it and made suggestions about its cutting had earlier made. It took strong self-assurance to follow his conviction but Mr Kaplan realized that there lay only one way in which the diamond could be cleaved. Calmly he marked the cleavage lines with Indian ink, a device which he originated but which some regarded as mere affectation on his part. Afterwards he stated that the Jonker was a freak of nature; what resembled the cleavage plane was not in fact the cleavage at all. At one point he had been about to split the stone when he noticed a microscopic bend in a slight surface crack. At the crucial moment all his calculations therefore went awry.

Finally the day came when the first cleavage took place. It was 27 April 1936 when a 35-carat section was split: this piece yielded the solitary marquise among the gems. Two more cleavings took place; the rest of the division was achieved by sawing. The figures (previous page) indicate the course of the cutting and polishing of the Jonker; it is of especial interest to note how close the final weights of the thirteen gems were to earlier estimates that Lazare Kaplan had given to Harry Winston.

The largest diamond, which has retained the name Jonker, originally weighed 142.9 carats, cut with 66 facets. Later the proportions were changed, to impart to it a more oblong outline and greater brilliance. It was thus reduced to a weight of 125.65 carats, cut with 58 facets. In the opinion of many who have inspected it, Jonker I is perhaps the most perfectly cut gem in existence. Whenever it was put on exhibition in various parts of the United States, it attracted even more attention than the rough stone had done before.

In 1949 King Farouk of Egypt bought the gem, but following his deposition and subsequent exile in 1952 its whereabouts became a mystery. It reappeared, however, in the ownership of Queen Ratna of Nepal. In 1977 it changed hands again when it was sold privately in Hong Kong for a reported US$2,259,400. So far as is known the 1977 buyer of the diamond still remains the owner of it today.

The exact disposition of the remaining gems is not known for sure. It was reported that the Maharajah of Indore was the purchaser of Jonkers V, VII, XI, and XII, while John D. Rockefeller Jr was rumoured to have been the buyer of Jonker X. On 16 October 1975 Jonker IV, set in a platinum ring, came up for auction at Sotheby Parke-Bernet Inc. in New York and was sold to a South American private collector for £276,609. On that occasion the gem was given a superb gemmological rating – a tribute both to the quality of the original rough stone and to the skill of the master who had fashioned it thirty years earlier. The same diamond came up for sale again in New York in December 1987, when it fetched $1,705,000. Finally, Jonker II, with a slightly reduced weight of 40.26 carats, was sold by Sotheby's in Geneva, in May 1994, for $1,974,830.

148

This magnificent colourless, cushion-cut diamond with a weight of 245.35 carats ranks as the sixth largest in the world. The original rough stone, in shape an irregular octahedron without definite faces, weighed 650.80 (metric) carats; it was found in the Jagersfontein mine towards the end of 1895. A syndicate of London diamond merchants comprising the firms Wernher, Beit & Co., Barnato Bros and Mosenthal Sons & Co., acquired the Jubilee together with the Excelsior. At first the stone was named the Reitz in honour of Francis William Reitz, then President of the Orange Free State in which Jagersfontein is situated.

In 1896 the syndicate sent the diamond to Amsterdam where it was polished by M. B. Barends, under the supervision of Messrs Metz. First, a piece weighing 40 carats or so was cleaved; this yielded a fine, clean pear shape of 13.34 carats which was bought by Dom Carlos I of Portugal as a present for his wife. The present whereabouts of this gem is unknown. The remaining large piece was then polished into the Jubilee. When during the cutting it became evident that a truly superb diamond of exceptional size and purity was being produced, it was planned to present it to Queen Victoria. In the end this did not happen and the

In celebration of Queen Victoria's Diamond Jubilee in 1897, the name of the Jubilee diamond was changed from the Reitz.

149

diamond remained with its owners. The following year marked the Diamond Jubilee of Queen Victoria so the gem was renamed the Jubilee to commemorate the occasion. In the world of diamonds the event was also marked by the introduction of the Jubilee cut; this has the characteristics of both the rose and brilliant cuts in that the table is replaced by eight star facets, the total number of facets being increased to 88. It is not often encountered today.

In 1900 the syndicate displayed the Jubilee at the Paris Exhibition, where it was one of the centres of attraction. It was then valued at 7,000,000 francs. Shortly afterwards Sir Dorabji Jamsetji Tata bought the diamond. He was the Indian industrialist and philanthropist who laid the foundation of his country's iron and steel industry; these and the cotton mills founded by his father formed the cornerstone of modern India's economic development.

Sir Dorabji Jamsetji Tata died in 1932. Three years later his heirs sent the Jubilee for sale at Cartier's, who in December of that year mounted it in a display of historic diamonds. For a buyer the firm looked first to the Gaekwar of Baroda who in 1928 had appointed Cartier as his sole advisers on purchases of precious stones. Their representatives were prepared to sell the Jubilee to the prince for £75,000. Having sought authorization from the treasury department in Baroda for the purchase, and despite the encouragement of its officials, the Gaekwar declined to buy the diamond. So in 1937 Cartier sold the Jubilee instead to M. Paul-Louis Weiller, the Paris industrialist and patron of the arts. The diamond's former setting was changed into a baguette diamond brooch, suggestive of either a six-pointed star or a stylized turtle.

M. Weiller was always generous in lending the Jubilee to exhibitions which included one staged at the Smithsonian Institution in Washington in 1960 and another held in Geneva in December of the same year. In 1966 the Jubilee returned to South Africa where it featured in the De Beers Diamond Pavilion in Johannesburg.

Mr Robert Mouawad has since bought the Jubilee which is now the largest item in his great collection. He is quoted as saying, 'If we refer to the human contribution brought to a diamond, my favourite would be the Jubilee for its outstanding cut for the period.'

The Jubilee possesses 88 facets and introduced a new diamond cut. It is the world's sixth largest polished diamond.

De Beers Archives.

Few cities occupy such a strategic position as Istanbul: to the West it represents the gateway to the East; to the East it stands as the gateway to the West. Consequently the city has for centuries played a vital part in trade between the two continents, a point of transit and a location for purchases. Among diamonds at least two, the Sancy and the Akbar Shah, have been acquired there and the likelihood is that many others from the East have come via this route.

Two other diamonds travelled no further west than Constantinople. Edwin Streeter named them the 'Turkey I' and 'Turkey II', and recorded their weights to be 147 and 84 carats. The larger of the two was called the Ottoman and was owned by the Grand Sultan in the middle of the nineteenth century; it was stated to have been a stone of great beauty and of the first water, valued at £156,800. Although its weight was reported to be 140 carats, slightly less than Streeter's figure, it was almost certainly none other than Turkey I. The whereabouts of this stone is not known today.

The other diamond, known as the 'Kasikci' or 'Spoonmaker's Diamond', is undoubtedly the 86-carat (metric) stone that is on view in the Topkapi Museum in Istanbul. This building, formerly the Sultan's seraglio, was begun in 1462 and served as the residence of the Sultans until the beginning of the nineteenth century. Nowadays it houses the treasures of the Sultans including collections of china, jewels, armour, textiles and manuscripts.

We are a little more fortunate than Edwin Streeter in knowing about the smaller diamond at least; his correspondent in Constantinople, whom he described as a 'gentleman holding an official position in the East' clearly found it hard to come by any information on the subject. On 19 July 1881, he wrote as follows:

In reply to yours of 11th inst., I beg to say that I shall endeavour to get the information you seek; but as the Turkish fast, the Ramadan, is now coming on, it is quite useless to attempt anything till after Bairam, that is in five weeks. I shall then apply, through the Embassy, for a firman to inspect the jewels, which may or may not be given. At that time I shall also endeavour to get such drawings and legends as you wish for. I may, however, say that of late years immense robberies have gone on; and very likely the stones you speak of have disappeared...'

Five months later Streeter's correspondent wrote:

I have your memorandum of 2nd inst., and can well understand that you are surprised at my long silence. I regret, however, to say that I am not one whit nearer the information you desire than when you first wrote to me about it; and I doubt very much if I shall ever get anything reliable to communicate to you. I have taken no inconsiderable amount of trouble in the matter, and have approached several high and influential men on the subject; but with absolutely no result. It is not at all a question of money, but simply this, that the reign of terror in the palace is so absolute, that no one would ever dare to ask a question referring to crown jewels.

The man responsible for this reign of terror was the Sultan Abd al-Hamid II, whose recourse to a spy system, censorship, imprisonment, exile and even the murder of his opponents was unprecedented. He owned several notable diamonds but when he was most in need of them, at his deposition, he was deprived of them by the treachery of one of his servants who had sold them. It is not known whether he regarded the Kasikci as a part of the Turkish regalia and therefore inviolable or whether he was thwarted in an attempt to remove that stone too.

The diamond is a pear shape, set in a frame of 49 diamonds. The alternative name of the gem, the Spoonmaker's Diamond, comes from its discovery in a part of Istanbul and its subsequent exchange for three spoons by a merchant. A goldsmith then bought it from the spoonmaker and showed it to one of his colleagues who recognized it as a diamond and demanded a part of its value. On learning about this dispute, the chief goldsmith removed the diamond and paid each of the two men 500 piastres. Soon after, the Sultan demanded to see the stone and decided to keep it for himself.

The Kasikci diamond, as now displayed at the Topkapi Museum in Istanbul.

De Beers Archives.

Khedive

The 36.61-carat Khedive ('Ruler') diamond named after Ismail Pasha during whose reign the Suez canal was completed.

The name of this diamond derives from Ismail Pasha (1830–95). Born in Cairo and educated in Paris, he succeeded his uncle as Viceroy of Egypt in 1863. Ismail obtained two concessions from the Ottoman Sultan. One was a right of direct succession in accordance with the principle of primogeniture: previously the succession had passed to the eldest member of the royal family. The other was the title of Khedive, an ancient Persian title meaning 'ruler'.

It was during the reign of Ismail Pasha that the Suez Canal was completed (1869). Work had begun on this project ten years earlier and it was eventually built at a cost of £29,725,000. Originally it was the French Consul who had obtained from Said Pasha, ruler of Egypt, a concession to establish La Compagnie Universelle du Canal Maritime de Suez. The company was formed in 1858 with a capital of 200,000,000 francs, most of the shares being bought by the French, Turks and Said Pasha himself. French involvement in the enterprise had been paramount so it was scarcely surprising that the Empress Eugénie should have been the recipient of gifts to mark the ceremony of the canal's opening. Among the items which she received were two brooches in the form of anchors pavé-set with diamonds; subsequently these came into the possession of Kathleen, Duchess of Newcastle, sister-in-law of the owner of the Hope diamond.

It has been asserted that the Empress Eugénie was also presented with the Khedive, a rectangular light yellow diamond of 36.61 carats, recut from its former weight of 43 carats to make it flawless. Now light yellow diamonds were known before the advent of diamonds in South Africa – they were poorly looked upon compared with white stones – but the Khedive has the appearance of a typical Cape stone. Therefore, if it had been found in Africa, it would have been one of the first recorded diamonds from that source; it would have helped to strengthen the belief of the Empress that diamonds from the Cape were usually yellowish in colour – a belief that she was later to express when she was confronted with the Porter Rhodes diamond in 1881.

Recent inquiries in France have failed to find any reference to the Khedive among the list of gifts exchanged at the opening of the Suez Canal. One writer has suggested that the linking of the diamond with the Empress Eugénie is totally fallacious and that it has been manufactured to impart 'colour' to its history. The same person has drawn attention to the film *Suez* made in the late 1930s, starring Tyrone Power and Loretta Young, and wondered whether somebody's imagination may have been fired by this piece of screenwork.

What is not disputed is the ownership of the Khedive by the Miami jeweller, Jack M. Werst. He sold it in 1953. In 1976 it was exhibited with other notable diamonds at the opening of the Hall of Minerals and Gems of the Museum of Natural History of New York. Thereafter it remained on display until put up for sale by Christie's in Geneva on 15 May 1986, when this light-yellow flawless, diamond fetched 484,000 Swiss francs (US$269,600).

Koh-i-noor

The Koh-i-noor, here out of its setting, is one of the oldest known diamonds, first recorded in 15th century Mogul India.

It has been said that whoever owned the Koh-i-noor ruled the world, a suitable epithet for this, the most famous of all diamonds and a veritable household name in many parts of the globe. Legend has suggested that the stone may date from before the time of Christ; theory indicates the possibility of its appearance in the early years of the fourteenth century; history confirms its existence for the past two and a half centuries. A propos the first, one writer has stated:

> Regarding its traditional history, which extends 5000 years further back, nothing need be said here; though it has afforded sundry imaginative writers with a subject for highly characteristic paragraphs we have no record of its having been at any time a cut stone.

The earliest authentic reference to a diamond which may be the Koh-i-noor is found in the *Baburnama*, the memoirs of Babur, first of the Mogul rulers in India. Born in 1483, Babur (meaning 'lion' – the name was not conferred on him at birth but appears to be a nickname, deriving from an Arabic or Persian word signifying 'lion' or 'tiger') was descended in the fifth generation from Tamerlane on the male side and in the fifteenth degree from Genghis Khan on the female side. With the blood in his veins of two of the greatest conquerors Asia had ever witnessed, it is not at all surprising that Babur should have become a great conqueror in his own right.

As a young man Babur owed his survival and success on the political and military battlefields to a combination of winning personal qualities and swift opportunism; these were to ensure his conquest of the plains of northern India. But in addition to being a warrior Babur was a cultured and civilized man – a writer and a poet.

In the *Baburnama*, Babur alluded to the Sultan Ala-ed-Din Khalji, the ruler of Delhi from 1295 to 1316. The year before his accession the Sultan had led an expedition to the Deccan or 'the South', the high and relatively cool plateau between the Narmada and the Tungabhadra-Krishna river, where he conquered Malwa and captured a large amount of booty. At that time, Ala-ed-Din was just a prince serving under his uncle, Jalal-ud-Din, but in 1295 he murdered his uncle in cold blood and became ruler himself. In 1297 Ala-ed-Din defeated the last king of Gujrat and secured more treasure. One account states that he got his hands on a great diamond at Gujrat; another says that he obtained the stone from the Deccan. The second version is not impossible because after his defeat the vanquished king fled southwards where he was plundered for the second time, on this occasion by Ala-ed-Din's generals.

More than two centuries later, at the time of Babur, northern India was divided among largely autonomous chiefs who were in no mood to resist a determined invader. After several probing raids into India, Babur was eventually invited by Daulat Khan, the ruler of the Punjab, to help him in his fight against his nephew Ibrahim Lodi, Sultan of Delhi, who was proving to be a despotic ruler. In 1526 Babur defeated and killed Ibrahim Lodi at the battle of Panipat; another who was slain was Vikramaditya, the former Rajah of Gwalior, who had fought on the side of Ibrahim Lodi. Before going into battle Vikramaditya had despatched all his jewels to the fort of Agra of which he was the Qilidar. Among these jewels was a notable diamond. It has been considered possible – though, in view of his disposition, improbable – that originally Ala-ed-Din may have rewarded Vikramaditya's ancestors, two faithful brothers, not only with Gwalior but also with the diamond.

Babur came to Agra on 4 May 1526, and the great diamond was most likely tendered to him there the

KOH-I-NOOR

156 Emperor Babur planning the Bah-i-Wafa near Jalalabad with his architects. Illustration from the *Baburnama* manuscript, 1589.

London, Victoria and Albert Museum. Photo AKG London.

next day. There is one reference to it recorded in the *Baburnama* which reads:

When Humayun [Babur's son] arrived, Vikramaditya's people attempted to escape, but were taken by the parties which Humayun had placed upon the watch, and put in custody. Humayun did not permit them to be plundered. Of their own free will they presented to Humayun a peshkash, consisting of a quantity of jewels and precious stones. Among them was one famous diamond which had been acquired by Sultan Alaeddin [Ala-ed-Din]. It is so valuable that a judge of diamonds valued it at half of the daily expense of the whole world. It is about eight mishquals. On my arrival, Humayun presented it to me as a peshkash, and I gave it back to him as a present.

There is another account which relates that the diamond was owned, not by Vikramaditya, but by Ibrahim Lodi. According to this version of events the mother of Ibrahim Lodi was responsible for handing it over to Humayun, the son and successor of Babur, who had been deputed to take possession of all the jewels that had belonged to the slain Sultan of Delhi. After Humayun's men had ransacked the Royal Treasury and failed to find the diamond, the servants and Treasury officials were questioned. They remained silent and, even after they had been threatened with dire punishments, none came forward with the information. In the end a servant pointed towards the royal palace.

When Humayun entered the palace the female members of Vikramaditya's family were weeping, so he assured them their honour would be safe in his hands and that he would treat them according to their high station. It was then that Ibrahim Lodi's mother went silently into a room and emerged with a gold box which, with trembling hands, she handed to the young prince. Humayun opened the box and took out the diamond.

This version, however, is not considered the true one by most writers, and the recovery of the diamond from the fort of Agra is regarded as the authentic one. There has also been much discussion and divergence of opinion concerning the method of calculating the weight of the diamond: its weight of around eight mishquals, as recorded by Babur, has given rise to a variety of mathematical equations. Of especial significance is the fact that a majority have arrived at a figure of around 186 (old) carats.

Four years after Babur's decisive victory at Panipat, Humayun fell ill. Doctors could do nothing for him; he continued to deteriorate. Then someone suggested to Babur that he should sacrifice his dearest possession to save his son. Doubtless this individual was hoping that the emperor would consider the diamond fulfilled such a role. If so, he was disappointed, because Babur did not fall in with this suggestion, maintaining that his most precious possession was his own life. The story goes that Babur moved around the bed of his ailing son, praying that Humayun's life

would be spared and his own life be sacrificed instead. From then on Humayun's condition improved while Babur declined and died in December 1530.

The reign of Humayun lasted for 26 years but it was subject to much interruption. After an initial period of about nine and a half years' rule he was driven out of India by the Afghan forces under Sher Khan. Humayun fled first to Sind, then to Persia, and did not return to India until after 15 years' exile. Having regained his throne his reign was fated to last a mere six months: one day, hearing the call to prayers, he hurriedly got up, but fell headlong down the stairs of his library, possibly under the effects of opium.

After his defeat by the Afghans and during his subsequent wanderings, there is evidence that

Emperor Babur.
Indian miniature, 16th century.

157

Humayun carried with him the great diamond that his father had handed back to him at Agra. For the next two hundred years or so, it came to be known as 'Babur's diamond'. Leaving behind his kingdom, his only daughter and his numerous wives – he even abandoned his son, Akbar, when fleeing from Afghanistan – Humayun clung to the diamond. His reverence for it is illustrated by one incident. The ruler of a domain where he had sought sanctuary wanted to acquire the gem so, taking advantage of the refugee's plight, he sent one of his courtiers, disguised as a merchant, to bargain with him. When this man presented himself and explained the purpose of his visit, Humayun was furious and replied:

'Such precious gems cannot be bought; either they fall to one by the arbitrament of the flashing sword, which is an expression of divine will, or else they come through the grace of mighty monarchs.'

The emissary departed quietly.

Humayun's wanderings finally took him to Persia where the country's ruler, Shah Tahmasp, received him cordially. The exiled Mogul Emperor was so kindly treated by the Shah that ultimately, as an expression of his gratitude, he gave him valuable jewels. One historian, Abul Fazal, who later was to be employed as secretary to Akbar, Humayun's successor, has told in his *Akbarnama* that among the jewels which Shah Tahmasp received was the gem known as 'Babur's diamond', so precious that it was worth the revenue of climes and countries. Another writer referred to Humayun's gift of a diamond and other jewels and related that Shah Tahmasp was so astonished at seeing them that he sent for his jewellers to appraise them. They told him that they were 'above all price'. This was the way in which Babur's diamond was always spoken of – the value of other diamonds could be estimated, but Babur's could not be appraised except by a fantastic reference to the expenditure of the world.

The presentation of this exceptional diamond to the ruler of Persia by Humayun was confirmed by Khur Shah, the ambassador of Ibrahim Qutb, King of Golconda, at the Persian court. He told of the gift of a diamond of six mishquals, that was reckoned to be worth the expenditure of the whole universe for two and a half days. However, he also stated that Shah Tahmasp did not think so highly of it and that afterwards he sent it to India as a present to Burhan Nizam, the Shah of Ahmednagar. But the emissary entrusted with the diamond, Mehtar Jamal, may have failed to deliver the stone because Shah Tahmasp later sent out orders for his arrest.

These events took place in 1547. From then on until the sack and plunder of Delhi in 1739 the diamond's history must be one of supposition and speculation. In the meantime a series of happenings took place which have an important bearing upon the history of Babur's diamond.

In the early 1650s the reigning Mogul Emperor was Shah Jahan, the great grandson of Humayun. He appointed his third son, Aurangzeb, to the governorship of the Deccan. Aurangzeb, in his turn, was keen to conquer the independent states in this region of India, one of which was Golconda, where the King's domain included the country's

principal diamond-mining area.

At that time the King of Golconda's First Minister was Mir Jumla, a diamond dealer of considerable repute in Persia who had travelled southwards, attracted by the lure and promise which the diamond fields held for him. Simultaneously with the administration of his master's State, Mir Jumla contrived to do a lot of business on his own behalf, above all in diamonds. The King put him in charge of most affairs pertaining to the mines and trading, and not surprisingly the Persian amassed a fortune. But Mir Jumla overstepped the bounds of caution, being caught in a compromising situation with the mother of the King. He was thus obliged to leave Golconda forthwith for his safety.

Mir Jumla met Aurangzeb early in 1656, then travelled to Delhi where he met Shah Jahan. According to an agent of the East India Company who happened to be in the vicinity at the time, Shah Jahan received Mir Jumla courteously and gifts were exchanged between the two – Jumla's to the Emperor including a diamond of 160 ratis in weight. Another account, by the French traveller Francois Bernier, records that:

Jumla, who had by his address contrived to obtain frequent invitations to the Court of Shah Jahan, proceeded at length to Agra and carried the most magnificent presents in the hope of inducing the Mogul Emperor to declare war against the Kings of Golconda and Bijapur and against the Portuguese. It was on this occasion that he presented Shah Jahan with that celebrated diamond which has been generally deemed unparalleled in size and beauty.

Yet a third writer has asserted that Mir Jumla gave one diamond to Shah Jahan and a second to Aurangzeb, the latter being an uncut specimen thought likely to have been cut later by the Venetian, Borgio.

Although the evidence is slender, the gift of a diamond by the wily Jumla to both father and son accords with his character and should not be dismissed out of hand: it would have been a means of ensuring his future whichever way the wind was to blow. In the event he chose to ally himself with Aurangzeb while Shah Jahan's last years were marked by his declining health and a struggle for power among his four sons. Aurangzeb emerged victorious and lost no time in ridding himself of his brothers and incarcerating his father in the fort at Agra. That the luckless Shah Jahan did possess some jewels during his imprisonment is confirmed by two sources. Bernier has stated that Shah Jahan, after he had been imprisoned, became so reconciled to Aurangzeb that he sent him some of the jewels which at first he had refused to do. Apparently Aurangzeb received them only after his father's death. Jean Baptiste Tavernier's version is different.

He wrote:

During his reign he [Shah Jahan] had begun to build the city of Jehanabad, though he had not quite finish'd it, and therefore he desir'd to see it once more before he dy'd; but Aurangzeb would not give him leave, unless he would be content to go and come back by water, or else to be confin'd to the Castle of Jehanabad, as he was at Agra, which refusal of his son did torment him, that it hasten'd his end. Which as soon as Aurangzeb heard of, he came to Agra and seiz'd upon all the jewels which he had not taken from his father while he liv'd. Begum Saheb had also a quantity of jewels, which he had not taken from her when he put her into the Castle. But now, because she had formerly taken her father's part, he found out a way to deprive her of them after a very plausible manner, making a show of bestowing very great Honours and Caresses upon his Sister, and taking her along with him to Jehanabad. But in a short time after we heard the news of her death; ... and all people suspected her to have been poisoned.

At this point in the story it is necessary to try to identify the large diamonds that figured among the jewels given to Shah Jahan and Aurangzeb. The big stone, said to have been uncut, must clearly be the Great Mogul which Aurangzeb showed Tavernier in 1665. But which is the diamond mentioned by Bernier as the one which Shah Jahan received from Mir Jumla, described as 'that celebrated diamond which has been generally deemed unparalleled in size and beauty'? Is it Babur's diamond? These and other questions were raised by several authorities following the arrival of the Koh-i-noor in England in 1850. First, there were those who maintained that the Koh-i-noor was the Great Mogul and that Babur's diamond was separate; secondly, there were those who believed that the Koh-i-noor was in fact Babur's diamond; thirdly, there were others who identified the Koh-i-noor with both Babur's diamond and the Great Mogul.

One of the first to air his views on the subject was the distinguished mineralogist James Tennant, who noted that in addition to its possessing defects similar to those decribed by Tavernier as having been in the Mogul's diamond,

the 'Koh-i-noor' had a flaw near the summit which, being on a line of cleavage parallel to the upper surface, may very possibly have been produced when the upper portion was removed – the weight of which, together with that of two portions removed from the sides, and the loss occasioned by the regrinding of four facets on the upper surface may very easily have represented the difference in the weights of the two stones, namely 82⅓ carats.

Another writer who discussed the matter of the Koh-i-noor's identity was Edwin Streeter, the nineteenth-century London jeweller and author of two most valuable books on diamonds and other gemstones. In his earlier book *Precious Stones and Gems* he stated that, 'any doubt as to the 'Mogul' and the 'Koh-i-noor' being identical is but rarely entertained'. But in his later work *The Great Diamonds of the World* he wrote that, 'all are agreed that Babur's

diamond and the 'Koh-i-noor' are identical and the Mogul's distinct'. This contradiction was pointed out by Valentine Ball who in 1889 published a further translation of Tavernier's *Six Voyages* with extensive notes and appendices. Ball ventured to believe that the view which Streeter had expressed in his earlier book was the sounder of the two:

It must be at once plainly stated that there is no direct evidence that a diamond of that weight (186 or 187 carats) [i.e. Babur's diamond] was in the possession of the Mogul Emperors at any subsequent period, up to the time of Nadir Shah's invasion. We know nothing as to the weight of the 'Koh-i-noor', as such, till about the time it was brought to England, namely the year 1850...

Tavernier did not see any stone of the weight above attributed to Babur's diamond in the possession of the Great Mogul, Aurangzeb, nor can we suppose that he heard of any such diamond being in the possession of Shah Jahan, who was confined in prison, where he retained a number of jewels in his own possession. If either he or Bernier had heard of such a stone he would surely have mentioned it... It is possible that Babur's diamond may have been in Shah Jahan's possession when Tavernier saw Aurangzeb's jewels and that the latter obtained possession of it when Shah Jahan died, and so ultimately it passed to Persia with other jewels taken by Nadir Shah...

Ball continued:

The necessary conclusion is that it is not the Mogul's diamond which, through failure of being historically traced as some authors assert, has disappeared, but it is Babur's diamond the history of which we are really left in doubt. The fixing of the weight of Babur's diamond at a figure identical, or nearly so, with that of the 'Koh-i-noor' when brought to England, though used as a link in the chain, has, as I think I have shown, effectively disposed of its claim to be identified with the Mogul's diamond in the first place, and secondly with the 'Koh-i-noor'.

In April 1899 an article entitled 'Babur's Diamond, was it the 'Koh-i-noor'?' appeared in the *Asiatic Quarterly Review*; it was written by Henry Beveridge, the husband of the translator of the *Baburnama*. Although in the end he was unable to decide whether or not Babur's diamond was the Koh-i-noor, Beveridge did make one relevant point: he drew attention to the unconscious confusion caused by there being two diamonds, which led Tavernier on one page to say that the great diamond was presented to Shah Jahan and on another page to say that it was presented to Aurangzeb. Hence the fact of there being two diamonds obviates many difficulties and may also explain the statement of a Persian nobleman, mentioned in Forbes's *Oriental Memoirs*, and quoted by Ball, about two large diamonds being carried off by Nadir Shah.

Almost a century later we are in the fortunate position of having information that was unavailable to earlier writers. In particular we now have details of the treasures amassed by the Czars, Shahs and miscellaneous monarchs. We know for

160

Opposite page: Shah Jahan in profile, seated in durbar, possibly at the Diwan-i-Am in Delhi, with Prince Aurangzeb on his left, c.1650.

Indian miniature. London, British Museum. By permission of the British Library.

KOH-I-NOOR

KOH-I-NOOR

162 Mohammed Shah, dressed in a white *jama*, being received by Nadir Shah. He had hidden the Koh-i-Noor in his headdress. Discovering this, Nadir Shah obliged his adversary to exchange headgear, thus gaining possession of the diamond.

Persian manuscript, Mogul School, c. 1740. Paris, Musée des Arts Asiatiques – Guimet. Photo © RMN – Arnaudet.

sure that there are three diamonds in existence which have a direct bearing upon the questions raised concerning the identities of the Great Mogul and Babur's diamond. They are the Orlov, weighing 189.62 metric carats, now in the Kremlin; the Darya-i Nur, estimated to weigh between 175 and 195 metric carats and presumed still to be among the Iranian Crown Jewels; and the Koh-i-noor, whose former weight before it was recut was 186 carats, equivalent to 190.3 metric carats.

Tavernier referred to the shape of the Great Mogul as 'of the same form as if one cut an egg through the middle', and drew it. Both Tavernier's drawing and description of the Great Mogul are applicable to the Orlov diamond as we know it to be today. There is, of course, an obvious discrepancy between the weights of the two stones,

that of the Great Mogul being almost 100 carats more. But if the diamond seen by Tavernier had been ground down the resemblance would become even more marked. The resultant loss of weight by the action of such grinding would bring the weight of the Great Mogul to approximately that of the Orlov.

Ball's reference to the Orlov is as follows:

Several writers, among them Professor Schrauf of Vienna (1869), have suggested that the Mogul's diamond is to be identified with the similarly shaped Orloff now belonging to Russia. Apart from the discrepancy in the weights and in the size, as shown by Tavernier's drawing, which was intended to represent the natural size of the former, it is tolerably certain that the Orloff was obtained from the temple of Srirangam on an island in the Cauvery river in Mysore. It was therefore a possession of the Hindus, and it is most improbable that it ever belonged to the Moguls.

Now this convenient dismissal of the Orlov by Professor Ball cannot be allowed to pass. Just as he alleges that Tavernier would have referred to the Koh-i-noor as a separate diamond if it had existed as such, equally would he not have referred to this huge gem at Srirangam as a separate diamond? For this is a diamond which even today, following the discoveries elsewhere, still ranks among the largest of undoubted authenticity. The temple at Srirangam is not situated so far from the diamondiferous regions of India that Tavernier, in his capacity both as a traveller and connoisseur of precious gems, could not have learned of the existence of such a notable stone.

But where Ball's theory concerning the identities of these diamonds falls down is in his reference to the Darya-i Nur, about which he wrote:

It has already been intimated that the Darya-i Nur, a flat stone which weighs 186 carats and is now in the Shah's Treasury, may very possibly be Babur's diamond… I have in vain sought for any well-authenticated fact which in the slightest degree controverts or even throws doubt on the suggestion that the Darya-i Nur, the 'Ocean of Light', may very possibly be Babur's diamond.

In the light of the examination of the contents of the Iranian Treasury undertaken in the 1960s, it has been conclusively proved that the Darya-i Nur constitutes the major portion of the Great Table diamond which Tavernier saw — and tried to buy — at Golconda. In all probability this diamond had been mined not long before his attempted purchase, thereby discounting it from having an earlier history, let alone one involving the Mogul Emperors. Furthermore the descriptions of Babur's diamond as being 'valued at half the daily expense of the whole world' and so forth are surely inapplicable to the flat rectangular-shaped Darya-i Nur: one would think that a more appropriate metaphor would have been to describe it as the source of half the water needed for the world per day. Curiously the sole point that suggests that the Darya-i Nur may be identified as Babur's diamond lies in a passage from a book on the life of Babur which reads:

The gifts were on a grand scale, being precious jewels, among these the great diamond now identified as the Koh-i-noor. This enormous rose-tinted stone weighed 320 ratis on Humayun's scales.

The Darya-i Nur is indeed rose-tinted but there has assuredly been a mistranslation here: 'rose-tinted' being substituted for 'rose-cut', the erstwhile shape of the Koh-i-noor.

Finally on the subject of identifying these truly historic diamonds with gems that we know exist today, the suggestion that the Koh-i-noor and the Great Mogul once formed parts of the same stone is impossible: the Koh-i-noor is a white diamond whereas the Orlov – if we assume it to be the Great Mogul – possesses a slight bluish-green tint. Therefore, the Darya-i Nur has been identified for sure as the Great Table diamond; a very strong case exists for identifying the Orlov as the Great Mogul; and a less strong, but nevertheless valid, case can be made for identifying the Koh-i-noor as Babur's diamond.

After lasting for nearly fifty years the reign of the strong and bigoted Aurangzeb ended in 1707. It marked the zenith of the rule of the Moguls: there followed a decline with no less than six weak Emperors reigning within a space of 13 years, each of them dying in an unnatural way. Contemporaneously with the setting of the sun on the Mogul Empire a new one was rising to the west in Persia. Nadir Kuli, or 'The Slave of the Wonderful' as he was called, was a young shepherd who, when eighteen, was abducted together with his mother by a raiding party of Uzbegs to Khiva. Four years later the mother died in slavery, but the young Nadir succeeded in escaping to Khorasan where his first step up the ladder of power was his entry into the service of the Governor of Abivard (then the capital of the district). Under Nadir Kuli, who in 1732 dethroned the weak ruler of Persia and usurped the throne in his stead four years later, Persia became a major power. After he had defeated the Afghans and the Turks and caused the Russians to evacuate the Caspian provinces, Nadir Shah turned his attention eastwards towards the declining empire of the Moguls. The reigning Emperor, Mohammed Shah, who had ascended the throne in 1719, was a wretched descendant of the once omnipotent Moguls; he was described as 'never without a mistress in his arms and a glass in his hand'. Rich pickings thus awaited the Persians as the Emperor realized his predicament far too late. The decisive battle of Karnal in 1738 was over

in two hours: the vast Indian army was routed, more than twenty thousand slain on the battlefield, a greater number taken prisoner and an immense hoard of spoils captured. In triumph Nadir Shah marched into Delhi where he was entertained sumptuously by the vanquished Mohammed Shah. Among the treasures which the Emperor handed over to Nadir Shah was the famed Peacock Throne which Tavernier described thus:

The largest throne, which is set up in the hall of the first court, is in form like one of our field beds, six feet long and four broad. The cushion at the base is round like a bolster: the cushions on the side are flat. The underpart of the canopy is all embroidered with pearls and diamonds, with a fringe of pearls round about. Upon the top of the canopy, which is made like an arch with four panes, stands a peacock with his tail spread, consisting all of saphirs and other proper coloured stones. The body is of beaten gold enchas'd with several jewels, and a great ruby upon his breast, at which hangs a pearl that weighs fifty carats. On each side of the peacock stand two nosegays as high as the bird, consisting of several sorts of flowers, all of beaten gold enamelled. When the king seats himself upon the throne there is a transparent jewel with a diamond appendant of eighty or ninety carats, encompass'd with rubies and emeralds, so hung that it is always in his eye. The twelve pillars also that uphold the canopy are set with rows of fair pearl, round, and of an excellent water, that weigh from six to ten carats apiece. This is the famous throne which Tamerlane began and Cha Jehan finish'd, which is really reported to have cost 160 million and 500,000 livres of our money.

The identity of the large diamond set as a pendant has always been a matter for conjecture: possibly it may have been the Shah. But nowhere in Tavernier's account is there a reference to the Koh-i-noor; indeed the Mogul Emperor must have taken steps to ensure that his treasured gem did not fall into the hands of his conqueror. However, Nadir Shah was fully equal to the task of finding the gem. There are two stories of how he procured it. One says that Mohammed Shah gave it to Nadir Shah, possibly in gratitude for sparing either his life or his empire. This seems unlikely, and in any event the second, which has come to be accepted as the true version, is both more plausible and more colourful.

The disclosure of the secret hiding place of the Koh-i-noor was made by one of the Emperor's harem; she told Nadir Shah that Mohammed always wore it hidden in his turban. So the cunning Nadir Shah had recourse to a clever trick. He ordered a grand feast to be celebrated a few days later to coincide with the restoration of Mohammed Shah to his throne. During the course of it Nadir Shah suddenly proposed an exchange of turbans, which is a well-known oriental custom signifying the creation of brotherly ties, sincerity and eternal friendship. Mohammed Shah was taken aback by his quick-thinking rival but at the same time was hardly in a position to resist such a request. With as much grace as he could summon –

Portrait of Prince Dhulip
Singh by Franz Winterhalter,
c.1850, for which the sittings
took place at Buckingham
Palace. He was amongst the
first to see the Koh-i-noor
diamond in its new form.

Osborne House, Isle of Wight.

his life were marked by growing avarice and cruelty,
so that he was detested by the very people whom he
had freed from the foreign yoke. In 1747 he was
murdered while asleep in his tent. With the murder
of Nadir Shah the unity of Persia collapsed and
the army broke up.

The next sixty years or so were the most
barbarous and blood-stained in the history of the
Koh-i-noor. The same pattern of events occurred
after the demise of Nadir Shah as after that of
Aurangzeb: a strong ruler was followed by a series
of weak ones. Nadir Shah's successor was Ali Kuli
who ascended the throne as Adil Shah, or 'The
Just'. His first act was to rid himself of all possible
claimants to the throne of Persia with the solitary
exception of Shah Rukh Mirza, the fourteen-year-
old grandson of Nadir Shah. But after a short and
inglorious reign, Adil Shah was dethroned and
blinded by his brother Ibrahim, who, in turn,
suffered the same fate before being captured and
put to death by his own troops. Then Shah Rukh
took the throne, but another pretender soon
emerged and the young king was defeated, also
having his eyes put out. Shah Rukh was to reign in
name, if not in fact, for almost fifty years; on
several occasions he was imprisoned by contenders
for the throne. One of his supporters was Ahmad
Abdali, an Afghan who had been one of Nadir
Shah's ablest generals before he returned to
Afghanistan, subdued it, and established himself as
its ruler. For the help which he had received from
him, Shah Rukh gave Ahmad Abdali important
jewels that included the Koh-i-noor.

Ahmad Abdali (later called Ahmad Shah) seems
to stand out like a shining beacon among the
various rulers which the people in that part of the
world were forced to endure at that point in their
history. In addition to being the unifier of
Afghanistan he also possessed an abundance of
civilized virtues, somewhat rare at the time. His
death in 1773 put an end to the comparative peace
which the sightless Shah Rukh had enjoyed. Civil
strife followed in Persia, culminating in the rule of
the individual usually regarded as the most horrible
and repulsive of all the characters connected with
the Koh-i-noor. This was Aga Mohammed Khan,
the first of the Qajar dynasty that was destined to
rule Persia from 1794 to 1825. As a boy of five he
had been captured and castrated by Adil Shah, a
misfortune that — somewhat naively, perhaps — has
been deemed to account for his extreme
vindictiveness and cruelty — qualites which are
evident in paintings of him.

Shah Rukh paid dearly for his gift of the Koh-i-
noor to Ahmad Shah because Aga Mohammed
Khan was convinced that the unfortunate man was
still in possession of it. Deserted by his sons, who

in fact his composure was such that Nadir Shah
thought he had been hoaxed — he accepted.
Eventually when Nadir Shah had retired to his
private apartment he unfolded the turban and
found the diamond concealed within. It was when
he set eyes on it that he exclaimed Koh-i-noor,
meaning 'Mountain of Light'. So the most famous
diamond in history acquired its name.

One observation must be made concerning
Nadir Shah's obtainment of the diamond. Clearly
he must have known of its existence beforehand
and must have eagerly sought it. This suggests that
it was known in Persia for generations, probably
from the time of Humayun's period of exile in that
land, and adds weight to the theory that it is
distinct from the Great Mogul diamond.

A peaceful end to Nadir Shah's sojourn in Delhi
was shattered by an outbreak of rioting, followed
by the dreadful sacking and pillaging of the city in
1739. The loot included the Koh-i-noor, which thus
left India for Persia for the second time, and one
other exceptional diamond which must have been
the Great Table. Further victories were secured by
the Persians in battle, but Nadir Shah became
corrupted by his success and the remaining years of

were unaware of the jewels that he had once owned, the blind Shah Rukh was forced to endure the most horrific torture by the cruel eunuch, who had an insatiable appetite for gems. As the torturing continued, jewels hitherto hidden were given up one by one. The final degradation which Shah Rukh suffered at the hands of the monstrous Aga Mohammed Shah was to have his head closely shaved and encircled with a thick paste upon which boiling water was then poured. The last gem he gave up was a great ruby which had once belonged to Aurangzeb. The torture then ceased, but Shah Rukh died from its terrible effects not long afterwards.

Meanwhile in Afghanistan, the country where the Koh-i-noor was being held, Ahmad Shah had been succeeded by his son Timur, a weak ruler but nevertheless a virile one since he left no less than twenty-three sons to contest his succession. Internecine warfare then broke out, with the eldest son, Zaman Shah, becoming king in 1793. Six years later his brother Mahmud blinded him and seized the throne; then in 1803 another brother, Shuja, imprisoned Mahmud and usurped the throne. Seven years after that event Mahmud escaped and resumed his reign, but he never obtained the Koh-i-noor because Zaman Shah had taken it with him and had had it embedded in the plaster of his prison cell's walls. Next Shah Shuja regained the throne and the Koh-i-noor – the latter's place of concealment having been pointed out to him by Zaman Shah. Finally, in 1810, the Saddozai of Afghanistan, founded by Ahmad Shah, broke up and the two ill-fated brothers, Zaman Shah and Shah Shuja, sought refuge with the Sikh leader Ranjit Singh, known as the 'Lion of the Punjab'.

Shah Shuja had the Koh-i-noor with him and the ruler of the Punjab must have known about the famous gem because he soon showed his desire to own it. He aimed to extort it from Shah Shuja as the price of giving him and his family sanctuary. However, the exiled Afghan tried by every means to prevent Ranjit Singh from getting hold of it. Once he told him that the stone had been pawned with a money-lender. On another occasion he said that it had been lost along with some other jewels. On a third occasion Shah Shuja sent Ranjit Singh a large topaz, saying that it was the diamond; when his court jewellers examined it and told him that it was not a diamond, the Lion of the Punjab was furious. He posted a guard around Shah Shuja's residence with orders that he was not to receive food or water for two days. In the end Shah Shuja, realizing his hopeless position, agreed to surrender the diamond to Ranjit Singh provided that he arrived in person to receive it from him.

Ranjit Singh accepted Shah Shuja's proposal and on 1 June 1813 went to his residence to claim the diamond. The customary greetings took place, then the two kings sat opposite each other in silence for some time before Ranjit Singh reminded Shah Shuja of the purpose of his visit. A servant was then ordered to fetch the gem from another room; when he returned with a bundle Ranjit Singh unwrapped it and found the Koh-i-noor inside. Without saying a word he left the room.

The Lion of the Punjab became very proud of the Koh-i-noor, wearing it set in an armlet between two smaller diamonds. He took great delight in showing the gem to distinguished visitors to his court. Shortly before his death in June 1839, an attempt was made to induce Ranjit Singh to seek the favour of the gods by presenting the diamond to the temple of Jaganath in Puri but his treasurer, Beli Ram, dissuaded him from doing so, maintaining that it was State property.

Ranjit Singh was the first and the last powerful Sikh king; he was followed by three weak kings, each of whom died prematurely. In 1843 Dhulip Singh, the last of Ranjit Singh's sons, then a minor, became the recognized ruler of the Punjab. During his reign the two Sikh Wars were fought, in due course leading to the annexation of the Punjab by the British. On 29 March 1849, the British colours were hoisted on the citadel of Lahore and the Punjab was formerly proclaimed to be a part of the British Empire in India. One of the terms of the Treaty of Lahore was that:

> The gem called the Koh-i-noor which was taken from Shah Shuja-ul-Mulk by Maharajah Ranjit Singh shall be surrendered by the Maharajah of Lahore to the Queen of England.

The Governor-General responsible for the ratification of this treaty was Lord Dalhousie who, on his arrival at Calcutta in January 1848, at the age of 35, had become the youngest holder of this office to set foot in India. More than anyone, Dalhousie was also responsible for the British acquisition of the Koh-i-noor, in which he continued to show great interest for the rest of his life. Not long after the signing of the Treaty of Lahore Dalhousie was to become embroiled in the controversy that raged in England concerning the acquisition of the diamond. Writing to his friend Sir George Cooper in August 1849, he stated:

> The Court [of the East India Company] you say, are ruffled by my having caused the Maharajah to cede to the Queen the Koh-i-noor; while the 'Daily News' and my Lord Ellenborough [Governor-General of India (1841–44)] are indignant because I did not confiscate everything to her Majesty, and censure me for leaving even a Roman Pearl to the Court. . . I was fully prepared to hear that the Court chafed at my not sending the diamond to them, and letting them present it to Her Majesty. They ought not to do so – they ought to enter into and cordially approve the sentiment on which I acted thus. The motive was simply this; that it was more for the

honour of the Queen that the Koh-i-noor should be surrendered directly from the hand of the conquered prince into the hands of the sovereign who was his conqueror, than that it should be presented to her as a gift — which is always a favour — by any joint-stock company among her subjects. So the Court ought to feel. As for their fretting and censuring, that I do not mind — so long as they do not disallow the article. I know I have acted best for the Sovereign, and for their honour too.

A British subject, Dr (later Sir) John Login, was entrusted with two charges: the responsibility for taking the Koh-i-noor out of the Toshakhana, the jewel-house, and the guardianship of the young Dhulip Singh. A cousin of Lady Login wrote to her that the old treasurer, Misr Maharaj, had given every assistance with regard to the former task and had said that it was a great relief to be free of responsibility for the diamond, adding that it had been the cause of so many deaths to so many of his own family that he never expected to be spared. The old man gave Login some advice on showing the jewel to visitors: he should not let it out of his own hand, and he should twist the ribbons that tied it as an armlet around his fingers. It was still set as in the time of Ranjit Singh.

The Koh-i-noor was formally handed over to the Punjab government consisting of three members: Sir Henry Lawrence, his younger brother John (afterwards Lord Lawrence), and C. C. Mausel. The other two members entrusted the safe-keeping of the diamond to John Lawrence, believing him to be the most practical and business-like of the trio. In their assessment they were to be proved totally wrong because the nearest the diamond came to being lost was while it was in John Lawrence's custody. He put the small box containing the diamond into his waistcoat pocket and continued working. Then when changing for dinner he threw his waist-coat aside and thought no more about the gem.

Some six weeks later a message came from Dalhousie saying that the Queen had ordered the Koh-i-noor to be transmitted to her. Henry Lawrence mentioned the subject at a Board meeting. When John Lawrence said quietly, 'Send for it at once,' his brother rejoined, 'Why, you've got it.' In a flash John Lawrence's carelessness struck him: he was horrified and, as he used to describe his feelings later when telling the story, he said quietly to himself, 'Well, this is the worst trouble I have ever got into.' But such was his composure that he gave no visible sign of trepidation. 'Oh yes, of course, I forgot about it,' he said, and went on with the meeting as if nothing had happened. However, he soon found an opportunity of slipping away to his private room and, with his heart in his mouth, sent for his old bearer, saying to him, 'Have you got a small box which was in my waistcoat pocket some time ago?'

The man replied, 'Yes, Sahib, I found it and put

it in one of your boxes.' 'Bring it here,' replied Lawrence, whereupon the old man went over to a broken-down tin box and produced the little one from it. 'Open it,' said Lawrence, 'and see what is inside.'

He watched the old man anxiously as fold after fold of small rags was taken off and was mightily relieved when the precious gem appeared. The bearer seemed to be unaware of the treasure which he had in his keeping and remarked, 'There is nothing here, Sahib, but a bit of glass.'

The Koh-i-noor was immediately shown to the board, who forthwith prepared for it to be despatched to the Queen. But first it had to travel from Lahore to Bombay, then a hazardous route swarming with robbers and other criminals. No less a person than the Governor-General, who, when he had first set eyes on the diamond had remarked, 'It is a superb gem,' was responsible for its transportation. On 16 May 1850, Dalhousie wrote:

The Koh-i-noor sailed from Bombay in H.M.S. Medea on the 6th April. I could not tell you at the time, for strict secrecy was observed, but I brought it from Lahore myself. I undertook the charge of it in a funk, and never was so happy in all my life as when I got it into the Treasury at Bombay. It was sewn and double sewn into a belt secured round my waist, one end of the belt fastened to a chain round my neck. It never left me day or night, except when I went to Ghazee Khan when I left it with Captain Ramsay (who now has joint charge of it) locked in a treasure chest till I came back. My stars! What a relief to get rid of it. It was detained at Bombay for two months for want of a ship, and I hope, please God, will now arrive safe in July. You had better say nothing about it, however, in your spheres, till you hear others announce it. I have reported it officially to the Court, and to her sacred Majesty by this mail.

The Koh-i-noor was placed in an iron box which was kept in a despatch box and deposited in the Government Treasury. For security reasons this piece of news was suppressed even among officers of the Treasury — and withheld from the ship's captain, Commander Lockyer. The only individuals who knew the truth were the two officers entrusted with the custody of the despatch box, Lieutenant-Colonel Mackeson and Captain Ramsay. Nevertheless HMS *Medea*'s voyage proved to be perilous and there were two occasions on which disaster was narrowly averted. When the ship reached Mauritius, cholera broke out on board and the local people refused to sell the necessary supplies to its crew, requesting the ship's immediate departure. When the *Medea* did not move, they asked their Governor to open fire and destroy the vessel. A few days after it had left Mauritius the *Medea* faced a new danger, a severe gale which lasted for about twelve hours before subsiding. Eventually the *Medea* reached Plymouth where the passengers and mail were landed but not the Koh-i-noor, which was forwarded to Portsmouth. From there the two officers took the diamond to East India House, handing it over to the Chairman and

Deputy Chairman of the Company. The latter delivered it to the Queen at Buckingham Palace on 3 July 1850.

In addition to giving rise to both historical and gemmological arguments, the arrival of the Koh-i-noor in England was accompanied by unease on the part of some, who were aware of superstitions attached to the gem. Unfortunately such people were presented with an early opportunity of voicing their feelings when a retired officer of the 10th Hussars lost his reason and struck Queen Victoria. Some promptly assigned the blame for this occurrence upon Dalhousie who, in a letter dated 1 September, was equally quick to reply thus:

I received your letter of 16th July yesterday. The several sad or foul events in England on which it touches have been mentioned by me heretofore, and they are too sad to refer to. You add that you knew these mishaps lie at my door, as I have sent the Koh-i-noor which always bring misfortune to its possessor. Whoever was the exquisite person from whom you heard this... he was rather lame both on his history and tradition... As for tradition, when Shah Shoojah [Shuja], from whom it was taken, was afterwards asked by Runjeat's [Ranjit Singh's] desire, 'What was the value of the Koh-i-noor?' he replied, 'Its value is Good Fortune, for whoever possesses it has been superior to all his enemies.' Perhaps your friend would favour you with his authority, after this, for his opposite statement. I sent the Queen a narrative of this conversation with Shah Shoojah, taken from the mouth of the messenger.

The directors of the British Museum wished to have a model made of the Koh-i-noor, so 19 April 1851 was appointed for removing the diamond from the setting in which it had arrived from India. The operation was performed by William Chapman (goldsmith) in the presence of Lord Breadalbane (the Lord Chamberlain), Lord Cawdor (the Trustee of the British Museum), Colonel Phipps (Keeper of Her Majesty's Privy Purse), and Sebastian Garrard (Keeper of Her Majesty's Jewels). After its removal Sebastian Garrard found it to weigh 186 1/10 carats instead of 279 as stated by Tavernier. This was probably the reason for an extraordinary passage which appeared in *The Times*

and read:

Some conversation took place respecting the doubts imputed to have been cast by Sir David Brewster upon the identity of the Koh-i-noor, but the general opinion among those best acquainted with the subject appeared to be that it was impossible for Dhulip Singh to have palmed off a fictitious diamond, when the constant habit of wearing it upon State occasions must have rendered it perfectly familiar to thousands who would instantly have detected any attempt at substitution. The more probable assumption was stated to be that the weight of 'The Mountain of Light' had been somewhat exaggerated.

The public were given an opportunity of seeing the Koh-i-noor when the Great Exhibition was staged in Hyde Park. The correspondent of *The Times* reported that:

The Koh-i-noor is at present decidedly the lion of the Exhibition. A mysterious interest appears to be attached to it, and now that so many precautions have been resorted to, and so much difficulty attends its inspection, the crowd is enormously enhanced, and the policemen at either end of the covered entrance have much trouble in restraining the struggling and impatient multitude. For some hours yesterday there were never less than a couple of hundred persons waiting their turn of admission, and yet, after all, the diamond does not satisfy. Either from the imperfect cutting or the difficulty of placing the lights advantageously, or the immovability of the stone itself, which should be made to revolve on its axis, few catch any of the brilliant rays that it reflects when viewed at a particular angle.

In India the Governor-General was continuing to take an interest in the diamond. On 13 July he wrote:

I see all sorts of sketches and pictures of the contents of the Exhibition. If you can get me anything presenting well the Koh-i-noor in its cage, coloured, I shall be much obliged.

Next month Dalhousie commented:

The Koh-i-noor is badly cut: it is rose-not-brilliant-cut, and of course won't sparkle like the latter. But it should not have been shown in a huge space. In the Toshakhana at Lahore Dr Login used to show it on a table covered with a black velvet cloth, the diamond alone appearing through a hole in the cloth, and relieved by the dark colour all round.

Another who was disappointed in the lack of brilliance of the Koh-i-noor was Prince Albert, the Prince Consort. He contacted Sir David Brewster, the scientist principally renowned for his investigation into the phenomenon of polarized light, as to how the diamond might best be recut. Brewster found several small caves within the stone which, in his view, were the result of the expansive force of condensed gases. Together with other flaws he thought that they would make the recutting, without a serious diminution of weight, a very difficult task. Professor Tennant and the Reverend W. Mitchell, Lecturer in Mineralogy at King's College, London, were also consulted. Accordingly they prepared a report wherein they admitted the improvement which the proposed alteration in

Indian armlet with a replica of the Koh-i-noor: Ranjit Singh wore the diamond on his arm, set in this manner between two smaller diamonds.

Crown copyright is reproduced with the permission of the Controller of Her Majesty's Stationery Office.

shape would have upon the stone, but at the same time they expressed fears lest any lateral cutting should endanger its integrity.

In the end it was decided to seek the advice of practical and experienced cutters, so Messrs Garrard, the Crown Jewellers, were instructed to obtain a report from such persons. Their choice fell upon Messrs Coster of Amsterdam who, while noting the accuracy of the fears expressed in the Tennant report, nevertheless considered that the dangers were not so formidable as to prevent the intended operation from being carried out. And so a small steam engine was set up at Garrard's while two gentlemen from Messrs Coster, Mr Voorzanger and Mr Fedder, travelled to London to undertake the recutting of the diamond.

Right: the Duke of Wellington, initiating the recutting of the Koh-i-noor on 17 July 1852.

170

On the afternoon of Friday 17 July 1852, the Duke of Wellington, who had shown great interest in the proposed recutting and attended several meetings during the course of the preparations, rode up on his favourite grey charger to Garrards, at Panton Street. The Koh-i-noor was embedded in lead, with the exception of one small salient angle that was intended to be the first to be submitted to the cutting operation. *The Times* reported that:

His Grace placed the gem upon the scaife, an horizontal wheel revolving with almost incalculable velocity, whereby the exposed angle was removed by friction, and the first facet of the new cutting was effected... The Koh-i-noor is intended to be converted into an oval brilliant, and the two smaller diamonds which accompany it are to be similarly treated as pendants. The present weight of the principal gem is 186 carats, and the process now in course of progress will not, it is anticipated, diminish in any material degree its weight, while it will largely increase its value and develop its beauties.

A day-by-day account of the operation that has been preserved discloses that on 19 July the cutters turned their attention to the flaw described by Tennant and Mitchell as having been made for the purpose of holding the stone more firmly in its setting and noted by them still to have had particles of gold adhering to it. Not being certain as to whether the flaw, or incision, was natural, the cutters decided to investigate it, so they altered the position of the stone and proceeded to cut directly into it. It was revealed to be a natural inclusion of a yellow tinge, common in smaller stones: the two experts considered that the part where the flaw was situated would prove to have been the external plane of the octahedron. Two weeks later, after examining the stone, Mitchell thought that it had become much whiter as the yellow had almost disappeared.

The cutting of the Koh-i-noor lasted for thirty-eight days and cost £8,000. The final yield was an oval brilliant weighing 108.93 metric carats, which represented a loss of weight of just under 43 per cent. There is no doubt that such a substantial reduction in the gem's weight came as a disappointment to many, not least to the Prince Consort who voiced his views on the matter in no uncertain terms. One authority observed that owing to the flattened and oval shape of the stone, the brilliant pattern selected by the Queen's advisers 'entailed the greatest possible waste', adding that Mr Coster himself would have preferred the drop form. There was also comment that the cutting of the Koh-i-noor revealed the painful fact that the art of diamond cutting was extinct in England, while even the cutters from Amsterdam and Paris had lost much of their former expertise.

One of the first to see the Koh-i-noor in its new form was Dhulip Singh, who was then living in London under the guardianship of Lady Login: she had been appointed to this post on the death of her husband. Since his arrival in England no one had broached the subject with the young Maharajah; it was realized that the diamond must have had a special meaning for him, something beyond a mere jewel of great value. But an opportunity of raising the subject presented itself. Lady Login was present at the sittings for a portrait of the young prince that took place at Buckingham Palace. At one of them the Queen asked Lady Login whether the Maharajah ever spoke of the Koh-i-noor and, if so, whether he regretted its loss. Lady Login replied that he had never spoken of it since his arrival in England although he had done so in India; at the same time he had been greatly interested in the descriptions of the operation of recutting it. The Queen then said that she hoped that before the next sitting Lady Login would ascertain Dhulip Singh's feelings on the subject and whether he would care to see it in its recut form. The Queen was informed that the prince would very much like to see the famed jewel.

During the following day's portrait session the Queen, who had heard Dhulip Singh's response, walked to the dais on which the Maharajah was posing, with the diamond in her hand. She asked if he thought it had been improved and whether he would have recognized it again. After he had finished his inspection, Dhulip Singh walked across the room, and with a low bow expressed in a few graceful words the pleasure it afforded him to have the opportunity of placing it in her hands.

The unease concerning the acquisition of the Koh-i-noor continued in Great Britain: some people considered that it had not been the property of the State, but the personal possession of Dhulip Singh. This may have arisen from the news of Dhulip Singh's presentation of the diamond to the Queen. The news reached Dalhousie who wrote from Government House on the 26 August 1854 saying that:

L—'s talk about the Koh-i-noor being a present from Dhuleep Singh to the Queen is arrant humbug. He knew as well as I did that it was nothing of the sort: and if I had been within a thousand miles of him he would not have dared to utter such a piece of trickery. Those 'beautiful eyes', with which Dhuleep has taken captive the court, are his mother's eyes — those with which she captivated and controlled the old lion of the Punjab. The officer who had charge of her from Lahore to Benares told me this. He said that hers were splendid orbs.

But the worries over the supposed misfortune that the Koh-i-noor was reputed to bring to its owner refused to die down and they ultimately led to Dalhousie writing his most extended and emphatic letter on the subject of the diamond. On his way home, he wrote from Malta on 7 January 1858 as follows:

The rumour you mention as to the Koh-i-noor I have seen in former years in an English paper, but never anywhere else. It is not only contrary to fact but contrary to native statements also. Did the Koh-i-noor bring ill luck to the great Akbar, who got it from Golconda, or to his son or grandson? Or to Aurangzeb, who rose to be the Great Mogul? And when that race of Emperors fell (not from the ill-fortune of the Koh-i-noor, but from their feeble hand) did it bring ill-fortune to Nadir Shah, who lived and died the greatest Eastern conqueror of modern times? Or to Ahmed Shah Doorani who got it at Nadir's death and founded the Afghan Empire? Or did it bring ill-fortune to Runjeet Singh, who got it from the Dooranis, and who rose from being a sower on twenty rupees a month at Goojeranwalla to be the Maharajah of the Punjab, swaying the greatest force in India next to ourselves? And has it brought ill-luck to the Queen? Especially representing the Punjab, has it shown that State an enemy to us? Has it not, on the contrary, shown it our fastest friend, by whose aid we have just put down the traitors of our own household? So much for the facts of history as to the Koh-i-noor. Now for the estimation in which its former owners held it. When Runjeet Singh seized it from Shah Shoojah [the Doorani Emperor] he was very anxious to ascertain its real value. He sent to merchants at Umritsir, but they said its value could not be estimated in money. He sent it to the Begum Shah, Shoojah's wife. Her answer was thus, 'If a strong man should take five stones, and should cast them, one east, one west, one north, and one south, and the last straight up in the air, and if all the space between those points were filled with gold and gems, that would not equal the value of the Koh-i-noor.' Runjeet (thinking this rather a vague estimate, I suppose) thus applied to Shah Shoojah. The old

man's answer was: 'The value of the Koh-i-noor is that whoever holds it is victorious over all his enemies.' And so it is. The Koh-i-noor has been of ill-fortune to the few who have lost it. To the long line of Emperors, Conquerors and potentates who through successive centuries have possessed it, it has been the symbol of victory and empire. And surely never more so than to our Queen, ever since she wore it, and at this moment... However, if Her Majesty thinks it brings bad luck let her give it back to me. I will take it and its ill-luck as speculation.

In the event Queen Victoria did not return the Koh-i-noor to Lord Dalhousie. Instead, in 1853 Garrards mounted it in a magnificent tiara for the Queen which contained more that two thousand diamonds. Five years later Queen Victoria ordered a new regal circlet for the Koh-i-noor which the Crown Jewellers delivered the following year. Then in 1911 Garrards made a new crown which Queen Mary wore for the Coronation: it contained only diamonds in its decoration, among them the Koh-i-noor. In 1937 the diamond was transferred to the crown made for Her Majesty, Queen Elizabeth, the Queen Mother, which was based on Queen Victoria's regal circlet. The Koh-i-noor is set in the Maltese Cross at the front of the crown.

The twentieth century has witnessed further controversy surrounding the Koh-i-noor, namely the question of its rightful ownership. It would not be uncharitable to suggest that, on the majority of occasions on which this subject has been raised, it has been due to the efforts of politicians anxious to score points off one another rather than to any initiative on the part of those who may harbour deep-seated feelings about the diamond.

In 1947 the government of India asked for the return of the Koh-i-noor: at the same time the Congress Ministry of Orissa claimed that the stone really belonged to the god Jaganath, despite the opinion of Ranjit Singh's treasurer that it was the property of the State. A further request followed in 1953 on the occasion of the Coronation of Her Majesty, Queen Elizabeth II. But the real furore erupted in 1976 when the Prime Minister of Pakistan, Zulfikar Ali Bhutto, in a letter to the British Prime Minister, James Callaghan, submitted a formal request for the return of the diamond to Pakistan. This was refused but was accompanied by an assurance by Callaghan to Bhutto that there was no question of Britain's handing it over to any other country. The view of the British government was reported at the time to have been that the history of the diamond is so confused and that Britain has a clear title, in that the diamond was not seized in war but was formally presented – the last statement being a somewhat curious interpretation of events in the nineteenth century. Pakistan's claim to the Koh-i-noor was disputed by India, which made another formal request for its restoration. Then an influential newspaper in Teheran stated that the gem ought to be returned to Iran.

The debate in the British Press provided evidence of the keen interest which the topic engendered. People and pressure groups hastened to put pen to paper. Lord Ballantrae, the great-grandson of Lord Dalhousie, submitted his own claim on the grounds that for just over a year his relative had been its owner. A second correspondent wrote that if the Koh-i-noor was to be handed back, then the marbles must be restored to Greece or Lord Elgin, the Isle of Man to Lord Derby and the Channel Islands to France – he was not sure to whom the Isle of Wight belonged but felt there would be a long and acrimonious dispute within the British Isles themselves. A third writer suggested that the solution to the problem was to partition the gem.

An authoritative and thoughtful contribution to the debate that raged in the Press was contained in a letter to *The Times* by Sir Olaf Caroe, a distinguished British administrator who had spent a lifetime's service in the East, including tenure of the post of Foreign Secretary to the Government of India from 1939 to 1945. Sir Olaf pointed out that the Koh-i-noor had been in Mogul possession in Delhi for two hundred and thirteen years, in Afghan possession in Kandahar and Kabul for sixty-six years, in Sikh possession in Lahore for thirty-six years and – at the time of writing – in British possession for one hundred and twenty seven years. He remarked that it is true that when acquired by the British it was at Lahore (now in Pakistan), but other and prior claimants in the field existed. The Moguls in Delhi were of Turkish origin and the rulers in Lahore, when the stone came into British hands, were Sikhs. Finally, he felt that the word 'return' was scarcely applicable.

Historically, therefore, it is difficult to pass judgement on the validity of the various claims. On the other hand, from a gemmological aspect, the Indian claim must be paramount because it was in that country that the Koh-i-noor first saw the light of day. However, his country's claim to the diamond was renounced by a man who was a statesman, not a mere politician; Jawaharlal Nehru, the first Prime Minister of independent India, once said, 'Diamonds are for Emperors and India does not need Emperors.'

In 1992 a new HM Stationery Office publication on the British Crown Jewels and Regalia gave the revised weight of 105.60 metric carats for the Koh-i-noor and not the 108.93 metric carat conversion figure previously published. The stone is set in the Maltese Cross at the front of the crown made for Her Majesty the Queen Mother and because of uncertainty as to the precise weight and the planned HMSO publication, the opportunity was taken in 1988 to have the stone removed during the maintenance and cleaning of the crown by the then Crown Jeweller, Mr Bill Summers, at Garrard and Co. It was weighed in the presence of witnesses on a modern certified electric balance.

172

The Koh-i-noor is now set in the Maltese Cross at the front of the crown made in 1937 for Her Majesty, Queen Elizabeth, the Queen Mother.

Crown copyright: Historic Royal Palaces

Reproduced by permission of Historic Royal Palaces under license from the Controller of Her Majesty's Stationery Office

Lesotho

The scene is set in a small country in southern Africa, Lesotho, formerly known as Basutoland and a British Protectorate until 1966. Lesotho, or the 'Mountain Kingdom' as it is popularly known, is 30,000 square km in area and has a population of 1.2 million. It is an enclave ringed by the Republic of South Africa and two of its eastern regions.

For many years the Basotho workers had provided the diamond mines at Kimberley with much of their labour force, and so had the opportunity to become acquainted with diamonds and 'blue ground'. Once back in their own country they had clearly put this knowledge to good use, because one day in 1954 a District Commissioner in a northern part of Lesotho received a report from the Kao Valley, in a remote part of his district, to the effect that a woman had died when a pit in which she had been working suddenly collapsed. Such an incident appeared unusual, to say the least, so the Commissioner despatched a police patrol to investigate. A week later the police reported that more than one hundred people were digging on a hill slope for diamonds and that diggers had been at work there for almost a year. Since some of the pits had extended to a depth of four metres the authorities forthwith banned further digging operations on the grounds of safety.

But the news of the digging was out. In 1955 Colonel Jack Scott, a colourful veteran of the South African mining scene, obtained a licence to prospect the whole country for diamonds. When they had been properly evaluated, the Kao diggings turned out to be a huge kimberlite pipe – then the sixth largest known in the world. More kimberlites were found eastward of Kao at a point known as Letseng-la-Terai, the 'turn by the swamp'. In 1959, however, confronted by ever increasing demands on his personal resources without expectation of an

early return, Colonel Scott entered into an agreement with De Beers, who undertook to assist him with the prospecting programme.

Lest it be thought that southern Africa for the most part consists of continuously sun-drenched terrain it would be as well to realize that the diamondiferous areas of Lesotho lie more than 3,000 metres above sea level and are exposed to every permutation of the elements – wind, sun, rain, cloud, hail, sleet, frost and snow. Thus a combination of an awkward and remote geographical location and an inhospitable climate rendered working conditions very difficult and frequently hazardous. Because the diamondiferous area was almost inaccessible, and appeared to be too low in grade for exploitation, De Beers chose to withdraw from the scene in 1960. The government at once set about establishing a public digging at Letseng-la-Terai. Claims three metres square were pegged out over the whole area of pipe and were offered to Basotho at the rate of 50 cents per month for each claim.

The early recovery of some fine quality diamonds exceeding 50 carats stirred up interest with the result that foreign diggers, bringing with them finance and skill gained from experience of the South African diggings, entered into partnerships with the local diggers. In addition, buyers, principally from South Africa, appeared on the scene, setting up offices and appointing representatives in Maseru, the capital of Lesotho. The buyers usually visited Maseru twice a month to buy from the diggers who made the long trip down from the mountain to the capital on foot or on pony. Some of the buyers would fly up to the diggings once a month using the air-strip that had been constructed on the top of a hill.

The method of mining was primitive but effective. In October 1965, a diamond weighing 527 carats was found by a 67-year-old digger who promptly fled to the hills, saying he feared for his life. The great moment of discovery, however, took place on Friday, 26 May 1967, when a brown gem weighing 601.26 carats was found. This was the Lesotho diamond, which ranks as the twelfth largest of gem quality in the world. Moreover it is the largest ever to have been discovered by a woman. Its finder was Mrs Ernestine Ramaboa, the wife of a 38-year-old digger, Petrus Ramaboa, of Thabana-Morena.

Since the start of their digging, the Ramaboas had experienced reasonable luck, finding several gems including one of 24 carats. Petrus Ramaboa decided to walk the 225 km to sell them and it was while he was away that his wife came upon the big diamond when sifting gravel from the deposit. When Mrs Ramaboa set eyes on the object, she knew at once that it was a diamond, even though at the time it was dull and cloudy. Without a word to her fellow diggers, she stuffed it into her dress pocket and departed to her hut to await her husband's return. When he saw it he decided they should set off at once for Maseru, Mrs Ramaboa telling the other diggers she was not well. The couple walked for four days and nights, stopping only briefly for sleep and food from villages. Petrus was obliged to use up most of the proceeds he had just received from his recent sale, so that by the time he and his wife reached Maseru he had only 28 shillings in his pocket. On arrival he at once showed the diamond to an independent buyer from Kimberley, who examined it, but made no offer for it. News of the find spread rapidly among the other buyers in Maseru and eventually the government stepped in for the Ramaboas' own protection.

A meeting was arranged between the Minister of Economic Development, Senator C. D. Molapo, and representatives of the registered diamond-buying firms for discussion on the government's procedure for selling the diamond. After the Minister had outlined the procedure to be followed, the buyers were allowed to discuss fully the new method of buying. The dealers were shown the diamond at a local bank and were requested to submit sealed tenders. Although it was pale brown in colour, the Lesotho was expected to realize between 150,000 and 200,000 rand (US$107,500– 143,500).

On the following Monday, the tenders were examined by a committee of three, consisting of the Minister of Economic Development, the Assistant Commissioner of Police and the Diamond Control Officer. Senator Molapo announced the amount offered by the highest bidder on the lawns of the Ministry of Home Affairs. The sum was 216,000 rand (US$150,000), offered by Eugene Serafini, a Bloemfontein buyer, who had been accompanied by a Dutch colleague,

J. W. Vermey. Mr Serafini had previously been the purchaser of the 527-carat diamond, for which he had paid 116,000 rand (US$83,500). Representatives of De Beers were among those unsuccessful at the Lesotho tender.

Shortly afterwards Mr Vermey contacted Harry Winston to ask whether he was interested in acquiring the Lesotho. He replied that he was, so the stone was sent to his office in Geneva, where it was put on display, thence to New York. The price was not divulged, but it was believed at the time that Mr Winston had paid roughly twice the amount Eugene Serafini had originally offered.

The arrival of the diamond in the United States was followed by that of Mr and Mrs Ramaboa who travelled to New York to watch the cleaving operation at the invitation of Mr Winston. They brought with them their only child, a nineteen-year-old girl who was deaf and spoke only with difficulty. The opportunity was taken of consulting top specialists over her affliction.

After weeks of study and the making of more than twenty replicas, the Lesotho was cleaved into two pieces by Harry Winston's cutter, Pastor Colon, Jnr, on 5 March 1968. According to Ronald Winston, the decision was made to cut 'at the point where nature left a crack in its surface'. The delicate operation of cleaving was shown live on television. The polishing of the Lesotho was completed the following year and resulted in eighteen gems weighing a total of 242.5 carats, equivalent to 40.33 per cent of the original rough weight. They were noticeably lighter in colour than had been expected.

Letseng-la-Terai in Lesotho where the gem was found. Later a diamond mine was constructed, but it only operated for five years.

De Beers Archives.

The details of the gems are as follows:

Lesotho	Carats	Cut
I	71.73	Emerald
II	60.67	Emerald
III	40.42	Marquise
IV	16.35	Pear
V	11.19	Pear
VI	6.98	Pear
VII	4.33	Pear
VIII	4.15	Pear
IX	4.07	Pear
X	3.87	Emerald
XI	3.50	Emerald
XII	3.22	Marquise
XIII	2.75	Square
XIV	2.32	Pear
XV	2.15	Emerald
XVI	1.86	Marquise
XVII	1.86	Pear
XVIII	1.08	Round

Lesotho II appeared in a jewellery sale held by Christie's in Geneva on 22 November 1979; it was accompanied by a Gemological Institute of America grading report: colour light brown, clarity flawless. Recently it has been revealed that Harry Winston sold Lesotho III to the Greek shipping magnate, Aristotle Onassis, who had it set in the engagement ring he gave to his wife, Jacqueline, the widow of President Kennedy. At the so-called 'Jackie Onassis' auction, held in New York by Sotheby's in April 1996, Mr Tony O'Reilly, the Irish businessman and former Irish rugby international, paid US$2,587,500 for the diamond as a present for his wife, Chryss.

Back in his own country, Petrus Ramaboa was able to expand his digging operation by increasing both the number of his claims and the number of men working for him. Asked whether he thought there was a chance of finding other large stones, he replied, 'I am sure of it. That diamond had broken off another one. You could see from the surfaces.

Somewhere there is another one just as big. But it's a hard life up there.'

In the late 1960s production at Letseng-la-Terai started to decline and soon the only mining operation in Lesotho was that being carried out at the Kao diggings, managed by a government agency with technical assistance given by De Beers. This too closed down in 1967. Six years later the country's ruler, Chief Jonathan, whose great ambition had been to see the creation of a large mining operation within Lesotho, asked Harry Oppenheimer whether De Beers might conduct yet a further evaluation of the Letseng-la-Terai deposit. Mr Oppenheimer referred the request to his colleagues and, after negotiation, De Beers agreed to proceed.

In November 1977 a modern mine was officially opened, at a capital cost of 36 million rand. Sadly its life was destined to be short. The Letseng-la-Terai deposit proved to be one of the lowest grade diamond mines in the world, producing only three carats per ton. But it also yielded an exceptional number of large stones: in the space of five years it produced more than one hundred diamonds weighing more than 100 carats, including one of 213 carats. However, due to the depressed state of the diamond market in the early 1980s, particularly for the larger, high quality stones produced at Letseng-la-Terai, the mine had been operating at a loss for some time. The partners examined the ways of keeping the mine open but it became apparent that any plan to extend the life of the mine by developing a satellite pit was uneconomic under the prevailing conditions. Reluctantly, the mine was closed.

One can only hope that Petrus Ramaboa's prediction that a missing part of his wife's great discovery will, one day, come true.

176 The cleaving of the Lesotho diamond in 1968 into two main pieces was shown live on American television.

De Beers Archives.

LESOTHO

Matan

An air of mystery has always surrounded the Matan – or the 'Mattam', as it has sometimes been called. Some accounts suggest it is not a diamond at all, merely a rock crystal. The stone takes its name from the Rajah of Matan, a town situated in the west of Borneo. This island, which has been called 'a treasure house of gems', has numbered gold, diamonds, antimony, mercury and gypsum among its diverse products. It is not recorded when diamonds were first found in Borneo; however, it must be one of the oldest sources since its existence as such was known to Tavernier who wrote:

> The principal reason that dissuaded me from going to the Island of Borneo was because I understood that the Queen of the Island would not permit any strangers to carry away any of those diamonds out of the Island. Those few that are exported, being carry'd out by stealth, and privately sold at Batavia. I say the Queen and not the King, because in that Island the Women have the Sovereign Command, and not the men.

The Bornean deposits are located principally in the western and southern regions of Kalimantan (Indonesian Borneo), close to the Landak river. Diamonds of varying hues – bottle green, pale blue, brown and even red – are said to have been found. The diggings are alluvial, the stones being recovered from river beds and deposits at the foot of the mountains. Work has usually been carried down to a depth of three to nine metres and it was ascertained that as the diggings went deeper, so the gems became both larger and more plentiful. The deposits have been worked ever since the Malays established settlements on the coast. In the nineteenth century there were ten mines at Landak, each worked by twenty to thirty labourers.

For a long period much of Borneo's trade was in the hands of the Dutch East India Company, founded in 1602 to regulate Dutch trade in the Indian Ocean. By the middle of the seventeenth century the Company had almost completely monopolized trade in this part of the world, setting up its headquarters at Batavia. For the year 1738, the Dutch East India Company exported diamonds to the value of 200,000 to 300,000 guilders from the Landak area. After the annexation of Holland by France, Dutch influence in the East declined, to be superseded by that of the British.

No one did more to secure the maritime supremacy of the Eastern Sea for Great Britain than Sir Thomas Stamford Raffles (1781–1826). This eminent man, with his resounding name, possessed an extensive knowledge of the East; his advice was constantly sought by his superiors in London, in particular by Lord Minto, the President of the Board of Trade. In 1810, Raffles was appointed Lieutenant-Governor of the island of Java. Seven years later he published a *History of Java* and, doubtless, would have written more had disaster not struck him. In 1824 the steamer in which he was sailing home caught fire with the result that he lost all his thousands of papers, drawings, notes and memoirs for an intended history of Borneo and Sumatra.

Concerning the Dutch dealings in diamonds Raffles wrote:

> Few courts of Europe could boast of a more brilliant display of diamonds than, in the prosperous times of the Dutch, was exhibited by the ladies of Batavia, the principal and only mart yet opened for the Bornean diamond mines and whence those known in the European world have been procured. With the decline of the Dutch government, however, the demand has decreased, and the mines are now much neglected, the numerous diamond-cutters not being able to obtain a livelihood. Formerly, when more Chinese were employed in the mines of Landak, diamonds from 10 to 13 carats were common in the public markets. The Pangéran (Rajah) of Landak now wears one of 18, and another of 14 carats.

For more than a century the mines in the west of

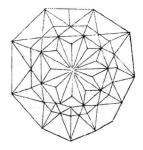

The drawing of a Bornean diamond entitled the 'Rajah' published in the Duke of Brunswick's catalogue. It is thought to have been the Matan.

Duc Souverain de Brunswick-Luneburg, *Catalogue: brilliants et autre pierres precieuses*, 1860.

Borneo were worked mainly by the Chinese. But in 1842 the 'Celestials', as they were known, were attacked, being either massacred or driven out of the country by the Dyaks (aborigines). It has been stated that the cause of the upheaval was the harsh treatment of the Dyaks by the Chinese.

It was a Dyak who was responsible for finding the legendary Matan. Again we are indebted to Raffles who wrote:

Among the larger diamonds which mines have produced, it may not be uninteresting to mention that the great diamond now in the possession of the Sultan of Matan, which has been seen and examined by Europeans, weighed 367 carats; it is of the shape of an egg, indented on one side. It is however, uncut... This celebrated diamond, known by the name of the 'Matan' diamond, was discovered by a Dyak and claimed as a droit of loyalty by the Sultan of the country, Gurn-Laya, but was handed over to the Pangéran of Landak, whose brother, having got possession of it, gave it as a bribe to the Sultan of Sukadana, in order that he might be placed upon the throne of Landak. The lawful prince, however, having fled to Bantam, by the aid of the prince of that country and the Dutch, succeeded in gaining possession of his district, and nearly destroyed Sukadana. It has remained as an heirloom in the family for four descents, and is almost the only appendage of royalty now remaining.

It is more than likely that Sir Thomas Stamford Raffles actually cast his eyes on the diamond and, therefore, was not relying upon a hearsay description of it. If that were so, then his description of its shape as ovoid adds to the confusion surrounding its history, because replicas that have been made of the Matan have always depicted it as a somewhat crudely shaped drop. However, a drawing which appeared among those of celebrated diamonds extant in 1860, when the Duke of Brunswick's jewels were catalogued, shows a gem of a more sophisticated cut. On the other

hand, it is possible that this drawing is of another Bornean diamond, known as the 'Star of Sarawak'. Edwin Streeter refers to its purchase around 1878 by the Rajah of Sarawak from a Chinese seller. The stone weighed 70 carats and was said to have been of the finest colour.

The supposition that the Matan was not a diamond but a rock crystal derives from the Sultan's habit of showing such a stone to strangers. It is said that since he had been robbed of so much of his territory, he did not want to lose this last remaining emblem of royalty to his powerful and greedy neighbours at Pontianak, to the north. Nevertheless John Mawe, in his book *A Treatise on Diamonds*, maintains that the Sultan did retain the real diamond; he tells of a friend who was permitted to see it, but asked not to touch it. The gem was about the size of a walnut, with a bluish metallic colour.

Further evidence that the Matan may have been a diamond is supplied by one of its owners who apparently valued it so highly that he refused to part with it. One particularly tempting offer came from the Dutch government anxious to obtain possession of a talisman associated with its former empire. Early in the nineteenth century the Governor sent an emissary to the Rajah to negotiate the purchase of the stone. The emissary offered 150,000 guilders, and two large war brigs, with a full complement of guns and ammunition, as well as other arms; but the Rajah declined to sell.

The truth about the Matan may never be known. During the Second World War, many homeward-bound Japanese vessels carried quantities of gems obtained during the occupation of Borneo. One cargo, reported to have had a value of nearly £4,000,000, was in the cruiser *Ashigara* when she was sunk off the coast of eastern Sumatra. According to survivors, at least one and possibly five boxes of diamonds were aboard at the time. In 1960, the president of Japan's largest salvage firm said that the wreck had been located under 30 metres of water and that it might be possible to salvage the ship's contents.

In the meantime Borneo has continued to yield diamonds. The most notable specimen that has emerged in the years following the war is the 166-carat Tri-Sakti, found in the Banjarmasin diggings of Kalimantan in the late 1960s. Asschers Diamant Maatschapij of Amsterdam fashioned an emerald cut weighing 50.53 carats, reported to be flawless and blue-white in colour, from the rough. Afterwards it was sold in Europe to an undisclosed buyer on behalf of the Indonesian government, whose leader at the time, President Sukarno, boldly predicted that there were more diamond deposits in Kalimantan than in Kimberley, South Africa.

Mazarins

Cardinal Jules Mazarin (1602–61) was the Chief Minister of France during the early part of the long reign of Louis XIV. He became a man of both power and affluence, leaving his fortune, which included pictures, books, houses, jewels and money, to the King. According to Nancy Mitford, biographer of Louis XIV, Mazarin considered that none of these equalled his most precious legacy to his Sovereign – Colbert. Jean Baptiste Colbert (1619–83) was the man who proved to be the most able minister in French history, particularly in financial affairs. Nevertheless, as an ardent collector of jewellery, Louis XIV would

have been an enthusiastic recipient of the eighteen diamonds left him by his former minister on the understanding that they became known as the 'Mazarins'. Two of the diamonds were the celebrated Sancy and Mirror of Portugal, which became Mazarins I and III respectively. The collection was recorded in the 1691 and 1791 inventories of the French Crown Jewels (following page).

It is apparent that several of the Mazarins were recut between 1691 and 1791, most likely in the years from 1774 to 1788 when numerous diamonds were sent to Amsterdam or Antwerp for recutting, a

The former Garde Meuble which once housed the Crown Jewels of France. Among them were the 18 Mazarins, all of which were stolen in the great 1792 robbery.

Paris, Musée Carnavalet. © Photothèque des musées de la Ville de Paris/cliché Toumazet.

179

MAZARINS

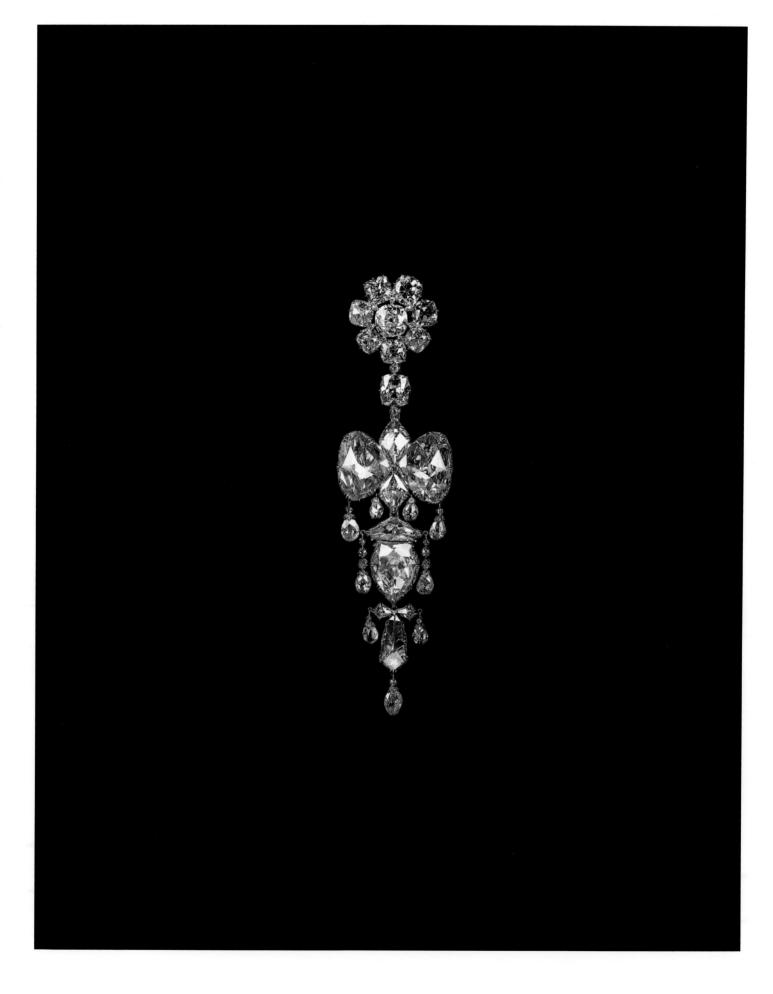

MAZARINS

	1691 Carats	1691 Value in livres	1791 Carats	1791 Value in livres	Carats (metric)	
I *Sancy*	53 3/4	600,000	53 12/16	1000,000	55.23	White pear shape
II	33 3/8	260,000	24 1/6	240,000	24.81	White table cut
III *Mirror of Portugal*	25 3/8	150,000	21 2/16	250,000	21.68	White square table cut
IV	24 1/4	100,000	13 10/16	60,000	13.97	Brownish heart-shape
V	21 5/8	120,000	22 6/16	160,000	22.97	'Crystalline' almond shape
VI	18 1/4	80,000	19 12/16	140,000	20.27	'Crystalline' almond shape
VII *Grand Mazarin*	21	75,000	18 9/16	75,000	19.10	Slightly yellowish square cut
VIII	18 1/4	55,000	14 12/16	30,000	15.14	White square cut
IX	15 1/4	75,000	14 14/16	150,000	15.27	'Crystalline' marquise
X	17	50,000	16	50,000	16.42	Greyish square cut
XI	17 3/4	40,000	20 6/16	50,000	20.91	White square cut
XII	17	50,000	17	50,000	17.45	'Crystalline' extended square cut with a reddish tinge
XIII	13	40,000	10 4/16	25,000	10.52	Brownish square cut
XIV	11 1/3	35,000	8 7/16	25,000	8.66	'Crystalline' square table cut
XV	10 3/4	20,000	8 16/32	12,000	8.72	A yellow/brownish square table cut
XVI	8 3/4	16,000	6	8,000	6.16	Yellowish square table cut
XVII	21 1/2	70,000	21 6/16	25,000	21.94	Brownish heart shape
XVIII	22	70,000	21 8/16	25,000	22.07	Brownish heart shape

procedure that, not surprisingly, was unpopular with the local cutters. Alterations must also have been made to the numbering of the stones since some of them had increased in weight by the time of the later inventory – great advances may have taken place in the technique of cutting diamonds but so far nobody has devised a method of increasing their weight!

Being part of the Crown Jewels of France, the Mazarins were housed in the Garde Meuble when thieves broke in on the night of 16 September 1792, stealing the jewels. In addition to the Sancy, numbers IV, VII, VIII, XIII and XVI were afterwards recovered. The Grand Mazarin, the seventh in the series, was set at the time of the First Empire in a diadem for the Empress.

Since the theft it has proved difficult to establish the whereabouts of the Cardinal's diamonds. From time to time a number of diamonds stated to have been owned by him have made their appearance, but on nearly every occasion their weights have not corresponded with those listed in the 1791 inventory. It is likely that many of the diamonds may have been recut so that, with one definite exception, it would be unwise to dismiss them as not being the original Mazarins.

At the sale of the former French Crown Jewels in 1887 a number of diamonds were listed as Mazarin diamonds. However, French authorities have stated that the only authentic Mazarin which figured in the sale was Number VII, the Grand Mazarin, which has been preserved and is now displayed in the Louvre. Later sightings have included the showing by Cartier's of two diamonds said to have been Mazarins, at an exhibition in 1900. Their weights are stated to have been 18 11/16 and 16 9/16 carats, so it is possible that they may have been recut from numbers II, III, V, VI, XI, XVII or XVIII. In 1928, the same firm showed another gem said to have been a Mazarin, weighing 15.88 carats. Finally, it was reported that an emerald cut of 30.58 carats which came up for auction in December 1964 was a former Mazarin; however, this cannot have been so because the only diamond in the collection known to have weighed as much as this was the Sancy.

Cardinal Mazarin, who bequeathed his fortune, which included a collection of 18 diamonds, to Louis XIV of France.

Opposite page: the Empress Eugénie's reliquary brooch dating from 1855 – designed by Alfred Bapst – into which it is believed the Mazarins XVII and XVIII are set.

Paris, Musée du Louvre. Photo © RMN – G. Blot/ H. Lewandowski.

McLean

The Duchess of
Windsor wearing the
McLean, photographed by
Dorothy Wilding in 1952.

By courtesy of the National
Portrait Gallery, London.

Thomas Cullinan may have failed in his attempt
to reach the United States but another
Irishman, Thomas W. Walsh, from Co. Tipperary,
did succeed in crossing the Atlantic. After spending
some time in a succession of mining camps, he
turned to prospecting on his own account and made
a fortune by his discovery of the lucrative Camp
Bird gold mine in the south-west of Colorado.
Later he sold the mine and became a friend of King
Leopold of the Belgians who tried, in vain, to
interest him in the mineralogical potential of the
territory then known as the Belgian Congo.
Through 'striking it rich' Thomas Walsh could
afford to have his daughter, Evalyn, born in Denver
on 1 March 1886, educated in style in Washington
DC and in Europe.

At the age of fifteen, Evalyn already showed signs
of the special attachment to jewellery which was to
make her almost a household name in the United
States. Her father noticed it and once remarked:
'Listen. The thing you want more than all else in the
world, I think, is a ring. I'm right? I'll give you a
diamond ring as will make you quite the envy of all
your friends.' During her visit to Europe in 1905 she
met the Pope. She also met Prince Altieri, a member
of an old Italian family, and clearly made a
favourable impression. But she wrote at the time
that 'I've got a plan to get from father an
automobile that I want right now, a lot more than I
want any man to be my husband. Actually I'm dying
for a Mercedes.' Nevertheless, the acquisition of a
suitable man rather than a motor car plainly figured
in her parents' plans and her father gave a big
dinner, at which an announcement was expected.
The Prince's mother was present wearing an Altieri
heirloom which Evalyn described as 'a necklace of
diamonds as large as hickory nuts, but those were
merely satellites of the orb that hung below the
cleft of her bosom. That stone was as large as a golf

ball. But she confided to her father that she would
rather have a Mercedes any day than Altieri.

On her return to America, Evalyn Walsh duly
received her Mercedes, but possession of it sparked
off the first of several family tragedies that were to
blight her life. When motoring in Rhode Island, a
tyre burst and her brother died in the accident. She
herself suffered serious injuries, which led to an
argument between her parents over the proposed
medical treatment. Mrs Walsh asked her husband,
'Which would you rather have Evalyn do: lose her
life or lose her leg?' She lost neither. Instead, she
gained a fiancé, Edward Beale McLean, whose
father, John R. McLean, was the millionaire owner
of numerous newspapers, including the *Washington
Post*. But the engagement proved to be a stormy one
and was broken off several times before their
eventual marriage in 1908. Evalyn said of Ned
McLean that he was in such a state of nerves from
drinking that he had to make a handkerchief sling
to steady the hand with which he lifted his glass.
Sadly, in later life, he suffered a complete
breakdown from drinking and died in a mental
institution.

Three years after the purchase of the Star of the
East in 1908 (see pp. 247–49) Mrs McLean bought
the Hope diamond, the gem with which her name
was to be most closely associated. Then she added
the 14.37-carat, kite-shaped Star of the South (not to
be confused with the much larger Brazilian diamond
of the same name) and a cushion-cut diamond
weighing 31.26 carats, later to become known as the
'McLean'. Perhaps Mrs McLean began to wish she
could emulate one of her acquaintances at Palm
Beach of whom she wrote: 'She was past sixty and all
her life had been accumulating jewellery. Tiffany
might have started a branch with what she wore even
when she was going swimming ...'

The McLeans became friends of President

Harding, whose wife would sometimes seek Mrs McLean's opinion about the clothes she should wear. But it was jewellery rather than the wardrobe which was foremost in Evalyn Walsh McLean's thoughts. She stated that 'One day when I was blue from all the trouble of making million-dollar ends meet, I remembered my old prescription for that state of mind, went to New York, and asked Cartier to show me something fine. He then dazzled me with a ruby and diamond bracelet – one that owed its existence to the Depression. However, it's no use for anyone to chide me for loving jewels. I cannot help it if I have passion for them. They make me feel comfortable and even happy. The truth is, when I neglect to wear jewels astute members of my family call in doctors because it is a sign I'm becoming ill.'

The Depression affected the McLeans along with many financially worse off families. Their bank was going to foreclose the mortgage and none of Mrs McLean's pleas counted. So she went home and declared, 'To the devil with them. I've got to have a hundred thousand dollars.' She went behind a large, heavily upholstered chair, ripped out the back and pushed her arm into some sort of squirrel's nest until her groping fingers found a cache of jewels, and she set out for New York with these stones. A pawnbroker let her have $50,000 on the jewellery taken from the chair and another $37,500 on the Hope. Later on she had the money to redeem them, pushed the cash across the counter, and when the jewellery had been bought, stuffed them into her dress. In her autobiography, published in 1936, she wrote: 'As for myself, I am pretty nearly broke now. I hope my acquaintances – I won't say my friends – are satisfied. The Hope diamond and every other jewel I have, have been in and out of New York pawnshops in recent years.'

Despite these misfortunes, at her death eleven years later, this eccentric, but endearing, lady, whose kindness and hospitality were well known in the war years, left no fewer than 74 items of jewellery. They included the four named diamonds – the Hope, the Star of the East, the Star of the South, and the McLean. In 1949 Harry Winston bought the entire collection from Mrs McLean's executors and the McLean diamond became part of his famous Court of Jewels, a fabulous collection that toured most of the major cities of the United States. In May 1959 Harry Winston sold the stone to the Duchess of Windsor. It was to become the most important item in her collection.

The Duchess died in April 1986. The sale of jewellery that had belonged to the woman referred to by uncrowned King Edward VIII, who abdicated, as the 'perfect woman' was held by Sotheby's on the evenings of the 2nd and 3rd April, 1987 – one of the most glamorous such events ever to have been staged. The sale, held in Geneva, realized $45,000,000, more than seven times the pre-sale estimate, resulting in a massive injection of funds for the Louis Pasteur Institute in Paris, the favourite charity of the Duchess of Windsor.

A suitable hush descended when the final, and most important, lot came up for sale. It was the McLean diamond, then set in a claw between tapered baguette diamond, single stone, shoulders. The sale catalogue included a report from the GIA to the effect that the stone was 'D' colour, with a clarity of VS2, and that its clarity was improvable. The report was accompanied by one from Gübelin which, interestingly, stated that the stone was a type IIA diamond and commented that diamonds showing a high degree of brilliancy like this specimen were sometimes called Golconda in trade circles, in recollection of the aspect of ancient fine diamonds. Certainly, the McLean has the appearance of an Indian diamond, which may in part explain the comparative dearth of information about its earlier history.

The pre-sale estimate for the McLean had been between 1,250,000 and 1,500,000 Swiss francs. In the event it fetched SFr. 4,730,000 (US$3,153,333). The buyer of the diamond was a Japanese gentleman, Mr Takagi, of the Heiwado Trading Company. Afterwards, he said he had bought the McLean 'for the romance it represents, for the extraordinary quality of the diamond and for the good cause which the money will go towards – the fight against the terrible disease, AIDS.'

The cushion-shaped McLean diamond.

Courtesy of Sotheby's Geneva.

Millennium Star

The newly discovered De Beers Millennium Star weighed an impressive 777 carats in the rough, making it the sixth largest rough diamond ever found.

De Beers Archive.

On 8 September 1999 De Beers unveiled to the world the 'De Beers Millennium Jewels', a truly unique collection of diamonds. The centrepiece was the De Beers Millennium Star, a 'D' colour, internally and externally flawless pear-shape weighing 203.04 carats. The remaining gems comprised eleven rare blue diamonds, cut in a variety of shapes, having a total weight of 118 carats. The largest was the Heart of Eternity, weighing 27.64 carats.

The De Beers Millennium Star was found by an alluvial digger in the early 1990s in the Mbuji-Mayi district of what was then known as Zaire, now the Democratic Republic of Congo. Its discovery set off a rush of diggers to the area hoping to find a similar stone. The diamond was purchased by De Beers on the open market and held in anticipation of the forthcoming Millennium. 'To be able to unveil not only one diamond, but a collection of such rarity that most of us will not see its like again is, I think, the only adequate way to mark the passage of 2,000 years of man's history', said Mr Nicholas Oppenheimer, Chairman of De Beers.

The diamond weighed 777 carats in the rough – a magic number – and ranks as the sixth largest authentic diamond of gem quality ever found.

The cutting of the De Beers Millennium Star took the Steinmetz Group of Companies three years and bears witness to the international nature of the modern diamond industry: it was split in Belgium, initially polished in South Africa and finally polished in New York. It proved necessary to construct a special room and devise special tools for the cutting operation. Some hundred plastic models of the rough stone were made so as to plan and design the optimum polished gem, in terms of both beauty and weight. After the cutting of the stone had been planned for many months, the rough, in shape an elongated cleavage, was cut into three pieces. Ultimately, the diamond was given the classic pear-shape with 54 facets.

Mr Harry Oppenheimer, the former Chairman of De Beers, who has probably handled more important diamonds in his 70-year career than anyone in the world, remarked of the Millennium Star: 'It is the most beautiful diamond I have ever seen'.

The De Beers Millennium Jewels were displayed in the Millennium Dome at Greenwich throughout the year 2000, and in public exhibitions in Tokyo and Dubai.

Mirror of Portugal

Queen Henrietta Maria by Sir Anthony Van Dyck. In the painting, she is wearing the Mirror of Portugal mounted in an enamelled gold chain surrounded by flowers.

The Royal Collection © Her Majesty the Queen.

After the death of the Cardinal King Henry of Portugal in 1580, his illegitimate nephew, Dom Antonio de Castro, known as the Prior of Crato, proclaimed himself King. Philip II, King of Spain, refused to recognize Dom Antonio's sovereignty and despatched an army which defeated him in 1580, resulting in the annexation of Portugal to Spain. The vanquished claimant then went to Paris; with French assistance he sent a naval expedition to the Azores, where he was still recognized as the King of Portugal, but was defeated by the Spanish squadrons. Dom Antonio escaped to London, taking with him some of the Portuguese Crown Jewels, for which, in his absence, he was condemned to death. Among these was the Mirror of Portugal, a rectangular table-cut diamond then reputed to have weighed around 30 carats. Dom Antonio hoped to interest Queen Elizabeth in the jewellery and raise sufficient funds to enable him to fight back. The Queen sent a fleet which landed near Lisbon in 1589, but the expedition proved a costly failure. Elizabeth nonetheless kept the Portuguese jewels; the Mirror of Portugal was mounted in a chain of gold, enamelled and surrounded by flowers. Impoverished and in poor health, Dom Antonio returned to Paris where he died in 1595.

In 1623 the Prince of Wales, later King Charles I, travelled to Spain to form an alliance; it was intended that it should be sealed by his betrothal to the Infanta. His father, James I, ordered that a selection of the finest jewels in the Tower of London be made available to his son so as to make a good impression. The Mirror of Portugal was chosen, set with a large pearl as a pendant. In the event, the Prince's suit proved to be unsuccessful, and in 1625, as Charles I, he married Henrietta Maria, daughter of Henry IV and Marie de Médicis of France.

Almost from the outset of his reign (1625–49), Charles I was short of money, the situation rendered even more difficult by his dispute with the Parliamentarians and the ensuing civil war. For her part, Queen Henrietta Maria, who was devoted to her husband, showed both courage and determination but never fully understood English politics. She believed that a military coup would serve to overthrow the Parliamentarians. In 1644 she sailed to the Netherlands to sell her jewels and raise funds for the king. Among the items she took from the Treasury were the Mirror of Portugal and the Sancy.

Neither diamond was sold in the Netherlands, so the Queen contracted loans with the Duke of Épernon amounting to 427,566 livres. Because he feared that he might not be repaid, the Queen pledged the Mirror of Portugal and the Sancy as surety. Alas, the Duke's fears proved to be justified and he was permitted to keep both diamonds. He sold them to Cardinal Mazarin, the Sancy becoming Mazarin I and the Mirror of Portugal named as Mazarin III in his famous collection. Cardinal Mazarin bequeathed them to the French Crown when he died in 1661.

At some stage the Mirror of Potugal was recut, most likely after its purchase by Cardinal Mazarin, since, in the 1691 inventory of the French Crown Jewels, its weight was recorded as $25\frac{3}{8}$ carats. It was then valued at 150,000 livres. The diamond must have been recut a second time, because in the inventory of the Crown Jewels a hundred years later its weight had been reduced to $21\frac{1}{8}$ carats, but its value had increased to 250,000 livres.

Unfortunately, the Mirror of Portugal was amongst the jewels stolen during the infamous robbery of the Garde Meuble on the night of 16 September 1792. Since then, there has been no trace of this historic diamond.

MIRROR OF PORTUGAL

Mouawad Magic

Above: the 108.81-carat Mouawad Magic, the largest diamond in Robert Mouawad's collection; it was found in Guinea and fashioned in Antwerp.

Courtesy of Mouawad Joailliers, Geneva.

Opposite: the 101.84-carat Mouawad Splendour, an 11-sided pear shape. Both diamonds are 'D' colour, internally flawless.

Courtesy of Mouawad Joailliers, Geneva.

It was in the early 1970s that the Lebanese Robert Mouawad first arrived on the jewellery auction scene. Soon his very presence in the sale-room was enough to send pulses racing when it was realised that a new, significant player had appeared. Along with his two contemporaries, Sheikh Ahmed Fitaihi of Jeddah and Laurence Graff of London, he has been responsible for some of the astonishing record diamond prices achieved in recent years.

The Mouawad family business dates from 1890 when Daoud Mouawad, Robert's grandfather, established a small jewellery workshop in Beirut, after learning the craft in New York and Mexico. Later, Daoud's son, Fayez, broadened the scope of the business by moving to Saudi Arabia in 1950. The timing proved excellent and it enabled the family to capitalize on the country's growing wealth and to benefit from increasing oil revenues in the Gulf. Once Fayez had handed over the reins to his son, Robert Mouwad was to enter Europe, develop North American and the Far Eastern connections, and to transform the family jewellery business into the global empire it has become today.

Born in 1945, Mr Mouawad has purchased a number of the world's great diamonds, including the Nassak, the Indore Pears, the Premier Rose, the Jubilee, the Queen of Holland, the Tereschenko and the Taylor-Burton. In reflecting on this remarkable collection, he has said:

'There are many motives behind the acquisition of these rare diamonds. Primarily, an admiration for rare diamonds as a result of being so conditioned by their magic. To collect exceptional stones has always been sought after by us to achieve self-satisfaction. To acquire unique and historic gems reflects our ego... however, those for which we have a very special admiration, we just enjoy looking at them, when we can spare a moment.'

One day, as is his wish, it is to be hoped that this legendary collection of diamonds will be housed in a new home, the Mouawad Museum in Beirut, and will be accessible to public view.

But Robert Mouawad has never been content with acquiring only historical diamonds, adding several modern-cut gems to his list. At a New York auction in 1988 he purchased the 59-carat 'D' flawless pear shape later to become known as the 'Star of Abdel-Aziz' after His Majesty King Fahd's youngest son. There have also been two fancy lilac-pink gems, the Mouawad Lilac, a step cut weighing 24.44 carats, and the Mouawad Pink, a cushion cut weighing 21.06 carats.

Others, in increasing order of sizes, include the Mouawad White, a 48.28-carat marquise; the Mouawad Splendour, an eleven-sided pear shape weighing 101.84 carats; the Mouawad Monolith, an emerald cut of 104.02 carats; the currently unnamed polygonal, a 106.00-carat modified pear shape.

Each diamond is unique and has personality traits, some more appealing than others. The whiteness or fancy colour, the size, the clarity, the cut, the immortal character, are all factors that contribute to the overall beauty of a stone. But it is the human touch that unveils its beauty. In its rough state it hides its true potential value. Also, the historical value of a gem, from its formation to its birth on the earth's surface, and the many lives it has affected, are all intangibles that add to its mystique.

Such are the thoughts of a great collector and diamond connoisseur.

Yet not all of Mr Mouawad's acquisitions have been made at auction. In March 1991, in Antwerp, he purchased a 284.6-carat rough diamond that had been found in the Aredor mine in Guinea. Through his own group's office in Belgium, it was fashioned into the largest of all his eponymous diamonds: a magnificent emerald cut later named the Mouawad Magic, weighing 108.81 carats. It measures 32.91 by 20.73 by 16.83 mm. This 'D' colour, internally flawless gem is considered a collection item and is consequently 'not for sale' at the present time.

Nassak

The Nassak diamond as an 80.60 carat triangular-cut. It was re-cut in 1937.

Courtesy Cartier Archive

The First Marquess of Westminster who purchased the Nassak and the Arcots in 1837.

About 180 km north-east of Bombay lies Nasik, the chief town of a district of Maharashtra. It lies on the Godavari river, some 48 km from its source. The name of the place has been variously written as Nassac, Nassik or Nessuck but the diamond named after it is nowadays known as the 'Nassak'.

Nasik is venerated by Hindus as one of the homes of Rama and Sita. Numerous cave-temples are found in the neighbourhood and, during the period of the Maratha's ascendancy, the town became a noted place of pilgrimage for worshippers of Siva. Siva is one of the principal deities of Hinduism and is worshipped as the paramount lord by the various Saiva sects of India. The god is one of the most complex, combining within himself seemingly contradictory qualities: he is both the destroyer and the creator. Siva's consort is known as Uma, Sati, Parvati, Durga or Kali; and it is said that the divine couple, together with their sons, dwell on Mount Kailasa in the Himalayas. Siva's mount is the bull, Nandi; a sculpture of Nandi sits opposite the main sanctuary of every Siva temple. In temples and private shrines Siva is worshipped in his fundamental form of the lingam, or phallus.

It is more than likely that one of the Maratha chieftains acquired the Nassak diamond and placed it in the eye of a statue of Siva, within one of the temples. So long as the power of the Maratha confederacy flourished, treasures accumulated in places of worship, but when that power was loosened, theft and pillage of sacred places took place.

In 1818 the British forces finally defeated the one remaining Peshwa (state) in the last of the Maratha Wars. Among the hoard of booty which they captured was the Nassak. The Peshwa had concealed the diamond from the British but it was brought to light by Colonel Briggs who forthwith handed it over to the Marquess of Hastings, the Governor-General and Commander in Chief of forces in India from 1813 to 1822, as part of the 'Deccan booty'.

Hastings presented the diamond to the East India Company, doubtless an honourable act only to be expected by a Commander in Chief, but one which he and his family might well have regretted. For Hastings, a friend and confidant of the Prince of Wales (later George IV), was a man of habitual extravagance and he left his family so badly off that, in 1827, the East India Company voted a further sum of £20,000 to his son, in addition to substantial funds allocated earlier.

When the Nassak arrived in England it was triangularly shaped and had been cut in the old, somewhat primitive, Indian style. Its weight was recorded as 89 carats and 2 grains. A noted authority on jewellery and precious stones at the time, John Mawe, described the Nassak as: 'a diamond of great purity but of a bad form... it is cut and polished, so as to retain the greatest possible weight, but it exhibits none of the qualities which it would so proudly display if it had been well proportioned.'

The East India Company handed the diamond into the custody of the famous firm of Rundell & Bridge, who had originally been appointed jewellers and silversmiths to the Crown by George III. Rundell & Bridge decided to have the Nassak recut, and this was successfully achieved with the loss of only 10 per cent of the diamond's original weight. They adhered to the policy of keeping as close as possible to the original triangular shape while at the same time increasing its brilliance. In July 1831 Emanuel Brothers bought the Nassak for £7,200: representing scarcely one third of the previous estimate of the gem's worth, the low figure is accounted for by the fact that the sale occurred during a period of severe financial depression.

Six years later, the Nassak came up for auction at an important sale held in Willis's Rooms in London. *The Times* reported that the room was:

filled with all the cognoscenti in precious stones and all the principal dealers, attracted by the announcement that the celebrated 'Nassak' diamond, the 'Arcot' diamonds and a variety of most other costly diamonds and pearls, the property of the late Mr Bridge, of Ludgate Hill, would be sold by auction by Mr Sharp. The sale commenced at 3 o'clock. Mr Sharp, previously to the sale, entered into a short description of the principal lots.

In all there were 24 lots and considerable competition ensued for some of them. Nevertheless, it was generally considered that the prices realized were far below expectations. The eventual purchaser of the Nassak was the first Marquess of Westminster.

The Marquess also bought the Arcot diamonds, two very fine pear shapes weighing a total of 57.35 carats that had originally been presented to Queen Charlotte, the consort of George III, by the Nawab of Arcot in 1777, as well as the brilliant weighing 32.20 carats which may have been cut from the diamond that fifty years before had caused so much embarrassment to that great colonial administrator Warren Hastings, and which is named after him (see p. 116). At the Drawing Room on Queen Victoria's eighteenth birthday, not long after she had ascended the throne in 1837, the Marquess wore the Nassak in the hilt of his sword. It was intended that the Marchioness should have worn the Arcot diamonds, but owing to indisposition she was unable to attend. The Nassak remained in the Grosvenor family until 1926, when the second Duke of Westminster sold it to Georges Mauboussin, the Paris jeweller.

In the same year the Nassak made the first of its voyages across the Atlantic when, after failing to find a European buyer for the gem, Mauboussin sent it to the United States for display as an 'artistic antique'. This caused the American jewellery industry to rise up in arms, because it was common knowledge that M. Mauboussin's intention was to offer the diamond for sale. However, the United States Customs Court upheld its importation as an 'artistic antique' and it came into the country duty free. The jewellery trade thereupon arranged an appeal to the Court of Customs and Patent Appeals and the former decision was reversed. The diamond was in the possession of Cartier London in 1933 when the designer Frederick A. Mew used it to enhance a five-row pearl and diamond necklace. The Nassak was shown at Cartier's Monte Carlo branch in 1936, which had been opened the year before. In 1937 the diamond was re-cut from an 80.60 carat triangular-cut to a 47.41 carat rectangular-cut. It was subsequently bought by Harry Winston who re-cut it once again tò 43.38 carats. He sold it to the New

York jewellers, Trabert and Hoeffer. In 1944 Mrs William B. Leeds of New York became the owner of the Nassak, wearing it in a ring set with two tapered baguettes.

The Nassak came up for auction again, on this occasion at the Parke-Bernet Galleries in New York, on 16 April 1970. Bidding started at $200,000: five bids and two minutes later it was all over. The buyer was Mr Edward J. Hand of Greenwich, Connecticut, who paid $500,000 for the diamond. It was reported that a large chain of jewellers had been the underbidder at $475,000. Mr Hand, who was once married to the tennis star Gussie Moran – older devotees of the game will recall the sartorial sensations she caused on court in the early 1950s – remarked: 'I think it was a bargain. I was prepared to go as high as $750,000.' Nevertheless, at the time

The town of Nasik on the Godavari river in India. The Nassak is thought to have been set in a statue in one of the temples there.

De Beers Archives.

the Nassak realized the second highest price ever paid for a gem at an auction, the amount only being exceeded by that which Cartier had paid the previous year for the diamond which had become the Taylor-Burton; perhaps earlier disappointments attached to the sale of the Nassak had been overcome and the true worth of the gem had at long last been recognized.

In due course, a partnership of J. & S.S. DeYoung, the Boston estate goods firm, and Bulgari of Italy acquired the Nassak. In 1977 they offered the diamond to the King of Saudi Arabia, but he declined to buy it, considering it unattractive – despite a grading report from the Gemological Institute of America stating that the stone was 'D' flawless. (It is considered today that its visible graining lines would disqualify the diamond from a flawless rating.) However, when the King was shown the Nassak a second time he was sufficiently impressed by its history to purchase it, together with a large Burma ruby.

Since then the diamond has been acquired by Mr Robert Mouawad.

Niarchos

Unlike the proverbial cat, one may expect the Premier mine to enjoy only four lives. The first lasted from the discovery of the diamond pipe just before 1902 – and the formation of the Premier (Transvaal) Diamond Mining Company – until the outbreak of the First World War when the mine was shut down and operated on a caretaker basis. By January 1916 it was working again and production continued up to 1932 when mining operations ceased due to the depressed state of the diamond industry.

Working resumed in 1945, but its fourth life really began in 1979 with the opening up of the mine below the 'gabbro' sill, a 70-metre geologic intrusion of barren rock which cuts right through the pipe some 400 metres below the surface. Production from this new source has not only given the mine its longest life, but one that should enable production to continue for a further fifteen years.

In the early years of its existence, the Premier mine produced many large diamonds including, of course, the Cullinan in 1905, and since working was restarted in 1945 the mine has continued to yield some exceptional stones. One of the most exciting moments occurred early on the morning of Saturday, 22 May 1954, when a diamond measuring just under 51 mm long, just over 25 mm wide and 19 mm thick unexpectedly appeared on the grease tables in the recovery plant. It was immediately apparent to the officials present that this was an exceptional find.

The diamond weighed 426.5 carats, was internally flawless, but was slightly chipped, probably due to contact with the mine's underground crusher. Sir Ernest Oppenheimer considered that it possessed the most perfect colour of any diamond he had seen, an opinion shared by others who were fortunate enough to view it.

In due course the unnamed diamond was shipped to London and in February 1956 it was announced by the Diamond Trading Company that a sale of rough diamonds totalling £3,000,000 had been made to the firm of Harry Winston Inc. of New York. At the time this transaction represented the largest single sale ever made to one of its clients.

The shipment comprised more than 50,000 individual gemstones and included the 426-carat diamond. The sale price was not disclosed but it was understood to be provisionally valued at over £100,000 – a significant sum in those days.

On 1 February 1956 the diamond was brought from Ildewild airport by a messenger for a customs broker and duly delivered to its purchaser in a brown paper bag. Accompanying him and, like him, unattended by any special guard, was a postman with three cardboard boxes containing the rest of the diamonds under his arm. The shipment had been made to New York by registered post and the actual postal charges amounted to the princely sum of approximately £1.75.

Harry Winston and his cutting staff spent weeks debating whether to fashion one large gem or several smaller stones from the rough. In the end they decided on a single diamond, Mr Winston stating that while it would have proved easier to sell the smaller stones, he felt that the historical value of creating one fine gem was more important.

Once this had been determined, plans were laid to ensure the cutting of a perfect final gem. The cutters made more than three hundred lead models of the proposed finished gem to guide them in their task. The actual operation was performed by Winston's chief cleaver, Bernard de Haan, who spent the entire year working on the project. The first severance took five weeks: from the 70-carat piece he removed, a 27.62-carat marquise was later polished. The second took equally long and produced another 70 carats from which a very significant emerald cut of 39.99 carats was obtained. Thus a rough piece weighing about

270 carats remained. For some 58 days, 'master diamond-cutter' de Haan first ground and then polished a great gem. Ultimately it yielded a pear shape weighing 128.25 carats, possessing a total of 144 facets. On 27 February 1957, the 'Ice Queen' was unveiled to the world.

Soon after, the late Stavros Niarchos, the Greek shipping magnate, bought the gem for his then wife, formerly Charlotte Ford, for a reported $2,000,000. Members of the Ford family were not polite, referring to the diamond as 'The Skating Rink', but Niarchos remained unperturbed, having also bought the two other gems that had been fashioned from the original 426-carat rough. For that amount

– and after they were divorced – he was surely entitled to bestow his name upon the diamond which he generously lent to many exhibitions. In 1966 the Niarchos returned to South Africa for the famous centennial 'Jewel Box 1966' exhibition. Since his death in April 1996, no further information about the Niarchos diamond has been forthcoming.

However, the 39.99-carat emerald cut, known today as the Ice Queen, was auctioned by Sotheby's in New York in October 1991. Having earlier been graded by the Gemological Institute of America as 'D' colour of VVS1 quality (the very smallest of inclusions), it was sold for $1,870,000 to Sheik Ahmed Hassan Fitaihi.

The Niarchos diamond, part of the original 426-carat rough, which was first observed in the final stages of recovery on the grease tables of the Premier mine.

De Beers Archives.

Nizam

Above top: the Nizam diamond drawn by Henry Piddington, geologist and curator of the Museum of Geology at Calcutta in the mid-19th century.

In *Famous Diamonds of the World*, R. M. Shipley, 1955.

Above bottom: L'Indien diamond referred to in the Duke of Brunswick's 1860 *Catalogue: Brilliants et autres pierres précieuses*.

Below: View of Hyderabad, formerly the largest princely state in India. Golconda and many alluvial deposits were located within it.

Founded in 1598 and lasting until 1948, Hyderabad was once the largest and most populous of the former princely states of India. The Nizams (princes) were Muslim rulers of the state, which included the country's principal alluvial diamond fields and the old fort of Golconda within its boundaries. It is perhaps hardly surprising that a diamond emanating from this region should bear the name 'Nizam'. The diamond so named is a stone shrouded in mystery, about which little appears to be known for sure; the one fact upon which all seem to agree is that the Nizam is only a partially cut diamond.

In his *Famous Diamonds of the World*, the distinguished American gemmologist Robert M. Shipley, the founder of the Gemological Institute of America, cites a meeting of the Asiatic Society held in 1847, at which Henry Piddington, a geologist and curator of the Museum of Geology at Calcutta, presented a model of an unusual stone together with some notes of a Captain Fitzgerald of the Bengal Artillery, attached to the Nizam's service. Captain Fitzgerald wrote:

About 12 years ago a large diamond was found in the Nizam's country... The model now shown is of a part only, a piece having been chipped off, which after passing through many hands was purchased by a native banker for 70,000 rupees. The larger piece, as represented by the model, is in the possession of his highness the Nizam.

Piddington estimated the weight of the diamond at '1,108 grains... equal to 277 carats of weight of the rough diamond. We shall then have 155¾ carats if it had been cut and polished entire...' Shipley has pointed out that Piddington's estimated weight is at variance with the model shown in his accompanying sketch. Another drawing of the same diamond, which shows a gemstone of a more sophisticated cut and is hard to reconcile with Piddington's sketch, appears in the second part of the Duke of Brunswick's 1860 catalogue. In this section, devoted to the celebrated diamonds extant at the time, the diamond is called 'L'Indien' and labelled as No. 1. The entry refers to: 'Un brillant, forme pendeloque, pesant 250 carats, se trouve aux Grandes-Indes, dans les mains d'un prince: valeur 12,500,000 fr.'

The most recent confirmation that the Nizam remains only semi-cut comes from an interview which Herbert L. Matthews, a well-known American newspaperman, had with the seventh Nizam, Sir Mir Osman Ali Khan Bahadur, in 1934. The Nizam stated that when he was a small boy the largest uncut diamond in the world was used as a paperweight on his father's desk. After the Nizam's death in 1967, the bulk of his jewels were placed in a bank vault and finally purchased by the Indian government in 1995. Today they are held in New Delhi and presumably the Nizam diamond remains among them, although there has never been confirmation of this.

Orlov

Legend, fact, supposition and theory – each must be accorded its place in any historical account of this celebrated diamond. Nowadays the Orlov is one of the most important items in one of the world's greatest collections of gems and jewellery, the Treasures of the Diamond Fund, Gokran, which is displayed within the buildings of the Kremlin in Moscow. The Diamond Fund, Gokran, comprises many of the historical jewels that were amassed by the rulers of Russia before the 1917 Revolution, as well as some of the exceptional diamonds unearthed during the past three decades that testify to Russia's current position as a leading world diamond producer.

The Orlov is mounted in the Imperial Sceptre, made during the reign of Catherine the Great (1762–96). Its weight has been recorded as 189.6 metric carats and it measures 47.6 mm in height, 31.75 mm in width and 34.92 mm in length. The clarity is typical of the finest Indian diamonds and its colour possesses a slightly bluish-green tint. The shape of the diamond has been described as resembling half of a pigeon's egg and its upper surface is marked by concentrated rows of triangular facets with corresponding four-sided facets appearing on the lower surface. The total number of facets is roughly 180. On one side of the diamond there exists a slight indentation.

The unusual shape of the Orlov, the pattern of its facets and the presence of this blemish intriguingly suggest that this diamond can be identified with a long-lost legendary stone.

Among the first Europeans who were permitted to examine the gems possessed by the Mogul rulers of India was Jean Baptiste Tavernier, who provided illustrations of several stones he had seen in his work *Six Voyages of Jean Baptiste Tavernier.*

Tavernier's drawing of the diamond which has come to be known as the Great Mogul is of particular interest and importance, because it is the only one of this legendary stone known to have survived. According to all the available accounts of its history the Great Mogul was found about the middle of the seventeenth century in the Kollur diamond deposits situated by the Kistna (or Krishna) river in Hyderabad, and weighed no less than 787½ carats. In due course it found its way into the Mogul treasury and was shown to Tavernier by Aurangzeb (1658–1707), the third son of Shah Jahan, who had successfully fought off the challenge of his three brothers and usurped his father's throne. The cutting of the Great Mogul was entrusted to an Italian, Hortensio Borgio, who reduced the weight of the stone to 279⁹/₁₆ carats. The results of the efforts of the cutter, however, so displeased Aurangzeb that instead of rewarding him for his services, he fined him 10,000 rupees – and would have extracted more had the wretched man possessed it. Tavernier makes several references to the Great Mogul, which are included under that entry.

It is clear that the Great Mogul was the leviathan of all the old Indian diamonds and that it was appreciated as such. But the mystery remains: what fate could have befallen such a great gem of which all trace appears to have been lost? Some have suggested that it was cut into several smaller gems. Others have suggested that it does exist today in the guise of another diamond, and the names of three in particular have been put forward: the Darya-i Nur, the Koh-i-noor and the Orlov.

The contents of the Iranian Treasury were opened up in the 1960s for examination and cataloguing by three Canadian experts. Their researches demonstrated that the Darya-i Nur, the most important gem in the whole collection, bears no resemblance whatsoever to the Great Mogul. The Darya-i Nur is light pink in colour, while its flat oblong shape has been demonstrably proved by

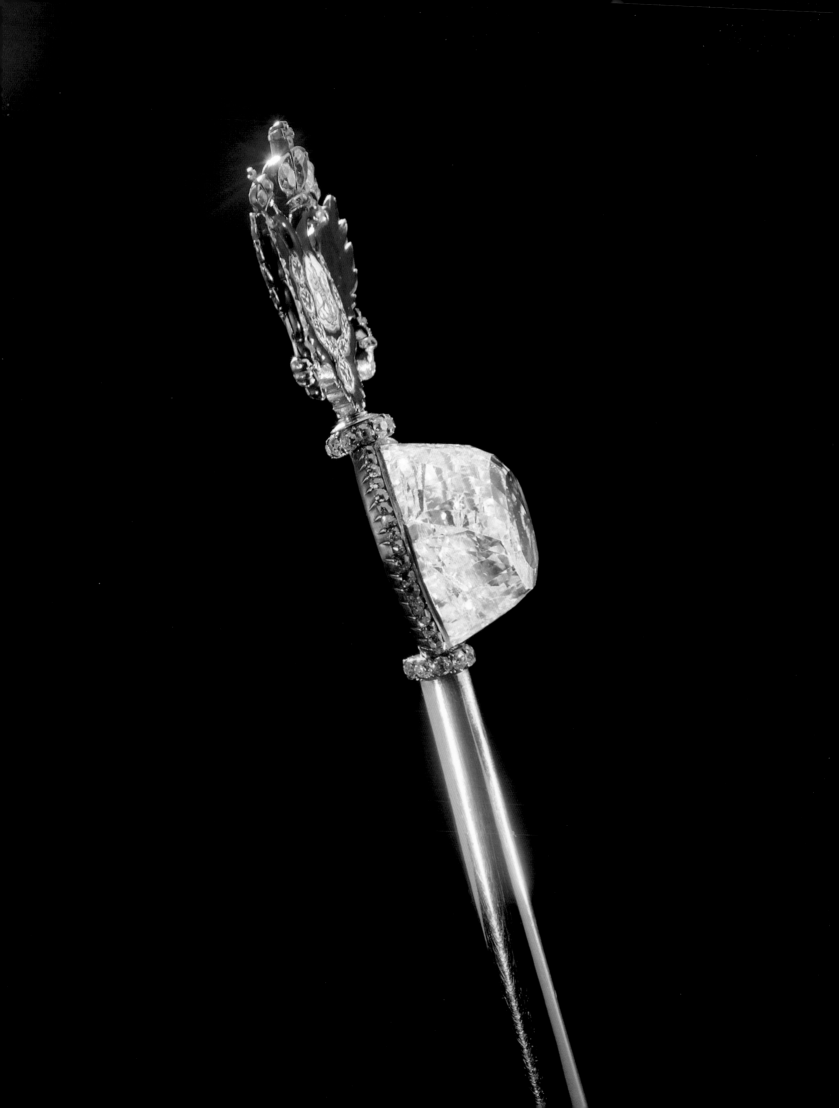

the Canadians to have been fashioned from the so-called Great Table diamond which figured as No. 3 in one of Tavernier's sets of drawings.

The evidence for identifying the Koh-i-noor with the Great Mogul is stronger. When that diamond was brought to England in 1850, drawings were made which showed that its diameter approximated to that of the Great Mogul. The gem was considerably flatter but it showed the surfaces whence portions had been removed by cleavage. On the other hand, some authorities have always maintained that the existence of the Koh-i-noor had been known long before the advent of the Great Mogul and have identified it as the great diamond owned by Babur (1483–1530), the first of the Mogul dynasty. Babur reigned about a century and a half before Aurangzeb. It is unlikely that anyone will ever know for certain one way or the other the truth about the earliest history of the Koh-i-noor.

There remains the Orlov. When a comparison is made between Tavernier's drawing of the Great Mogul and photographs of the diamond in the Kremlin, it immediately becomes apparent that there are similarities. The first lies in the shape. It will be recalled that the Orlov has been described as resembling half of a pigeon's egg and that Tavernier referred to the Great Mogul as presenting 'the form of an egg cut in half'. Throughout history there cannot have been many diamonds of such an unusual form. Secondly, the pattern of facets of the two stones is not dissimilar. Thirdly, the previously mentioned slight indentation that exists in the Orlov must correspond to Tavernier's note to the effect that 'there is a slight crack and a little flaw in it'. In addition, as will shortly be shown, the story of the Great Mogul would appear to have no known ending while that of the Orlov has no clear beginning – further historical evidence that they are probably one and the same diamond.

On the other hand, there is the discrepancy between the weights of the two stones. After being cut by the Venetian, Borgio, the Great Mogul's weight was reduced to around 280 carats, whereas the Orlov is estimated to be less than 200 carats. In this connection two points must be made. First, it has been shown by others that Tavernier may not always have recorded with accuracy the weights of the various stones he examined; for example, it is almost certain that he erred in the weight he gave for the Great Table diamond. Secondly, it is not at all unlikely that at some point in its complicated history a further attempt may have been made to alter the state of the Orlov – to improve upon the efforts of Hortensio Borgio, by grinding away a portion of the top of Tavernier's diamond to resemble the shape of the Orlov today.

Finally, the noted Soviet authority on gems, Academician Alexander E. Fersman, who examined all the former Crown Jewels from a gemmological point of view, was in no doubt that the Orlov was the same diamond as the Great Mogul.

According to one account, the earliest known fact about the Orlov is that it was set as one of the eyes of an idol in a sacred temple in the south of India. This temple is stated to have been situated at a site alternatively spelled by past authors as 'Srirangen', 'Sherigan', 'Scheringham' and 'Sheringham'. But its true location is Srirangam, a town in the Tiruchirapalli (Trichinopoly) district of Madras which stands on an island formed by the tranching of the Cauvery river, about 3.2 km north of Tiruchirapalli city. The island, measuring 27 km long and 1.5 to 2 km wide, was strategically

Catherine the Great, who had the Orlov set at the top of the Imperial Sceptre designed by Troitnoki. Portrait by Fjodor Stepanowitsch, 1763.

Moscow, Tretyakov Gallery. Photo AKG London.

Opposite: The Orlov set in the Imperial Sceptre.

Photo © Nikolai Rachmaninov.

important as a base during the struggle between the English and French forces for Trichinopoly in the eighteenth century.

The great temple at Srirangam, dating from the seventeenth century, is dedicated to Vishnu and is regarded as one of the most sacred shrines of southern India. It is composed of seven rectangular enclosures, one within another, the outermost having a perimeter exceeding 11.25 km in length. A remarkable feature is the Hall of a Thousand Pillars, with its colonnade of rearing horses.

A French soldier, who deserted and found employment in the neighbourhood of Srirangam, learnt that the temple contained a celebrated idol of a Hindu god, the eyes of which were formed by two large diamonds of inestimable value. Thereupon he made a plan to seize these gems, a feat which necessitated years rather than months of planning, since no Christian was ever admitted beyond the fourth of the seven enclosures. So in order to effect his evil purpose, he embraced the Hindu faith and eventually obtained employment within the walls of the temple. By degrees he gained the confidence of the unsuspecting Brahmins and was allowed in as a frequent worshipper at the inner shrine, because of his apparent veneration for this particular divinity. Ultimately, he secured the appointment of guardian to the innermost shrine within which lay the object of his attention.

Then came the moment for which the Frenchman had waited so long, a stormy night that masked the idol in fitful shadows. He laid his sacrilegious hands upon the deity entrusted to his care and prized one of the diamond eyes out of its socket. Losing courage, he then fled from the scene leaving the other diamond behind. He scaled the walls of the temple, swam the river and escaped through the surrounding jungle to the comparative safety of the English army encamped at Trichinopoly, and all the while the tempest raged. Finally, he made his way to Madras where he sold the diamond for £2,000 to an English sea captain who brought it to London and sold it to a Jewish merchant for £12,000. The merchant, in turn, is said to have sold it to an Armenian by the name of Khojeh Raphael, who had left Persia as a young man, sailed to Surat and then travelled eastwards towards Bengal. After residing there, he travelled by sea to England and then to Russia, passing through Amsterdam. Apparently, his travels had taken him to most European countries before he decided to settle as a merchant in the Italian port of Leghorn. According to a Persian traveller, Khojeh was 'a complete old scoundrel, who had seen a great deal of the world and understood a number of languages'.

This colourful account of the Orlov cannot be relied upon as authoritative. The real point of interest concerns the identity of the second diamond set in the idol. Which diamond could possibly have been set as an eye? The candidates are few, with the Koh-i-noor foremost among them, but we know that this historic gem had been taken from Delhi in 1739 by the Persian Nadir Shah. Perhaps the second eye of the idol was filled by some other precious stone – or had the idol itself at some time suffered the fate of Nelson at Calvi?

Another version of the Orlov's journey to Europe is even more lurid. This account begins with the diamond belonging to the Mogul rulers and being amongst the loot carried off from Delhi by the Persians under Nadir Shah. Shortly after Nadir Shah had been murdered in 1747, an Afghan soldier, formerly in his service, appeared in Bassorah, a large town situated on the Shatt-el-Arab, some 112 km north of the Persian Gulf. The original city of Bassorah, of *Thousand and One Nights* fame, was founded by Caliph Omar I in AD 636, some 13 km from the modern city of Basra, which, like its predecessor, is an important port and trading centre for produce from the east.

As well as the diamond, the Afghan brought with him many other expensive jewels, all of which he offered to an Armenian merchant called Grigori Safras, then residing with his two brothers in Bassorah. Safras was astonished at such a valuable hoard in the hands of a poor soldier who was obviously unaware of its true value. He was obliged to postpone the chance of doing business with the soldier in order to find sufficient funds. In the meantime, the Afghan became suspicious of the merchant's delay and, believing that a trap was being laid for him, disappeared from the city as mysteriously as he had entered.

The soldier made his way to Baghdad where he met a Jewish trader to whom he sold his treasure for 65,000 piastres (then about £500) and two fine Arab horses. But instead of returning home, he proceeded to squander his newly acquired riches in a bout of dissipation. Unfortunately, in the middle of his revels he met up again with Safras who this time determined not to lose sight of his man. Disappointed to learn that the Afghan had sold his treasure, however, he was able to learn from the soldier the whereabouts of the trader's residence, and lost no time in calling on him. Safras offered the merchant twice the amount he had paid for the diamond but the trader was unwilling to part with it. Thereupon Safras consulted his two brothers who by now had joined him in Baghdad; they decided to acquire the diamond by foul means. Having successfully accomplished this, it became obvious that the Afghan would also need to be disposed of, because his evidence would incriminate the brothers. So, taking advantage of his liking for riotous living, they induced him to join them the next day in a bout of drinking during the course of which they administered poison. The bodies of the Jewish trader and the Afghan soldier were placed together in a sack and thrown by night into the River Tigris.

The slaughter had not yet finished. Events had run smoothly for the murderers up to that point, but when it came to the distribution of the plunder each of the three brothers insisted on having the diamond. As it was impossible to divide the gem into three equal parts, and as neither of his brothers was prepared to waive his claim, the wily Safras treated them in exactly the same way that they had treated their unfortunate victims. So Safras perpetrated a double fratricide and another sack was dumped in the Tigris. After such a spate of killings, the Armenian wisely considered it prudent to move on; accordingly he made his way to Constantinople, then through Hungary and Silesia, before arriving in Amsterdam. Here he set himself up as a dealer in precious stones. One can only hope that it was the city's pre-eminence as a trading centre that attracted him, rather than its aqueous situation.

Now according to Edwin Streeter's book *The Great Diamonds of the World*, this second version of the history of the Orlov diamond does not refer to the Orlov at all but to a totally different diamond called the 'Moon of Mountains', which weighed 120 carats. However, no trace exists of such a diamond today, least of all in the Kremlin Diamond Fund. In addition the Russian authorities have brought to light records which indicate that around 1768 their great diamond had indeed passed into the hands of an individual by the name of Safras. Moreover they have also referred to the city of Astrakhan in their account of the Orlov, a reference which is possibly explained by Streeter.

He states that after setting up in Amsterdam as a dealer, Safras drew the attention of certain European rulers, among them Catherine the Great of Russia, to his jewels. The Empress was apparently much taken by the description of the Armenian's great diamond and invited Safras to her capital, St Petersburg, where she put him in touch with the Court jeweller, I. L. Lazarev. Negotiations broke down over an agreed price for the gem, the amount requested by Safras being considered exorbitant. However, Count Panin, the favourite minister of the Empress at the time, proved equal to the occasion and ultimately showed himself to be more than a match for the astute Armenian. The demands of Safras were neither agreed to nor rejected; instead he was gradually led into a style of living which proved beyond his means, with the result that he ran heavily into debt. When his means were exhausted, Panin abruptly terminated the negotiations and informed Safras that he could not leave Russia, or even St Petersburg, until all his creditors had been paid. Safras was thus at the mercy of the minister; nevertheless he was determined not to sacrifice his diamond and he succeeded in raising enough money to settle his outstanding debts by selling other gems among the Armenian community in St Petersburg. Thereupon he withdrew from the Russian capital.

A few years later the Russian Court learned that Safras was residing in Astrakhan and negotiations were reopened for the sale of the diamond, which he was induced to part with, apparently on the original terms. However, at this point in the diamond's history there is yet more confusion. It has always been thought that the diamond's much travelled purchaser bought the gem in Amsterdam; there were reports in the London press to that effect.

So the conclusion to be drawn is that the business was not successfully completed in Astrakhan – Count Orlov had to travel to Amsterdam to finalize the arrangements. By this time the gem had become known as the Amsterdam diamond.

Count Grigori Grigorievich Orlov (1723–83) was a Russian nobleman and an army officer of great distinction. He was wounded no less than three times during the various campaigns of the Seven Years War. On one occasion he was detailed to escort an important Prussian officer as a prisoner-of-war to St Petersburg where in 1759 he was presented to the Grand Duke Peter and his consort, Catherine. Leading a riotous life in the capital, he caught the fancy of the Grand Duchess and became her lover. After the accession of Catherine's husband to the throne as Peter III, Orlov and his

younger brother, Count Aleksei Grigorievich, organized the coup of July 1762 whereby the weak Peter III was dethroned in favour of Catherine and then murdered.

Catherine appointed her lover adjutant-general, director-general of engineers and general-in-chief, but Count Panin, who was then her political mentor, frustrated the intention of the Empress to marry Orlov. Continuing to serve Catherine in various official capacities, Orlov became deeply resentful when she took Aleksander Vassilchikov, then Grigori Potemkin, as lovers in his place. He left Russia in 1775.

Two years earlier Orlov had visited Amsterdam, where he came to learn of the existence of Safras' great diamond. He bought it for a sum reputed to have been 1,400,000 florins, equivalent to 400,000 roubles. Such a purchase, doubtless, would have been made both to remind Catherine of the role which Orlov had played in her accession to the throne and hopefully to restore himself to his former position as her favourite. This possibility appeared even stronger at the time, because Catherine herself had refused to accept Safras' original asking price for the diamond. Orlov presented the diamond to the Empress on her Saint's Day; she accepted it and had it set in the Imperial Sceptre, designed by Troitnoki, immediately beneath the golden eagle. The Empress gave Orlov a marble palace at St Petersburg, but she never rewarded him with his former position as her favourite. In 1777 Count Orlov married his cousin, but following her death in Lausanne five years later he became mentally deranged and returned to Russia to die the following year.

Interestingly, there is supposed to exist a document signed by both Orlov and Lazarev, the court jeweller at St Petersburg, which places an entirely different interpretation upon the circumstances surrounding the former's purchase of the diamond. The Russian author suggests that the role of Count Orlov was merely that of a go-between in the transaction and that it was Catherine the Great herself who purchased the diamond. The Empress employed intermediaries for two reasons: first, she wished to contrast her own alleged 'German frugality' (she had been born a German princess) with the reckless spending habits of her predecessors, and secondly, she considered that it would not have been proper for a monarch to bargain over the purchase price – something which Orlov himself could do. And it was for this service to the Empress that Orlov earned the honour of giving his name to the diamond.

There is a legend concerning the diamond, dating from the time of Napoleon. As the Emperor of France's forces were approaching Moscow during the campaign of 1812, the Orlov was secreted in the tomb of a priest in the Kremlin. When Napoleon entered Moscow he gave orders that the gem be sought. After he had learned of its whereabouts, Napoleon in person, accompanied by his body-guards, proceeded to the Kremlin to secure the diamond. The tomb was opened to reveal the great gem. One of the bodyguards stretched out a hand to take the diamond, but before he had touched it the ghost of the priest rose up and cursed the invaders. Napoleon and his bodyguards are then supposed to have fled empty-handed from the Kremlin. Now, on almost all counts this would appear to be nothing more than a legend, but it adds yet one more detail to this already complex and most colourful story.

Count Grigori Grigorievich Orlov, one of Catherine the Great's greatest allies and her lover, after whom the diamond is named.

Penthièvre

This fine quality, yellow oval-cut diamond, weighing 10 carats, is named after Louis-Jean-Marie de Bourbon, Duke of Penthièvre (1725–95). Neither the circumstances nor the date of the Duke's acquisition of the gem appear to be known.

Born at Rambouillet, the Duke of Penthièvre was heir to the last of the legitimate sons of Louis XIV. He became Governor of Brittany and his service in the French army saw him fight with great bravery in the battles of Dettingen, Fontenoy and Raucoux. He possessed an immense fortune of which he made generous use and he was the sole prince of his family to remain popular up to the time of his death. This occurred just 36 days before the ruling Convention passed a decree placing all the princes of the Bourbon dynasty under arrest and ordering the sequestration of their property.

The Duke of Penthièvre had six children but only one survived: his daughter Louise-Marie Adelaïde de Bourbon. She married Philippe, Duke of Orleans, who came to be known as 'Egalité', and became the mother – that is if the following account of events is disregarded – of Louis Philippe, the future King of France. The Duke of Orleans adopted the name of 'Egalité' in accordance with his pronounced liberal views, voted for the execution of his kinsman, Louis XVI, in 1793, but went to the scaffold himself later the same year. The marriage between 'Egalité' and the daughter of the Duke of Penthièvre was not a happy one. In the event, the alleged efforts of 'Egalité' to prevent his wife's rich inheritance from reverting to her relations, if she should die early, proved to be responsible for one of the most extraordinary and bizarre episodes ever to have taken place within the confines of a prominent European royal family.

The story centred on Maria Stella Petronilla who, in October 1786, became the second wife of the first Lord Newborough. After his death she married another nobleman, Baron Angern-Sternberg, before dying in Paris in 1843 in obscurity and poverty. One day in 1821 she received the following letter:

Miladi:

The day on which you were born to a person, whom I cannot name, and who is dead, a son was born to me. I was requested to make an exchange of children, and in the then state of my finances, I agreed to the profitable proposals that were made to me, and adopted you for my daughter, my son being taken by the other party. Heaven has repaired my fault, since you are in a better position than your real father, although he was of almost similar rank, and this makes me quit life in some peace... I pray you to keep this information concealed, to prevent the world from discussing a matter beyond remedy. This will reach you only after my death.

Lorenzo Chiappini.

Louis-Jean-Marie de Bourbon, Duke of Penthièvre, with his daughter Louise-Marie Adelaïde de Bourbon. Portrait by Jean-Baptiste Carpentier le Vieux.

Versailles and Trianon. Photo © RMN – G. Blot.

201

PENTHIÈVRE

But the world did begin to discuss the matter, while Maria Stella was astounded by the contents of the letter she had received. At once she saw all the difficulties of her early life cleared up, in particular the harsh treatment meted out to her and the difference between her upbringing and that of the other Chiappini children. Furthermore she remembered that when she was beside the dying Chiappini he had uttered three, at that time, incomprehensible final syllables: 'Dio mio. Baranto.' Finally, after she had received the above letter she came to understand the full meaning of the word 'baranto': evidently it was a mispronunciation of 'baratto', meaning in Italian a 'substitution' or 'tricky exchange'.

But if Maria Stella was not a Chiappini then who was she? Henceforth the whole purpose of her life was to resolve this question. After her enquiries and investigation into the affair, Maria Stella contended that:

(1) She was the legitimate daughter and eldest child of the Duke and Duchess of Orleans ('Egalité').

(2) In 1772, 'Egalité' and his wife, at that time the Duke and Duchess of Châtres, were travelling incognito in Italy as Comte and Comtesse of Joinville.

(3) In 1773 at Modigliana, in Tuscany, the so-called Comtesse of Joinville gave birth to a daughter.

(4) A son being greatly desired as an heir, chiefly for pecuniary reasons, his infant daughter was exchanged for a son, born the same day to the wife of one Lorenzo Chiappini, constable of the village of Modigliana. (If the Duke's wife had predeceased him without leaving a son, a large proportion of her great wealth would have reverted to her family into which he had married. 'Egalité' may have had cause to fear that his wife, who was very delicate, might not produce a healthy boy.)

(5) This girl was brought up in the constable's family and passed for his daughter. She was married at Florence, at an early age, to the first Lord Newborough.

(6) The son of Lorenzo Chiappini was, for a monetary consideration, handed over to the Comte de Joinville, otherwise the Duke of Châtres, who ever after fraudulently represented him to be his own child, and that this changeling eventually became Louis Philippe, King of the French.

(7) In person, manner and in the contour of his physiognomy, Louis Philippe resembled an Italian peasant; this characteristic resemblance being strikingly apparent in his dark and coarse skin, very common appearance, and heavy under-bred physique, while Philippe 'Egalité', his reputed father, was, when young, said to have been the most handsome man in France, especially in figure and carriage.

(8) The younger children of Philippe 'Egalité' – the Duke of Montpensier, the Count of Beaujolais and Madame Adelaïde – were handsome, fair and refined and bore no resemblance to his so-called eldest son, Louis Philippe.

(9) Maria Stella's likeness to many members of the House of Orleans, particularly to the children of 'Egalité', excepting Louis Philippe, was most striking, and that in evidence of this she was repeatedly accosted by old domestics of the Orleans family.

(10) She bore no likeness whatever, in form or face, in mind or in character, to the real and undoubted offspring of Chiappini, the village constable, who passed for her father.

The story told by Maria Stella was chiefly based on circumstantial evidence; however, it was admitted at the time that there were numerous statements vaguely recorded by her the truth of which had come to be proved beyond question. This fact supported her argument to some extent. Her first success was the judgement of the episcopal court at Faenza which, in 1824, declared that the Comte de Joinville had exchanged his daughter for Lorenzo Chiappini's son. When Maria Stella published proofs of her identity, in 1830, some people were only too ready to support her claim and use it as a weapon to pour scorn and ridicule upon the 'bourgeois monarch', as they termed the King. The publication coincided with the accession to the French throne of Louis Philippe who, for his part, treated the whole story with amused contempt.

Among those who would never have believed Lady Newborough's story was Queen Victoria. After Louis Philippe had been forced to give up his throne and flee the country, in 1848, he sought refuge in England where a mansion in Surrey was placed at his disposal. Queen Victoria, who came to know the exiled monarch, categorized both his virtues and his failings but of one thing she was certain: he was the epitome of a true Frenchman. Many years after the deaths of the main protagonists in the episode a book was published in Paris in 1907 based on unpublished material in the National Archives. It refuted Maria Stella's claims, dismissed her version of the events and asserted that her real father had been a certain Count Carlo Battaglini of Rimini who had died in 1796. The case had been not so much one of substitution as of 'farming out' so as to avoid a scandal.

While the mystery of Maria Stella, Lady Newborough, may never be solved, the alleged protagonist, Philippe 'Egalité', would have been pleased with the turn of events had he survived the guillotine. His wife's inheritance did not revert to members of her family and at least one item, the Penthièvre diamond, came into the possession of their future daughter-in-law, Queen Marie-Amélie the consort of Louis Philippe. On 25 November 1839, the Crown Jeweller, Constant Bapst, assisted by the Inspector of the Crown Jewels, drew up an inventory of the Queen's jewellery: one of the items was recorded as a 'pin with yellow brilliant in basket mounting, valued at 10,000 francs'.

Queen Marie-Amélie owned an extensive

The yellow oval cut Penthièvre now set in a bandeau with the pink pear-shaped Condé diamond at the centre.

Chantilly, Musée Condé. De Beers Archives.

203

collection of jewels which were valued at 629,000 francs in the 1839 inventory. Together with other valuables belonging to the family of Louis Philippe, they were kept in the Tuileries. In another part of the palace were the Crown Jewels which remained locked in the vaults of the Civil List from 1832 until the end of Louis Philippe's reign. Neither the King nor the Queen made use of them, the former eschewing all forms of ostentation and having no taste for luxury. Moreover, it would have been politically unwise for the monarch to have had anything to do with them. The King's discretion in the matter, however, was not enough to prevent yet further misfortune befalling the jewels in the final months of his reign. In February 1848 a mob besieged the Tuileries – on this occasion in search of wine, not jewels. They succeeded in breaking into the cellars of the Commandant of the National Guard where they eagerly fell upon 10,000 bottles. The next morning twelve corpses, including one of a very beautiful girl of nineteen, were found among a mass of broken bottles and a veritable sea of wine. In the following month an inventory was made and it was

ascertained that three items of jewellery were missing. Despite a widespread search they were never recovered.

The jewellery belonging to members of Louis Philippe's family escaped the misadventure that befell the Crown Jewels so that the next recorded owner of the Penthièvre was the Count of Paris (1838–94), the grandson of the 'bourgeois king'. The gem appeared as a 'pin with daffodil yellow stone known by the name of Penthièvre' among the jewels which he bequeathed to his own son, the Duke of Orleans. Then, at some point, the Duke of Orleans sold the diamond to his great-uncle, the Duke of Aumale, the fifth son of King Louis Philippe. This royal personage inherited the fortune of the Condé family, which included the famous pink Condé diamond. In 1886, the Duke of Aumale bequeathed his entire fortune, including both the Condé and the Penthièvre diamonds to L'Institut de France, as well as the park and Château de Chantilly, now an important museum.

Today the Penthièvre is retained by the Musée Condé in Chantilly, outside Paris, and is set in a large oval-shaped motif on a flat bandeau.

204 Louis-Philippe, King of France, whose wife Marie-Amélie, owned the Penthièvre. Wearing general's uniform, his hand is placed on the *Charte* of 1830.

Painting by Gérard Baron François. Versailles and Trianon. Photo © RMN – Arnaudet.

Pigot

The name of one of the most controversial figures in the annals of the British administration of India is perpetuated by this diamond. Born in 1719, George Pigot joined the East India Company at the age of seventeen as a writer and was sent out to Madras. In 1755 he was appointed Governor and Commander-in-chief of Madras, becoming responsible for its defence when in the winter of 1758–59 the French forces, led by Lally, besieged the city. Pigot is deemed to have defended the city efficiently if not brilliantly. In 1763 Pigot resigned and returned home. Two years later he entered the House of Commons and remained a Member until his death – despite his service overseas and his elevation to the peerage in 1766. Since he had received an Irish peerage, he was not debarred from membership of the Lower House.

In 1775 Pigot was appointed to a second term as Governor and Commander-in-chief of Madras, but on resuming office immediately found himself at odds with some members of his council. The dispute centred on the contest between the Nawab of Arcot and the Rajah of Tanjore, each member of the council taking a side. The situation deteriorated and matters came to a head in August 1776, when Pigot was arrested by Colonel Stuart, leader of the refractory members of the council, and imprisoned at St Thomas's Mount, nine miles from Madras.

The news of these events caused much discussion in England. At a meeting of the directors of the East India Company in April 1777, it was resolved that the powers assumed by Lord Pigot were 'neither known in the constitution of the Company nor authorized by charter, nor warranted by any orders or instructions of the Court of Directors'. But Pigot's friends successfully resisted the passing of this resolution: instead, they carried two resolutions condemning Pigot's imprisonment and calling for the suspension of those members of the

council who had supported the action. At the same time a resolution was passed which condemned Pigot's conduct in receiving certain trifling presents from the Nawab of Arcot, receipt of which he had openly avowed in a letter to the court of directors. Pigot died in jail in May 1777, his health impaired by his experiences and the climate.

Two years after his death, one of his brothers brought the subject of his deposition before the House of Commons. The Commons supported his case, and recommended the prosecution of Pigot's opponents on the council, then residing in England. They were tried and found guilty of arresting, imprisoning and deposing the Governor: each was fined £1,000, upon payment of which they were discharged.

During his years in India, Pigot obtained at least two diamonds, including the gem which bears his name. Some say that he received them from the Rajah of Tanjore or from the Rajah's mother, but a contemporary of Pigot's remarked, 'Can it be believed that this great man would betray his trust to the Company for to receive a present from the Rajah of Tanjore? No it cannot!' Others have declared that the diamonds were among the 'trifling presents' which he admitted to receiving from the Nawab of Arcot, the same prince who had given seven diamonds to Queen Charlotte including the two notable pear shapes that have become known as the Arcot diamonds. But, whoever the donor was, the receipt of such gifts was frowned upon by the directors of the East India Company.

Pigot bequeathed his eponymous diamond to his sister and two brothers, but thirteen years after his death, his surviving brother, sister and the widow of his elder brother disposed of the Pigot diamond in a most unusual manner. They promoted a Private Act of Parliament to sell it by lottery. Hansard (the

George Pigot, controversial Governor of Madras, condemned for accepting gifts from the Nawab of Arcot, including the Pigot diamond.

Portrait by George Willinson, 1777. By courtesy of the National Portrait Gallery.

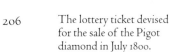

The lottery ticket devised for the sale of the Pigot diamond in July 1800.

Courtesy of Dr Jack Ogden.

official printed record of British parliamentary debates) records as follows:

An Act to enable Sir George Pigot Baronet, Margaret Fisher, and Frances Pigot, to dispose of a certain Diamond therein mentioned, by a lottery.

[20 July 1800.]

Whereas the Right Honourable George Lord Pigot, being possessed, at the time of his Decease, amongst other Things, of a Diamond of very considerable Value, duly made and published his last will and Testament in Writing, bearing Date the Sixteenth Day of April in the Year One thousand seven hundred and seventy five and thereby gave and bequeathed all the Rest, Residue and Remainder of his Personal Estate and Effects (whereof the said Diamond was Part) unto his brothers Sir Robert Pigot Baronet (then Robert Pigot) and Hugh Pigot, late Vice Admiral in His Majesty's Navy, and his sister Margaret Fisher widow, their Executors, Administrators and Assigns, in equal Shares and proportions, Share and Share alike…

And whereas the said Diamond is esteemed by skilful Lapidists to be but little inferior in weight, and equal in Water and Brilliancy, to any known Diamond in Europe; and the value thereof is now estimated at a Sum little short of Thirty thousand Pounds: And whereas the said Diamond has at various times been shown for Sale, but owing to its very great Value, no Individual hath yet been willing to purchase it; whereby the several Persons interested therein have, for a great Number of Years, lost all the Benefit and Advantage which they otherwise would have derived therefrom, had the same been sold and disposed of: And whereas there is not now any Prospect of selling and disposing of the same, to the best Advantage, other than and except by way of Lottery or Chance; in order therefore, that the said Sir George Pigot, Margaret Fisher and Frances Pigot, may be enabled to sell and dispose of the said Diamond, to the best Advantage; May it please your Majesty… that it may be enacted; and be it enacted by the King's Most Excellent Majesty, by and with the Advice and Consent of the Lords Spiritual and Temporal, and Commons, in this present Parliament assembled, and by the Authority of the same…

II. Provided always, and be it enacted, That the Money so to be raised shall not exceed the Sum of Twenty three thousand nine hundred and ninety eight Pounds and Sixteen Shillings upon the Sale of the said Diamond; and that the Number of Tickets shall not in the whole exceed Eleven thousand four hundred and twenty eight, to be numbered respectively from One to Eleven thousand four hundred and twenty eight, both inclusive, at and for the Price of Two Guineas for each ticket.

The winner of the lottery was a consortium whose members had bought a fair number of tickets.

At this point in the diamond's history there are two different versions of what transpired. George Fox, the author of the history of Rundell & Co., the noted firm who were to be appointed Crown Jewellers in 1804, has stated that after a great deal of negotiation the Pigot was sold by the consortium – he refers to it as a 'Club' – to Rundell's and to a Mr Parker of Fleet Street for around £10,000. On the other hand *The Times* recorded its sale by Christie's on 12 May 1802 for 9,500 guineas to Parker. The auctioneer gave a poetical description of the diamond for the occasion and remarked that it was unfortunate for the owners to be selling at a time when prices were so low in a place 'where the charms of the fair needed not such ornaments and whose sparkling eyes outshone all the diamonds of Golconda'. The diamond, however, did become the joint property of Rundell's and Parker and was described in the following glowing terms:

Its form is of a perfect oval about one and a quarter inches [31.75 mm] in length by three-quarters of an inch [19.05mm] broad. The water of it is of the most pure description and there is but only one imperfection in it and that does not interfere in the least with either its colour or brilliancy and must indeed be pointed out before it can be discerned. The defect alluded to is a very small red foul (so called by Jewellers) very near the girdle or edge of the diamond. The weight of this most beautiful Jem is 187½ gr.

The scene now switches to France where, in May 1804, Napoleon Bonaparte was proclaimed Emperor. Napoleon attached great importance to his forthcoming coronation in December of that year; it was arranged that he should be annointed by the Pope before being crowned in the Cathedral of Notre-Dame. Rundell & Co. were also taking a keen interest in the ceremonies, particularly as it was known that Napoleon was buying gemstones for the occasion. So, with the consent of Parker, they decided to send the Pigot to Paris in the strong expectation that they might be able to dispose of it to the new Emperor. But the state in which Europe then found itself – England and France were at war – made it no easy matter for them to accomplish their plans. After much consideration, the firm decided to send the gem over in the custody of one of their employees, Philip Liebart, an accomplished diamond setter who came from Liège, but who had left his native city during the time of the Revolution.

Liebart left for France with the Pigot safely sewn up in the 'waistband of his small clothes' to prevent either its loss or discovery. His route took him via Holland to Liège where some of his family were still living. One of them was his brother, a priest, whom he consulted on the best way to travel to Paris without attracting the attention of Napoleon's ever-active and vigilant police. He managed to arrive there successfully and, in accordance with his instructions, to deposit the diamond with Messrs Lafitte & Co., the eminent bankers, and to deliver his letter of introduction and instruction to those gentlemen. Soon after, the diamond was shown to Napoleon, whose vanity was greatly excited by having it offered to him and who, at first, appeared keen to buy it.

But something must have aroused Napoleon's suspicions: having taken time to consider the subject, he became fully persuaded that the diamond was English property and that it had lately been smuggled into France. He refused to have any more to do with it and the police started to inquire as to how Lafitte's had obtained the stone. The unfortunate Liebart, therefore, had to get out of Paris secretly, leaving the diamond behind. He was obliged to travel by the least public routes so that it was only after much delay and discomfort that he was able to reach his brother in Liège and then with his assistance to pass through Holland, thence to London.

None of the parties in London involved in the abortive transaction blamed Liebart, who indeed had done his utmost for his employers. It was the opinion of some that, had they been endowed with sufficient foresight and forethought, they would never have embarked on such a scheme. In 1804 the diamond left Paris in the custody of Lafitte & Co. and did not return until twelve years later. Apart from the loss of interest in it during this period the diamond became the subject of three Chancery suits, one in England, two in France. The first of them, in London, was Parker versus Rundell & Co., which, after years of litigation, ended by giving Rundell's the entire property of the diamond and in their paying to Parker a sum of money to indemnify his claim for his interest in it.

After the restoration of Louis XVIII to the French throne, Mr J. W. Rundell went to Paris and initiated a lawsuit in the French courts for the recovery of the diamond which Lafitte & Co. had improperly allowed to pass out of their hands. The suit, prosecuted with zeal and ability by Rundell's lawyers, was about to be closed when news came of Napoleon's escape from Elba. Everything in Paris was thrown into turmoil and Rundell was glad to make a hasty retreat from the city, even without the diamond. After the so-called Hundred Days, which culminated in Napoleon's defeat at the decisive battle of Waterloo in June 1815, Rundell again visited Paris, fully expecting to have the Pigot delivered to him without further trouble and expense. In this he was to be disappointed: he was obliged to begin the action for the restoration of the diamond all over again. Finally, after several months' delay, he obtained possession of the stone and returned to London with it at the end of 1816.

Rundell & Bridge, as the firm had now become, made new efforts to sell the Pigot; they tried to interest the Prince Regent, members of the Royal Family and several European monarchs. Models of it were cut in glass and crystal and despatched with suitable letters to many famous and distinguished persons in Europe, Egypt and India.

Below: A model of the missing Pigot diamond.

De Beers Archives

207

A long and protracted correspondence with the Pasha of Egypt, conducted through the firm of Briggs Brothers & Co., of the Minories in the City of London, ultimately brought its reward with the sale of the diamond to that ruler in 1822. He paid £30,000 for it on which Rundell & Bridge agreed a commission of five per cent to Briggs Brothers. During the course of the negotiations, the Pasha showed that he was very keen to obtain the Pigot and he urged every argument he could summon up to induce Rundell & Bridge to accept consignments of corn and cotton in exchange. However, the jewellers had too often experienced the unsatisfactory effects of accepting various commodities in lieu of money and were having nothing of it.

George Fox, in his history of Rundell & Bridge, summed up the firm's experiences with the Pigot diamond as follows:

It had long been the opinion of those best acquainted with the Pigot's history during the time Rundell & Co. had an interest in it that if those gentlemen had made a present of £10,000 at the time they became the purchasers of it instead of having that sum for the diamond, that they would have been considerable gainers in the end notwithstanding they got so large a sum for it from the Pasha. And this appears very probable when the great loss of interest and the enormous expense of the three lawsuits are taken into account, not to say anything about travelling expenses, and the expense of living many months in Paris and leaving out of consideration the anxiety and great loss of time to the partners of the house as well as of many of the persons employed by them whose time would have been more beneficially employed but for their engagements in respect of the Pigot diamond.

Travellers to Egypt who visited the Pasha stated that after he had received the Pigot diamond from England he presented it to the Grand Signor (the Sultan of the Ottoman Empire) to induce him to acknowledge the Pasha's right to be Governor of Egypt. This indicates that the buyer of the stone was Mohammed Ali (1769–1849), Ottoman Viceroy of Egypt from 1805 to 1848 and the founder of the dynasty that ruled Egypt until 1952. His origins are disputed: most have concluded that because of his association with Albanian troops he was Albanian, but according to family tradition, his ancestors were Turks from Anatolia who later settled in Konya. From there his grandfather emigrated to Macedonia where he was born.

When Napoleon landed in Egypt at the head of a French army in 1798, Mohammed Ali accompanied a contingent of Macedonian Albanians that was sent with an Ottoman expeditionary force to resist the invaders. After disembarking at Aboukir they were repelled into the sea and the future Pasha was nearly drowned. He survived the defeat and by 1801 had risen to be one of the two officers commanding the Albanian forces in Egypt. Following the departure of the French, Egypt lapsed into anarchy. By force and intrigue

Mohammed Ali systematically disposed of his rivals for power so that in July 1805 the Sultan bowed to reality by appointing him Viceroy of Egypt. In 1831 Mohammed Ali invaded Syria and declared war on his Imperial master, gaining a succession of victories which demoralized the Ottoman Empire. Ten years later the Sultan granted Mohammed Ali the hereditary rule of Egypt in exchange for his ceding certain territories.

Whether or not it was Mohammed Ali who purchased the Pigot and presented it to the Sultan of Turkey is a question that has been much debated among gem historians. There are those who have maintained that the buyer was another Albanian, just as cunning and ruthless as the ruler of Egypt; this was Ali Pasha (1741–1822), called 'The Lion of Janina', who succeeded eventually in establishing his

authority over large areas of the Ottoman Empire. But if Ali Pasha was the buyer he would not have had long to contemplate the diamond's beauties because Rundell & Bridge only managed to sell it in 1822, the year of Ali's death. Moreover it should be noted that he was never the Pasha of Egypt, the title of the ruler specifically stated by the jewellers as the purchaser of the diamond. But the name of Ali Pasha does feature in the most memorable episode of the Pigot's history.

Ali Pasha followed in his mother's footsteps, becoming a notorious brigand leader. In 1768, he married the daughter of the rich Pasha of Delvino but turned treachery and murder to his own account, in the process neglecting the interests of his father-in-law. He obtained the Pashalik of Janina; then by intriguing with the Greeks and the Albanians he further extended his authority, as well as increasing his own wealth. Although he progressed further up the ladder of power by being appointed Viceroy of Rumelia, Ali Pasha repeatedly failed to carry out the orders of his master, the Sultan: instead he sent him presents and plausible excuses. By 1819 the Sultan, Mahmud II (1808–39), who had decided to centralise the government of

The Battle of Aboukir Bay, 1794, where Mohammed Ali, thought to have been the purchaser of the Pigot diamond, almost drowned.

the Ottoman Empire, considered that the time was ripe for getting rid of Ali Pasha.

An old adversary of Ali Pasha's, Ismail Pasha Bey, was appointed to Janina to remove him, but when he found the task beyond him, Khurshid Ali was chosen to undertake it. There are differing accounts of how Ali Pasha met his end on 5 February 1822, each one more lurid than the last. One has it that he was shot by Khurshid's men at a small island monastery in the lake of Janina. Another states that Ali Pasha was induced by a ruse to admit an emissary from the Sultan whose attendants succeeded in overpowering and killing him. He was decapitated and his head was sent to the Sultan at Constantinople. The best known – and the least plausible, though surely worthy of dramatic adaptation – relates how on his deathbed, after being wounded, he desired that his favourite wife, Vasilika, should be poisoned. Then he gave the Pigot diamond, which he always wore in a green silk purse attached to his girdle, to a certain Captain D'Anglas, with orders that it be crushed to powder in his presence. Vasilika survived, as did the obedient officer, who bitterly regretted his folly; the destroyed diamond haunted his dreams for months afterwards.

Ali Pasha's reputation is colourful and varied. His barbarism and cruelty are said to have surpassed those of Mohammed Ali. He has been described as the most monstrous being that ever walked on earth – his customary methods of achieving his ends having been beheading, impaling and roasting. But in 1809 the poet Byron, who commemorated him in his *Childe Harold's Pilgrimage*, wrote of him:

He said he was certain I was a man of birth, because I had small ears, curling hair and little white hands… He told me to consider him as a father whilst I was in Turkey, and he said he looked on me as his son.

Then in 1822, after Ali Pasha's death, Byron wrote,

I never judge from manners, for once I had my pocket picked by the civillest gentleman I ever met with: and one of the mildest persons I ever saw was Ali Pasha.

It is more than likely that the Pigot found its way to Turkey, whether Mohammed Ali or Ali Pasha was its buyer. If it was Mohammed Ali, we have the reliable statement of Rundell & Bridge to the effect that soon after he bought the stone, he presented it to the Sultan of Turkey. This would undoubtedly have been before 1831, because in that year he sent his army into Syria and declared war against the Sultan. If Ali Pasha had bought the Pigot then it is probable that his Turkish assassins would have been obliged to take the diamond back with them to the Sultan, who undoubtedly would have been aware of the existence of such a renowned gem. The story of

the diamond's destruction must be viewed as not only a historical improbability but also a technical impossibility; although diamonds are brittle and can be damaged, they cannot easily be pulverized. Somehow one doubts that the necessary technical apparatus was available on the island in Janina to have fulfilled the wish of the dying Ali Pasha.

A final question about the Pigot remains: its weight, which has been variously reported as being from 47 to 85⅘ (old) carats. But Fox has stated clearly that it weighed 187½ grains, which is equivalent to 47⅜ (old) or 48.63 (metric) carats, and that was the weight of the diamond given in the notes accompanying the glass models of celebrated diamonds that attracted such interest when displayed in the Great Exhibition of 1851. Perhaps the reports of the stone weighing considerably more derive from rather optimistic models made at the behest of Rundell & Bridge. The mineralogist James Gregory – who was destined to play a notorious role in connection with the early diamond discoveries in South Africa – presented one to the Natural History Museum in London: it is equivalent to a diamond weighing 93.3 carats.

Although the Pigot must for the moment be considered as having vanished, efforts to locate it have continued. In the early 1960s a leading firm of auctioneers heard of the existence in Egypt of a diamond identical in weight to the Pigot, but unfortunately neither its shape nor its colour bore resemblance to it. Then a 49.03-carat pear shape came up for sale in London. It was said to have been sent for sale by a royal personage, rumoured to have ruled over 'a small Adriatic country', so Janina, Ali Pasha's locality, sprang to mind. But once more the shape, colour, and in this instance, the weight could not be reconciled to those of the Pigot. Then a mysterious stone, said to have weighed 49 carats, featured in a court case in London; no other details were made available. Finally, a diamond weighing exactly 48.63 metric carats came up for sale in New York in 1984, but its weight was the sole point of resemblance between it and the missing diamond. Provided that it has not suffered recutting, this gem, which has such a varied and interesting history, may still come to light.

Polar Star

Right: Prince Youssopov, who had helped instigate the murder of Rasputin, fled Russia after the Revolution, taking the Polar Star with him.

Opposite: the Polar Star diamond, last sold at Christie's, Geneva, in 1980.

The Polar Star derives its name from the eight-pointed star cut on its pavilion. A Golconda cushion-shaped diamond, weighing 41.28 metric carats, it has been described as the 'brightest diamond ever seen'. The symmetry of its cutting is so perfect that it can be balanced on its culet.

The history of the gem can be traced back to its ownership by Joseph Bonaparte, the elder brother of Napoleon, who ruled as the king of Naples, then of Spain for a short time. A great lover of gems, he acquired the Polar Star from an unnamed source. After losing both his crown and kingdom he sold the diamond and set sail for America where he spent the remaining years of his life.

At some time the Polar Star was bought by Princess Tatiana Youssoupov (1769–1841), a member of one of the richest and most influential families in Imperial Russia, later related to the Imperial family. The diamond has also been known as the 'Youssoupov'. The Youssoupov family is perhaps best known for its involvement with the strange figure of Rasputin, the Russian courtier and religious figure whose influence at the Russian Court was for a time paramount. Rasputin was credited with alleviating the haemophilia of the young Czarevich, thereby gaining influence over the Empress Alexandra and, through her, the Czar Nicholas II. He further used his influence indiscriminately and, during the First World War, made and unmade cabinet ministers at will: all who opposed him suffered disgrace and banishment.

Alarmed by the harmful effect Rasputin was having upon the Court, Prince Felix Youssoupov and others conspired to kill him. On the night of 29–30 December 1916, the Prince entertained Rasputin to dinner, poisoning his wine. When this attempt failed, the conspirators shot him and threw his body into a tributary of the River Neva.

After the Revolution, Prince Felix Youssoupov

POLAR STAR

fled from Russia, taking the Polar Star with him. In 1925 the jewellery cache of the Youssoupovs in their former palace was discovered. According to reports, the whereabouts of the hiding-place were betrayed to the authorities by the son of the mason who had originally devised it in 1917. Secret passages from the picture gallery led to two underground dungeons which contained a huge collection of jewels and other treasures. However, Prince Felix had by that time succeeded in getting other family jewels out of Russia. These included two other notable diamonds: the Sultan of Morocco, a steel-coloured diamond of 35.67 metric carats said to have been owned by the Youssoupov family since 1840, and the Ram's Head, a light pinkish gem of 17.47 carats.

In 1924 Prince Felix embarked upon a series of negotiations with Cartier's. The Polar Star was lodged, intermittently, with their London branch, before being pledged, along with other family jewels, with the London firm of T. M. Sutton, until Cartier's redeemed it. In 1928 they sold the diamond to Lady Deterding, the wife of the oil magnate Sir Henry Deterding, who was the founder of Royal Dutch Shell. Finally, after her death and acting on the instructions of her executors, Christie's auctioned the Polar Star in Geneva on 20 November 1980. On that occasion a dealer from Sri Lanka paid eight million Swiss Francs (then $5,086,705) for the gem.

The sole contentious point concerning the Polar Star is the date of its acquisition by the Youssoupovs. In 1949 Prince Felix stated that it had been in his family's ownership for a century, a fact corroborated by Dieulafait, who published his *Diamonds and Precious Stones* in 1874.

But Streeter considered this to be a 'curious statement', maintaining that the Polar Star had been purchased in England for the Imperial Regalia of Russia. However, the existence of another oval-cut diamond among the former Russian Crown Jewels is confirmed by Twining in *A History of the Crown Jewels of Europe*. He has listed a fine oval brilliant with a rosy-white or light-pinkish tint weighing $40^{12}/_{32}$ (old) carats; at the same time he points to it being too long in the oval. Now, if the weight of this stone is converted into metric carats, it is less than that of the Polar Star, which certainly cannot be described as being irregular in length – indeed it is beautifully proportioned. It is clear that the diamond described by Twining is the principal stone among the former Crown Jewels that were put up for sale by Christie's in London in 1927. Consequently there are two different diamonds: the declarations of both Prince Felix Youssoupov and Streeter are thereby validated.

Above: the Polar Star showing the eight-pointed star cut on the pavilion.

De Beers Archives

Right: Lady Deterding, wife of the oil magnate Henry Deterding, bought the Polar Star from Cartier in 1928. It remained in her possession until her death.

212

Porter Rhodes

Although mining operations ceased as long ago as August 1914, the famous Kimberley mine, or the 'Big Hole' as it is affectionately known to many, remains a truly awesome sight – the largest hand-excavated hole in the world. No wonder that civil aircraft often make a detour to allow passengers a sight of it. A few statistics will suffice to give some idea of its size: the area at the surface is over 15 hectares; the perimeter 1.6 km; the depth of the mine (underground) 1,100 metres; the ground excavated 25,400,000 tonnes; diamonds produced totalled 14,504,566 carats. Before it was pumped dry, water used to rise at the rate of 76 mm a week.

An examination of the diamonds produced by the Kimberley mine, made in the year of its closure, revealed the following characteristics of its output: fairly considerable quantities of boart and shot boart (a term used in South Africa to describe spheres of translucent diamond of somewhat oily lustre and matted surface, the colour varying from light to dark grey, sometimes with a tinge of pink, sometimes inclining to stone brown); numerous large maccles or twin crystals; diamonds of a peculiar pinkish-brown colour; white octahedral stones; a small percentage of fine white cleavages, and peculiar aggregates of diamond crystals held together by boart.

In comparison with other South African diamond mines, the Kimberley mine produced few very large stones. This can be seen by an examination of the table of large diamonds found in South Africa which appears in *The Genesis of the Diamond*, the monumental work of Alpheus Williams, a former General Manager of De Beers. A gem that figured in Williams's list, however, has come to be regarded as one of the finest ever to have been discovered in South Africa. This was the Porter Rhodes, which was found during the early days of mining at Kimberley. Discovered on

12 February 1880, in the claim of Mr Porter Rhodes, it was a beautiful, colourless octahedron, weighing 153.5 metric carats and valued at £200,000.

Porter Rhodes, who was not related to Cecil Rhodes, later became one of the first directors of De Beers Consolidated Mines; at the second Annual General Meeting of the company in 1890, Julius Wernher was appointed in his place.

Following the discovery of his diamond, Porter Rhodes travelled to London where the gem was exhibited at the Bond Street museum of Edwin Streeter. He sent Streeter a letter containing details of the discovery of the diamond which included the following information.

It transpired that on the day of the discovery Porter Rhodes had been detained by proceedings at the local Magistrates' Court and could not leave until after noon, by which time mining activity had come to a halt for the dinner break. So he went in the direction where he was most likely to meet up with his chief overseer; fortunately he saw him in the street and at a glance was able to tell that something unusual had occurred. In reply to his question, 'Anything good today?' the overseer produced a stone which was so uncommonly white that Porter Rhodes thought someone was playing a joke on him – until he realized it was genuine.

Porter Rhodes had always impressed upon his overseers the need to maintain silence in the event of something unusual turning up. The reason for this lay in the fact that the members of the diamond-dealing community liked to be in the position of knowing that a diamond, or a parcel of diamonds, purchased from the claim-holder had not been shown to anyone else. By these means Porter Rhodes firmly believed that he was able to obtain higher prices. Accordingly, he kept news of the finding of the diamond to himself for four months. Eventually when the news was released and

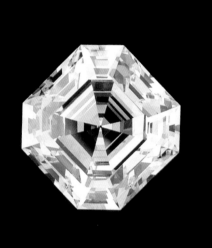

the diamond displayed in an office, it became difficult to restrain the crowd, each of whom was eager to handle the gem. People willingly paid a sovereign to examine it, and within one hour £100 had been taken; in the end almost £500 was donated to the management committee of the local hospital on the diamond fields. Porter Rhodes noticed that most of the dealers kept 'test stones', equivalent to the modern sample parcels, for making colour comparisons of gems offered to them. Many produced such samples, but when placed next to Porter Rhodes' diamond none could compare with it for perfection of colour.

When Porter Rhodes arrived in England, the Colonel in charge of the Crown Jewels made arrangements for him to visit Queen Victoria, then residing at Osborne House in the Isle of Wight, to show her the diamond. On 19 January 1881, Porter Rhodes was presented to the Queen, who was accompanied by her son, Prince Leopold, and her daughter, Princess Beatrice. The Queen immediately recognized the stone's beauty, but asked whether it could really have come from the Cape. Next, Porter Rhodes was taken to Osborne Cottage, then the temporary residence of the Empress Eugénie, to show her the diamond too. In view of her knowledge of diamonds, she cast doubts upon the origin of the diamond, being under the impression that Cape stones were generally yellowish in colour and, therefore, of comparatively little value.

The Porter Rhodes diamond thereby helped to dispel the myth that South African diamonds were inferior in colour to those found in India and Brazil; it also aroused great interest while it was on display in London. In due course, it was fashioned into an old-mine cut without the faintest tinge of blue in it – simply a dead white gem. The original 73-carat diamond was believed to have been sold by the Duke of Westminster and re-cut by the London jewellers Jerwood & Ward to 56.60 carats. Cartier acquired it from the estate of Solly B. Joel and sold it to Sir Ernest Oppenheimer. The Porter Rhodes was then acquired by the Maharajah of Indore, from whom Harry Winston bought it in 1946, and sold it on to an American client. In 1957 Winston repurchased the Porter Rhodes and sold it to another client in Texas. Finally, the gem came up for auction in New York in October 1987 where it was sold by Sotheby's to Laurence Graff, the London jeweller, for $3,800,000.

The Porter Rhodes, a 'D' colour diamond, twice recut and polished, now weighs 54. 99 carats.

Courtesy Laurence Graff.

Portuguese

Peggy Hopkins Joyce, a former Ziegfield Follies Girl, reknowned for collecting diamonds and husbands. She bought the Portuguese in 1928, set in a diamond choker by Black, Starr & Frost.

Photograph by Edward Steichen for the *Vanity Fair* issue of March 1931. © Edward Steichen Estate. Courtesy *Vanity Fair*.

The February 1924 issue of *Vogue* carried an advertisement for the New York jewellers, Black, Starr & Frost, which stated the following: 'Another historic jewel is the Black Starr and Frost diamond. It is a blue diamond, of particular intensity of color, and weighs 127 carats – larger than the Koh-i-noor. More than that it is the largest blue diamond ever discovered. It is absolutely perfect in every way, and it is the largest diamond of any kind which is offered for sale. Price $300,000.'

Although this very fine stone still retains its name, no information has been uncovered to substantiate its ownership by the Portuguese kings; nor is it likely that it originated in Brazil, which supplied most of the Crown Jewels of Portugal. Instead it is easier to believe, as has been asserted, that it was recut to its present shape from a cushion cut that had weighed 150 carats. The rough gem is said to have been unearthed in South Africa in 1910 or 1912. No large diamonds are reported to have been found in 1910 but one large piece weighing 565¾ (old) carats was found in the Jagersfontein mine two years later, which could have been manufactured to produce a polished diamond of 150 carats.

According to Laurence Krashes, author of *Harry Winston, The Ultimate Jeweller*, the New York newspapers of 13 March 1928 reported the sale of this diamond to Peggy Hopkins Joyce, a lady who was renowned for her acquisition of both husbands and jewels. In 1951 Harry Winston bought the Portuguese from her and then frequently displayed it in the United States in his Court of Jewels. In 1957 an international industrialist purchased the diamond from him, but five years later traded it back. In 1965 the Smithsonian Institution in Washington DC acquired the Portuguese from Mr Winston.

The diamond has been described as the 'unknown' among the great collection housed there, an epithet which it does not deserve because it is a very fine gem. Its shape is unusual: it has a nearly octagonal outline, the corners being almost the same length as the sides and ends. Its exact weight is 127.01 metric carats and it measures 32.75 by 29.65 mm and is 16.01 mm deep. In addition to its brilliant colour flashes, the diamond has a slight milky fluorescence that causes it to 'glow', both in daylight and under artificial light.

The Portuguese diamond, which is now considered to be of South African, rather than Brazilian, origin.

Courtesy of the Smithsonian Institution, Washington DC.

PORTUGUESE

Premier Rose

In March 1978 the Premier mine yielded yet another remarkable diamond, a triangular-shaped cleavage of the finest colour, weighing 353.9 carats. Like an earlier gem found at the Premier, the Niarchos, this one too travelled right through the various stages of mining recovery only to emerge at the final one, the grease table in the recovery plant. A spokesman for De Beers stated that the stone had been mined at a depth of 450 metres, thus seemingly discounting any possible connection with the Cullinan diamond, which had been found merely two metres below the surface.

For reasons of security, the news of the finding of the diamond was not released for two months. After it had been disclosed, the Press lost no time in speculating about possible destinations for the eventual polished gem. Prince Rainier of Monaco was obliged to deny reports that he was planning to buy it as a wedding present for his daughter, Princess Caroline, who was shortly to be married; another European royal family was rumoured to be interested; finally Emperor Bokassa of the Central African Empire, who had already spent £20,000,000 on his coronation, was said to have made an offer. In the end the Johannesburg firm, Mouw Diamond Cutting Works, purchased it, naming it after Mrs Rose Mouw. She was renowned for her prowess in marking diamonds, the first process before cleaving or sawing a gem. Mouws then contacted their American partner, William Goldberg, who promptly purchased a

share in the diamond. When he set eyes upon it, Mr Goldberg exclaimed, 'A lot of people are going to be interested – this is an unusually exciting diamond.'

The cutting was carried out in South Africa and produced three gems which became known as members of the Premier Rose family. The largest, which has retained the name Premier Rose, is a pear shape weighing 137.02 carats, cut with 189 facets and measuring approximately 43.40 by 23.20 by 18.93 mm. It was submitted to the Gemological Institute of America for certification where it received a 'D' flawless rating, symbols for the finest qualities of colour and clarity. It was then the largest stone of this calibre to have been certified by the GIA. The weight of the Premier Rose makes it the sixth biggest pear-shaped diamond in existence. The Little Rose is also a pear-shape and weighs 31.48 carats, while the Baby Rose is a brilliant of 2.11 carats. The final polished yield of 48 per cent was a high figure to obtain from what had been considered a very difficult, awkwardly shaped piece of rough.

The William Goldberg Diamond Corporation of New York handled the sale of the gems. The Premier Rose was sold in 1979 to an undisclosed buyer for about $10,000,000; the sale of the two smaller diamonds followed shortly after. Recently, Mr Robert Mouawad has added the Premier Rose to his great collection of important diamonds.

The Premier Rose, sixth largest pear-shaped diamond in the world.

De Beers Archives.

President Vargas

Opposite: the President Vargas, the largest gem diamond ever to be discovered in Brazil.

© 1989 Sotheby's, Inc.

Diamonds have been found in several of Brazil's twenty-seven provinces but Minas Gerais (General Mines) remains the principal source. Gems from the various areas often exhibit their own peculiar characteristics. One unusual deposit exists in the province of Bahia where a species of very tough, generally black, industrial diamond known as *carbonado* is found. In 1905 one such monster known as the 'Sergio' was recovered; it weighed no less than 3,167 carats, thereby surpassing the weight of the great Cullinan diamond.

On 13 August 1938 Terra Magica (Brazil) revealed her greatest gem when a diamond weighing 726.6 carats was picked up in the gravels of the San Antonio River in the Coromandel district of Minas Gerais, an area that was destined to produce several other large stones. Two garimpeiros (diamond diggers or prospectors), Joaquim Venancio Tiago and Manoel Miguel Domingues, were the lucky finders. Yet their good fortune, alas, did not extend very far, because not long after they had sold the diamond to a broker for $56,000, the same man went to the provincial capital, Belo Horizonte, where it was sold for £235,000. The buyer was a merchant named Oswaldo Dantes dos Reis who, in turn, sold the gem to a Dutch syndicate represented by the Dutch Union Bank (Hollandsche Bankunie) of Amsterdam. By then the diamond had been named 'President Vargas' in honour of Getúlio Dornelles Vargas, President of Brazil (1930–45 and 1951–54).

While the stone remained in the bank's safety deposit vault Harry Winston learned of its existence through his brokers in Brazil; they advised him of its rare quality and exceptional size. After negotiations by wire and telephone, Mr Winston left for Brazil only to find upon arrival that the diamond had been sent to Amsterdam. He travelled to London, then on to Amsterdam, where he finally purchased the President Vargas. The diamond was duly shipped to New York by ordinary registered mail at a cost of seventy cents although it had been insured by Lloyds for $750,000.

The President Vargas was a very fine piece of rough – without imperfections and of excellent colour except for a faint yellowish tinge on two of its edges. The only blemish was a slight incipient fracture which suggested that in the process of its recovery some tool, perhaps a pickaxe, had struck the stone. The shape of the diamond was unusual, being somewhat flattened and strangely bearing some resemblance to the outline of Brazil. It showed two faces of the rhombic dodecahedron and a large cleavage face: it measured 71 mm long, 56 mm wide and 22.8 mm thick. Under ultraviolet light the diamond displayed a beautiful bluish-violet fluorescence.

On account of its unusual formation it was decided to cleave the President Vargas. The grain, though visible at the top, suddenly disappeared into the stone and did not meet with any similar graining coming from the opposite direction. Accordingly, a 20-carat piece was sawn from the top before the first cleaving; from this a pear shape, weighing 10.05 carats, was fashioned. After that, the cleaving grain appeared on a 45-degree angle from the sawing plane. A propos the cleaving of the diamond into two pieces, one of 150 carats and the other of 550 carats, Harry Winston was quoted as follows:

My chief cleaver was nervous about breaking up the $700,000 diamond, so I didn't dare tell him in advance when we were going to cut. Then one day I suggested casually that he practise a bit with the steel rod that we use to strike the cleaving wedge. After about twenty minutes, he said the stroke felt just right, so I told him to go ahead. Just as he brought the rod down to strike it was as though an invisible hand had stopped his arm, for the tap he gave the 'Vargas' wouldn't have dented a cream puff. He was the colour of the stone itself and I yelled, 'Hit it!

Hit it!' so he upped again with the rod and came down with the neatest blow I ever saw. The diamond couldn't have fallen apart better and neither could that cleaver. He took one look at the job and passed out cold.

In all, twenty-nine gems were fashioned from the President Vargas, nineteen sizeable and ten smaller ones weighing a total of 411.06 carats. They comprised sixteen emerald cuts, one pear shape, one marquise and among the lesser gems, ten triangles and one baguette.

The name 'President Vargas' has been retained by the largest gem, an emerald-cut weighing 48.26 carats. For a number of years this diamond was owned by Mrs Robert W. Windfohr of Fort Worth, Texas, who purchased it in 1944. In 1958 Harry Winston repurchased and recut it to a flawless 44.17-carat stone, selling it again to an undisclosed buyer

in 1961. The identities of the other buyers are not known, but in 1948 it was reported that the Gaekwar of Baroda had bought one of the Vargas gems.

As a sequel to the discovery of the President Vargas, another large diamond, weighing 460 carats, was found on 8 June 1939, just 2 km from the site of the earlier find. A garimpeiro, Ramiro Martines Lemos, found this large brown diamond, which was happily named the 'Darcy Vargas' after the wife of the President.

In recent years two of the emerald cuts have come up for sale at Sotheby's in New York. In April 1989 President Vargas IV, weighing 28.03 carats, formerly among the jewels of Lydia Morrison, was sold for $781,000, then again in October 1997 for $745,000. President Vargas VI, weighing 25.34 carats, fetched $396,000 in October 1992.

QUEEN OF HOLLAND

Queen of Holland

There are differing opinions concerning the provenance of this 135.92-carat cushion-cut diamond. The Dutch firm F. Friedman & Co. cut it into its present shape in 1904. They owned it for several years, exhibiting it at the 1925 Paris Exhibition of Arts and Industry. The Dutch sovereign from whom the stone takes its name was Queen Wilhelmina, who reigned from 1890 to 1948.

This suggests the possibility that the Queen of Holland was mined in South Africa. Nothing is known of the diamond's earlier history until it arrived in Amsterdam at a time when numerous South African diamonds were finding their way there. Yet there are experts who think that the Queen of Holland is a typical Golconda stone. Although it is a white diamond it does possess a definite blue tint. The Gemological Institute of America had graded it as 'internally flawless' and 'D' colour, and it must be one of the largest of that calibre it has seen.

Whatever the truth may be, the diamond does have an Indian connection. In 1930 it attracted the attention of Shri Kumar Ranjitsinhji, the Maharajah of Nawanagar (1872–1933). He made his name first as a great cricketer then as an enlightened ruler. It was recorded that whenever he batted 'he evoked an atmosphere of magic by the effortless grace and speed with which he scored runs'. After Ranjitsinhji succeeded as Maharajah of Nawanagar in 1906, he became a progressive ruler and statesman. He represented the Indian States at the League of Nations Assembly in 1920 and, ten years later, he attended the first Round Table Conference to consider the constitution of India.

The Maharajah's interest in the Queen of Holland diamond was aroused in 1930. In his book *The Magic of Diamonds* Albert Monnickendam relates how he received a telephone call from the Prince's Court Jeweller asking him to visit the Maharajah at his magnificent house at Staines, outside London. After lunch he accompanied the Maharajah to a large room flooded with north light from a bay window. As well as the Maharajah, his ADC and the Court Jeweller were present:

The reason for my attendance was soon explained. A very important diamond had been offered to Ranji Singh for purchase; and although he was a keen judge himself, and had already consulted several experts, he wished to have a final opinion before making a decision… His Highness asked me to sit near him and to my amazement opened the lid of the box and took out a magnificent diamond of about 130 carats set in a pendant. He placed it in my hands asking, 'What do you think of this?'

On examination I found the stone to be absolutely perfect, of the finest colour and quality. In fact it resembled the famous Regent diamond in every way. Whilst I was examining the diamond, I felt the Maharajah's eyes continually watching me, and when I looked up there was an expression of pleasure and hope on his face. It was obvious that he was greatly fascinated by the stone. When I told him that it was one of the finest diamonds in the world, and that it must be a famous stone, he told me that it came from the Russian crown jewels, but did not mention its name. When I was asked its value I put it at approximately £250,000, though no true market price can be given for such a stone.

The Maharajah of Nawanagar did purchase the Queen of Holland and Cartier set it as the centrepiece of the pendant to the magnificent ceremonial necklace of the Prince. Jacques Cartier, who assembled the necklace, referred to it as 'a really superb realization of a connoisseur's dream.' Cartier eventually bought the diamond from the Maharajah's family and sent it to their London branch in 1960 where it was put on offer. In 1978 Mr William Goldberg of New York purchased the diamond and it was recut, with minor alterations, from 136.25 carats to its present weight. Later that year it was sold for a reputed $7,000,000. The Queen of Holland is now owned by Mr Robert Mouawad.

Opposite: The Queen of Holland, a 'D' colour flawless diamond tinged with blue, suggesting Golconda as its place of origin.

De Beers Archives.

Below: Ranjitsinhji, the Maharaja of Nawanangar, a renowned cricketer and enlightened statesman who, fascinated by this diamond, purchased it in 1930.

Red Cross

The Red Cross diamond which was presented as a gift to the art sale held by Christie's on behalf of the British Red Cross Society.

This canary-coloured square diamond weighs 205.07 (metric) carats. It is said to have weighed 375 carats in the rough and to have come from one of the Kimberley mines in 1901. The largest rough found that year weighed only 307 carats, but two more, weighing 337½ and 363 carats, had been discovered at the De Beers mine in 1899. Whichever may be incorrect – the date of discovery or the rough weight – there is no doubting the fact that the Red Cross is a typical South African diamond.

The original syndicate of dealing firms who bought the output of De Beers presented the diamond as a gift to the art sale held in London by Christie's in April 1918, on behalf of the British Red Cross Society and the Order of St John. The gem had been cut in Amsterdam; *The Times* wrote:

Large and square-shaped, it has been cut with many facets and is of that pale canary yellow colour which is so much sought after by Indian Princes. The play of the stone is very vivid. In artificial light it is much more luminous than a white stone. After exposure to brilliant light it emits the rays it has absorbed, and thus becomes self-luminous in the dark. Another rare feature is that a Maltese Cross is distinctly visible in the top facet. Hence the double appropriateness of its name, the Red Cross Diamond.

The Red Cross was the highlight of the third day of the sale which brought £35,575 out of the total proceeds of £52,238. It was reported that:

The hope expressed by the auctioneer that this jewel would fetch 'a price worthy of its name' was fulfilled. The first bid was £3000, from which a quick advance was made to £6000. Thence by two hundreds, it was taken to £8000: from that, by two and three hundreds, to £9000; and at £10,000 the diamond was knocked down to S. J. Phillips. On behalf of the anonymous purchaser they state that he is willing to hold the diamond for one month at the purchase price of £10,000, at the disposal of any buyer who will guarantee to hand it back to the British Red Cross Society and the Order of St John to be used as the societies think best for the benefit of their funds.

In due course, it was stated that a member of a European royal family had bought the Red Cross; however, it was an undisclosed American businessman who put it up for sale half a century later. In June 1973 the stone was auctioned in Tokyo, but as the highest bid only reached £820,000 it was withdrawn from sale. The auctioneers had expected it to be sold for £2,000,000. Since then the diamond has 'been around a bit' – that is, most of the diamond trade have been aware that it is on the market and many have viewed it. In November 1973 Christie's put it up for sale in Geneva. It was then deposited in Switzerland before being put up for sale again in 1977. The identity of its present owner remains unknown.

Red Diamond

226

Among diamonds of unusual colour those of a red hue are extremely rare. Edwin Streeter related that he had bought one weighing just a carat, which he subsequently sold for £800. It was known as the 'Halphen Red Diamond', presumably because it was once owned by that prominent nineteenth century dealer in Paris. Streeter adds that a fine red specimen was found in Borneo, but was not of so deep a red as the Halphen diamond. This diamond, weighing 5.05 metric carats, is therefore probably the largest example of its kind.

In 1913 a South African geologist, Dr H. Harger, predicted that rich alluvial deposits awaited discovery in an area of the Western Transvaal. His prophecy was fulfilled in 1926 when he found fifty diamonds in river-gravels on a farm near Lichtenburg.

The result of Harger's find was to cause several of the most spectacular diamond rushes in South Africa, in 1926 and 1927. When so many diggers sought to establish claims on the diggings, such rushes were organized on an official basis; an official appeared, read a proclamation, raised his hand and gave the signal to start. With a roar, the line surged forward: there may not have been any sprinters – sometimes there were men on crutches participating – but within moments the runners had come to a halt and thousands of pegs had been stuck into the ground, each one demonstrating somebody's hope of making a fortune.

The main rush at Lichtenburg took place on 20 August 1926 when 6,000 people (the number may have been as high as 10,000) ran off in response to the starter's signal to peg claims in the alluvial soil. Within 3¼ years Lichtenburg had produced more than £10,000,000 worth of diamonds, which were sold by diggers impervious to the current state of the diamond market. Coming as it did then, the production from the Lichtenburg field contributed hugely to the ensuing weakness and almost collapse

of the diamond trade in the late 1920s. Today a few diggers remain on the site, producing just a handful of diamonds each month.

One unusual gem at least came from Lichtenburg: it was a 35-carat piece of boart. After some haggling over the price, a diamond broker named Houthakker, who was a regular visitor to the diggings, paid £8 per carat for it. Houthakker showed it to Sir Ernest Oppenheimer who, recognizing its unusual qualities, suggested that it might be sent to Amsterdam for cleaving or polishing. So the diamond was sent to the office of the Goudvis brothers in that city. When it arrived and the brothers looked at it, the youngest brother at once said that the broker must have been crazy to have bought such an object. The eldest demurred and suggested they should examine it more closely. 'I see light,' he said, holding the stone up under lamplight.

The firm's master cutter was then called in and after further discussion it was decided to make two windows on each side of the stone: 2 carats were lost but the stone still remained black. Once more the eldest brother maintained he saw light. Windows were then made on all sides of the diamond which by now had been reduced to 23 carats. The gem remained merely brownish. Then the cutter made a sort of crystal shape out of the stone and he too saw a beam of light within. Under a strong lamp a reddish glow could now be seen in the diamond.

After animated discussion concerning the eventual shape of the stone and seven months of studying and polishing it, there emerged an emerald cut weighing 5.05 carats. By now all the brothers had become excited. When the diamond was eventually finished they looked at it by candlelight. Except for the candle the room was totally dark, and in the flicker of its beam it was as if a drop of blood had

RED DIAMOND

fallen upon the hand that held the gem. It was of an extraordinary deep ruby red colour.

There was no dealer in Amsterdam who would make a firm estimate of the diamond's value. The Goudvis brothers themselves thought that it might fetch 100,000 guilders, but Hugo Prins, the famous authority on polished stones, placed its value much higher. So the brothers decided to send the diamond to New York in the custody of the youngest. In New York no one showed any interest, so back it came to Europe. No sooner had it arrived than a cable was received from Tiffany's: 'Have customer for red stone.' Again it crossed the Atlantic to be shown to Tiffany's client who was looking for an expensive present for his fiancée. He offered $100,000. Cables then flashed to and fro: the eldest brother wanted to sell but the others demanded $150,000 — a special price for something extra special. The customer then withdrew his offer and was no longer interested. So once more the diamond made the by-now-familiar crossing.

With the onset of the war the Red Diamond was placed in a safe in the city of Arnhem. In 1944, together with all the other diamonds, it was stolen from the safe and disappeared. Two years later the US army found a parcel which they said contained a lot of diamonds and one ruby in a salt mine in Germany. This solitary 'ruby' was the Red Diamond. Its identification was facilitated because of the certainty that part of the parcel had come directly from the Goudvis brothers. The diamond, in turn, helped to identify many others.

By the end of the War all the Goudvis brothers were dead and, as their heirs owed money to the bank, the diamond was sold by tender for 57,000 guilders. The buyer was the well-known broker, George Prins. In 1968 the Red Diamond was offered for sale and bought by Asscher's Diamant Maatschappij who had tried to buy it many years before. Finally, in 1970, Asscher's sold the diamond to a private collector of fancy-coloured stones.

The spectacular 'diamond rush' in Lichtenburg in 1926, which led to over 6,000 people staking their claims.

De Beers Archives.

RED DIAMOND

Regent

The Regent, bought in 1717
by the Duke of Orleans,
now displayed at the Musée
du Louvre in Paris.

Photo © RMN, Paris.

A few years ago it was rumoured that this beautiful and historic diamond was up for sale. A French journalist, confronted with this news, expressed his utter disbelief at such a possibility, adding that it was tantamount to Great Britain disposing of Cullinan I from among the Crown Jewels. He was wholly justified in drawing such an analogy because the Regent diamond, as well as being the best-loved and most important item in the French Crown Jewels, has played its part in helping to shape the fortunes of France.

The rumour of a sale proved entirely without foundation. It transpired that the diamond had been removed temporarily from its place in the Musée du Louvre in Paris so as to allow certain alterations to be made.

While the history of the Regent is primarily linked with France, it must be remembered that before it became the property of France it had been owned by an Englishman, Thomas Pitt. The gem was, therefore, known for some years as the Pitt diamond and its owner became known as 'Diamond Pitt'. Thomas Pitt (1653–1726) was a British merchant whose persistent involvement in Oriental trade frequently brought him into conflict with the mighty East India Company. Indeed, in 1674 the Company had Pitt arrested and fined. Such an action, however, did not prevent Thomas Pitt's election to Parliament nor his success in procuring a seat for his family through the purchase of the manor of Old Sarum. In 1693 he embarked on another venture in the East; finally, as it was unable to curb his activities, the East India Company made him President of Fort Madras.

During his tenure of office, Pitt became involved in the diamond trade, but complained bitterly to the Company of the limitations that were being placed on him. He entertained hopes of realizing

an income of £3,000 per year from this source, but was disappointed in that respect. Nevertheless, he did manage to acquire the great diamond of 410 carats that was unearthed in the Partial deposits in 1701. Situated on the lower Kistna river, these deposits formed part of what have become known over the years as the Golconda mines, although Golconda itself is the name of a mountain fortress near Hyderabad. It was here that diamonds were traded, giving rise to the term 'Golconda', which is still widely used today for a type of transparent diamond often possessing a bluish tinge.

There are differing accounts of how Pitt obtained his great diamond. One relates how a slave found the diamond and, in order to secure his find, cut a hole in the calf of his leg and concealed it either in the wound itself or in the bandages tied around the injury. Since the diamond weighed over 400 carats, it seems reasonable to suppose that the bandages hid it rather more than the cavity. The slave escaped to sea where he met an English captain and took him into his confidence regarding the diamond. In return for his freedom, which was to be procured by passage to another country, the slave offered the captain a half-share in the value of the diamond. The latter took the slave on board but then, after getting hold of the diamond, murdered the poor wretch and threw his body overboard. Afterwards the captain sold the diamond to Thomas Pitt for £1,000 but, overcome by remorse, he squandered the money and then hanged himself.

It may never be known to what extent the facts contained in this account represent the truth. However, it is known for certain that soon after Pitt had returned to England ugly rumours began to circulate. All suggested that he had obtained the diamond by foul means rather than fair play. It is generally considered that the poet and satirist, Alexander Pope, was alluding to Pitt when he

penned the following lines in his 'Epistle to Bathurst':

> Asleep and naked as an Indian lay,
> An honest factor stole a gem away;
> He pledged it to the Knight, the Knight had wit,
> So kept the diamond, and the rogue was bit.

The stink of dead fish surrounding the diamond reached Pitt while he was visiting Norway. Accordingly, in October 1710, he despatched a letter from Bergen setting forth the true facts concerning its acquisition. Thomas Pitt's family preserved a copy of this document and they arranged for its publication in the *Daily Post* of 3 November 1743, seventeen years after Pitt's death, when once again rumours about the diamond were fuelled by political opponents of his family.

In this account Pitt relates how, soon after his arrival in Madras, he learned of reports concerning the discovery and sale of large diamonds in the country and how, three years later, one of the most eminent Indian diamond merchants named Jamchund appeared with a large stone of 305 mangelins (equivalent to 410 old carats) and a number of smaller ones. After much bargaining they eventually agreed upon a figure of 48,000 pagodas, or a little over £20,000, for its sale. No mention is made in the account of any slave and his accompanying misadventures. On the back of this declaration the following words were written: 'In case of the death of me, Thomas Pitt, I direct that this paper, sealed as it is, be delivered to my son, Robert Pitt.'

Pitt's account of this acquisition of the diamond is said to have been confirmed by a 'Mr Salmon' who was present on the occasion. The name of this gentleman may have been 'Salomon' or 'Salamons'; whereas 'Salmon' is by no means a name often encountered in English, the others frequently occur in Jewish commercial circles. This is substantiated by a book entitled *Diamonds and Coral* by Dr Gedalia Yogev, which constitutes the most exhaustive and enthralling account of the prominent part played by English Jews in international trade during the eighteenth century.

Dr Yogev has disclosed that there were few firms among the Jewish-Portuguese community of London which did not at one time or another become involved in the diamond trade. The East India Company gave permission for a number or Jews to settle at Madras while another succeeded, without the Company's permission, in settling at Golconda. Therefore it comes as no surprise to learn that Thomas Pitt came to rely upon advice from Jewish experts during the course of acquiring his great diamond. Pitt consigned it to London in October 1702, addressed jointly to his son Robert, his chief agent, Sir Stephen Evance, and one of the Jewish merchants, Alvaro da Fonseca. Earlier Pitt

had requested a Dutch Jew, Isaac Abendana at Madras, to make a model of the stone to facilitate its eventual cutting; this was duly sent to London together with Abendana's opinion of the diamond.

The important contribution made by the Jewish community to the trading in diamonds extended to their cutting. Thus Pitt's diamond was duly cut in London by Joseph Cope, who was thought of as the only person in England capable of undertaking the task. Cope, who maintained that he had never seen a model as bad as that made by Isaac Abendana, spent two years cutting the stone, the whole operation costing £5,000. The result was a cushion-shaped brilliant, weighing 140.5 (metric) carats and measuring 25.4 mm in breadth, 25.4 mm in length and 19 mm in thickness, which may lay claim to being considered the most perfectly cut of all the celebrated diamonds of old. The Regent possesses that unique limpidity characteristic of so many of the finest Indian diamonds, together with a beautiful light blue tinge. Contemporaries of the cutter noted the only flaw as being a speck which was invisible in its setting, but later on the French Court Jeweller Bapst stated that there were two almost invisible cracks within the gem. The cleavage and dust resulting from the cutting was valued at between £7,000 and £8,000 and sold to Abraham Nathan. According to Lord Twining's *A History of the Crown Jewels of Europe*, rose-cut diamonds were fashioned from the cleaved material and sold to Peter the Great of Russia.

The possession of the magnificent gem, however, gave Thomas Pitt no peace of mind. Even after he had refuted the calumnies on his name and reputation – a man of merely naked ambition in commerce generally needs to count his enemies simultaneously with his cash – he was constantly haunted by fear of losing or being robbed of the diamond, which had already become famous throughout the West. While he kept possession of the gem, Pitt never spent two nights running under one roof and moved about in disguise, never giving notice of his arrival nor departure from London. Consequently it was not surprising that he endeavoured to sell the diamond. Such a transaction, however, proved to be infinitely more difficult and lengthy than the cutting and polishing of the gem. It proved almost impossible to determine a price because the gem was so much bigger than any customarily on offer at the time. Robert Pitt consulted several experts in Amsterdam, but all to no avail.

In 1712 another merchant, Marcus Moses, travelled to Paris taking with him a model of the cut diamond. Pitt had arranged for Moses to meet Pierre Dulivier, the Governor of Pondicherry, who was then in Paris. Marcus Moses worked in partnership with the banker and goldsmith,

Thomas Pitt, the British merchant and President of Fort Madras whose involvement in the Oriental diamond trade consequently earned him the sobriquet of 'Diamond Pitt'.

Sir Richard Hoare. Sir Richard, as well as dealing in jewellery in France and Germany, also dealt in diamonds; he was the founder of C. Hoare & Co., the oldest private deposit bank in Great Britain.

Pitt continued to try to interest various European royal families in purchasing his diamond, then considered incomparably the finest seen. In October 1714 it was shown to the jewellery-loving Louis XIV of France at Fontainebleau, but even he declined to buy it, presumably because his finances and those of his country were at a low ebb after thirteen years of continual warfare.

But Pitt's chances of selling it improved the following year with the accession of Louis XV to the throne of France. Following the deaths of other male members of the royal family, Louis XV succeeded his great-grandfather Louis XIV as King of France at the tender age of five. Until he attained his legal majority in February 1723, France was governed by Philippe II, Duke of Orleans.

Accordingly, in 1717, a model of Pitt's gem was once again despatched to Paris, on this occasion to John Law, a Scottish banker and financier who from 1716 to 1720 tried unsuccessfully to extricate the French government from its financial difficulties. Law took the model first to the Duke of St Simon, who agreed with him that France ought to possess such a gem. The Regent of France, the Duke of Orleans, was shown the gem but because of the parlous state of the Treasury, he was reluctant to spend a large sum on it. In the end the Duke of Orleans yielded to the combined blandishments of St Simon and Law and consented to the sum of 2,500,000 livres, or £135,000, being spent upon the purchase of the Pitt diamond.

The French Crown Jeweller, Rondé, came to London to take delivery of Pitt's diamond and, accompanied by an escort of Grenadiers, it crossed the Channel to Calais. Its purchase proved popular in France and the name was changed to the 'Regent'. As a first instalment on the payment, Thomas Pitt received £40,000, and the complete transaction restored the fortunes of his family. It is ironic to recall the great part that this same family was destined to play in the wars against France later that century. John Law also profited by the deal to the extent of £5,000; but his fortunes later declined sharply, to the detriment of France, so much so that after his death in Venice in 1729 the *Mercure de France* contained the following epitaph:

> … cet Ecossais célèbre
> Ce calculateur sans égal
> Qui par les règles de l'algèbre
> A mis la France à l'hôpital.

Thanks principally to Louis XIV, the Crown Jewels of France represented the richest collection in Europe early in the eighteenth century. It must have been a dazzling occasion when Louis XV appeared. on 21 March 1721, at a magnificent reception held at Versailles marking the arrival of Turkish ambassadors. The young monarch wore the Regent diamond set in a knot of pearls and diamonds as a shoulder ornament, another famous diamond, the Sancy, in his hat, and a flame-coloured coat with the diamond buttons and buttonholes of his predecessor. The following year he attended a solemn *Te Deum* at Notre Dame, celebrating the conclusion of an alliance between France and Spain, wearing a lilac velvet costume and the same diamond ornaments.

In September 1725 Louis XV married Marie Leszcynska, daughter of the exiled King of Poland. The Crown Jewels were reset for the ceremony: the ornaments formerly worn by the King were broken up and adapted for the Queen as various items of

Charles X, the last Bourbon King of France, whose ostentatious tastes dictated his desire to wear the Regent set in the surmounting fleur-de-lis of his crown at his coronation .

231

jewellery. The Regent shone in a headband. The next Queen of France, Marie Antoinette, consort of Louis XVI, had entirely different tastes in jewellery; she preferred light and delicate settings to heavy ornaments, so that many of the Crown Jewels were reset. They were often reset again and again at the behest of the Queen. The most important change to the Crown Jewels during the reign of Louis XVI was the recutting of a number of large gems in the Low Countries; fortunately, the Regent did not figure among them.

Events moved quickly during the reign of Louis

XVI, culminating in the French Revolution of 1789 and the subsequent imprisonment and execution of the King and Queen in 1793. The Crown Jewels were removed from Versailles to the Garde Meuble in Paris which served both as museum to house the royal treasures and as a furniture store. The guardian of the jewels, Thierry de la Ville-d'Avray, made frequent representations to the authorities concerning the lack of security and, after it was rumoured that there had been a plan to carry them off, a new inventory of the jewels was made in June 1791. The Regent was valued at 12,000,000 francs. Thierry perished in the massacre of 2 September 1792, so that the supervision of the Crown Jewels became the responsibility of a man named Santerre, assisted by two Commissioners of the Commune who were present on the pretext that they were representatives of the interests of the State.

The fears for the safety of the jewels entertained by Thierry proved only too well founded when, on the morning of 17 September 1792, it was discovered that thieves had entered the Garde Meuble during the night and had carried off most of the treasures. Of the great diamonds in the collection – which had included the Sancy, the Mirror of Portugal, the Blue Diamond of the Crown and the Côte de Bretagne as well as the Regent – some disappeared forever. Others only came to light many years later. Fortunately the Regent, which had exceeded all the others in weight and importance, was discovered in a Paris attic a year later.

All the jewellery which had been recovered was placed in the coffers of the Public Treasury, to which were added many items confiscated from private owners. During this period of French history the country was ruled by the Directory, who were faced with the enormous cost of arming and maintaining fourteen armies in the field. It was at this point in its history that the Regent truly became the National Diamond of France, being employed in a number of complicated financial transactions. The most important was the double loan agreement concluded by Parceval, the Adjutant-General in charge of army recruitment; in the first, he pawned the Regent to Treskow, a Berlin banker, for 4,000,000 francs. The diamond was taken to Berlin but was redeemed, and then given to a Dutchman named Vandenberg as a guarantee for a series of loans. Apparently this gentleman lived lavishly in Amsterdam and entertained 'everybody who was anybody' at the time, displaying the diamond prominently in one of his reception rooms. On returning the Regent to the French government, he confessed that it was only a model that had been displayed: the real gem had been constantly worn by his wife round her neck, under her bodice.

When Napoleon Bonaparte came to power in

1799, he and the Minister of Finance redeemed all the diamonds, except the Sancy, in an effort to put the country's finances in order. The Regent certainly played its part in putting the French armies in order and in assisting Bonaparte to win the decisive battle of Marengo in 1800, because the cavalry there had been mounted on horses procured by the Crown Jewels. In 1802 Napoleon ordered the Regent to be set in the hilt of his sword, which he carried at his coronation as Emperor of France two years later.

At the dawn of the Napoleonic era it should be remembered that the man who had led Britain throughout the turbulent years of the French Revolution and was to lead her at the beginning of the Napoleonic Wars was none other than William Pitt the Younger, the great-grandson of Thomas Pitt, the former owner of the Regent.

After Napoleon's exile in 1814 the diamond experienced numerous adventures. Along with other Crown Jewels it was carried off by the Empress Marie-Louise, Napoleon's second wife, first to the Château of Blois, thence to Austria. But her father, the Emperor Francis I, returned the diamond to Louis XVIII of France. On hearing of Napoleon's escape from Elba and landing in France, Louis XVIII fled by night to Ghent, taking many of the Crown Jewels with him. Napoleon gave him a safeguard to leave the country and demanded the jewels back, but they were not returned to him. After Napoleon's defeat at Waterloo and the Second Restoration of the Bourbon dynasty, Louis XVIII ordered a new inventory to be made. His younger brother, who succeeded him as Charles X in 1824, was a lover of ostentation and he decided to revive the coronation ceremony, which was held with great splendour the following May. Charles X wore the Regent set in the surmounting fleur-de-lis of his crown.

The Regent remained in this crown until the advent of the Second Empire. On the occasion of the marriage of Napoleon III to Eugenie on 29 January 1853, the Crown Jewels were dismantled and new ornaments were designed. Two important diadems, the 'Russian' and the 'Greek', were made for the Empress; the latter contained a socket in which the Regent could be inserted when not set in another item of jewellery. A degree of opulence and extravagance returned to the French Court, greatly enhanced by the Crown Jewels worn by the beautiful Empress Eugénie. Some of the jewellery, including the Regent, was displayed to the public at the Paris Exhibition of 1855.

The Second Empire came to an abrupt end in 1870 with the defeat of France in the Franco-Prussian War and the ensuing insurrection in Paris. At the beginning of the Third Republic, a proposal for the sale of the Crown Jewels was laid before the

Opposite: Portrait of Napoleon Bonaparte by Jean-Auguste-Dominique Ingres, 1804. The Regent, set in the hilt of his sword, was carried at his coronation as Emperor of France.

Liège, Musée des Beaux Arts. Photo AKG London.

Commune by a deputy named Benjamin Raspail. Twenty years before, his father had unsuccessfully brought a similar proposal before the National Assembly. But the son finally triumphed, the motion being approved on 20 June 1882; it took a further four years to be passed by the Senate.

The sale of the Crown Jewels of France began in 1887. *The Times* of London reported that 'there are 48 lots but the "Regent" diamond and others of most historical interest are not included in the sale, though their time may perhaps come if this first instalment succeeds'. Whether or not it proved successful – the net proceeds amounted to 6,927,509 francs – considerable relief was expressed by the jewellery trade when it was all over since the announcement of the sale so long before had depressed the market.

The Regent diamond, which according to the valuation of the Crown Jewels represented two thirds of their value, was fortunately not included in the sale. The unique position occupied in French history by this wonderful diamond was recognized: instead it was decided to display it permanently in the Galerie d'Apollon of the Louvre.

The only period during which the Regent has not been on display there occurred during the Second World War when, shortly before the fall of Paris in 1940, the diamond was removed and taken to Chambord, one of the most famous châteaux of the Loire. It remained hidden behind a stone panel, but was eventually returned to its former home in 1945. People queued to take another look at it.

A particularly memorable occasion was the exhibition entitled 'Ten Centuries of French Jewellery' held in the Louvre in May 1962. Not only was the Regent displayed, but also several other famous diamonds, including the Sancy and the Hope, which had last been together in the Garde Meuble on that fateful night in September 1792. Sir Ernest Oppenheimer, when expressing his love of diamonds, once remarked 'diamonds speak to me'. If diamonds were given the gift of speech how revealing it would have been to eavesdrop on a conversation between these three historic gems and to learn the truth about their adventures during the previous two centuries!

Sancy

The Sancy has the most confused history of all the famous diamonds. It is, as Edwin Streeter so aptly described it, 'the very sphinx of diamonds'. At several points in the story, which spans four centuries of European history, there are varying accounts of what may have occurred, while there are at least three diamonds which have borne the name Sancy (four, in fact, if one recalls that some have referred to a diamond called the 'Cent-six' – presumably evidence of faulty dictation or hard hearing). The diamond which has come to be recognized today as the authentic Sancy weighs 55.23 metric carats.

The diamond takes its name from Nicolas Harlay de Sancy, a descendant of the younger branch of the family of Harlay. Born in 1546, he rose to become the Master of Requests to the French Parliament in 1573, a position within the Council of State. Two years later, King Henry III appointed him ambassador to Switzerland. Sancy pursued a versatile career as lawyer, diplomat and, above all, financier. At a time of religious strife within his homeland, it was noted that he had few scruples over this particular subject and that he was prepared to change his religion according to circumstances, a fact which led to the writing of a biting satire entitled *The Confession of M. de Sancy* by the poet Agrippa d'Aubigne.

It is not known for sure when, where or from whom Sancy acquired his diamond. One version has it that he bought the stone from Dom Antonio de Castro, the natural son of the Infante Dom Luis of Portugal who, following the death of the Cardinal King Henry in 1580, had proclaimed himself King. Philip II of Spain refused to recognize Dom Antonio's claim to the throne and despatched an army under the command of the Duke of Alba, which defeated him in 1580 and led to the annexation of Portugal to Spain. The

vanquished Dom Antonio escaped to London with some of the Portuguese Crown Jewels with which he hoped to raise funds, so as to carry on the struggle against his rival. He tried to interest Elizabeth I in the jewels, among which was a large table-cut diamond known as the 'Mirror of Portugal'. There is no record of the Sancy among this collection although, as will be seen later, it was destined to play a part in English history.

A second account of how Sancy obtained his diamond is probably nearer the truth, but at the same time raises several questions. In his invaluable book *The Great Diamonds of the World*, Edwin Streeter tells of a statement made by Robert van Bercken, among others, to the effect that the diamond was brought from the East by M. de Sancy, the French ambassador at the Ottoman Court, after he had purchased it for a large sum in Constantinople about the year 1570. Three pages later, Streeter quotes an extract from Robert van Bercken's book *Merveilles des Indes*, published in 1669, which reads:

There are some [diamonds] of extraordinary size and perfection. The present Queen of England has the one brought by the late M. de Sancy from his embassy in the Levant, which is almond-shaped, cut in facets on both sides, perfectly white and pure, and weighing 100 carats.

There are three errors in van Bercken's account. First, Nicolas de Sancy – who died in 1627 – never held the post of French ambassador to Turkey, although his second son Achille de Sancy did. Secondly, if it is taken to mean that in 1669 the English Queen owned the diamond, then that statement is not true, because by then the Dowager Queen had already pawned it and the reigning Queen never had possession of it. Thirdly, the Sancy diamond known to us today has never approximated to a weight of 100 carats. It is, of course, possible that Achille de Sancy may have owned such a diamond when he returned from his

embassy in 1617 but there is no record of his own interest or involvement in diamonds. On the other hand, it is likely that during his travels in the Far East the elder Sancy may have acquired his eponymous diamond with others in Constantinople since that city served as an important trading centre for produce emanating from countries to to the east.

Robert van Bercken's ancestor was the celebrated cutter Lodewyck van Berquiem who, around the year 1476, is said to have cut three exceptional diamonds for that celebrated warrior Charles the Bold, Duke of Burgundy. Charles was defeated and killed by the Swiss at the battle of Nancy in 1477 and he is said to have lost these three diamonds among all his possessions on the battle field. Some authorities have maintained that the Sancy was one of the three diamonds, but Robert van

Bercken's description of the diamond owned by the Queen of England as almond-shaped and cut in facets on both sides disproves this theory, because that was a shape and cut peculiar to India and then unknown in Europe.

Nicolas de Sancy served two French monarchs loyally, the first being Henry III (1574–89), the third son of the notorious Catherine de Médicis. During the reign of his elder brother, Charles IX, he assisted his mother, the instigator of the holocaust which resulted in the killing of many Huguenots (French Protestants) throughout the kingdom on

the night of 23 to 24 August 1572. This infamous deed has become known as the Massacre of St Bartholomew's Day. The reign of Henry III was characterized principally by his struggle with the Huguenots, while his own indolence, vice and vanity – he became prematurely bald and wore a little turban on his head, his 'toque' as it was called, ornamented in front with a large diamond – contributed to the popularity of Henry of Lorraine, Duke of Guise, who aspired to the throne of France. In 1588 Henry III arranged the murder of the Duke and his brother. By the following year, which witnessed the death of the dominant Catherine de Médicis, many provinces were in rebellion.

In 1589 Henry III was assassinated by a Dominican monk and, as he died childless, the House of Valois which had ruled France since 1328 came to an end. On his deathbed, he nominated as his successor Henry of Navarre, who ascended the throne as Henry IV, the first of the Bourbon dynasty. By the time of the new monarch's accession, Nicolas de Sancy had become Colonel General of the Swiss troops which he had raised for Henry III, and he was able to perform a singular service for his new sovereign by bringing them over to his side. Brought up as a Protestant, Henry IV was obliged to spend several years fighting against the forces of Spain and the Catholic league in order to secure his position on the throne. In July 1593 he became a Catholic and the papal absolution two years later facilitated the conquest of his kingdom which was predominantly Roman Catholic. He expressed the motive behind his conversion in the celebrated remark attributed to him: 'Paris is worth a mass.'

Henry IV sought to pacify domestic disturbances and restore prosperity to France; one of his first acts was to appoint Sancy as his Superintendent of Finance. On numerous occasions Sancy employed his diamond on behalf of his sovereign. In 1593 the gem was pledged to Rodericques, a money-lender, for a third of its value. Next year it passed to a citizen of Lucca from whom Sancy redeemed it in 1595.

By 1596 Sancy found that he was in need of money himself and spent much of the next few years endeavouring to sell the Sancy and the Beau Sancy. On three occasions he despatched either or both to Constantinople without selling them. He also tried to sell them to the Grand Duke of Muscovy but again to no avail. All the time he was trying to interest the Duke of Mantua in the sale. This nobleman lived in great splendour and was a connoisseur of valuable gems. But by January 1604 Sancy had endured enough of the protracted negotiations and gave up. Sancy's own sovereign, Henry IV, had also expressed a wish to buy both gems and had offered 70,000 ecus for them; Sancy found this sum insufficient. He was asking the Duke of Mantua for 140,000 ecus.

Doubtless as a last resort, in March 1604, Sancy sent his brother to England with the large diamond and a model of the smaller one, hoping to interest King James I (1603–25) in them. He would sell or exchange them for smaller diamonds or merchandise. Ultimately it was M. de Montglat, Sancy's cousin and French ambassador in London, who successfully negotiated with the King, and bought the larger diamond for 60,000 ecus, in three instalments.

In the *Inventory of the Jewels in the Tower of London* dated 22 March 1605 appears an item described as:

A greate and ryche jewell of golde called teh 'Myrror of Greate Brytayne' conteyninge one verie fayre table dyamonde, one verie fayre table rubye, twoe other lardge dyamondes cut lozenge wyse, the one of them called the 'Stone of the letter H of Scotlande' garnyshed wyth smalle dyamandes, twoe rounde perles fixed and one fayre dyamonde cutt in fawcettis, bought of Sauncey.

In the same year James I promulgated a decree in which he named the Imperial Crown and a number of royal and princely ornaments, including the Mirror of Great Britain, to be 'indivisible and inseparate, for ever hereafter annexed to the kingdom of this realm'. It represented an attempt to preserve the Crown Jewels for posterity but it proved to be a short-lived move because almost from the start of his reign, his son and successor Charles I (1625–1649) was short of money. In 1625 Charles I disposed of the Mirror of Great Britain but retained the Sancy diamond. The ensuing Civil War between the Royalist forces and those of the Parliamentarians rendered the King's financial position even more desperate. In 1644, his consort, Queen Henrietta Maria, the daughter of Henry IV of France, left for her home country taking with her many of the jewels in the Royal Treasury. Then she negotiated with the Netherlands for the purchase of supplies and ammunitions needed to assist the Royalist cause. Mr Herbert Tillander has suggested that Thomas Cletscher, the Crown Jeweller and Mayor in the Hague, was probably acting as the Queen's agent: he has drawn attention to the sketchbook of Cletscher in which the Sancy is illustrated in three different settings.

Neither the Sancy nor the Mirror of Portugal which the Queen had taken with her were sold in the Netherlands. Instead the Queen contracted loans to a total of 427,566 livres with the Duke of Épernon, and among the jewels which she gave as surety were these two diamonds. As she was unable to repay the loans, the Duke was allowed to retain or sell the diamonds in return for the extinction of 360,000 livres of this debt. Therefore, on 19 May 1657, the Duke of Épernon bought both of these historic stones and discharged the exiled Queen from payment of the rest of the debt which at the time was outstanding. He, in turn, sold the Sancy and the Mirror of Portugal to Cardinal Mazarin.

Cardinal Jules Mazarin was an outstanding figure in seventeenth-century France. Following the death of Cardinal Richelieu in 1642, Mazarin took on the function of First Minister of the Crown, a position which he held until his death. His foreign policy led to the establishment of peace on the basis of French pre-eminence in Europe. He acquired great personal wealth during his ministry and became one of the biggest landowners in France. He was also an important patron of the arts, an avid collector of books, paintings – and diamonds. Before his purchases from the Duke of Épernon, Mazarin had already bought some jewels which had belonged to Charles I and others formerly owned by Queen Christina of Sweden. In his will he bequeathed the Sancy and the Mirror of Portugal to the French Crown, requesting that they be added to the other sixteen which he had also bequeathed to the Crown, and that they should thereafter be known as the 'Mazarin' diamonds.

So the Sancy, which was the largest of the Mazarins, became not only Mazarin I but also a Crown Jewel of France. However, some writers have preferred a different version of how the Sancy came into the royal collection. According to them, Queen Henrietta Maria presented Edward Somerset, third Marquess of Worcester, with some jewels in token of the valuable service which he had rendered to the Royalist cause. In 1682 he was created Duke of Beaufort and remained in exile, refusing to subscribe to the oaths of allegiance to William III. In about 1695 he is said to have sold these jewels, which included the Sancy, to that diamond-loving monarch, King Louis XIV of France, for 625,000 francs. However, this version of events does contain a number of assumptions and unsubstantiated statements, and makes no mention of Cardinal Mazarin's acquisition of the Sancy, a fact which has been well documented. Hence it is the first version which is today considered to be the authentic one.

In the inventory of the Crown Jewels of France made in 1691, the Sancy was valued at 600,000 livres and its weight was recorded as 53¾ (old) carats. Undoubtedly, its most splendid setting was in the great crown made by the Crown Jewellers for the coronation of Louis XV in 1722. This also contained the Regent diamond which henceforth was considered the principal gem in the Crown collection. Louis XV also wore the Sancy in a large agraffe (loop and hook fastening) in his hat, with the Regent set in a knot of pearls and diamonds on a shoulder ornament. His Queen, Marie Leszcynska, also wore the Sancy, set in a pendant to a necklace, at many of the great state

Marie Leszcynska, Queen of France – portrayed here in 1747 by Carle Van Loo – wore the Sancy set in a pendant to a necklace.

Versailles and Trianon. Photo © RMN – G. Blot/ H. Lewandowski.

occasions at which she was obliged to appear.

During the reign of the next king, Louis XVI, the great crowns and other jewels were broken up and the diamonds employed in more delicate ornaments worn by the Queen, Marie Antoinette. In the 1791 inventory of the Crown Jewels, the Sancy was valued at 1,000,000 livres and its weight recorded as 53^{12}/$_{16}$ carats. By this time the French Revolution, culminating in the execution of the King in 1793, had broken out. The ruling authorities employed some of the jewels in financial transactions. A diamond weighing 53¾ carats, which can only have been the Sancy, was pawned to the Marquess of Iranda in Madrid to raise 1,000,000 francs. This Spanish nobleman was one of several persons who supplied horses to the army. Thereafter some authorities have stated that the diamond came into the hands of the widow of Charles IV of Spain who is then said to have given it to her lover, Godoy, known as the 'Prince of Peace'. Godoy is said to have tried to resell the stone to Charles X of France in 1828 through the intermediary of a Paris lawyer, but negotiations broke down.

That same year, Prince Nicholas Demidoff bought the Sancy. The Demidoffs were the owners of large industries and silver mines in Russia – one member of the family married Princess Mathilde, the daughter of Jerome Bonaparte. In 1829 Prince Nicholas died and the Sancy passed to his son Paul who, in 1836, married a Finnish lady by the name of Aurora Stjernvall, a maid of honour at the Russian court. According to the renowned Finnish gemmologist Herbert Tillander, it is customary in the Nordic countries for the bride to receive a 'morning gift' on the morning after the wedding ceremonies. On this occasion the bride was the fortunate recipient of the Sancy diamond. Paul Demidoff died in 1840, and six years later his widow married Andrew Karamsin, a captain of the guards. In 1854 she was widowed once more and finally settled in Helsinki.

While the Sancy was in the ownership of Paul Demidoff, it featured in a famous lawsuit. The Director of the Society of the Mines and Forges of the Grisons, Switzerland, M. Levrat, agreed to buy the diamond for £24,000 but a dispute arose over its value. Levrat maintained that the gem was not worth a third of that sum since it had been recut as a brilliant and its weight greatly reduced. Demidoff accordingly consented to accept 145,800 francs (£5,830) payable in three instalments, at intervals of six months. But Levrat failed to honour the first instalment whereupon Demidoff brought an action against him to have the contract cancelled and recover possession of the diamond which Levrat had by then placed in the hands of the State Pawning Establishment, known as the Mont de Piété. Judgement was given in Demidoff's favour and he was authorized to withdraw the diamond on payment of the customary expenses to the Mont de Piété while Levrat was obliged to pay the legal costs of the action.

The facts surrounding this case are strange. There is no record of the Sancy either having been recut as a brilliant or its weight having been reduced. It is quite possible in the circumstances, therefore, that the litigation may have revolved around a totally different diamond, because confirmation that the Sancy retained the same cut and the same weight is supplied by a drawing which appeared in the issue dated 11 March 1865 of the *Illustrated London News*. Part of the accompanying note read:

The illustration shows the exact shape of the celebrated Sancy diamond which has been purchased for £20,000 by Messrs R. and S. Garrard & Co of the Haymarket for Sir Jamsetjee Jejeebhoy, the great Parsee merchant of Bombay... This diamond is of peculiar form, being neither a brilliant nor a perfect rose cut. It is what is called a briolette – that is, a solid drop; but it differs from a briolette in having flattened tables back and front, a perfect briolette being cut to a point. The facets are very regular and well cut, which leads to the belief that, although the stone retains its original form, the work has been gone over and improved at no very distant date. We are more inclined to this idea from the fact that the stone was said to weigh originally 55 carats, but its weight is now only 53¼ carats.

The weight of the diamond in Paris, which is considered to be the authentic Sancy, is 55.23 metric carats, equivalent to 53⅘ old carats. Over the centuries, there has thus been no diminution in its weight while it still retains the same shape.

The reference above to Sir Jamsetjee Jejeebhoy now inaugurates another chapter in the confused history of the Sancy. In 1867 the stone was exhibited by Bapst, the French jeweller, at the Paris exhibition: it was on offer for 1,000,000 francs. But at this same exhibition the Maharajah of Patiala – a keen collector of diamonds who two decades later was to purchase the great De Beers diamond, exceeding 200 carats – is said to have bought the Sancy. In addition, he is said to have worn the Sancy on his turban with other large diamonds at the Durbar held during the visit to India by the Prince of Wales, afterwards King Edward VII, in 1911. Some have maintained that the Patiala 'Sancy' is the famous historical diamond, but this belief is not held by most individuals who have examined the question.

Recent information which has come to light suggests that the diamond bought by Sir Jamsetjee Jejeebhoy was probably in his family's possession until the late 1880s. In 1889 the Sancy was bought by Lucien Falize, goldsmith, historian, archaeo-logist and painter. Three years later, William Waldorf Astor bought it for his wife. Astor had served a term in the legislature of the State of New York and from 1881 to 1885 had been Minister for the United States in Italy. In 1899 he became a naturalized British citizen and in 1917 was created Viscount Astor. His daughter-in-law achieved fame when, in 1919, she became the first woman to sit as an MP in the House of Commons.

In 1962 the Sancy was exhibited at the Louvre with two other famous diamonds that have featured in French history, the Regent and the Hope, at the exhibition entitled 'Ten Centuries of French Jewellery'. In 1978 the fourth and present Viscount Astor sold the Sancy, reputedly for $1,000,000, to the Banque de France and Musées de France. This famous gem is now on view at the Gallerie d'Apollon in the Musée du Louvre. The belief held by the French authorities that this diamond is the authentic Sancy is shared by the Gemological Institute of America whose officials had earlier stated:

The diamond which is in the possession of Lord Astor weighs 53¾ (old) carats and has dimensions identical with models generally accepted as authentic. The diamond owned by the Indian potentate weights 60.40 carats and, although pear-shaped, actual measurements do not correspond to the accepted ones.

The exact measurements and other details of the Sancy were released in 1976 after the diamond had been examined in London. Mr E. A. Jobbins, formely of the Institute of Geological Sciences, has kindly supplied the following information:

The 'Sancy' diamond is pear-shaped and approximates to a double rose cut, with mostly triangular facets but with a central pentagonal facet on each side, the latter facets roughly parallel to each other. There are slight scratches on one of the pentagonal facets. The maximum dimensions of the stone are 25.7 mm long, 20.6 mm wide and 14.3 mm deep. The weight is 11.046 grams or 55.23 metric carats, and the specific gravity (determined in toluene) is 3.519.

The stone is reasonably clean, apart from a small flaw near the surface (repeated by reflection in the facets). Comparison stones were not available to us and we were, therefore, unable to colour-grade the stone, but the general appearance suggests a good colour. The stone is lively and the fire (dispersion) is well displayed...

The fluorescences of the stone by ultraviolet light are extremely interesting. By short-wave (235.77 mm) UV light, the stone fluoresces a deep yellow, but we saw no phosphorescence on cutting off the radiation. By contrast, under long-wave (365 mm) radiation, the stone fluoresces a pale salmon pink, with a very noticeable greenish-yellow phosphorescence. This behaviour is not common and, in itself, would serve as a good identification test for the stone. We were unable to detect any absorption spectrum when white light was passsed through the stone.

Contact immersion photographs (by exposing photographic paper upon which the stone rests in water to short UV light) reveal that the stone is transparent to this radiation (235.7 mm) and would appear, therefore, to be a Type II diamond, as are many other large diamonds.

Although we may remain in the dark about much of its past history, the 'sphinx of diamonds' has given up the secrets of its physical aspect.

Below: Lady Astor, who received the Sancy from her husband in 1922 and wore it in a tiara for State occasions.

Hulton Getty Picture Collection.

239

Shah

Right: Czar Nicholas I Pawlowitsch, who received the Shah from the Persian ruler Fath Ali Shah. Portrait by Franz Krueger, 1840.

Sammlung E. Werner Johanniter Ordeus, Berlin. Photo AKG London.

Opposite page: the Shah, one of the few existing historic diamonds with an engraved inscription to have remained partially uncut.

Photo © Nikolai Rachmaninov.

Below: the unfortunate Russian diplomat and dramatist, Alexander Griboedov, murdered whilst Minister of Persia. The Shah diamond was subsequently offered to Czar Nicholas I as a token of grief by Fath Ali Shah.

This historic gem is not a cut diamond: it has been partly polished from its original weight of 95 carats to its present one of 88.7 metric carats. The Shah is light yellowish in colour but possesses the limpidity characteristic of so many fine Indian diamonds. The stone has variously been described as a table cut, a portrait stone or bar-shaped; it has three cleavage faces and one that has been facetted. It represents, therefore, an early form, albeit somewhat primitive to our modern taste, of the art of diamond cutting that was practised in the East centuries ago.

However, the Shah is of exceptional interest for a different reason. The diamond's three cleavage faces are beautifully engraved with the names of three rulers who once owned it. As such the gem is one or the few diamonds still in existence having engraved inscriptions, other notable ones being the Jahangir and the Darya-i Nur.

The three inscriptions tell us something about the history of the Shah. The first date is that of the year 1000 in the Muslim calendar, which corresponds to our 1591, and refers to Burhan II, the ruler of Ahmadnagar. This old kingdom, situated in the north-west Deccan of India between Gujarat and Bijapur, fell to the Mogul Emperor Shah Jahan in 1636.

The second inscription reads 'Son of Jahangir Shah. Jahan Shah 1051', corresponding to 1641. Shah Jahan (1628–58) was, of course, the ruler who built the Taj Mahal at Agra. After many disputes he was succeeded by Aurangzeb (1658–1707), the third of his four sons, into whose hands the diamond passed. The famous French traveller and connoisseur of gems Jean Baptiste Tavernier visited the Emperor's court in 1665 and described the scene as follows: 'On the side of the throne which is opposite the Court, there is to be seen a jewel consisting of a diamond of about 80 to 90 carats weight, with rubies and emeralds around it, and

Александръ Сергѣевичъ
ГРИБОѢДОВъ.

SHAH

when the king is seated he has the jewel in full view.' This diamond was almost certainly the Shah, for around its upper edge runs a small groove probably made for the purpose of securing the cord with which it was suspended.

The third inscription is that of the Persian ruler Fath Ali Shah (1797–1834), Shah of Persia in the year 1824. Undoubtedly the Persians must have acquired the diamond following their invasion of India in 1739 under Nadir Shah; they sacked Delhi and plundered much booty including many jewels, one of them being the most famous diamond of all, the Koh-i-noor. But whereas that gem eventually found its way to Great Britain, the Shah travelled to Russia to become part of that country's Crown Jewels.

There are two differing accounts of how the Shah became Russian property. Some authorities have stated that a grandson of Fath Ali Shah presented the gem to Czar Nicholas I during the course of a visit to St Petersburg in 1843. But, considering the value and pride of ownership attached to great diamonds by Eastern potentates, it is difficult to envisage the gift of such a precious object. The other account, which is the one agreed upon by its Russian owners, seems altogether more plausible.

After a dispute between Russia and Persia, war was declared in 1827. At first, the Persians carried all before them, recovering much lost territory, but due to the parsimony of Fath Ali Shah most of his troops had to be disbanded when the Shah refused payment during the winter. Thereupon the Russians gained the upper hand and forced the ignominious treaty of Turkmanchai upon the Persians in 1828. The man who successfully negotiated the treaty, whereby the Russians gained much territory, was Alexander Sergeyevich Griboedov, a diplomat and dramatist, best known in the latter role as the author of a satirical play in verse called 'The Misfortune of Being Clever' – perhaps the nineteenth century's equivalent of today's 'too clever by half'.

Griboedov was decorated by the Russians and appointed Minister of Persia. He tried scrupulously and energetically to enforce the treaty of Turkmanchai, but the Persians considered its terms harsh and feelings of resentment towards Griboedov were intense. Insult was added to injury when two Armenian girls escaped from the Shah's harem and took refuge in the Russian Legation. Originally they had come from Russian Armenia and wished to return there. Griboedov had no choice but to give them shelter, an act which inflamed the situation to such an extent that a mob stormed the legation on 30 January 1829 and killed Griboedov.

As a 'token of grief' Fath Ali Shah despatched the Shah diamond to Czar Nicholas I. It not only helped to placate the Czar but undoubtedly averted further warfare between the two countries.

In July 1914 the diamond was removed from the Diamond Room in the White Palace at St Petersburg and taken to Moscow for safekeeping. After the Revolution in 1917, the strong-boxes containing the jewels were unlocked and the Shah diamond was found. It remains today one of the most important treasures in the Diamond Fund and is on display in the Kremlin. May the day never come when cutters, either from the East or the West, get their hands upon this historic gem just for the sake of recutting it!

243

Above: the diamond is engraved with the names of three rulers who once owned it: Burhan II in 1591, Shah Jahan in 1641, and Fath Ali Shah in 1824.

Photo © Nikolai Rachmaninov.

Opposite page: Fath Ali Shah, the Persian ruler, who inherited the diamond long after Nadir Shah's infamous Sack of Delhi in 1739. Within five years of its being inscribed with his name, the diamond was in Moscow.

Oil on canvas, Paris, Musée du Louvre. Photo © RMN – H. Lewandowski.

On 16 May 1985, Christie's put up for sale in Geneva what was described as 'a spectacular historic table-cut diamond'. It was an unmounted table cut of octagonal outline, weighing 56.71 (metric) carats, and measuring 44.6 by 33 by 3.6mm. The vendor thought that such a stone might once have formed a part of the Great Table diamond which Tavernier had seen at Golconda in 1642. However, as the result of the examination of the Iranian Crown Jewels undertaken by leading Canadian gemmologists in the late 1960s, it has been proved that two diamonds, the Darya-i Nur and the Nur ul-Ain, have almost certainly been cut from that legendary diamond. Nevertheless this gem has been demonstrated to possess a history of its own, every bit as fascinating as that of the Great Table.

Before the sale, the owner of the diamond showed it to Anna Somers-Cocks, of the Victoria and Albert Museum, London, who suggested that it might be taken to the Institute of Geological Sciences for further examination. It was examined there by Mr E. A. Jobbins and Dr R. R. Harding, whose attention was then drawn by Susan Stronge, also of the Victoria and Albert Museum, to paintings in the Freer Gallery, Washington, of Jahangir Shah, the fourth Mogul emperor who reigned from 1605 to 1627. Jahangir is depicted wearing wrist bracelets containing flat table-cut stones which were similar to the stone Mr Jobbins and Dr Harding were examining. But even more revealing is a miniature dated 1616–17 in the Victoria and Albert Museum; this shows Shah Jahan, the third son and successor to Jahangir Shah, displaying a *sarpech* (turban ornament) in his left hand, made of gold and set with a cushion-shaped emerald with pearl and gold sprays. The octagonal diamond below the emerald closely resembles this table cut. The resemblance becomes even more convincing when the hand of Shah Jahan is enlarged to almost actual size. The contours and size of the two stones become unquestionably one and the same. As Christie's pointed out in the catalogue of the sale, the accuracy of this pictorial rendering is the more admirable as Nadir uz-Zaman, the artist, endeavoured to convey an artistic vision which did not primarily rely upon gemmological precision. Nonetheless, the court miniaturists in the Mogul Empire enjoyed the confidence of the Emperor, which enabled them to study precious stones in detail before portraying them.

In 1657 Shah Jahan fell ill, precipitating a struggle for power among his four sons: Dara Shikoh, Murad Shikoh, Aurangzeb and Shah Shuja. It was the third son who emerged victorious and declared himself Emperor in 1658, confining his father in the Agra Fort until his death there in 1666. The French traveller and jeweller Jean Baptiste Tavernier was received at the court of Aurangzeb in 1665, where he was shown some of the Emperor's jewels. After inspecting the Great Mogul diamond, the chief treasurer of the jewels showed him:

… another diamond of pear shape of very good form and fine water, with three other diamonds, table-shaped, two of them clean and the third with some little black specks. Each weighs fifty-five to sixty ratis, and the pear sixty-two and a half.

In *The Great Diamonds of the World*, Edwin Streeter included an entry headed 'The Three Tables' wherein he calculated that, according to Tavernier's scale of reduction, the weights of the three stones would be from 48 to 52 old (49.5 to 54.05 metric) carats. As Christie's observed in the sale catalogue, the similarity to the weight of Shah Jahan's Table-Cut is more than coincidental, even though it is difficult to ascertain the accuracy of Tavernier's assessment in India over three hundred years ago.

Streeter concluded his account of the three table cuts by stating that none of them had been traced since the time of Tavernier nor had any stones

The unusual Shah Jahan Table-Cut which was put up for sale in 1985 but surprisingly remained unsold.

De Beers Archives.

245

246   Shah Jahan, the fifth Mogul
Emperor, holding a turban
ornament. The octagonal
diamond below the emerald
closely resembles the
Table-Cut diamond.

Mogul manuscript, 17th century.

but that is all. Its existence is chronicled, and its size; but we know of no person who has seen it, and as yet have not unearthed a single 'biographic' incident connected with it. Possibly in future editions of the present work, our correspondents may help us. The secrets of Russian jewels are in some cases as well kept as those of Turkey. The 'Table' is reported to be a fine stone, though of course its form is the least attractive style of diamond cutting. It weighs 68 carats.

Two discrepancies obviously exist between the model and the real stone: the weights and the position of the drill holes. These holes were drilled near one edge of the diamond to allow wire, or some form of cord, to be threaded through, enabling it to be worn as a pendant.

In 1985, at the time of the sale, it was stated that the Shah Jahan Table-Cut came into ownership of the vendor's family in 1893 when his father had it in his possession during a visit to Paris. Therefore, the display of a model of the diamond at the Great Exhibition denotes that its existence was known at least forty years before. Its attribution to Russia in the notes that accompanied the models may have been correct as it is most likely that the stone travelled westwards to that country from India. In 1741 Nadir Shah sent an emissary to the recently proclaimed Empress Elizabeth at St Petersburg with gifts that included various jewelled artefacts, among them a ring once worn by Shah Jahan. It is a moot point whether or not the table-cut diamond became a Russian Crown Jewel; if it did enter the Treasury, then clearly it was one of the jewels which were given away, usually as political presents. It is of interest to note that a smaller and less imposing diamond, cut in a style not altogether dissimilar from that of Shah Jahan's diamond, has been retained in the Russian Treasury called the 'Russian Table Portrait' diamond, weighing 25 carats.

A description of the Shah Jahan Table-Cut by Mr Jobbins and Dr Harding appeared in 1984 in *The Journal of Gemmology*. They noted that the diamond shows a distinct pale pink colour: a grading might be 'fancy light pink' but the stone was not examined under ideal grading conditions. The corners by the drill holes appear to have been ground away, while there is some evidence from marks along the edge of the diamond of earlier drill holes. Therefore, there may have been attempts to drill more widely spaced holes which failed because of fracturing, and the stone may have weighed considerably more before the existing set of holes was drilled. There are no prominent inclusions, but iron staining is present in cracks near one corner. Cleavage traces are present in several areas, and these were carefully noted with a view to orientating the stone within an octahedral framework. Since its appearance at the 1985 auction, the location of this diamond has been unknown.

answering to their description ever been seen in Europe. In both respects he was wrong – at least one of the table cuts was known to have existed during his lifetime. However, he was probably right in suggesting that they had been carried off by Nadir Shah after the Sack of Delhi in 1739.

In June 1851 *The Times* wrote, at the occasion of the Great Exhibition in Hyde Park, London:

In the British department, among the gorgeous and costly display of jewellery and gold and silver plate, there is a small case which attracts considerable attention. It contains imitations in crystal of all the largest diamonds in the world.

Among these models was one that is clearly Shah Jahan's Table-Cut. The notes that accompanied it placed it under 'Russia' and described it as:

A flat Table Diamond Scollop'd at the Corners adorns the Gripe of the Emperor's sword: – 68 carats. £36,992.

The existence of the Russian Table was known to Streeter who wrote:

A Russian Secret
It is not a little remarkable that it should often be so difficult to discover the whereabouts of a great and famous diamond, the more so when we discover its financial value. The 'Russian Table' is in evidence, both in works of history and of travel,

SHAH JAHAN TABLE-CUT

Star of the East

After their marriage in 1908, Edward B. McLean and his bride travelled to Europe for their honeymoon. Each had received $100,000 from their respective fathers as a wedding present. Among the countries they visited was Turkey where Evalyn McLean expressed a wish to see the treasures of the jewellery-loving Sultan of the Ottoman Empire, Abd al-Hamid II. When the American ambassador heard of her wish, he told her: 'He may tap you for his harem,' to which she replied: 'The way they tap a boy for some society at Yale? Is that the way he gets them?'

When the couple reached Paris Mrs McLean was able to buy the wedding present which her father had told her to get. Pierre Cartier showed her the 'Star of the East', a fine 94.80-carat, pear-shaped diamond, mounted on a chain beneath a hexagonal emerald of 34 carats and a pearl of 32 grains, which may once have belonged to Sultan Abd al-Hamid. 'Ned,' she said to her husband, 'it's got me. I'll never get away from the spell of this.' Her husband – who was unimpressed by jewels – replied, 'A shock may break the spell. Suppose you ask the price of this magnificence.' But the young bride refused to listen to him and purchased the Star of the East for $120,000, in the process using up some of his paternal wedding present money. Mrs McLean pointed out the diamond's merits as an investment and that she could tell her own father that it represented a double gift to cover both her wedding and her Christmas presents.

On her return home the following exchange between Thomas Walsh and his daughter took place:

Walsh: Did you buy a wedding present?
Mrs McLean: Yes
Walsh: Did you pay the duty?
Mrs McLean: No, I smuggled it.
Walsh: You take the cake.

STAR OF THE EAST

Later Thomas Walsh said: 'Don't worry. I'll send you my lawyer down tomorrow and let him declare the trinket. Hell, I am glad to buy it for Evalyn. There won't be a bit of trouble. I'll send the word to the Customs that she is not all there.'

The Star of the East remained in Evalyn Walsh McLean's ownership for 40 years or so. On one occasion she was photographed wearing the diamond as an aigrette with what appeared to be a feather from some exotic bird in a diamond bandeau. The Hope lay somewhat lower as a pendant to a pearl necklace. After her death, Harry Winston bought both diamonds and, in 1951, he sold the Star of the East and a fancy-coloured oval-cut diamond to King Farouk of Egypt. By the time of the King's overthrow in 1952, Mr Winston had still not received payment for the two gems, but three years later an Egyptian government legal board, entrusted with the disposal of the former royal assets, ruled in his favour. Nevertheless, it needed several years of litigation before he was able to reclaim the Star of the East from a safe-deposit box in Switzerland.

In 1969 Harry Winston sold the Star of the East, the new owner asking him to remount the gem as a pendant to a V-shaped diamond necklace to which two flawless matching pear shapes could be attached. The Star of the East was displayed at the Metropolitan Museum of Art, New York, in 1978, at a reception marking the fiftieth anniversary of Harry Winston Inc. Six years later the diamond came back into the ownership of Harry Winston Inc.

Opposite: in 1969 the Star of the East was remounted in a necklace to which two matching pear shapes could later be attached.

Courtesy Harry Winston Inc., New York.

Previous page: Evalyn Walsh McLean – wearing the Star of the East on a diamond bandeau and the Hope as a necklace – whose passion for fine jewels was well-known: 'When I neglect to wear jewels, astute members of my family call in doctors, because it is a sign I'm becoming ill.'

Photo © Hulton Getty Picture Library.

Star of the Season

Opposite: the 101.10-carat Star of the Season was the most expensive diamond ever to be sold at auction when it came under the hammer in 1995.

Photo Sotheby's Geneva. Courtesy Ahmed H. Fitaihi Co. Ltd.

In recent years Sheikh Ahmed Hassan Fitaihi has been a major force at international jewellery auctions. The Sheikh's family business dates from 1907 when his grandfather opened a jewellery emporium in Makkah. At that time, Abdul Aziz Al-Saud (known in the West as Ibn Saud) was battling to reconquer and reunite the numerous and disparate tribes of the Arabian peninsula. The family of Al-Saud had in fact reigned over a large part of Arabia in the early nineteenth century but later lost much of its territory to Turkey. Eventually, in 1927, Abdul Aziz Al-Saud was proclaimed king and in 1932 the country was named the Kingdom of Saudi Arabia.

During that period, Sheikh Fitaihi's father moved both his family and business to Jeddah where initially he opened a small trading shop. Known affectionately as 'The Red Sea Bride', Jeddah is the main Saudi port and through the centuries has maintained its tradition as a trading city. Ahmed Hassan Fitaihi began working in his father's shop at an early age; before long he was compelled to manage the shop alone. The Sheikh recalls one occasion when he sold almost all the stock. His father returned surprised, if not pained, to see all the windows empty. Then and there his father taught him his first lesson: 'Before selling, think of buying.' Jeddah has remained the base for Sheikh Fitaihi's activities: the Fitaihi Center was opened in April 1984 and a new Fitaihi Center was added in 1993 at Riyadh, the capital of Saudi Arabia.

Applying his father's dictum in recent years, Sheikh Fitaihi has bought more than two thousand pieces of jewellery, as well as many large diamonds, at international auctions. These include an 80.02-carat emerald cut fashioned by Harry Winston Inc. from a rough diamond weighing 416 carats that had recently been unearthed in South Africa. This gem measures 30.86 by 21.53 by 13.51 mm and was graded as 'D' colour and internally flawless by the GIA. Purchased in New York for $7,150,000 in October 1991, it was named by Sheikh Fitaihi the 'Jeddah Bride' in honour of his beloved city. The first of his important acquisitions, it retains a special place in his affections.

Other purchases have included the Ice Queen in October 1991, the second gem that was cut from the 426-carat rough stone that yielded the Niarchos diamond; the Red Sea Star in November 1992, an emerald cut of 50.83 carats; the Star of the Desert in April 1993, a pear shape of 66.29 carats; the larger of the two celebrated Arcot pear-shapes in November 1993; the Heart of the Desert in November 1994, a heart shape of 62.42 carats.

The largest diamond which Sheikh Fitaihi has bought is a cut-cornered rectangular modified brilliant-cut, 'D' colour and internally flawless, which weighs 100.36 carats and measures 28.50 by 25.96 by 16.35 mm. The Sheikh paid $11,882,333 for this gem in Geneva in November 1993, subsequently naming it the Star of Happiness.

His most expensive acquisition has been the Star of the Season: a pear-shape of 100.10 carats, bought at Sotheby's in Geneva during May 1995. A final price of US$16.5 million for this 'D' colour, internally flawless diamond turned out to be the maximum amount paid for any single piece of jewellery in the auction world. This world record price stands intact as of now, reached after a very hard fought competition among the numerous international bidders present in the packed auction hall. The electrifying atmosphere of that night added to the intensity of bidding for this rare piece. Just after its acquisition by Sheikh Fitaihi, he received an instant offer to sell it with a sizeable premium added to its final price. As an international collector, fond of such great rarities, he turned down the offer.

Star of Sierra Leone

The feast of Saint Valentine, which falls on 14 February, appears to be intended to commemorate two saints of the same name. According to legend, one was a Roman priest who suffered martyrdom during the persecution of the Emperor Claudius, and the other a Bishop who apparently was also martyred in Rome. The events of both martyrdoms are legendary, but appear to be based on historical events. It is possible that they may actually be different developments of the same original account and refer to only one individual.

The present significance of St Valentine's day as a lovers' festival – and doubtless a boon to the coffers of the Post Office which is obliged to handle a surfeit of mail in the form of greetings cards – has no connection with the saint or with any incident in his life. However, if a diamond is considered to be a token of love and affection, on what more suitable day of the year could one first make its appearance? And that was precisely what occurred in Sierra Leone on 14 February 1972, in the once rich diamond fields of the Kono area, situated in the country's Eastern Province, some 320 km east of Freetown.

On that day, Mr E. O. Williams, the Sierra Leone engineer in charge of the separator plant operated by the National Diamond Mining Company Limited (Diminco), and Mr W. D. Adams, the Security Officer, were astonished to see a huge diamond appear on the glass-enclosed picking table which forms the final stage in the long and arduous process the recovery of diamonds. It is reported that on seeing it their first words were unprintable! No wonder, because the stone weighed 968.9 carats, which is approximately 0.22 kg and measured 63.5 mm long by 38.1 mm wide. It was a cleavage, the size of a hen's egg and roughly rectangular.

As soon as it became clear that this was an exceptional discovery of great value, the diamond was conveyed under close security escort to Freetown where the country's President, Dr Siaka Stevens, named it the 'Star of Sierra Leone'.

The Star of Sierra Leone is the third largest diamond of gem quality to have been found, being surpassed only by the Cullinan and the Excelsior. Since both of those great stones originated in diamond pipes, the Star of Sierra Leone thus remains to this day the largest diamond ever to have been recovered from an alluvial source. The record had previously been held by another great stone from Sierra Leone, the 770-carat Woyie River diamond. Although the Star of Sierra Leone contained inclusions with several dark imperfections, numerous black spots and oxidization in one corner, it also possessed a marvellous colour, characteristic of so many very fine diamonds found in Sierra Leone.

Diminco was owned jointly by the Sierra Leone government and the Sierra Leone Selection Trust Limited. The joint owners requested the De Beers Central Selling Organisation to handle the sale of the diamond on their behalf. Representatives of the CSO flew out from London to Sierra Leone to view the stone and early in May it was transferred to their headquarters in London. On 30 June, at the Sierra Leone High Commission in London, Dr Davidson Nicol, the High Commissioner, showed the Star of Sierra Leone to a gathering of some hundred journalists, photographers, and radio and television reporters.

Arrangements were then made by the Central Selling Organisation for the world's diamond dealers and merchants to be given the opportunity of viewing the gem, and the date for the sale by tender was set up for mid-July. At the time it was understood that those invited to view included a few important dealers who were not on the Diamond Trading Company's accredited list of buyers.

Opposite: the Star of Sierra Leone.

© 1988 Sotheby's Inc.

253

The formal conditions of the tender were as follows:

1. Persons tendering must produce bank guarantees of ability to raise not less than £1,000,000.
2. Any sealed bids must be accompanied by a deposit of £100,000.
3. The Star of Sierra Leone will be sold to the highest bidder, provided that: his bid is not less than the reserve price, and payment in full is made to NDMC [National Diamond Mining Company] within fifteen days following the date when the tender bids are opened. Should payment in full not be received within the stated period, the deposit will be forfeited to NDMC and the procedure repeated with the second highest bidder as if he had submitted the highest bid and so on.
4. Unsuccessful bidders' deposits will be returned to them on completion of the sale.
5. The successful bidder to give reasonable publicity to Sierra Leone.

On 18 July the sealed tenders submitted by the prospective buyers were opened by the Sierra Leone Minister of Mines, Mr S. B. Kawusu-Conteh, in the presence of Mr A. E. Oppenheimer and Dr Nicol. Alas, expectations were not fulfilled: the diamond had failed in the five bids submitted to reach its reserve price. Thereupon the Minister decided not to proceed with the sale but to report back to the President and other members of the government.

A period of silence ensued. Then, on 3 October, the President of Sierra Leone announced that the diamond had been sold to Harry Winston of New York and that the price paid was well in excess of any tender received. The purchase price has never been revealed, but according to Mr Winston it was 'in the vicinity of several million dollars'.

So the Star of Sierra Leone had found its buyer and it is perhaps stating the obvious to assert that it could not have found a more suitable one. Harry Winston had bought and cut so many of the world's greatest diamonds – the Jonker, President Vargas, Niarchos and Lesotho, for instance – and had purchased many other historical diamonds, such as the Hope, Nepal, Portuguese and the Star of the East. In addition he had assisted in building up the great collection of diamonds housed in the Smithsonian Institution in Washington DC, and how appropriate it is that its new gallery should now

be named after him. But the Star of Sierra Leone was surely his most significant purchase. His name, coupled with that of the diamond itself, helped to arouse the maximum publicity in the various capitals of the world where the Star of Sierra Leone was put on exhibition – the proceeds going to various charities in its country of origin.

After several months of study, the Star of Sierra Leone was cut in New York. Herein lies one of the recent tragedies of diamond cutting, for it was Mr Winston's intention, regardless of the difficulty in finding a buyer, to have the diamond cut so as to yield one exceptional gem. Sadly the great emerald cut, which weighed 143.20 carats, was found on completion to be flawed. Consequently Harry Winston, being a perfectionist, decided that the gem must be recut. The final yield was seventeen gems totalling 238.48 carats.

No.	Cut	Carats
I	Pear	53.96
II	Emerald	32.52
III	Emerald	30.15
IV	Marquise	27.34
V	Emerald	23.01
VI	Pear	22.27
VII	Marquise	11.35
VIII	Pear	6.44
IX	Pear	5.70
X	Marquise	4.29
XI	Marquise	3.92
XII	Marquise	3.73
XIII	Pear	3.25
XIV	Marquise	2.97
XV	Marquise	2.87
XVI	Marquise	2.86
XVII	Pear	1.85

Thirteen of the seventeen gems were flawless. All were sold in 1975. The seven which resulted from the recutting of the big emerald cut were the numbers II, X, XII, XIII, XIV and XVI and, with the exception of the largest, they are now set in the Star of Sierra Leone Brooch. In recent years, Sotheby's have sold two of the Star of Sierra Leone gems in New York; Star of Sierra Leone II, set in a ring, was sold in October 1988 for $320,000, while Star of Sierra Leone III fetched $1,872,500 in October 1999.

Star of the South

Women as well as men have played an important part in the discovery of diamond deposits. The dramatic discoveries made by the Russian geologist Larissa Popugayeva near Daaldinsk on the Siberian platform in August 1954 have culminated in the opening up of Russia's huge diamond field situated in the remote region of Yakutia. Exactly a quarter of a century later, Maureen Muggeridge found two diamonds at Smoke Creek in a trail that was to lead up-stream and to the pegging of Western Australia's massive Argyle pipe.

Women have made discoveries in yet other parts of the world – not of diamond deposits but of spectacular diamonds. In the early 1850s, long before Mrs Ernestine Ramaboa unearthed the Lesotho Brown, a black slave, whose name is unknown, at work in the alluvial deposits of Brazil, picked up a stone weighing 254 carats, equivalent to 261.24 metric carats.

She found the diamond in diggings situated near the small town of Bagagem in Minas Gerais, approximately 480 km north-west of the provincial capital, Belo Horizonte. In honour of the diamond, the name of the town was later changed to Estrêla do Sul, meaning in Portuguese 'Star of the South'. This area has over the years yielded several large diamonds, one being a cape-coloured stone of 260 carats, discovered by a garimpeiro, the Brazilian term for a digger or prospector, early in 1983.

According to the prevailing custom in Brazil, the fortunate finder was rewarded with her freedom and, in view of the exceptional size of the diamond, with a pension for life. It remains the policy of most diamond mining companies to reward honest employees. Concerning the practice employed in Brazil in the last century, Edwin Streeter wrote:

There are many laws and regulations to prevent the negroes concealing and smuggling diamonds. As a means of encouraging honesty, if a negro finds a stone of 17½ carats, he is crowned with a wreath of flowers and led in procession to the manager. Then his freedom is bestowed upon him, plus a suit of clothes and permission to work for wages. If a negro finds one from eight to ten carats weight, he receives two new shirts, a suit of clothes, a hat and a handsome knife. For smaller but valuable stones, other rewards are given. For unfaithfulness, the negroes are beaten with sticks, or have iron bands fastened round their throats; and on repetition of the fault, they are not admitted to the works again. Notwithstanding all these rewards and punishments, one third of the produce is supposed to be surreptitiously disposed of by the labourers. Manifold are the tricks used by the negroes to appropriate and barter the gems they discover. In the very presence of overseers they manage to conceal them in their hair, their mouths, their ears or between their fingers. Not infrequently they will throw them away and return for them at the dead of night.

Whether or not Streeter considered it somewhat indelicate to pursue the matter further – it must be remembered that his book was published in 1882 during the middle of the so-called moralistic Victorian era – any mine manager or customs official will confirm the fact that the corporal places of concealment employed by smugglers today are rather more diverse than Streeter specified.

The slave's master, Casimiro de Tal, did not perceive the true value of the diamond his slave had found and was induced to part with it for a mere £3,000. But the buyer, who promptly deposited the stone in the Bank of Rio de Janeiro, received an advance of no less than £30,000 on its security alone. The diamond was examined by several mineralogists, including the Frenchman Dufrénoy, who described it as being an irregular rhombic dodecahedron with convex faces. In a few places it showed small octahedral impressions of other diamonds, as if the larger diamond had once formed one of a group of crystals; in other places the octahedral cleavage was discernible. The few small inclusions within the gem were considered to have been ilmenite (titaniferous iron ore) since they

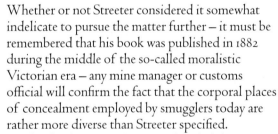

The Star of the South

256 Mulhar Rao, the Gaekwar of
Baroda, who owned the Star
of the South. He was the
principal figure in a famous
poison case involving smaller
diamonds.

are one of the most common to be enclosed in
diamonds.

After being the subject of several deals, the
diamond was eventually sent to Amsterdam to be
cut. The cutting operation lasted three months and
was undertaken by Mr Voorzanger of the famous
firm of Coster. Only a year or two previously he
had been entrusted with the task of recutting the
Koh-i-noor. The Brazilian diamond was fashioned
into a beautiful elongated cushion shape of great
purity, weighing 129 (metric) carats and measuring
34.24 mm long, 29.81 mm wide and 19.87 mm thick.
The reflected light is perfectly white but assumes a
rose tint when refraction takes place.

It has been stated that this phenomenon is
doubtless due to the peculiar prismatic form
imparted to the crystal, perhaps unconsciously, by
the cutter. Confirmation of this came from
Dr Raal, formerly of the De Beers Diamond
Research Laboratory, who kindly supplied the
following explanation:

The rose tint evidenced by the diamond when viewed in a
certain way is indeed most probably due to its 'peculiar
prismatic form'. White light is comprised of violet, indigo,

blue, green, yellow, orange and red components, the so-called
spectral colours also to be seen in a rainbow. A regular
diamond prism would disperse or split a white light into these
colours. The reason for this is that red light has a longer
wavelength than violet light which has the shortest wavelength.
The prism bends light according to its wavelength, thereby
effecting a split into spectral colours with the violet light being
bent most and the red least.

Dependent upon the angle of the prism and that of the
incidental white light, it is quite feasible for the violet, indigo
and blue components, say, to be bent so much that they do not
emerge on the other side of the prism but get reflected internally.
This phenomenon is known as total internal reflection.

The emergent light now consists of the longer
wavelengths, viz. red, orange, yellow, and if they overlap or
merge to a certain degree, the resultant colour could easily be a
'decided rose tint'.

Following the cutting of the diamond in the
Netherlands, a Paris syndicate of dealers bought
the gem and appropriately named it the Star of the
South. The syndicate displayed the diamond at the
London Exhibition of 1862 and the Paris Exhibition
of 1867; on both occasions it attracted considerable
attention on account of its great beauty. The principal member of this syndicate was a Mr Halphen
who was later to be one of the buyers at the 1874
sale of jewellery belonging to the eccentric Duke
of Brunswick. That celebrated collector of jewels
made an offer to buy the Star of the South which,
valued at 3,250,800 francs, figured as number six in a
survey of the world's largest diamonds included in
the 1860 catalogue of his jewellery.

However, it was not to be: instead the diamond
was despatched to India for possible purchase by an
Indian prince. But the prince's offer of £100,000
proved unacceptable to its owners, so the gem
returned to Paris.

It was while negotiations were proceeding in
India for its sale that news of the existence of the
Star of the South reached Khande Rao, the
Gaekwar of Baroda. Next to the Duke of
Brunswick, he was probably the most notable
collector of jewellery during the nineteenth century.
The Gaekwar gave a commission for buying the
diamond to the London dealer Edward Dresden
who, four years later, was to become the owner of
another Brazilian diamond, the English Dresden.

A propos the Gaekwar's purchase of the Star of
the South, Dresden informed Edwin Streeter that:

A few years after the death of the late Emperor Napoleon, his
Empress sold through Smith, Fleming and Co. her famous
collection of diamonds (amongst which was a pair of splendid
drops), to that same ruler of Baroda so that he now possesses a
matchless quantity of diamonds, including the 'Star of the
South', which I had the commission to buy, and for which I
paid Halphen in Paris, two million francs (£80,000), inclusive,
of course, of the mountings which were very costly.

It will be noted that the Gaekwar of Baroda's
price for the Star of the South was £20,000 less
than the amount the other Indian prince had

offered the Paris syndicate. No reasons have been given for their acceptance of the lower offer so one must assume that Mr Dresden was, to say the least, an extremely persuasive agent.

Khande Rao was succeeded in 1870 by his estranged brother, Mulhar Rao, whose involvement in a sinister episode to do with smaller diamonds ensured that he was destined for notoriety. The Gaekwar's rule did not begin auspiciously. Having been kept a close prisoner for seven years by his late brother, he was charged with the murder of his predecessor's favourite, the commander-in-chief and other influential personages; nothing came of these charges which were semi-officially denied in the Indian press. But the Gaekwar's principal activities were to become centred on Colonel Phayre, then the British Political Resident at Baroda. It transpired that every morning the Resident was in the habit of drinking a glass of sherbet. On several occasions he had noticed an unusual taste and consequently had thrown away the contents of the glass. At last his attention was drawn to a sediment at the bottom, which, on being submitted to chemical analysis, was found to consist of a mixture of arsenic, diamond dust and copper. Several persons were arrested on suspicion and the general impression remained that the attempt to poison the Resident was due to political and not to private motives. A Police Commissioner was duly sent to Baroda to investigate the matter.

Not unnaturally the Indian press discussed the affair at great length while *The Times* in London continued to report it regularly. In its issue dated 15 December 1874, the latter contained the following despatch from its Indian correspondent:

In the absence of any official statement as to the facts ascertained by the recent investigation held at the Residency relative to the attempt to poison Colonel Phayre, the strangest rumours fill the air in Baroda. It is asserted that no less than two persons who were in a position to be useful witnesses have died by poison and have been burnt. It is needless to say that it is not imagined that they committed suicide. Two other possible witnesses are spoken of as having been spirited away. The one thing which is certain is that the affair is universally regarded as most serious.

Six days later *The Times* reported:

The official inquiry has been closed and the report presented to the Bombay Government but it has not yet been made public ... It is said that the man who brought the poisoned glass to the Resident died almost immediately after, and his body was burnt in great haste, and the new conclusion drawn from this circumstance is that he knew too much to be safe and was therefore put out of the way by the conspirators. Another report is that one of the persons implicated has confessed, stating that he was offered £10,000 to be paid on the death of Colonel Phayre, and that he actually received £150 by way of earnest and it is added that he pointed out where this money is hidden. Search was made and the exact sum was found in the place indicated.

Then on 31 December 1874, this dramatic item appeared in *The Times*:

The Police Commissioner sent to Baroda to investigate the late attempt to poison Colonel Phayre has returned here. The *Bombay Gazette* believes his report will show that the Guicowar [*sic*] of Baroda was directly implicated in the attempted crime.

The Gaekwar was duly indicted on a charge of complicity in the attempt to poison the Resident and the trial opened at Calcutta on 23 February 1875, before a jury comprising three Britons and three Indians. The trial lasted a month, with the proceedings being reported almost daily in *The Times*. Readers were regaled with accounts of an endless series of bizarre goings-on and revelations such as are of the very essence of drama; in fact they provided a perfect demonstration of Byron's words that the truth is always strange: stranger than fiction. One of the revelations in court came from the Gaekwar's Private Secretary. He stated that on two occasions he had bought arsenic, diamonds and diamond dust on the orders of the Gaekwar. The prince had said the diamonds were for a crown for the High Priest of Akulkote.

In the end the jury could not agree on a unanimous verdict. However, the Viceroy, Lord Northbrook, deposed the Gaekwar on the grounds of his unsatisfactory governance of Baroda and placed his ten-year-old son on the throne. Since Mulhar Rao had left no legitimate descendants, his predecessor's widow was given permission to adopt a boy from another branch of the Gaekwar lineage. The choice fell upon a boy of 12, the second son of a farmer from a remote village, who became Sayaji Rao III of Baroda and who reigned from 1875 to 1939. Although it appeared to be universally agreed that a bad ruler had rightly been dismissed, it was also thought in India that neither the Viceroy nor the government of India had handled the affair in a dextrous manner.

In 1934 the new Gaekwar of Baroda, then an elderly and greatly respected ruler, informed Robert M. Shipley that both the Star of the South and the English Dresden were mounted in a necklace among his family's jewels. In recent years it has been reported that the Star of the South is owned by Mr Rustomjee Jamsetjee of Bombay, but this has not been confirmed.

257

Lord Northbrook, the Viceroy of India, who was responsible for the Gaekwar of Baroda's deposition.

Star of South Africa

258

Opposite: the Star of South Africa, whose discovery in 1889 is seen as the symbol of the country's mineral development.

De Beers Archives.

More than 130 years have passed since the discovery of the Eureka in 1866, so that we are now able to assess the historical significance of that event. It is doubtful if anyone then living in either South Africa or Great Britain could have foretold what lay ahead for the southern land or the chain of events following the find of this diamond.

Indeed there were numerous influential persons in England who were sceptical about the provenance of the Eureka and who, even when it was proved to be of African origin, remained unaware of the importance it held for the future of the country. When Queen Victoria examined the diamond at Windsor she doubted its origin, being under the impression that diamonds came only from India or Brazil. Sir Roderick Murchison, a noted geologist who twice held office as President of the Geological Society, doubted whether the matrix of the diamond existed in South Africa. In 1867, Penrose Julyan, the London agent for the Cape Colony, wrote to Richard Southey, the Colonial Secretary at Cape Colony:

All the Diamond Merchants of London have I think seen the real Stone, and short paragraphs have appeared in some of the Newspapers about it, but it is almost impossible to get them to take any interest in the matter.

Despite their valuation of the stone, Messrs Garrards expressed their lack of interest in investigating the discoveries unless diamonds were found in sufficient quantities. Lastly, at governmental level, the Secretary of State for the Colonies seemed to take little interest in the matter: after a few more diamonds had been picked up he merely requested the Foreign Office to ascertain from its representative in Rio de Janeiro what system the Brazilian government employed to license diamond dealers.

The prevailing lack of interest shown in London appeared to be shared by persons in authority within South Africa. The Governor, Sir Philip Wodehouse, displayed more interest in buying the best specimens that came to light than in any form of systematic exploration of possible diamond deposits. He shared the interest shown by members of the Legislative Assembly and the Legislative Council in the possibility of locating gold deposits to the north. But at the time the Eureka was discovered, Sir Philip's principal preoccupation centred on the silver discoveries in South West Africa. Believing that the territory along the coast northwards of the Cape Colony might prove to be rich in certain minerals, principally silver, he enquired whether the British government might be prepared to annexe the territory. Sir Philip considered that in the event of mineral deposits being found there, it would be undesirable if the region were left without the presence of any constituted authority capable of governing it and, on the other hand, that such a valuable territory situated next to a British possession ought not to fall into the hands of a foreign power. But the Secretary of State replied discouragingly on the matter so the question of annexation was dropped.

Similarly the attentions of Sir Richard Southey, a man with a lively mind and of many interests, were for the most part devoted to matters other than diamonds, despite his own involvement in the Eureka. In particular, Southey was keenly interested in the possibilities of developing deposits of copper and gold and in the promotion of the silk industry, a project first attempted in the days of the Dutch East India Company.

Therefore, it was fortunate that there were individuals of lesser standing in South Africa alive to the significance of the diamond's discovery. One of them was the itinerant hunter and trader, John O'Reilly. While on his way to Hopetown he passed a farm where he was shown a crystal, together with other stones, that had been picked up some

STAR OF SOUTH AFRICA

450 metres from the Orange River. Through the knowledge which he had acquired from the finding of the Eureka, he was at once able to perceive that the crystal was a diamond and he promptly bought it and forwarded it to Cape Town. It was verified as a gem of the first water weighing $8^{13}/_{16}$ carats and its discovery prompted the Governor to send the following message, dated 17 June 1867, to Parliament on the subject of mineral rights in the Colony:

The Governor thinks it right in consequence of the discovery of another Diamond in the Northern part of the Colony, to bring to the notice of the Honourable House of Assembly that the ownership of precious stones found, is by Law, as he understands, vested in the Crown. Looking, however, to the great difficulty of enforcing this claim, and considering how desirable it is to encourage all efforts at developing the mineral resources of the Colony, the Government does not propose, unless requested so to do by the Honourable House to impose, for the present at least, any restrictions on the researches of private individuals, or to make any claim on the fruits of their labours.

This discovery was followed by others which showed a growing awareness on the part of some people in the neighbourhood of the presence of diamonds and their potential value. In particular the finder of the eighth diamond, weighing 15½ carats and afterwards pronounced by Dr Guybon Atherstone to be a gem of the finest quality and for which the Governor offered £400, was a Griqua who declined to reveal where he had found the diamond, beyond the fact that he had picked it up by the Vaal River. Furthermore he refused to sell it until he had ascertained its full value. At the same time perhaps the clearest evidence that the village of Hopetown was starting to assume some importance as a trading centre for diamonds was supplied by the Dutch cutter, Louis Hond, who had left Cape Town and journeyed north to make his headquarters there. He thus became one of the few on the spot who possessed the ability to identify and appraise a diamond – a true professional among the amateurs. From what is known about him, Hond was not likely to have missed out on any business opportunities which presented themselves, nor were his persistence and determination ever in doubt, for he continued to press for the fee he claimed for his part in valuing the Eureka.

Before Hond arrived in Hopetown another firm, Lilienfeld Bros, had already established itself there. This concern, which began dealing in diamonds some time in 1868, maintained a business connection with A. Mosenthal and Co., who were leading wholesale merchants in Port Elizabeth. This city was starting to become an important centre for the marketing of diamonds, which were acquired by various trading firms from Griquas and others inland. The clearest evidence of this fact is supplied

by the diaries of Sir Lewis Michell, who had arrived in South Africa in 1864 to join the London and South African Bank, to which he was appointed General Manager two years later. He wrote:

Our commercial troubles were ere long terminated by the discovery of diamonds though at the outset it led to unlimited gambling and heavy losses. Both the Queenstown banks applied to me for support and early in 1869 I met their Managers in Grahamstown and with them proceeded to Queenstown to discuss the situation... The Queenstown trip... resulted in my affording both banks the support they desired, but my Board, always timid in the wrong place, viewed my action with undisguised alarm and passed a resolution after the style of the Medes and Persians, that under no circumstance whatever were diamonds to be regarded as any security for advances... This was the last straw... I endeavoured to reduce my Board to mitigate their drastic decision... and then, failing to carry the Board with me, I resigned.

This far-sighted man joined the Standard Bank, becoming one of their most famous General Managers and the confidant of Cecil Rhodes, whom he succeeded as Chairman of De Beers Consolidated Mines in 1902. It is evident that diamonds were appearing in 1868 and 1869 in sufficient quantities to impress a leading bank manager. In 1868 one diamond worth £150 featured among the Cape Colony's list of exports; the Governor's own diamonds were not listed – probably discretion reigned in this matter – nor, it would appear, were most of the others found in that year. In 1869, 147 diamonds were listed, their value of £34,813 making them the Colony's sixth largest export.

The news of the importance which Port Elizabeth was starting to assume in matters pertaining to diamonds in due course reached the ears of the Colonial Secretary at Cape Town. Although gold fever raged and in August 1868 Parliament had decided a commission should be sent to the gold fields, Southey had begun to appreciate the implications of the diamond discoveries because in a letter to Chalmers – then Commissioner and Resident Magistrate at Hopetown – dated 5 June of that year, he had written:

I wish you would give me as near as you can the exact position of where each of the diamonds that have been sent from Hopetown were found and the relative position of this one... I want by and by to publish a short history of each with a view to benefit the country by dispelling the idea now existing that these gems have been brought here from Foreign parts...

Now the idea that there were people who deliberately shipped diamonds from an existing source to another part of the world where new deposits had been found so as to disguise the discovery was not a novel one. Certainly the London diamond merchant, Harry Emanuel, of Bond Street, was aware of it since in his book *Diamonds and Precious Stones*, published in 1867, he had written as follows concerning the discovery of diamonds in Brazil in the early part of the preceding century:

The European traders, who had never seen or dreamt of any other but the Indian diamond, and who feared that if an indefinite number were thrown on the market by this discovery of new mines, their stocks would thus be depreciated, and perhaps become valueless, endeavoured by every means to discourage their sale and spread a report that the so-called Brazilian diamonds were only the refuse of the Indian mines exported from Goa to Brazil, and thence to Europe; and at first succeeded in preventing the sale. The Portuguese merchants, however, turned the tables on them by exporting them from Brazil to Goa and then offering them for sale as Indian diamonds.

Undoubtedly Emanuel would have recalled these events when diamonds allegedly of South African origin started to make their appearance on the London market. In 1868 the quantities were sufficient for him to appoint J. R. Gregory to travel to South Africa to investigate the diamond situation there. In her book *Diamond Fever, South African Diamond History 1866-69 from Primary Sources*, the South African writer Marian Robertson considers that there is only circumstantial evidence to suggest that Emanuel was receiving diamonds from that source; nevertheless his reputation in gemmological circles was such that he would have been a front-runner among candidates to whom someone in South Africa might have chosen to send diamonds.

Gregory, described in the *Journal of the Society of Arts* as 'a gentleman well known in geological and mineralogical circles', duly arrived in South Africa. Once there he kept his movements as quiet as possible; it would appear that others were prepared to keep quiet about them too. However, in July 1868 he did meet Southey in Cape Town, and told him he was unimpressed by the mineralogical investigations then being undertaken. In November Emanuel's notorious denial of the existence of diamonds in South Africa was published in the *Journal of the Society of Arts*. It contained the following choice extracts:

Sir, As the report of diamonds having been found at the Cape has excited considerable interest, and as it is possible that some unfortunate persons may thereby be induced to embark on a fruitless errand, I think it advisable to make public some facts with which I have become acquainted in connection with this subject. Some months ago my attention was called to the report of diamonds having been discovered in or near to the Orange River and I was shown a diamond of fair quality (resembling Indian Rough material) said to have been found thereabouts. Being naturally desirous of discovering or developing a new source of supply to supplement the gradually decreasing yield of the Brazilian and Indian mines, I commissioned Mr J. R. Gregory... thoroughly to explore the districts where diamonds were said to have been found.

Mr Gregory has just returned and reports having carefully visited the Orange, Vaal, Buffalo and Fish Rivers, as well as the adjacent country as far as 120 miles into Griqualand, and has failed to find anywhere these geological and mineralogical signs which have hitherto been invariably seen whenever diamonds have been found and nowhere does the formation of the country warrant the inference that diamonds could exist there...

Mr Gregory, who is a perfectly competent authority, after exploring all the places said to be 'diamondiferous' and over 2000 miles of other Cape territory is clearly of opinion that no diamonds have or ever will be found in the Cape Colony – saving such as are deposited there for a purpose...

These so termed 'diamond (and gold) discoveries' have been extremely puffed and unless the true facts are made apparent, I fear that many adventurous persons might be induced to risk all in emigrating to a Colony where everything is very dear and subsistence hardly to be earned; and I fancy they would derive small comfort in their ruin from the consideration that emigrating might eventually lower the price of labour and thereby benefit the established colonists.

The Countess of Dudley, second wife of the first Earl, owned the Star of South Africa. She wore it in a hair ornament.

Courtesy of the National Portrait Gallery, London.

Predictably the contents of this letter aroused the utmost indignation and scorn among those persons in South Africa who had become involved in the diamond scene. It was alleged that Gregory had never visited the sites of the discoveries; that he had only spent a fortnight in trekking 200 km beyond the Orange River; and that when a diamond was brought to him while he was visiting Hopetown he made the extraordinary assertion that it must have been dropped by an ostrich and that if other diamonds were found in that part of the country they must all have been brought there and dropped by ostriches.

Dr Atherstone lost no time in refuting Gregory's theories one by one. Altogether the so-called expert's pronouncements upon the existence – or rather the non-existence – of both gold and diamonds within South Africa constitute one of the most erroneous and outrageous statements ever delivered in this particular field of science: no wonder that for years to come the expression 'to do a Gregory' was common-place in southern Africa. Yet, as will be shown later on, there was a motive behind the whole of Gregory's involvement which O'Reilly, for one, did not lose sight of. In a letter which he sent to the *Colesburg Advertiser*, he wrote:

Mr Gregory entertains the hope of turning the discovery to his own particular benefit, in which perhaps his learned and charitable sponsor might share. I shall simply remark that Mr Gregory told several persons here that he expected to return to the Cape very shortly, and leave the public to draw their own conclusions and judge for themselves which is most likely to be the true way of accounting for the nature and style of his reports.

Gregory's theories were soon blown sky-high by an event which the new Civil Commissioner and Resident Magistrate of Hopetown, H. F. Burton, who had replaced Chalmers, mentioned in a postscript to a letter dated 18 March 1869, to Richard Southey:

P.S. Since writing the above a diamond has been brought in weighing about 83 (eighty three) carats. It is said to have been found in the Colony. Schalk van Niekerk who found the first diamond brought it in.

On the same day Burton's clerk wrote excitedly and rather more extensively on the same topic to Richard Southey:

My Dear Sir,
*   I sit down to communicate to you the fact that the largest diamond yet found has been brought in here by Mr Schalk van Niekerk of 'De Kalk' the same party who found the first No.1 which was bought by the Governor for £500. That brought in today weighs 83½ (eighty three and a half) carats and has been valued by some amateurs at between £25 and £30,000 – it is a real beauty. Mr Schalk van Niekerk gave for it 500 sheep, 10 head of cattle and 1 horse (value about £150). This is the gem which I am told a year ago was in possession of a native doctor who used it as a talisman in his professional visits. It was found (the seller assures Niekerk) in the Colony below Niekerk's farm 'De Kalk'. Mr Niekerk himself told me this, so you may rely upon its being the truth. Hond has not yet valued the stone. The inhabitants are in a great state of excitement and Gregory's name has not been made use of in very favourable terms. It is not very likely that this*

stone was dropped by an ostrich, or placed where it was found by the native to enhance the value of the farm.
*   Pray excuse this hurried note, my object is to be the first to inform you of this good news.*

*   Yours my dear Sir,*
*   very truly,*
*   Fred Steytler*

Mr Niekerk intends taking up the diamond to Cape Town himself, as advised by me, and you will be enabled to have a good view of it there. Perhaps I shall have to apply for leave of absence to go with him to take it to the Governor and yourself – this is by no means certain however.

It was ironic that Southey should have received these letters only a few days after he had written to Julyan saying that he did not feel they should 'be in too much hurry' to publish anything about diamonds officially. As was to be expected the news of the discovery of such a large stone caused the greatest excitement at Hopetown and other places. Some lost no time in calling the diamond the 'S. A. Koh-i-noor' while others referred to it as 'Niekerk's Pandalok'.

According to Louis Hond he was the first person to call the diamond by the name by which it is chiefly known, the Star of South Africa . Hond was shortly to play an important part in the purchase of the diamond, but not before James Wykeham, the Deputy Sheriff for Hopetown, had made determined efforts to buy it. Wykeham offered van Niekerk £11,000 but Lilienfeld Bros, assisted by Hond, offered £100 more. Van Niekerk did not go back to Wykeham and his partner in search of a higher offer – they had been prepared to go as high as £13,000 – and it appears as if either Lilienfeld or Hond cast doubt on Wykeham's ability to raise the sum he had offered for the stone. Van Niekerk was talked into accepting the lower figure and he was probably informed of the business connection between Lilienfeld Bros and Mosenthal's in Port Elizabeth, itself a guarantee of payment. In the end, van Niekerk accepted £11,200 for the diamond and signed a bill of sale with Lilienfeld's, but it was drawn up in such a manner that Wykeham feared van Niekerk had lost the security of Mosenthal's.

The purchase of the Star of South Africa by Lilienfeld's soon gave rise to legal proceedings, initiated by the Diamond Metal and Mineral Association. This company, which was wholly South African, had obtained the concession from Waterboer, the Chief of the Griquas, to the sole prospecting rights in the territory which lay to the north of the Orange River. It was the DMMA's submission that the diamond had been found on this side of the river, thus entitling Waterboer to the ensuing financial benefit from the diamond. Accordingly on 31 March 1868 an application was made in Colesberg by Waterboer and others to restrain Lilienfeld Bros from selling, parting with, or in any way disposing of the 83½carat diamond which they had recently purchased.

Before the case came to the Supreme Court extraordinary scenes had taken place in the Colesberg and Hopetown districts of the Colony. Most of them centred on the finder of the diamond, a Griqua boy named Swartboy (his name has been variously spelled Swaartboy, Zwartboy, Zwartbooy and Swartbooi).

His statement to the effect that he had found the diamond within 200 yards of a hut on a kopje situated on the northern side of the Orange River appeared in an affidavit provided by a government land surveyor to assist the cause of the DMMA and Waterboer. However, Lilienfeld's lost no time in collecting evidence which showed that the boy had picked the stone up on the south, i.e. Colonial, side of the river. Affidavits were collected by both sides and appeared like leaves on trees. But the most astonishing fact was the virtual kidnapping of Swartboy on two occasions, one by each side, so as to induce him to alter this story of the discovery of the diamond. No wonder that it was reported of him:

…before and since he had sold the… diamond he was repeatedly asked by several persons where he had found the… stone but was always very reluctant in describing the locality where he had found it… that when persons residing on the other side of the Orange River asked where he had found it, he invariably told them that he had found it on this side of the river in the Colony, and when persons residing in this Colony asked him where he had found it, he invariably told them that he had found it on the opposite side of the river in Waterboer's territory because he was afraid that the stone might be claimed and taken from him.

On 19 May 1869 the case was heard by the Supreme Court in Cape Town. Almost the first thing the Judges did was to rule that the affidavits produced by the DMMA were based on hearsay evidence and that they were therefore inadmissible. But the principal reason for the DMMA's losing the case – or as the *Cape Argus* put it, why they 'came to grief' – lay in the alleged concession granted by Waterboer. This raised territorial questions outside the jurisdiction of the Court which presented difficulties in granting the DMMA's application. After the Court had found in favour of Lilienfeld Bros, they asked for their costs to be paid by the DMMA and Waterboer. The losing side had insufficient financial resources to risk any further Court actions, so the Star of South Africa could then be disposed of. The result of the hearing was duly reported in the *Colesburg Advertiser* which noted that many citizens went to Leopold Lilienfeld to wish him good luck. The Union Jack floated before his house and in the evening the inhabitants 'testified their joy by throwing turpentine balls and fireworks and by serenading Mr Lilienfeld'. An anonymous letter appeared in the press pointing out the dangers of such amusement – although it appears that one of the Municipal Commissioners had supplied the materials for making the fireballs!

On 2 June 1869 the Star of South Africa was exhibited at the Commercial Exchange in Adderley Street, Cape Town. Not surprisingly the diamond was also shown to the Governor, who on this occasion, it appears, did not make an offer to buy such a gem. The Star of South Africa made its final appearance in South Africa at an exhibition in Port Elizabeth before being shipped to Great Britain on 4 June in the steamship *Celt*, the same vessel which two years before had carried the Eureka. On the later trip the cargo included wool, feathers, hides, sheep and goat skins, oil, wine, raisins, ivory, a box of diamonds from Adler & Co. of Port Elizabeth and five live zebras.

It has been recounted how, at some time before the Star of South Africa left the shores of Africa, the diamond was placed upon the table in Parliament during the session and that the Colonial Secretary uttered the oft-quoted words: 'This diamond, gentlemen, is the rock upon which the future prosperity of South Africa will be built.' In this connection Mrs Robertson has pointed out that the parliamentary session did not open until 23 June, by which time the *Celt* had sailed for London. Furthermore, no record exists among the parliamentary papers of Southey having spoken these words after the diamond had left and the session had begun, nor in the minutes of the Executive Council. But even if he did not utter these resounding words there is no doubting their accuracy. The discovery of the Star of South Africa was the momentous event which successfully led to a horde of people appearing on the alluvial diggings by the Orange and Vaal Rivers, the discovery of the dry or pipe deposits in the area of Kimberley leading to the formation of De Beers Consolidated Mines in 1888. The finance engendered by the diamond discoveries in turn led to the development of the gold field on the Witwatersrand and the opening up of the territories to the north. In a nutshell, the Star of South Africa transformed South Africa from the pastoral land it was once to its position as the most industrialized country of the whole continent today.

The news of the finding of the diamond involved Southey in correspondence with several individuals in London. In a letter which he received from Julyan he read:

The finding of your Great Diamond has created quite an excitement among those interested in such matters and desire is expressed by the knowing ones to see it. If genuine, Mr Gregory's opinions will henceforth have little weight.

263

But Southey must have drawn particular satisfaction from a letter he received from the diamond merchant Emanuel which read as follows:

18 New Bond Street, May 18, 1869

Sir, I have to acknowledge the receipt of your letter for which I am much obliged. I am happy to see that you do not share the absurd notions entertained by the Colonial newspapers viz that I had any interest in preventing the discovery of diamonds in the Cape becoming known. The facts are these. I had a firm belief that diamonds were found at the Cape and under that impression engaged Mr Gregory, who is favourably known to the Geological Society officials and to the Authorities at the Museum to examine into the matter. When I tell you that I had to remunerate him for his time and for the loss of his business which was at a standstill till his return you will readily believe it was at no inconsiderable expense to myself that I induced him to go out. On his return (long before the time specified) he made a report which I published verbatim, giving his name so that I cannot consent to bear the onus of my misstatement on his part.

I had no means of judging excepting through his statements, but yet at a meeting of the Society of the Arts I publicly stated that I was not bold enough to assert that diamonds were not existent in South Africa but that if so they occurred (according to Mr Gregory's statements and if the minerals he brought home were a fair sample) in a deposit in which as yet no diamonds had been hitherto found. I am perfectly ready to admit that facts are far too strong for any hypothesis based on Scientific knowledge. After your kind communication I can no longer have any doubt of the fact of Diamonds being found in your Colony, and shall be very glad if you can keep me informed of the progress being made in the discovery. In return if my poor services can be of any use to you, I shall be happy to place them at your disposition. I have the honour to remain, Sir,

Your obedient servant,
Harry Emanuel

P.S. If you think fit I shall have no objection to the publication of this letter.

However, although the somewhat obsequious tone of this letter appears to indicate that Emanuel was merely eating humble pie, the suspicion must remain that the merchant's conduct was rather more disingenuous in the matter. This is borne out by the July 1869 issue of the *Geological Magazine* which contained Gregory's reply to Dr Atherstone's letter. In this Gregory admitted to having purposely deceived him and everyone in the Colony as to the real purpose of his visit. In August Atherstone wrote an indignant letter which probably came near to the truth: he accused Gregory of '…ministering to the interests of his monied friend the Diamond Merchant to try to stamp out the diamond discovery here and so keep up for a time at least the price of diamonds, of which I am told Emmanuel [sic] had a very large stock on hand.'

So it seems as if the suspicions which O'Reilly had held concerning the real motive for Gregory's visit and which he had aired in his letter to the *Colesburg Advertiser* were entirely justified. At the same time the whole episode can have done little to enhance the standing of diamond merchants in London; one suspects that this was not high even before the discovery of the Eureka, and the events pertaining to the Star of South Africa clearly led to its further debasement.

In due course Lilienfeld's despatched the Star of South Africa to Amsterdam where it was cut into a flawless pear shape weighing 47.69 (metric) carats. The diamond was sold to the second wife of the first Earl of Dudley who wore it as a hair ornament: since then it has sometimes been known as the 'Dudley'. After nothing had been heard for some years, this historic gem reappeared in 1974 when Christie's put it up for sale in Geneva on 2 May. The seller's name was not disclosed, but as the sale catalogue stated that the diamond had been owned by the family of the vendor for more than 60 years, Lady Dudley must have sold it before her death in February 1929. At the time of the sale, the Star of South Africa was suspended from a detachable pendant set with brilliant-cut diamond collets with round-cut diamond intersections: the pendant bow-shaped with vertical suspension-link and calyx-shaped terminals. It was expected that this jewel would fetch well over £100,000: in the event it was sold for £225,000. The buyer, a private collector, has retained it in this setting.

Diamonds have no mercy. 'They will show up the wearer if they can,' says one character in *The Sandcastle*, an early novel by the distinguished British writer, Iris Murdoch. Now this may be true of some ladies – usually sporting an outrageously large item of jewellery which imparts a degree of unwholesome vulgarity to themselves – but is it applicable to Elizabeth Taylor? Those well-publicized gifts which she received from her fifth husband, the late Richard Burton, certainly enhance her appearance and do not look out of place on her. A rapport is established between the jewel and its wearer.

Richard Burton's first purchase for Miss Taylor was the 33.19-carat emerald-cut Krupp diamond, in 1968. This had formerly been part of the estate of Vera Krupp, second wife of the steel magnate, Alfred Krupp. Miss Taylor wore this stone in a ring. Next came the magnificent pearl known as La Peregrina for which Burton paid £15,000. For Elizabeth Taylor's fortieth birthday in 1972 Richard Burton gave her a heart-shaped diamond set with rubies in a pendant. 'I would have liked to buy her the Taj Mahal,' he remarked, 'but it would cost too much to transport. This diamond has so many carats, it's almost a turnip.' Then he added, 'Diamonds are an investment. When people no longer want to see Liz and I on the screen, then we can sell off a few baubles.'

By far the best known of Richard Burton's purchases was the 69.42-carat pear shape, later to be called the Taylor-Burton diamond. It was cut from a rough stone weighing 240.80 carats found in the Premier mine in 1966 and subsequently bought by Harry Winston. Here there is a coincidence. Eight years before, another cleavage of almost identical weight (240.75 carats) had been found in the Premier. Harry Winston bought this stone too, remarking at the time, 'I don't think there have been half a dozen stones in the world of this quality.'

Not for the first time the Premier mine was to have the last word because the 69.42-carat gem cut from the later discovery is a beautiful 'D' flawless.

After the rough piece of 240.80 carats had arrived in New York, Harry Winston and his cleaver, Pastor Colon Jr, studied it for six months. Markings were made, erased and redrawn to show where the stone should be cleaved. There came the day appointed for the cleaving. In this instance the usual tension that surrounds such an operation was increased by the heat and the glare of the television lights that had been allowed into the workroom. After he had cleaved the stone, the 50-year-old cleaver said nothing: he reached across the workbench for the piece of diamond that had been separated and looked at it through horn-rimmed glasses for a fraction of a second before exclaiming 'Beautiful!' This piece of 78 carats was expected to yield a gem weighing around 24 carats, while the larger piece, of 162 carats, was destined to produce the pear shape whose weight had originally been expected to be about 75 carats.

In 1967 Winston sold the pear shape to Mrs Harriet Annenberg Ames, the sister of Walter Annenberg, the American ambassador in London during the Presidency of Richard Nixon. Two years later, she sent the diamond to Parke-Bernet Galleries in New York for auction explaining her decision thus:

I found myself positively cringing and keeping my gloves on for fear it would have been seen, I have always been an extremely gregarious person and I did not enjoy that feeling. It sat in a bank vault for years. It seemed foolish to keep it if one could not use it. As things are in New York one could not possibly wear it publicly.

The diamond was put up for auction on 23 October 1969, on the understanding that it could be named by the buyer. Before the sale speculation was rife as to who was going to bid for the gem, with the usual international names being bandied about by the columnists. The name of Miss Taylor was among them and she did indeed have a preview of the diamond when it was flown to Switzerland for her to have a look at, then back to New York under precautions delicately described as 'unusual'.

The auctioneer began the bidding by asking if anyone would offer $200,000, at which the crowded room erupted with 'Yes'. Bidding then continued to climb and with nine bidders active, rushed to $500,000. At $500,000 the individual bids increased in $10,000 steps. At $650,000 only two bidders remained in the fray. When the bidding reached $1,000,000, Al Yugler of Frank Pollack, who was representing Richard Burton, dropped out. Pandemonium broke out when the hammer fell and the entire room stood up, so that the auctioneer could not identify who had won the prize, and he had to call for order. The winner was Robert Kenmore, the Chairman of the Board of Kenmore Corporation, the owners of Cartier Inc., who paid the record price of $1,050,000 for the gem, which he promptly named the 'Cartier'. The previous record price for a jewel had been $305,000 for a diamond necklace from the Rovensky estate in 1957.

As well as Richard Burton, Harry Winston had also been an under-bidder at the sale. But the former was not finished yet and he was determined to acquire the diamond. So, speaking from the pay-phone of a well-known hotel in the south of England, he spoke to Mr Kenmore's agent. Sandwiched between the lounge bar and the saloon, Burton negotiated for the gem while continually shoving coins into the box. Patrons quietly putting away their drinks would have heard the actor's ringing tones exclaiming, 'I don't care how much it is; go and buy it.' In the end Robert Kenmore agreed to sell it, but on condition that Cartier were able to display the stone, by now named the 'Taylor-Burton', in New York and Chicago. He did not deny that Cartier had made a profit: 'We're businessmen, and we're happy that Miss Taylor is happy.'

More than 6,000 people a day flocked to Cartier's New York store to see the Taylor-Burton, the crowds stretching down the block. But an article in the *New York Times* was distinctly acidulous on the subject. Under the heading 'The Million Dollar Diamond' appeared the following comment:

The peasants have been lining up outside Cartier's this week to gawk at a diamond as big as the Ritz that cost well over a million dollars. It is destined to hang around the neck of Mrs Richard Burton. As someone said, it would have been nice to wear in the tumbril on the way to the guillotine.

Shortly afterwards Miss Taylor wore the Taylor-Burton in public for the first time, when she attended Princess Grace's fortieth birthday party in Monaco. It was flown from New York to Nice in the company of two armed guards hired by Burton and Cartier. In 1978, following her divorce from Richard Burton, Miss Taylor announced she was putting the diamond up for sale and was planning to use part of the proceeds to build a hospital in Botswana. Dare one hope this received adequate coverage in the *New York Times*? In June of the following year Henry Lambert, the New York jeweller, stated that he had bought the Taylor-Burton for nearly $5,000,000.

By December he had sold the Taylor-Burton to its present owner, Mr Robert Mouawad.

Opposite: The Taylor-Burton Diamond as mounted by Cartier.

Courtesy Cartier Archive.

Below: Richard Burton and Elizabeth Taylor at the Scorpio Ball in New York, to which she wore the necklace containing the diamond.

Photo © SYGMA, New York.

TAYLOR-BURTON

Tereschenko

To gem historians and, judging by the reaction of the Press, to the general public as well, it is always something of an event when the existence of an unusual stone, hitherto known only to a handful of people, becomes more widely known. That is what occurred in 1984 when Christie's announced that they would be auctioning this fancy-blue, pear-shaped diamond of 42.92 metric carats, the fourth largest recorded fancy-blue diamond.

The original owners of the gem, the Tereschenko family, were sugar-kings in pre-1917 Russia. One member, Mikhail (1886–1956), who held advanced political views, became Kerensky's Minister of Foreign Affairs in 1917. Four years before, Mikhail had deposited the diamond with Cartier's in Paris. In 1915 he instructed Cartier's to mount the gem as the centrepiece in a necklace containing a variety of fancy-coloured diamonds. The jewel was unique in combining forty-six marquise, round, pear and heart-shaped diamonds ranging from 0.13 to 2.88 carats. Their various colours were described as 'jonquil, lemon, aquamarine, sultana-green, gold button, grey, blue, crevet, lilac, rose, old port, madeira and topaz'. As such, the necklace ranked among the most important creations of this century in fancy-coloured diamonds.

In 1916, on the eve of the Russian Revolution, the Tereschenko diamond was secretly taken out of Russia. Then it passed into private ownership.

Like other fancy-blues, the Tereschenko belongs to the rare category of Type IIb diamonds. It is not known where it was found: theoretically, it may have come from either the Kollur alluvial deposits in India or from the Premier mine in South Africa. However, by 1913 the Premier mine had been in existence for barely ten years and, since there is no report or record of it having yielded such a rare and unusual gem, it must be assumed that the diamond is of Indian origin.

Days before the sale in Geneva, four dealers contacted Christie's separately, offering to buy the diamond directly at the estimated price, between three and four million Swiss francs, thereby saving at least the ten per cent charge added to the selling price. Christie's refused the offers. In addition, a syndicate suggested that the auctioneers ought to have the diamond graded by the Gemological Institute of America. They pointed out that while the report of the Swiss laboratory in Lucerne, mentioned in the sale catalogue, was impeccable it would make commercial sense to have the diamond graded by the GIA because its certificate was better known, particularly in the Middle East and Asia. A sale would thus be made easier in those regions. Christie's duly obliged: the gem was flown to the New York laboratory of the GIA and was returned with the necessary documents.

The Tereschenko came up for sale on 14 November 1984. At 10 p.m. excitement ran high in the brightly lit ballroom of the Hotel Richmond when the Chairman of Christie's announced: 'We are now selling Lot 454. We shall start the bidding at three million Swiss francs.' The price seemed to surprise no one in the room, which was full of important dealers from all over the world and several billionaires too. It took forty seconds for the bidding to reach six and a half million Swiss francs, a figure far in excess of Christie's most optimistic estimate. Ultimately a shout of 'Ten million Swiss francs' came from the back of the room and the auctioneer brought down his hammer. For $4,508,196 , Mr Robert Mouawad had made a new addition to his growing collection.

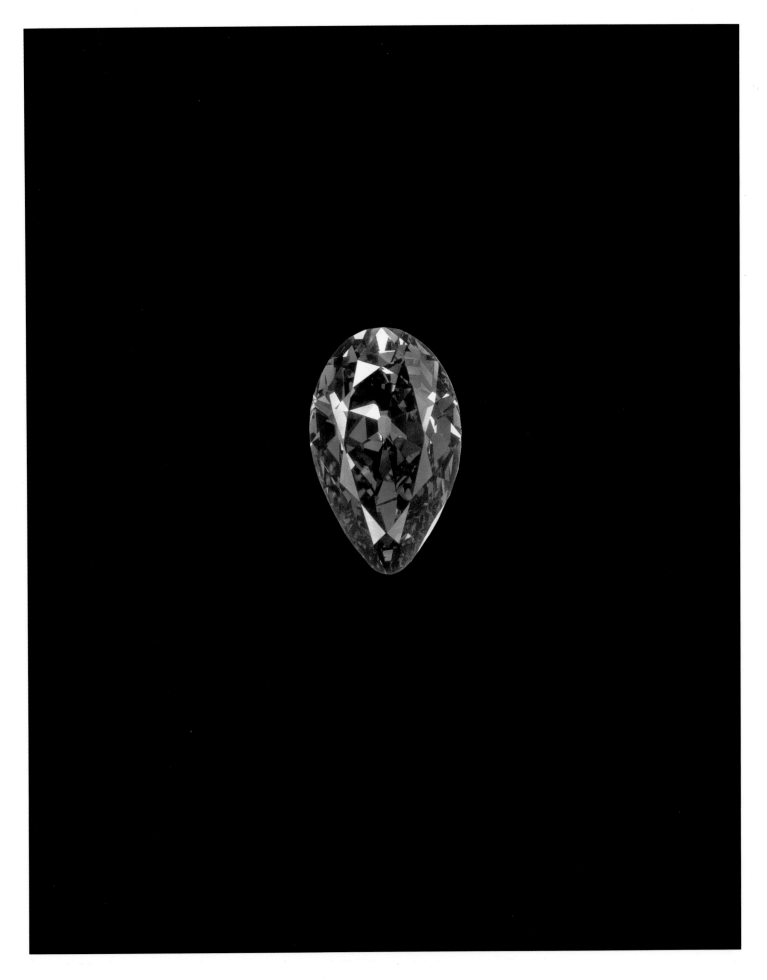

TERESCHENKO

Tiffany

Above: the flamboyant Barney Barnato, one of the most colourful figures in South Africa's early diamond days.

De Beers Archives.

Opposite: the Tiffany.

Courtesy of Tiffany & Co., New York.

It is debatable whether Truman Capote's novel *Breakfast at Tiffany's* did much to increase the prestige of this famous New York jewellery store because long before 1958, the year of the book's publication, it had become a household name within the United States and a well-known one outside. Doubtless some people continue to enquire whether the store does serve breakfast to its clientele, but of course what the delightfully-named heroine, Holly Golightly, sought was not refreshment of the stomach but of the spirit, which was supplied by the sight of the magnificent gems on display in the showcases.

Founded by Charles Louis Tiffany in 1837, Tiffany & Co. came to the fore among diamond merchants during the second half of the last century. During the political disturbances in Paris in 1848, which culminated in the overthrow of King Louis Philippe, the firm bought a large quantity of jewels. At the sale of the French Crown Jewels in 1887, Tiffany's bought the great diamond necklace of the Empress Eugénie, considered at the time to have been the finest single item to go on sale, four diamonds which may have been among the former Mazarins, as well as several other pieces. In the end, Tiffany's emerged as the largest buyer, with 24 out of a total of 69 lots.

Between these two events in French history came the discovery of diamonds in South Africa. Tiffany's were active there too, buying a light-yellow cushion cut of 77 (old) carats cut from a rough stone weighing fractionally less than 125 (old) carats and another fine yellow gem weighing 51⅞ (old) carats. Both of these two diamonds were among the first large stones to be cut in New York City. They were surpassed, however, by the famous gem named after its owners. In the rough, the Tiffany was a beautiful canary-yellow octahedron weighing 287.42 (metric) carats.

It is believed that the Tiffany was found either in 1877 or 1878. The lack of exact information concerning the correct date of its discovery extends to its location as well; this has variously been described as the 'De Beers Mine', the 'Kimberley Mine', 'the De Beers mines' or 'the Kimberley mines'. The finding of the Tiffany took place before accurate records of the discovery of large diamonds from South Africa were kept. However, the clue to its location is surely supplied by one writer who has stated that it was found in the mines of the French Company. This was the colloquial name for the Compagnie Française de Diamant du Cap, an important mining concern, the existence of which sparked off the most momentous financial struggle which the diamond industry has witnessed.

In the belief that the only solution to the problems posed by the inefficient and haphazard mining methods employed in the Kimberley deposits lay in the amalgamation of the multitude of claims into one unit, by 1887 Cecil Rhodes and his colleagues had succeeded in making the De Beers Mining Company, formed seven years before, the sole owner of the De Beers mine. Rhodes's second objective was the amalgamation of all the principal mines in the vicinity of Kimberley into one company, thereby ensuring a rational system of both producing and selling diamonds. With this aim in view Rhodes turned his attention to the Kimberley mine, by far the richest deposit in the area. The largest mining concern within this mine was the Kimberley Central Mining Company, which was then headed by the flamboyant Barney Barnato.

Born Barnett Isaacs in 1852, the son of a small shopkeeper off Petticoat Lane, one of the best-known streets of London's East End, Barnato was in every respect the complete antithesis of Rhodes. Barnato was an extrovert, imbued with Jewish-Cockney wit and humour. After leaving school at

fourteen, he obtained a number of odd jobs including being a 'bouncer' at a public house and appearing on the stage at a music hall. Several of his relatives left for South Africa on hearing of the discovery of diamonds there, so Barney eventually followed them. His only capital on arrival at the diamond fields consisted of boxes of cigars – of doubtful quality – which he hoped to sell to the diggers. He became an itinerant buyer of diamonds, his genial personality proving a useful asset. In time, he bought four claims in the centre of the Kimberley mine and prospered so that he was able to form the Barnato Diamond Mining Company. Like Rhodes, Barnato kept on buying up claims. In 1885 Barnato merged his company with that of Baring-Gould's Kimberley Central Mining Company, thus giving him as strong a hold in the Kimberley mine as that of Rhodes in the De Beers mine.

Since his company was doing so well, Barney Barnato saw no reason at all why he should join any scheme of Rhodes for amalgamation. However, one obstacle lay in the path of the Kimberley Central, namely the Compagnie Française de Diamant du Cap. By virtue of its position within the Kimberley mine and the policy it pursued, the French Company impeded any success of future operations by Barnato's company. Consequently Barnato made proposals to the French: but Rhodes had already done likewise and had succeeded in raising the finance necessary for the purchase of the French Company in Paris. Rhodes then laid a trap for his rival. He told Barnato that he could acquire the French Company if he wanted it and would not ask for cash in payment, only the equivalent of the price paid in Kimberley Central's recently issued new shares. By this means Rhodes was able to secure a useful foothold in the form of one-fifth of Kimberley Central's issued capital; all the time this had been his real objective, not the control of the French Company. Barnato acquiesced in this plan, falling right into the trap Rhodes had set for him.

The stage was now set for a titanic battle for the remainder of the Kimberley Central's issued capital. Both Rhodes and Barnato bought recklessly, and at a time when the price of diamonds barely covered the cost of production, the company's shares soared from £14 to £49 within a few months. Eventually Rhodes and his associates could claim to own three-fifths of the Kimberley Central's issued capital and Barnato realized he had been beaten. He surrendered in March 1888, accepting terms which gave Rhodes the control he had sought. On 12 March, De Beers Consolidated Mines Limited was formerly incorporated. The new company took over assets representing the whole of the De Beers mine, three-quarters of the Kimberley mine and a controlling interest in the Bultfontein and Dutoitspan mines. Cecil Rhodes and Barney Barnato were appointed among the company's first Life Governors.

Some of Kimberley Central's shareholders, however, disapproved of Barnato selling out to Cecil Rhodes and challenged the merger in the Courts. It was the judge who told them that if Barnato agreed to put Kimberley Central into voluntary liquidation, De Beers could simply purchase its assets. Accordingly this is what the company did: Rhodes wrote out a cheque for £5,338,650 for the assets of Kimberley Central, which, in those days, was the largest sum of money ever covered by a single cheque.

Further evidence that the Tiffany diamond must have originated in the claims of the historically important French Company is shown by the fact that the gem was shipped to Paris. Experts there studied it for one year before it was cut under the supervision of the distinguished gemmologist George F. Kunz in 1878. It yielded a cushion-cut brilliant of 128.51 (metric) carats, measuring 27 mm wide, 28.5 mm long, and 22.2 mm high. It was given a total of 90 facets: 48 on the pavilion, 40 on the crown, a table and a culet. The extra facets were cut not to give the diamond more sparkle, rather to make it smoulder as if it were on fire. The gem is high in fluorescence and retains this rich colour in artificial light but is even more beautiful by day.

The head of Tiffany's office in Paris, Mr Gideon Reed, bought the Tiffany for $18,000, on behalf of his firm, whence it was imported into the United States in 1879. Initially, little publicity attended the diamond after its arrival there, a deliberate policy which has been ascribed to Charles Tiffany's fears that, as yellowish diamonds were being produced in South Africa in greater quantities than ever before, this particular diamond might merely be one of many such stones. However, it is important to draw a distinction between light yellow and yellowish diamonds and those of the rare deeper canary yellow; the Tiffany remains one of the finest examples of the latter category.

It was not long before the existence of the Tiffany did become widely known. In 1896 one of the triumvirate who ruled China, the Viceroy Li Hung-Chang – about whom President Grant is said to have remarked, 'There are three great men in the world, Gladstone, Bismarck and Chang, but the greatest of these is Chang' – visited New York. He announced that the one thing he wished to see was the Tiffany diamond, a request that was duly met by the firm.

Since being viewed by this distinguished visitor, the Tiffany has been seen by millions of others in almost seventy years of continuous display in

Tiffany's store. It has also been shown at numerous exhibitions: they include the Chicago Columbian in 1893, the Pan-American in 1901, the Chicago Century of Progress in 1933–34 and the New York World's Fair in 1939. The first occasion on which the diamond was worn was in 1957 at the Tiffany Ball held in Newport, Rhode Island, when the chairwoman of the ball had the honour of wearing it, mounted for the occasion in a necklace of white diamonds. In 1971 the Tiffany returned to South Africa for the exhibition which marked the centennial celebrations of the Kimberley mine. After an absence of forty years from London, Tiffany's re-opened their branch in Old Bond Street in 1986, and displayed the diamond to herald its return.

Left: The facade of Tiffany's in New York.

Photo Elliot Kaufman. Courtesy of Tiffany & Co., New York.

Opposite page: the late Audrey Hepburn wearing Jean Schlumberger's 'Ribbons' necklace in which the Tiffany diamond was set. She wore the diamond in the publicity stills for the release of the film *Breakfast at Tiffany's* in 1961.

Courtesy of Tiffany & Co.

The sole disturbance in the otherwise uneventful history of the Tiffany diamond concerns reported attempts to sell the stone, which was valued at $12,000,000 at the end of 1983. In 1951 the new chairman of Tiffany's recommended that the gem should be sold, a decision which not surprisingly horrified certain members of the old Board. A buyer agreed to pay $500,000 for the stone but the deal fell through because the chairman wanted a cheque in full whereas the prospective buyer wished for other financial arrangements to be made. Then in 1973 the *New York Times* carried an advertisement by Tiffany's offering to sell the diamond for $5,000,000. However, in the circumstances it would be as well to recall the story of the eager new salesman who, when asked what he would get if he sold the famous gem, was promptly told by the head of the firm 'Fired!'

Victoria

Drawing of the Victoria
diamond in the rough,
shortly after its discovery.

Published in W. R. Cattelle's
The Diamond, in 1911.

From the very beginning an aura of mystery attended the discovery of this gem, which weighed 457 ½ (old) carats in the rough. Also called the 'Imperial' or 'Great White', it remained the biggest octahedral diamond from South Africa until 1896 when it was surpassed by one weighing 503¼ (old) carats that was found in the De Beers mine.

The doubts about its origin were clearly expressed early on because under the heading of 'A Large Diamond' two letters from correspondents appeared in *The Times* in London. The first, dated 20 August 1884, read as follows:

Sir. This gem is of a blue-white colour, similar to the finest stones from the Jagersfontein Mine, which is said to be (and most probably is) the true locality of this gem. There is somewhat of a mystery attached to the true origin of the stone, and from the secrecy displayed at its first discovery, it is not improbable that it has been procured through an 'illicit' at the mine from which it is reported to come.

By the existing laws in connexion with diamond mines, it is necessary for persons to hold licences for the traffic in diamonds, but, unfortunately, the jurisdiction extends only to a limited circle. For instance, in the Cape Colony proper, the purchasing and selling of gems is unrestricted, no such law existing. The Jagersfontein Mine, in the Orange Free State, has for some time been only partially worked, and I believe many diggers could tell a rueful tale of their unsuccessful operations. If this monster stone has been found and sold in a strictly legitimate manner, it seems astonishing that all the diamond world has not heard of this wondrous gem before. It also seems peculiar that it should have been consigned to this country by a Port Elizabeth house...

Report says that it was purchased in the first instance for £15,000, and the syndicate now possessing it ask £200,000. Should it prove to be the wondrous gem reported this latter sum is certainly not too high a valuation for such a marvellous and unique stone.

That letter drew the following forthright reply which appeared two days later.

Sir: It may preserve your columns from further fiction, may satisfy public curiosity, and give the unrivalled beauty a fair start in society if the simple pedigree is given, for which I am indebted to a letter, dated 30 June, from my near relative, Mr Allenberg, of Port Elizabeth, who shipped the stone for sale to the London market.

The diamond was found on a Dutchman's farm in the Orange Free State by one of his 'belongings' and kept in secret by him for nearly a year, purely from a dread that, if known, his farm would be 'jumped' by a crowd of diggers and he driven from house and home. At length — by what arguments is not given in the letter — an old friend of Mr Allenberg's obtained sight of the stone and induced the owner to forward it for sale.

No doubt presumably the exact locality must become known. I am ignorant of it, and cannot therefore gratify the curious or the money-making...

It is true that the stone was sold to a syndicate of the leading diamond merchants in London. There has been no secrecy from first to last.

The guess of the price in The Times *is not correct.*

Despite the affirmative tone of the second letter, experts continued to harbour doubts about the source of the Victoria . In this connection, it is important to note that while the Jagersfontein mine definitely did produce many fine white stones, they were nearly always cleavages in the rough; octahedral diamonds were characteristic of three of the Kimberley mines: De Beers mine, Kimberley mine and Dutoitspan mine.

In the issue of *Science* dated 5 August 1887, an interesting article entitled 'Four Large South African Diamonds' appeared under the name of George F. Kunz, the distinguished gemmologist under whose supervision the Tiffany diamond was cut. Mr Kunz first discussed the Victoria. Aware of the correspondence in *The Times* indicating the Orange Free State as the source of the stone, he wrote:

It is, however, believed that it was found by someone in one of the Kimberley mines, South Africa. The first intimation that any of the various mining companies had of its existence was when they heard of its safe arrival in London. It is generally supposed that in the month of June or July 1884, the stone had been found by one of the surveillance officers of the Central Mining Company in the Kimberley mines. It being his duty to search others, he had the privilege of not being searched himself, and so the stone was passed through the searching-house, and he was afterwards supposed to have found means of communicating with four illicit diamond-buyers. Owing to the stringency of the diamond laws of Griqualand West, the trading in rough diamonds is forbidden to any one not owning one of the 'patents' or 'licences', as they are called, costing £200 and a guaranty of £500. All purchases made by them must also be entered in a special registry, and are duly signed each week by the police authorities. £3000 was the price paid to obtain the stone from the first possessor. To prepare themselves for the ordeal of transporting the stone out of the district, they assembled at night, commenced drinking, then gambling, and after a night's debauch two of the party lost their share in the big stone. The other two reached Cape Town in safety, where the diamond laws are not in force, and from a dealer there received £19,000 cash for their stone. An outward duty of one-half per cent is collected on shipments of diamonds from Cape Colony; but this diamond is said to have been carried by one of the passengers of a mail steamer, and was hence undeclared. We next hear from it in London, causing considerable sensation in Hatton Garden, the great diamond market. After considerable time had been spent in trying to find a capitalist who could afford to buy such a gem, it was at last arranged by a former resident of the Cape mines to form a company of eight persons, who bought the stone together for £45,000 cash, on condition that if they should dispose of it each should receive a ninth share in the eventual profits.

Mr Kunz went on to add that it was finally decided to cut it into the largest possible brilliant, rather than into numerous small stones, and that Amsterdam was selected as the place where the gem could best be cut.

The Victoria was despatched to the firm of Jacques Metz where a special workshop was constructed for its cutting. First, a piece was cleaved off which eventually yielded a brilliant of 19 (old) carats. This stone was later bought by the King of Portugal; its location is unknown today but it may be one of the brilliants among the former Crown Jewels on display in the Ajuda Palace in Lisbon.

The cutting of the largest piece of the Victoria began on 9 April 1887, in the presence of the Queen of Holland: the operation took about a year because the preliminary processes in cutting a diamond were by-passed and it was polished solely on the scaife. A great deal of time was consumed by the cooling of the stone as it became heated after an hour's running on the wheel. The cutter was Mr M. B. Barends.

The finished gem was a slightly oval-shaped brilliant cut with 58 facets. It measured 39.5 mm long, 30 mm wide and 23 mm thick. In his article, Mr Kunz noted that the form of the Victoria was not entirely even and that on one side of the girdle there was quite a flat place, a natural unpolished surface, necessary, in cutting, to preserve the large weight of the stone. Its weight was ultimately 184.5 (metric) carats.

The sixth Nizam of Hyderabad, Mahbub Ali Khan, bought the Victoria which was believed to bring good luck: this belief later prompted the Prince to reject an offer for it from the Aga Khan. But the Nizam's purchase was to inaugurate a second period of mystery surrounding the diamond.

When the British withdrew from India in 1947 and the Indian sub-continent was partitioned into India and Pakistan, the ruling Nizam of Hyderabad, the son of the purchaser of the

Victoria diamond, chose to remain independent, refusing to join to either of those two countries. Eventually, after the breakdown of negotiations and subsequent armed interventions by Indian forces, Hyderabad acceded to the Indian Union as a state in January 1950. Later Hyderabad was partitioned among three neighbouring states. The Nizam, General His Excellent Highness Sir Mir Osman Ali Khan Bahadur, who had loyally supported the Allied cause during the Second World War, retired to Bombay (now Mumbai) to live on a pension granted him by the government of India. It was said that the Nizam lived so frugally that his personal expenses amounted to merely 7s. 6d (37½ pence) a day.

The Nizam placed his collection of jewels, stated unofficially at the time to have been worth between £13,000,000 and £15,000,000, under trust, dividing them into two groups: the first comprised forty pieces which the trustees could sell; the second and slightly larger group consisted of pieces that were not for sale, unless, in the Nizam's own words, some unforseen calamity should befall his family. There was no mention of the Victoria. On the other hand a diamond called the Jacob was specifically included in the second category.

On more than one occasion there were reports that the Nizam was experiencing financial difficulties, caused apparently by his family and his dependants, of whom there were said to be more than a thousand. Then in April 1951 it was stated that the Jacob was to be offered for sale along with other jewels. The Indian States Minister told Parliament that the proceeds from the sale would be invested in government securities and used to benefit Hyderabad. Simultaneously came reports that the Indian government was refusing to allow any more of the famous jewels to leave the country and that the Jacob diamond would almost certainly be listed as 'national treasure'. Again, there was no mention of the Victoria.

Five years later it was reported that the Jacob, then held by the Bank of India, was for sale. An American dealer described it as 'white, not blue' in colour, adding that it was not the most brilliant gem which he had seen.

After the death of the Nizam in 1967 his jewels were again in the news. The trustees wished to sell some of them to help meet the family's staggering tax liabilities. Millionaires flocked to India to attend the sale. Certain conditions were laid down for prospective buyers: anyone who wanted to examine a single jewel on sale was obliged to pay a non-refundable fee of £100; no one could bid without depositing £2,000 security which would be refunded only after all transactions had been completed; one-tenth of the price offered for each

275

The Nizam of Hyderabad, reputedly the richest man in the world during his reign (1911–48), who inherited the Victoria diamond. His jewels – 137 pieces – were purchased by the Indian government in 1995 and are currently held in a bank vault in New Delhi.

piece of jewellery had to be furnished with the bid, the remainder within ten days of an offer's acceptance.

The auction was stalled because of public outcry. Many Indians felt that, like the British Crown Jewels and the jewellery collection housed in the Smithsonian Institution in Washington, the jewels that had belonged to the Nizam of Hyderabad should be regarded as a part of the country's national heritage and, therefore, should be preserved in India.

There the matter rested until 1993 when the Indian government decided to buy the fabled collection. The two sides reached final agreement on the price and the government said that payment for the jewels would be made in six instalments, but the trustees rejected this arrangement and their argument was upheld by the Supreme Court, who directed the government to pay in full.

Once again events stalled until the Supreme Court intervened at the behest of the trustees. It forced the government's hand by directing that the trustees could invite bids from foreign buyers.

Earlier the Supreme Court had given a deadline but yielded to an appeal from the government for more time. The Lower House of the Indian Parliament gave its approval for funds to buy the collection but the Upper House did not get around to ratifying the decision in the session. The impasse was fortunately resolved by the discovery of a loophole in the parliamentary rule book which allowed the money to be handed over to the appropriate government department; all that was left to do was to work out the final details of the agreement. The government was required to produce the cash by 16 January, 1995, or the deal would collapse.

On 12 January, the Indian government paid approximately Rs 218 crore ($70 million) for the Nizam's jewels, which comprised 137 items. Privately the trustees and the beneficiaries considered that the best price had not been obtained for the collection, which had earlier been valued much higher by international auctioneers.

Throughout these proceedings there was no mention of a diamond entitled Victoria, Imperial or Great White. On the other hand mention continued to be made of the Jacob, its weight being reported variously as 100, 150 and, more significantly, 184½ carats. The last figure is, of course, the reported weight of the Victoria. Is it possible then that a diamond with a somewhat mundane name is the same stone as another with such a resounding title? The answer is supplied by John Lord in his book *The Maharajahs*, published in 1972, where he recounts the strange story of A. M. Jacob. Alexander Jacob was an Armenian Jew who arrived in Simla in 1871, where he became a dealer in precious stones. Lord writes:

Jacob was notorious, from Simla to the fashionable spa of Homburg, for his powers of magic. The gullible credited him with the ability to walk on water and even the least credulous granted him powers of mesmerism and telepathy. It was generally believed by British and Indians alike that he practised white magic, and it was variously supposed that he was a Jew, an Armenian, a Russian agent, a British agent. It was obvious to all that he was the most important dealer in jewels and antiquities in India, and known to a few that he had in fact undertaken missions for the Secret Department of the government of India. He travelled by private train. His little store in Simla was a pantechnicon of riches, blazing with gold and smokey with incense, and in it Jacob squatted, pale and subtle, keeping a diary full of secrets.

It is not surprising that such a character as Jacob should have served as the model for at least three characters in fiction, the most celebrated being Lurgan in Rudyard Kipling's novel *Kim*. This tale was published in 1901, ten years after the lawsuit that had spelled ruin for Jacob. John Lord describes the case as follows:

Jacob had agreed to purchase for the Nizam a famous diamond kept in England, then called 'the Imperial' (and later 'the Jacob'), for the sum of three hundred thousand pounds, half of which His Highness had paid as a deposit. Now Jacob delivered the diamond in person with only the Nizam's valet as a witness. He left, with the Nizam still owing half the purchase price. Unknown to Jacob, the Resident had heard about the transaction. A worthy, wordy man whose lust was legalities and propriety, the Resident sought to save the Nizam's almost bankrupt government from the folly of buying yet another bauble. The Nizam froze. He was not allowed to pay the rest of the money and he would not return the diamond. He wrapped it in an ink-stained cloth and dropped it into a drawer. Jacob was forced to defend his investment by suing a Calcutta court; though he won the case he was broken. His legal expenses were great. No prince in India would deal with him again and he died in penury, even his magic spent, in Bombay.

As the twenty-first century opens, more and more does it appear to be the age of collectivity. Fortunately, there have been a few individuals who have survived to make their mark in their own fields, to the ultimate benefit of the community as a whole. One who did so in the field of diamonds was a Canadian geologist, Dr John Thorburn Williamson.

Williamson was born in Quebec in 1907. At first he studied law but then changed to geology, in which he graduated from McGill University, Montreal, that eminent cradle of geologists the world over. For a time he pursued his career as a geologist in Canada before transferring his attention to Africa. He obtained a post with a mining company in what was then Northern Rhodesia, now Zambia, but resigned in 1936. His interest in geological possibilities spurred him on in a northerly direction, so that he joined the Tanganyika Diamond and Gold Development Company, owners of the Mabuki diamond mine near Mwanza, a port situated on the southern shores of Lake Victoria.

After the Tanganyika Diamond and Gold Development Company closed down their operations in Tanganyika, Williamson became self-employed, carrying out his own private prospecting; he paid particular attention to the region of Shinyanga, some 180 km to the south of Mwanza. Williamson was convinced that a rich diamond deposit existed in this area, an opinion not shared by surveyors employed by the British government: they scoffed at the idea and informed him that 'the area was valueless from a mineralogical point of view'. This was despite the publication in 1939 of a Tanganyika Geological Survey, written by a New Zealand geologist, G. J. Williams, employed by the colonial government, which specifically drew attention to the area geologically favourable for

Dr John Williamson, the Canadian geologist whose belief in the existence of an important diamond deposit in Tanzania was to be proved correct.

diamonds, namely the Shinyanga district.

One day in March 1940, Williamson and his party, which included two local prospectors whom he had trained and were working for him, camped under a baobab tree at a remote spot called Mwadui, situated in what is today Tanzania but was then the territory of Tanganyika. Now the Creator must have been seized by a fit of imagination when the baobab – or monkey-bread tree, as it is sometimes called – was made because it looks as if it had been planted upside down. It is planted to give shade in some tropical countries since its trunk sometimes attains a diameter of over nine metres and the span of its branches may provide foliage over 45 metres.

One of the two prospectors, James Ashton, was the first to notice some typical kimberlite minerals on the surface in the area later to prove so rich in diamonds. When he reported this find, Williamson despatched him to the place with some labourers and a 1.2-metre diameter, hand-operated, diamond pan (with the Swahili name of *Malaya*, i.e. 'the wandering one'). There Ashton washed some gravels and found the first diamond.

Following this, Williamson started prospecting and developing the deposit. A private company, Williamson Diamonds Limited, was formed in March 1942, with Dr Williamson as the sole governing Director and General Manager. It resulted in the opening up of what has proved to be the kimberlite pipe with the largest area ever to have been found at the surface.

During its life, approximately one half of the diamonds recovered from the Mwadui pipe have proved to be of gem quality. They contain mostly clear and colourless stones but do include a few small 'fancy' diamonds, in colours such as green and pink. A few large gems have also been unearthed, notably one of 155 carats in 1945, an exceptionally fine blue-white piece of 114 carats in 1948, and the largest to date, a fine stone weighing 256.07 carats that was valued at £30,725. On one occasion in 1945, the Governor of Tanganyika, Sir William Battershill, chanced to visit Mwadui when a 65-carat gem was found: it was suitably named after the visitor.

But all these discoveries were eclipsed in October 1947 by that of the diamond which bears Dr Williamson's name. This was a beautiful pink gem, weighing 54.5 carats, which was found by a child in the dust beneath a baobab tree. In shape it was a cleavage, almost circular at its widest part and rounded over the top but tapered in the short conical lower half.

The pride which Williamson took in his mine was equalled by the affection which he felt for this diamond. Long after it had travelled overseas the mine's chief security officer related how Dr Williamson used to hide a replica of the stone in the topsoil. Then he would take an unsuspecting visitor to the spot, halt for a moment and start to shuffle his feet in the dust. The visitor would share in the ensuing excitement when the hidden object was revealed, only for him to learn that it was merely a plastic replica of the famous diamond. Some poignancy is added to this charade when it is recalled that the discovery remains unique to this day, no other pink stone of comparable size ever having come to light at Mwadui.

Dr Williamson was struck by the beauty of the diamond. He was also a passionate admirer of the Crown, and its discovery enabled him to present a sumptuous gift to Princess Elizabeth (now Queen Elizabeth II) on the occasion of her wedding on 20 November 1947. Such a gift was undoubtedly among the most valuable wedding presents that she received.

The task of cutting the valuable diamond was entrusted to the firm of Briefel and Lemer, whose premises were located in Clerkenwell, one of the oldest parts of London, where diamond cutting had long been carried out. One of the partners, Sidney Briefel, had a theory about the origin of pink diamonds, namely that they were coloured by the first sunset ever to have shone on carbon crystals still swimming in seas of lava!

However, Mr Briefel was a gentleman imbued with practical as well as imaginative qualities and he soon realized that prolonged study of the diamond would be necessary before deciding how best to cut it. There was no doubt in his mind that it ought to be cut as a brilliant so as to make the most of its size and colour. But its shape presented a special problem because in the lower half of the diamond there was a deep cavity, equal in size to about 3 carats. It was thought that the cutting needed to remove all trace of this pit would be such that the final polished gem could not possibly weigh more than 18 carats. Some experts in fact doubted whether the eventual yield would exceed 14 carats.

An unusual feature of the cutting of the Williamson Pink lay in the fact that neither of the initial processes of shaping a diamond, cleaving or sawing, was employed. Mr Briefel devised a method of grinding the rough stone in such a way as to retain its natural maximum diameter. It was cut and polished entirely on the scaife and the future shape of the gem was achieved by the polisher grinding away the circumference in a series of small straight facets. First, the rounded tip was slowly polished away until the largest possible table was obtained above the girdle. Then, fraction by fraction, other parts of the diamond were removed.

Accompanied by her grandmother, Queen Mary, the Princess visited the factory on 10 March 1948 to see how the work was progressing. The cavity had been much reduced and now appeared merely as a blemish on one of the facets. So far nothing had been lost from the maximum diameter of the stone.

By the end of March 1948, after two months' work, the time had come when the polisher knew he dared not leave the stone on the scaife a moment longer. The facet had reached its correct forty-one degree angle and its top edge was defined clearly and sharply, together with the bottom of the girdle. If any sign of the pit then remained, the entire stone would have had to have been reduced proportionally.

He lifted the gem and examined it. The last vestige of the cavity had disappeared.

The work continued until 14 April, when the Princess's private secretary was informed: 'The finished brilliant has achieved a weight of 23.60 carats and it has retained the pink colour which it displayed in the rough.' The gem, indeed, was completely pure and flawless.

Opposite: the Williamson diamond which Queen Elizabeth II chose to have set in the centre of a flower spray brooch designed by Cartier.

Photograph by Rosemary May. Reproduced by Gracious Permission of Her Majesty the Queen.

For some time Princess Elizabeth was undecided about the manner in which the pink gem should be set. Eventually, in 1953, the year of her coronation, the Queen had the diamond set in the centre of a flower spray brooch created by Cartier. It was jonquil shaped, with curved petals of marquises: one on each side of the stalk represented the leaves. The brooch was made of platinum and measured 114.3 mm long. All the accompanying white diamonds originated from the mine at Mwadui and included:

> 21 marquises, with a total weight of 9.73 carats
> 12 baguettes, with a total weight of 4.64 carats
> 170 brilliants, with a total weight of 12.40 carats

This most beautiful jewel was displayed at 'The Ageless Diamond' exhibition held in London in the summer of 1959. Subsequently Her Majesty wore the brooch on one of her tours to Africa and on the occasion of the wedding of her first cousin, the Duke of Kent, in York Minster in 1961. But the event which surely provided most evidence of the affection which the Queen clearly feels for the pink diamond was the wedding of the Prince of Wales on 29 July 1981. Millions of viewers worldwide who watched the ceremony on television saw Her Majesty wearing the brooch set against the background of a blue dress. It is safe to assume that no famous diamond has ever been seen by so many people at the same time.

Sadly, after a long illness, Dr Williamson died from cancer of the throat in 1958. His grave lies under the foot of a baobab tree at Mwadui. Not long afterwards the government of Tanganyika and De Beers Consolidated Mines became joint owners of the mine, with Harry Oppenheimer becoming chairman of the reconstituted board of directors. Mr Oppenheimer paid tribute to the founder of the mine when he said, 'I am sure that Dr Williamson will finally be recognized as the man who set going a process which will eventually, in its repercussions, raise the standard of living generally throughout the territory.' Although with the passage of time, production has declined significantly at Mwadui, it has made an important contribution to the economy of Tanzania. But it is difficult to forget what the situation would be today if the opinions of government officials had been allowed to triumph over those of an individual.

A 'legend in his lifetime', the 'twentieth-century Tavernier', the 'King of Diamonds' are just a few of the epithets to have been applied to Harry Winston. He deserved them all, for no one in this century did more to promote and to preserve the numerous celebrated diamonds which he and his firm handled.

The origins of the family business date from soon after 1890 when Harry Winston's father, Jacob, opened a small jewellery shop in Maiden Lane, then the centre of the jewellery business in New York before the advent of 47th Street. He used to make his own clocks and watches. For reasons of health – he suffered from asthma – he was obliged to move west to Los Angeles where he again opened a jewellery shop, but in due course returned east where Harry Winston was born, in New York City, in March 1896.

In 1920 Harry Winston used the $20,000 which he had saved in California to set up a one-man firm, Premier Diamond Company, in a small office on Fifth Avenue in New York. Thirteen years later he started his own retail business but soon found it hard to break into the tightly controlled diamond market. He decided to look beyond the conventional sources of fine gemstones to what was then decidedly unconventional: estate jewellery. During the 1920s there was an abundance of estate jewellery on the market, expensive pieces that people had begun to liquidate for various reasons after the First World War. Winston purchased the outdated items, removed the gems from their settings and recut them in the modern style to show off more sparkle and brilliance. They were then mounted in contemporary settings to appeal to the taste of the thirties.

Highly successful in this field, Harry Winston achieved the financial independence he sought, and by 1933 began to manufacture his own jewellery; that same year he closed the Premier Diamond Company

and became incorporated as Harry Winston Inc. In 1935 he purchased the first of the many great diamonds which he was destined to acquire: this was the 726-carat Jonker, found in South Africa the previous year. It was followed by the purchase of the President Vargas – identical in weight to the Jonker – in 1938. Then, in 1949, he made his most famous purchase of all, that of the Hope diamond which he bought from the estate of Mrs Evalyn Walsh McLean, a prominent figure in Washington society. The Hope was just one of the pieces included in 'The Court of Jewels', a display of historic stones which Winston created and which travelled around the country to raise money for various charities. In this he was conspicuously successful.

Harry Winston presented the Hope diamond as a gift to the Smithsonian Institution in Washington in 1958, where he wished to establish a collection of fine jewels for the nation. It is entirely appropriate, therefore, that the Hall of Gems and Minerals in the Smithsonian, after its renovation, reopened in September 1997 with a Harry Winston Gallery.

The diamond which bears the name of Winston is a fine blue-white and flawless pear shape of 62.05 carats, cut, in 1954, from a rough stone weighing 154.5 carats that had come to light in the Jagersfontein mine two years earlier. Of this gem Harry Winston remarked: 'I'm going to keep this one quiet. I want to keep it to myself. This stone is like a great painting. You want to keep looking at it.' However, in 1959 the Winston was sold to King Saud of Saudi Arabia for a reported $600,000. Eighteen months later, the King asked Mr Winston to come to Boston, Massachusetts, where he was undergoing eye surgery, and handed the diamond back to him. He explained: 'I have four wives, and if I give one stone to one wife, well, my life won't be worth a moment's peace – unless of course you have three others like this.' Unfortunately Harry Winston

Harry Winston, a legend throughout the diamond world.

Courtesy Harry Winston Ltd., New York.

The fine blue-white, flawless Winston diamond.

De Beers Archives.

did not have available any stones which would have eased the predicament of the King, an extremely valuable client of his, and was obliged to take the diamond back. He loaned it for display at the 'International Exhibition of Modern Jewellery 1890–1961', held in Goldsmiths Hall, London, in 1961.

Three years later, Harry Winston had a luckier stroke. Asked to value some jewellery that had belonged to a daughter of Jack Chrysler, the automobile tycoon, he came across a pear shape weighing 59.46 carats. This diamond made an almost perfect match with the Winston, with the result that they were set as a pair of earrings and subsequently sold to a Canadian client. In November 1980 they came up for auction in Geneva where they fetched $7,300,000.

Wittelsbach

How often does one sadly come across phrases such as 'present location unknown' or 'all trace of the diamond has been lost' when undertaking research into the histories of famous diamonds. It is all the more satisfying, therefore, to recall an item in a newspaper that appeared in January 1962, under the heading of 'Rare diamond reappears'. This referred to the Wittelsbach, a diamond of a rare dark blue colour whose reappearance, admittedly after a mere three decades, was nevertheless an exciting and welcome event. The Wittelsbach weighs 35.50 metric carats and measures 24.40 mm in diameter and 8.29 mm in depth; it is pure apart from a few surface scratches that were probably caused during removal from its setting. The diamond has been cut with 50 facets arranged in an unusual pattern.

The first record of the Wittelsbach dates from the latter part of the seventeenth century. One fact is thus certain: the diamond must be of Indian origin. Furthermore, it has been suggested that a diamond of such a rare colour must once have formed part of the famous French Blue diamond, weighing 112½ old carats, which Tavernier bought in India and later sold to Louis XIV of France. The principal gem which this yielded is the Hope, weighing 45.52 carats, so that technical reasons alone clearly preclude the possibility of the Wittelsbach having been fashioned from the same piece of rough. The sole possibility of a connection between the Wittelsbach and the Hope lies in Tavernier's French Blue diamond being merely part of a much larger piece of rough that had at some time been split into two (a most unlikely occurrence). However, it would be interesting to ascertain whether the Wittelsbach has physical properties similar to the Hope.

The history of the Wittelsbach has been uneventful; for the most part it has been passed down from one royal owner to another. The gem formed part of the gift which Philip IV of Spain gave to his fifteen-year-old daughter, the Infanta Margareta Teresa, upon the occasion of her betrothal to the Emperor Leopold I of Austria in 1664. (Any chance of tracing the earlier history of the Wittelsbach was lost when the Madrid archives were destroyed during the Spanish Civil War of 1936–39.) The bride's father commanded the Treasurer to compose a dowry from a recent acquisition of precious stones from India and Portugal. The resulting selection included a large blue diamond. Unfortunately, the marriage between the Emperor and the Infanta ended with her early death in 1675. Her jewels passed to her husband, and are listed in a document dated 23 March 1673:

Diamond ornament… consisting of… a large brooch with a Great Blue Diamond in the centre, to which belongs a bow-shaped jewel set with rubies.

Leopold I later gave all the jewellery he had inherited from the Infanta to his third wife, the Empress Eleonore Magdalena, daughter of the Elector Palatine. The Empress outlived her husband, dying in 1720. By then she had already made arrangements to bequeath the 'Great Blue Diamond' to her younger grand-daughter, the Archduchess Maria Amelia, daughter of the Emperor Joseph I.

In 1717 the Archduchess made the acquaintance of the man she was destined to marry, the Bavarian Crown Prince Charles Albert. Born in Brussels in 1697, he was subsequently brought up and educated in Austria. Their wedding in 1722 was an event that heralded an important change in the future of the blue diamond. Henceforth it became the 'family diamond' of the ruling House of Bavaria, the Wittelsbachs; it remained so until the abdication of the last king in 1918. The diamond was the principal item in Maria Amelia's dowry and was described under the heading of diamond ornaments as, 'No. 1. A large blue brilliant encircled with small brilliants', and valued at 240,000 guilders, proof of the value attached to the gem, especially when its worth is compared to that of other valuables recorded in contemporary inventories.

It was not long after the wedding of the Crown Prince to the Archduchess that his father, the Elector Maximilian Emmanuel, found himself in financial difficulties. As the head of a Royal Family, he was responsible for the welfare of its members which, in turn, meant that he was free to do as he pleased with all their worldly goods. Borrowing money from a banker named Oppenheim, he thus pledged both the Wittelsbach diamond and a golden dinner service. They were redeemed four years later for 543,781 guilders, but the Elector, who died shortly afterwards, left his son and successor the task of covering this amount. In addition, the Elector left his family an impoverished one; the redemption of the diamond raised the total deficit to 4,000,000 guilders.

The new Elector, Charles Albert, clearly had an affection for the Wittelsbach because during his lifetime he had its setting altered several times, each one more beautiful than the last. His successor, Maximilian III, ordered yet another setting for the gem which was undertaken by a Munich jeweller. The Wittelsbach was set in a circle of brilliants with a border of larger brilliants in a floral design. Suspended from this was a loop or bow of brilliants with horizontal rays radiating from a large oblong brilliant-cut diamond of a pinkish tint in the centre. Altogether a total of 700 brilliants were employed in this extravagant setting.

The last King of Bavaria to wear the blue diamond was Louis III, who reigned until 1918 when Germany became a republic. After his abdication he retired to his estate in Hungary, dying there in 1921. His interment in the Theatinerkirche in Munich was a ceremonial occasion of splendour and it marked the last time that the Wittelsbach diamond accompanied a monarch to his final place of rest.

In the aftermath of the First World War, Bavaria became a republic and the possessions of the former House of Wittelsbach were placed under the control of an equalization fund. The members of the Royal Family received an indemnity which, however, was soon to prove worthless in the ensuing period of inflation, and since legislation did not permit the conversion of landed property into

money, the members of the Royal House were soon left in an impoverished state. Accordingly, the State agreed in 1931 that certain Crown Jewels of the House of Wittelsbach should be sold to alleviate the hardship experienced by descendants of the last king.

The honour of auctioning the Bavarian Crown Jewels fell to Christie's in London, who, in November 1931, announced that the sale would take place the following month and that the contents would include 'a famous Blue diamond'. Public interest was remarkable; the sale comprised thirteen lots and lasted for over two hours. The first lot consisted of the blue diamond; it had what was apparently considered to be a good start at £3,000 and the bidding rose to £5,400. Although it was knocked down at that figure to a purchaser named 'Thorp' the general impression was that the diamond remained unsold. Among the items that were sold, was one described as 'a fine cinnamon-yellow oblong brilliant' for £1,500 which may have been the previously mentioned diamond of a pinkish tint that featured in the jewel made for Maximilian III.

Now the mystery of the whereabouts of the Wittelsbach truly begins. Whatever transpired at Christie's in December 1931, the diamond did not return to its former place of display in Munich; in its place visitors were shown a worthless piece of blue cut glass. Rumours included one that the stone had been sold illegally in 1932 through a Munich jeweller and had reappeared in Holland. Later research unveiled the fact that the Wittelsbach had been sold in Belgium in 1951 and that it had changed hands again in 1955. Three years later millions of visitors came to Brussels for the World Exhibition and many must have cast eyes upon the exhibition of jewellery which included a large blue diamond. But not one person appeared to have had any inkling that this was in fact a missing famous gem – the Wittelsbach diamond.

Credit for the recognition of the true identity of the blue diamond must go to the late Mr Joseph Komkommer, a leading figure in the Belgian diamond industry and the fourth generation of a diamond family.

In January 1962 Mr Komkommer received a telephone call asking him to look at an old-mine cut diamond with a view to its recutting. When he opened the envelope he received a shock – a dark blue diamond is among the rarest and most precious gems. Mr Komkommer at once recognized that the diamond was one of historical significance and that it would be sacrilegious to recut it. With the assistance of his son, Mr Jacques Komkommer, he identified the diamond as the 'lost' blue diamond

284   Opposite: the Wittelsbach.

Photo Ernst Heiniger, in
Le Grand Livre des Bijoux, 1974.

Las Meninas by Velazquez, depicting the Spanish royal family with the Infanta Margareta and her maids of honour in the artist's studio, 1656. She received the Wittelsbach from her father, Philip IV, on her betrothal.

Madrid, Museo del Prado. Photo AKG London/Erich Lessing.

that was formerly owned by the House of Wittelsbach. Mr Komkommer thereupon formed a consortium of diamond buyers from Belgium and the USA which purchased the diamond, then valued at £180,000. The vendors were the trustees of an estate whose identity remained undisclosed. Finally, the Wittelsbach was acquired by a private collector in 1964.

'What was he doing, the great god Pan, Down in the reeds by the river?' asks Elizabeth Barrett Browning in her poem, 'The Musical Instrument'. To which one can only surmise that if the river chanced to be the Woyie in Sierra Leone, then it is more than probable that Pan was on the look-out for diamonds, for this particular river has been a prolific source of large stones. In reality, the Woyie is neither quite one thing nor the other; at some sections it gives the appearance of being a very small river, while at some other sections illicit mining has turned it into a morass where the outline of the original stream has been obliterated.

During the 1940s the recovery plant operated by Sierra Leone Selection Trust Limited unearthed three exceptional diamonds from the river gravels. The first, weighing 249.25 carats, was found in March 1943, and the second, weighing 532 carats, was found in the following June. The third and largest weighed 770 carats, equivalent to 154 g, and was discovered on 6 January 1945 (almost forty years after the discovery of the Cullinan). As well as becoming known as the Woyie River diamond, it was also called the 'Victory', in commemoration of the ending of the war in Europe four months later. There were also suggestions at the time that the gem might be called 'The Star of Sierra Leone'; however, that name was to be kept on ice and not to be bestowed until more than a quarter of a century later when the great 968.9-carat diamond was found. Nevertheless, until the discovery of that diamond the Woyie River remained the largest alluvial diamond to have ever been found.

The diamond was somewhat lozenge-shaped and measured 71 mm long, 53 mm broad and 32 mm thick. It was not clean internally, possessing numerous inclusions, but it was of the finest colour. A conspicuous feature of the rough was the presence of pronounced triangular pits, known as

trigons, on one of its faces. This was one of the points underlined in the very thorough and interesting account of the three large diamonds of Sierra Leone, written in 1945 by the late Professor W. T. Gordon, then Professor of Geology, University of London. He wrote as follows:

As with diamonds from other localities, the crystal faces are pitted. Octahedral faces have triangular or, rarely, hexagonal pits and the triangles are equilateral in shape; cube faces have square pits with their edges diagonal to the cube edges... The largest and latest to be found [in Sierra Leone] has one octahedral face with triangular pits that are larger and deeper than any previously recorded. Some of them measure nearly 6mm on edge and are about 1 mm deep. They are arranged in parallel position as usual and set with their sides towards the points of the ideal octahedra. The spacing of the pits is such that the areas between them assume raised shield-shaped, triangular forms; the points of the shields and those of the pits are in ranks facing opposite directions.

Another unusual feature of the Woyie River, an exceptionally smooth face, drew this comment from Professor Gordon:

The area of this cleavage face is 11.5 sq.cm., and it is so clean a fracture that the blow which produced it must have been a sudden, sharp impact in precisely the correct direction. The surface is exceedingly smooth, whereas most cleavage faces show a certain stepping from layer to layer while keeping in the same general direction. The blow need not have been a heavy one, but the marvel of the smoothness of the fracture-face can only be appreciated by those who have tried to cleave a diamond using the cleaver's tools.

In conclusion, Professor Gordon suggested that the stone might once have been larger, but that there was no sign of it having been merely the smaller piece of a much larger diamond.

The Diamond Corporation subsequently purchased the Woyie River and included it among a display of rough diamonds shown to Queen Mary when she visited the Company's offices in October 1947. The public was given an opportunity of viewing the diamond when it was exhibited at the

British Industries Fair of May 1949. Eventually the task of cutting the Woyie River was entrusted to the London firm of Briefel and Lemer. They had previously cut the pink-coloured Williamson diamond, presented to Princess Elizabeth (now Queen Elizabeth II) on the occasion of her marriage in 1947. As had been the case with other large diamonds, prolonged study of the gem was necessary and a cement model of it was made; a special machine for the sawing operation was also devised.

Because of the number of its inclusions the Woyie River was destined not to be one of those diamonds fashioned into one principal gem. Instead, initially it was separated into 30 different pieces weighing 695.71 carats, from which 30 gems weighing a total of 282.36 carats were cut; this represented 36.67 per cent of the weight of the original diamond – a very fair yield for one containing so many imperfections and a tribute to the skill and expertise of the late Sidney Briefel, who was in charge of the cleaving operation. Ten of the gems weighed over 20 carats, seven between 5 and 10 carats and thirteen less than 5 carats; they comprised ten brilliants, eight emerald cuts, five marquises, two pear shapes and five others of various fancy shapes. All the gems, which were of the finest colour, were sold privately.

The largest gem cut from the Woyie River, an emerald cut weighing 31.35 carats, has retained the name 'Victory'. It reappeared at the jewellery sale held in New York by Christie's on 11 April 1984, as one of the jewels owned by Florence J. Gould, having since been graded 'D' colour, internally flawless. It was purchased for $880,000 by a buyer from Saudi Arabia.

The largest gem cut from the Woyie River – the Victory.

Left: The 'vivid blue' 27.64-carat Heart of Eternity, the largest of the eleven blue diamonds of the 'De Beers Millennium Jewels' display in the Millennium Dome in London during 2000.

De Beers Archive

Abbas Mirza

Abbas Mirza, a member of the Persian royal family, was the second son of Fath Ali Shah (1797–1834) and a leader of his country's forces. He was formally recognized as heir to the throne of Persia, but he died one year before his father. During his final campaign in Khorassan, in the eastern part of the country, where Abbas Mirza was entrusted with the task of restoring order and defending Persian rights, the Abbas Mirza diamond came to light. In 1832, following the capture of Goocha, a large diamond weighing 130 carats was found among the jewels of the harem of Reeza Kooli Khan. This information was conveyed to a meeting of the British Association in 1851 when Dr Beke, of the Chemical Section, made a statement entitled 'On a diamond slab supposed to have been cut from the Koh-i-noor.'

Dr Beke's theory that the Abbas Mirza diamond had been cut from the Koh-i-noor was endorsed by Professor James Tennant, the London mineralogist, while Tennant's statement was followed by some observations by Sir David Brewster, the Scottish physicist and inventor of the kaleidoscope. Sir David concurred with the opinion put forth that the Abbas Mirza was only a part of a much larger and very fine diamond but he did not specify that the crystal was necessarily the Koh-i-noor.

Whatever the origins of the Abbas Mirza may have been, it cannot be identified with any existing diamond; the gemmologists who were able to examine the Iranian Crown Jewels in the 1960s have stated that no diamond approximates to the Abbas Mirza in that legendary collection. It is more than likely that its somewhat primitive shape, judging by previous accounts, would have been recut to suit the more sophisticated tastes of a later age.

Aga Khan

This fine pear-shaped diamond, weighing 33.13 carats, is named after Sir Sultan Mohammad Shah Aga Khan III (1877–1957). The Aga Khan is the title of the Imam, or spiritual leader, of the Shia Ismaili Muslims; the Aga Khan III, who was the 48th Imam, was a much respected political and spiritual leader of his people.

Like many other Eastern rulers, the Aga Khan was attracted to gems and commissioned Cartier to mount some of the best gemstones which he had inherited from his mother, a Qajar princess; in addition he requested the firm to sell unwanted stones from his collection. In 1928 he sent 38 brilliant cuts and three pear shapes, weighing 40, 38 and 35 carats, for sale, which Cartier set in a spectacular necklace, first displayed at the French Exhibition in Cairo in 1929. Later that year, on the eve of the Wall Street Crash, the necklace was broken up; Cartier acquired the 35-carat pear shape while the 38-carat diamond was returned to the Aga Khan and the 40-carat gem was set as the centre-piece of a necklace for his son, Prince Aly Khan.

The Aga Khan III is the 38-carat diamond, subsequently recut to its present weight, and has been certified by the GIA as 'E' colour and internally flawless. It was the last of the six items of jewellery from the Aga Khan's collection which Christie's sold in Geneva in May 1988 and on that occasion it fetched $1,807,143. The proceeds from this collection went to the Bellerive Foundation which, established in 1977, is concerned with a wide range of topics from environmental protection and conservation of natural resources to the safeguarding of human and animal rights.

Ahmadabad

Today Ahmadabad, the capital of the State of Gujarat, is situated 550 km north of Bombay on the Sabarmati river. The city has long been a centre for trading and cutting diamonds, both of which are still pursued today. One visitor to Ahmadabad in the seventeenth century was the celebrated French traveller and historian, Jean Baptiste Tavernier who, within the space of forty years, undertook six expeditions to the East. In chapter XXII of Part II of his *Travels to India*, Tavernier described some of the notable diamonds and rubies which he had seen during the course of his travels, often with illustrations, from which the following is extracted:

'No. 4 represents a diamond which I bought at Ahmadabad for one of my friends. It weighed 178 ratis, or 157¼ of our carats... [no.5] represents the shape of the above mentioned diamond after it had been cut on both sides. Its weight was then 94½ carats, the water being perfect. The flat side, where there were two flaws at the base, was as thin as a sheet of thick paper. When I had the stone cut I had all this thin portion removed, together with a part of the point above, where a small speck of flaw still remains.'

This is the sole instance of Tavernier supplying drawings of both the rough and polished states of a diamond. This briolette-shaped diamond was presumably cut in Ahmadabad: after that, its history is uncertain. Who was the friend for whom Tavernier purchased the diamond? The most likely person was his sovereign, Louis XIV of France, to whom he had sold several diamonds which included two briolettes. But there has never been any reference to a diamond such as the Ahmadabad entering the Crown Jewels of France. Others, including Edwin Streeter, the author of two books on celebrated diamonds, have indicated that the diamond may have found its way to Persia via one of the numerous ports of Gujarat which served as a gateway to the Persian Gulf and Arabia, but no trace of it has been found among the Iranian Crown Jewels. A 'friend' is an unlikely epithet to apply to the mighty Aurengzeb, last of the Mughal emperors (1659–1707) and a noted collector of diamonds, of which one is reputed to have been the Ahmadabad. It is more probable that the 'friend' was one of the emperor's courtiers, who would have bought the gem for the emperor.

The Ahmadabad is next reported to have belonged to the Begum, Hazrat Mahal, the wife of King Wajid Ali Shah of Oudh, who had been exiled to Calcutta by the British following his refusal to sign a treaty of abdication at the time of the Indian Mutiny of 1857. She was a beautiful woman and an outspoken rebel leader at the time of the Mutiny. When British forces regained control after the rebellion, she was obliged to flee to Nepal where, it is said, she traded the diamond in return for her safe passage.

It is unlikely that the diamond has completely disappeared. It should be noted that its weight is lighter than that of the recorded weight of 90.5 carats of the Ahmadabad; however, such a reduction may be explained by its transformation from a briolette to a pear shape. But of greater significance is the fact that this gem possesses a minor flaw at its base. Is it not probable that this is one of the two small specks of flaw which Tavernier stated had remained after the cutting had taken place? Therefore, it is possible that this diamond, besides possessing an inherent beauty found in the finest diamonds from the historic Golconda mines of India, is also a long lost gem.

The Ahmadabad has been certified by the GIA as 'D' colour, VS1 clarity and was accompanied by a working diagram indicating that the clarity is improvable. It came up for sale by Christie's in Geneva in November 1995 when it was bought by Robert Mouawad for $4,324,554.

Algeiba Star

In November 1983 Christie's auctioned in Geneva two very fine yellow diamonds, both of South African origin: a cushion shape of 139.38 carats and a rectangular cushion shape of 132.42 carats. The larger of the two, then called the Mahjal, was sold for 1,320,000 Swiss Francs (£412,500). It is said to have been worn as a turban piece by Jagatjit Singh Bahadur, Maharajah of Kapurthala, a small princely state in the Punjab.

The Maharajah of Kapurthala (1872–1949) was a colourful figure. He was entitled to a personal salute of 15 guns. On a quieter note he owned a vast array of clocks which necessitated the employment of a servant for the express purpose of keeping them wound up. He was also a great lover of France which led him to build a palace closely modelled on Versailles. The incongruity of such a building within the sight of the snow-capped Himalayas was not unnaturally apt to take visitors by surprise.

In 1984 the Mahjal was recut to 133.03 carats and renamed the Algeiba Star.

Amsterdam

In 1972 one of the leading firms in the field of industrial diamonds, D. Drukker & Zn, of Amsterdam, purchased a black gem, weighing 55.85 metric carats. At the time it was not recognized as having an unusual value and was destined either to be used for a specific industrial purpose or to be crushed into diamond powder. The gem passed through the hands of several experts without comment. Its value was not more than six dollars per carat. Drukker's tried to cleave the diamond. However, its great hardness at once became apparent as well as the fact that every splinter was of the deepest black and not transparent. Subsequently the diamond was polished laboriously over several months into a pear shape weighing 33.74 metric carats, with the normal proportions of that cut. It was given a total of 145 facets, the extra facets being polished on the girdle. The Amsterdam is remarkable because even with optimal lighting it is absolutely opaque – most black diamonds possess grey imperfections and are translucent when put under strong light. The colour is probably caused by dispersion of ultra-fine submicroscopic inclusions, but the depth and quality of blackness are such that it must be an unusually uniform dispersion.

In February 1973 the diamond was publicly displayed for the first time and named the 'Amsterdam' by the wife of the Burgomaster of that city. It was set in a specially designed piece of jewellery and was exhibited on the occasion of the 700th anniversary of the city. Soon after its first public appearance a photograph of the diamond was printed in a well-known French magazine: this led to an offer of purchase from someone in France who had not even set eyes on it.

The offer was refused as were subsequent ones from other countries. Since then, the Amsterdam has been shown in numerous occasions for charitable purposes.

Ashberg

It is said that this amber, cushion-shaped diamond, weighing 102.48 metric carats, was formerly part of the Russian Crown Jewels. It must then have been a late addition to that collection because the stone bears all the characteristics of one from South Africa. In 1934 the Russian Trade Delegation sold the diamond to Mr Ashberg, a leading Stockholm banker. The Stockholm firm of Bolin, former Crown Jewellers to the Court of St Petersburg, mounted it as a pendant. In 1949 the Ashberg was displayed, mounted in a necklace containing diamonds and other gemstones, at the Amsterdam Exhibition, the aim of which was to attract new workers to the diamond industry.

Ten years later the Bukowski auction house in Stockholm put the Ashberg up for sale but it failed to reach its reserve and was withdrawn. Then its owner succeeded in selling the gem to a private buyer whose name was not revealed. Finally, in May 1981, Christie's auctioned the diamond in Geneva where once again it failed to reach its reserve and was withdrawn from sale.

Black Orlov

Regrettably most accounts of the early history of this diamond must be treated with the utmost scepticism. It has been stated that the stone, also known as the 'Eye of Brahma', weighed 195 carats in the rough and was then set in an idol near Pondicherry before being owned for a time in the middle of the eighteenth century by the Russian Princess Nadia Vyegin-Orlov. However, there is no evidence of black diamonds being found in India, let alone one of such size, and it is unlikely that a black diamond would have been retained because by and large black is not considered an auspicious colour among Hindus. Furthermore, there was never a prince or princess of the aforementioned name because all Princes Orlov descend from the brothers of Catherine the Great's lover, Count Grigor Grigorievich Orlov, and finally, the cushion shape of the diamond indicates that it has been polished probably within the past hundred years.

Weighing 67.5 carats, the cushion-shaped Black Orlov – so named due to its colour which has been described as 'dark gunmetal' – is by no means an uninteresting diamond. Charles F. Winson, a dealer from New York City, owned the gem for many years, exhibiting it at numerous events, including the display mounted by the American Museum of Natural History in 1951, the 1964 Texas State Fair in Dallas, and the Diamond Pavilion in Johanesburg in 1967. In July 1969 Winson sold the Black Orlov, then valued at $300,000, and set it in a diamond and platinum necklace. Auctioned in New York by Sotheby's in December 1990, it is now in private ownership.

Carlotta

This 40-carat pink pear-shaped diamond was named in memory of Mrs Lazare Kaplan, formerly Miss Charlotte Kittower. It was cut from a rough stone that had been found in Lesotho.

Lazare Kaplan died in 1986 aged 102. During his lifetime he came to be looked upon in the industry as the doyen of diamond cutters. Apprenticed to an uncle in Antwerp in 1897, he soon established a reputation as an outstanding cleaver and cutter: he was known for his insistence upon the maximum fire and brilliance as being the essential prerequisites of a finished gem even if it led to a slightly greater loss in weight. As he once said: 'The diamond is the gem that can render the most brilliance. Sapphires and rubies are beautiful for their colour but with the diamond the reflection is its beauty and that is why the cut is so important.' Kaplan's prowess and fame as a cleaver were fully put to the test in the 1930s when he was entrusted by Harry Winston with

the cutting of first the Pohl, then the Jonker diamond. Another of his accomplishments was the development in 1954 of the oval cut, a shape which, in the opinion of some, rivals that of the round cut in its brilliance.

Copenhagen Blue

This beautiful dark blue emerald-cut was named after the Danish capital during an exhibition staged there in 1960. Danish jewellers were quick off the mark to name it thus – it could equally have been named after some of the other locations where it had been exhibited. The gem weighs 45.85 metric carats and was fashioned from a piece of rough found in the Premier mine in South Africa. It ranks as the second largest dark blue diamond, being surpassed by an unnamed brilliant weighing 51.84 carats. The emerald cut is set in a bracelet with white diamonds, weighing a total of 87 carats, while the brilliant is set as the pendant to a diamond necklace containing 116 white diamonds, weighing a total of a 120 carats. In addition two other dark blue brilliants, whose combined weight is 23.39 carats, are set as earrings together with 26 white diamonds weighing a total of 28 carats. The whole of this unique suite of diamonds is in private ownership today.

Deepdene

'Deepdene', derived from the old English meaning 'deep valley', was the name given to this lovely, golden yellow, treated diamond of 104.88 carats. It was named after the country estate of the Bok family, one of its former owners, in Montgomery County, Pennsylvania, USA. The diamond was purchased from Martin Ehrmann, a Los Angeles jewellery dealer, who had earlier acquired it from its first known owner, Lazare Kaplan, the legendary New York diamantaire. Believed to have been mined in South Africa around 1890,

the diamond was subsequently cut by I.J. Asscher in Amsterdam.

The Deepdene was displayed at the museum of the Philadelphia Academy of Science in 1938 and was on public view for several years. Its impressive size and attractive colour captured the imagination of all who saw it, as is evident from an article in Philadelphia's *Evening Ledger* of 29 September 1939. Following its long exhibition, the diamond was duly returned to Mr Cary W. Bok, who sold it to Harry Winston in 1954. Then, having been mounted in a clip surrounded by 13 diamonds, it was purchased by a Canadian buyer, Mrs Eleanor Loder, the following year.

The original weight of the Deepdene was stated as having been 104.88 carats, yet today it is 104.53. The discrepancy is explained by the fact that after the diamond passed out of the Bok's possession, it was subjected to brief bombardment by cyclotron, artificially enhancing its hue, an experiment undertaken by the renowned mineralogist and gem authority Dr Frederick H. Pough. After the treatment, the pavilion and culet were then slightly recut to remove the pattern of concentrated colour around the culet, known as the 'umbrella effect'.

In 1970 the diamond was acquired by the jeweller Karl Friedrich, of Frankfurt, father of its present owners. At that time, the diamond had not been graded by a gemmological laboratory for few then issued reports, giving opinions instead. Prior to buying the gem, however, Mr Friedrich had sent it to the German National Gemmological Institute in Idar-Oberstein and to the University of Mainz. Both certified that the diamond was natural.

On 27 May 1971, Mr Friedrich offered the Deepdene for sale at a Christie's Geneva auction, where it was purchased by Van Cleef & Arpels for SFr 1.9 million. According to contemporary press reports, their bid was on behalf of the Greek shipping magnate, Mr Aristotle Onassis.

Just before the sale, however, Dr Eduard Gübelin came forward, insisting that he had previously examined the diamond and was convinced that it had been treated. As a consequence, the diamond was sent to the London Chamber of Commerce's

Precious Stones Laboratory where its then director and leading authority, Mr Basil Anderson, agreed with Dr Gübelin. After they had both concluded the diamond was treated, the sale was rescinded.

For a long while, the controversy raged in gemmological circles over whether the diamond had been treated, or not. Only when Dr Pough eventually heard about the aborted sale did he appreciate that the 104.88-carat diamond on which he had experimented must have been the Deepdene. The mystery was ended, and the issue was finally resolved, when he contacted Karl Friedrich and explained what had happened.

Prior to Dr Pough's realization, however, the diamond had already been confirmed to be the Deepdene, despite the loss in weight. An old photograph of the original gem had been obtained from Mr Bok's second wife and widow and compared with the actual 104.53-carat diamond under a Leitzsch 'crime macroscope'. This had enabled both to be magnified 12½ times in a single visual field. Evidence of their being one and the same diamond came from an identical 'natural', a thin sliver left of the original rough, approximately 1 mm in length and 1.5 mm in width, just above both girdles.

The diamond, thus confirmed as the Deepdene, was sold by Christie's Geneva in November 1997 to Laurence Graff for $715,320.

Earth Star

The Earth Star was fashioned from a rough gem of 248.9 carats found in the Jagersfontein mine on 16 May 1967. It travelled right through the recovery process until it appeared on the grease table in the recovery plant. Not surprisingly its appearance caused a stir at the mine; it caused surprise to many in the industry too because among the numerous fine diamonds produced by Jagersfontein, there had been few brown gemstones. In all its long existence, the mine had never been noted for yielding large stones of this colour. Moreover this specimen came from the 2,500-foot level of the mine workings,

which is exceptionally deep in a diamond pipe for a gem of such size to be found.

Messrs Baumgold Bros of New York purchased the stone and cut it into a pear shape weighing 111.59 carats, then the biggest cut brown diamond in the world. The gem was found to possess a greater degree of brilliance than is usually found in a gem of such a strong colour: the combination of colour and brilliance led to Joseph Baumgold naming it the 'Earth Star'. The diamond returned to South Africa in 1971 for display at the exhibition held to commemorate the centenary of the discovery of the Kimberley mine. It was bought by Stephen Zbova of Naples, Florida, for $900,000 in 1983.

English Dresden

Edward Z. Dresden of Gracechurch Street, London, the man who gave his name to this diamond, was listed in the Post Office directory simply as 'merchant'. However, as the stone was shipped to Holland for cutting, one can assume that he was connected with the diamond-dealing firm Gebr. Dresden & Co., of Keizersgracht, Amsterdam.

The English Dresden was found in 1857 in diggings by the Bagagem river in the state of Minas Gerais, Brazil, close to where the Star of the South had been found four years earlier. In fact the two diamonds were destined to follow similar historical paths. Agents acting on behalf of Dresden purchased the stone in Rio de Janeiro, whence it was sent first to London, then to Amsterdam to be cut by Messrs Coster. After a great deal of preliminary study, they cut it into a finely proportioned pear shape, both colourless and flawless, which weighed 76½ (old) carats, 78.53 metric. Since the rough piece had weighed 119½ carats, little more than a third was lost in the cutting.

Contemporary accounts have testified to the fact that the English Dresden was regarded as a very fine gem. Mr Dresden himself wrote: 'There is no diamond known in the world to come

up to it. I matched my drop with the Koh-i-noor at Garrards one day, and to the surprise of all present, the latter's colour turned almost yellowish: a proof of how perfectly white my diamond must be.'

Another person declared: 'It is perfectly pure, free from defects, and has extraordinary play and brilliancy. Indeed the quality of the stone is superior to the Koh-i-noor. Yet when a half share in this magnificent jewel was offered to a noted West End jeweller for the relatively small sum of £12,000 he declined it.'

After this refusal the English Dresden was apparently offered to, and refused by, members of several European ruling houses. Then it came to be much admired by an Indian prince, but, unable to meet the asking price of £40,000, he was reluctantly compelled to decline the purchase. However, on this occasion he was accompanied by an English merchant from Bombay who, upon seeing Dresden's diamond, immediately expressed a desire to own it. At the time no one paid attention to his wish, but within a year the merchant found himself in a position to buy the diamond. It chanced that he was a holder of substantial stocks of cotton when, as the result of the American Civil War, there was a steep rise in the price of this commodity. After he had sold off his stock at enormous prices and thus realized a fortune, he wrote to Mr Dresden with an offer to purchase his diamond.

The handling of the negotiations was entrusted to an agent of the Bombay merchant who took the opportunity of doing a stroke of business on his own account. He persuaded Dresden to accept a figure of £32,000 for the diamond: then he informed the cotton dealer that the original price of £40,000 had to be paid without question, thereby lining his own pockets comfortably. Unfortunately this merchant was destined to enjoy ownership of the diamond for only a short time. He continued to do a substantial business in cotton and found himself a large holder when the price collapsed as suddenly as it had risen. After this misfortune he died and his estate had to be wound up; his executors were fortunate in being able to recover the £40,000 by selling the diamond to that avid collector, Khande Rao, the Gaekwar of Baroda. The English Dresden remained among the jewels of the rulers of Baroda until 1934 when it was reported to have been acquired by Cursetjee Fardoonji. So far as it is known, the diamond still remains in India.

Frankfurt Solitaire

In 1764 the Emperor Francis I of Austria bought this diamond, together with a ring, at Frankfurt-am-Main, for 28,000 louis-d'or. He had the diamond, a brilliant cut of fine colour weighing 44⅝ (old) carats, mounted in a hat buckle. After his death, his widow, the Empress Maria Theresa, ordered all her late consort's jewellery, including the Frankfurt Solitaire, to be handed over to the Treasury for safe custody. The diamond was subsequently set as the centre-piece of a diamond tiara.

The Frankfurt Solitaire remained in the Treasury until November 1918, when the last Habsburg Emperor, Charles, ordered the High Chamberlain of the Imperial Court to remove those jewels that constituted the personal property of the Imperial family. In addition to the Frankfurt Solitaire they included the Florentine diamond, the Baden Solitaire of 30 carats, and a rose-coloured brilliant of just over 26 carats.

Some of these jewels were sold to help in paying the expenses of the Imperial family which had gone into exile in Switzerland in 1918, while others were unfortunately stolen by an unfaithful employee. It is not known into which category the Frankfurt Solitaire fell but there has been no news of its whereabouts since that time.

Golconda Doré

On 17 May 1962, Sotheby's of London auctioned this diamond which was bought by a London dealer for £8,200. The sale catalogue contained the following: 'Salomon Habib was a notable French collector of unusual diamonds, part of whose collection, including the famous blue Hope diamond, was sold by auction in Paris on 24 June 1909.

'The gemstone being offered is understood at one time to have belonged to the Sultan Abdul Hamid [Abd al-Hamid] who wore it as an armlet. It is believed to have been purchased by M. Habib in 1909 and to have been recut in Amsterdam at a later date. This gem with others from M. Habib's collection was put up for sale at auction by the Credit Municipal de Paris at the Hotel Drouot on 8 February 1933 as Lot 5 by the description of 'Golconda Doré', the weight in the catalogue being incorrectly given as 95.35 carats, whereas the true weight is 95.40 carats. The stone was withdrawn from sale and remained in the ownership of M. Habib until his death in 1961. For a diamond of such exceptionally large size it possessed a high degree of purity.'

Some have asserted that I.J. Asscher, of Amsterdam, cut the Golconda Doré: however, this famous firm neither cut nor recut the diamond. In 1962 Dunklings the Jewellers of Melbourne, Australia, purchased the gem and they were its owners when thieves stole it during an exhibition in Sydney Lower Town Hall in October 1980. Since then there has been no news of the Golconda Doré.

Le Grand Cœur d'Afrique

The British jewellery firm Graff has received the Queen's Award for Export Achievement on three occasions. Its founder, Laurence Graff, has enjoyed 36 years in the industry since beginning as a jewellery apprentice at the age of 14. In 1960 he founded his own business in Hatton Garden, London, opening his first retail outlet in Knights-bridge 14 years later. Since his auction debut in 1975, Laurence Graff has risen to become one of the foremost buyers of important stones: the Idol's Eye, the Emperor Maximilian, the Porter Rhodes, the Begum Blue and Excelsior I are among the notable diamonds which have passed through his

hands. As well as handling these celebrated diamonds, Laurence Graff himself has added to the tally of fine gems.

The West African state of Guinea has had a somewhat chequered existence as a diamond producer: this has been due to a combination of interference in the industry and output being smuggled out of the country to realize hard currency. But Guinea has been the source in recent years of some very fine stones, notably in 1982 when a cleavage, weighing 278 carats, was found some 645 km east of the capital, Conakry. After protracted negotiations, Laurence Graff bought the stone and despatched it to New York for cutting. First, two smaller gems were cut, a marquise of 14.25 carats, which was sold at once in New York, and a flawless heart shape of 25.22 carats. The latter became known as 'Le Petit Cœur' and was set in a necklace. Work then started on the major part of the diamond which ultimately yielded a flawless heart shape weighing 70.03 carats. It was named 'Le Grand Cœur d'Afrique' and was set in a spectacular necklace containing almost 70 carats of smaller heart shapes. In August 1983 newspapers reported that two billionaires were interested in buying it to present to their wives. At the same time, it was stated that 'both need to be a little more generous towards their beautiful wives, however'. In the end somebody must have shown the required degree of generosity because in December of that year Graff sold the diamond to a buyer whose name was not disclosed.

Great Chrysanthemum

In 1963 a brown diamond weighing 198.28 carats came to light in South Africa and was bought by Julius Cohen of New York. He entrusted its cutting to the firm of S. & M. Kaufman, who polished a pear shape of 104.15 carats, measuring 25 mm wide, 39 mm long and 16 mm deep. The diamond has a total of 189 facets: 67 on the crown, 65 on the girdle and 57 on the pavilion. After it had been cut, the gems colour turned out to be a deep, rich golden-brown, with overtones of sienna and burnt orange, hence its name. The Great Chrysanthemum was mounted as the centre stone in a yellow-gold necklace containing 410 oval and marquise-cut diamonds, valued by its owner at $540,000. As well as being exhibited in the USA the diamond has twice returned to South Africa, for display at the Kimberley Centenary Exhibition in 1971 and the Diamond Pavilion in Johannesburg six years earlier.

Great Table

The examination and documentation of the contents of the Iranian Treasury in 1966 by a team of Canadians, experts in various fields, resulted in the disclosure of much valuable and fascinating information. Subsequently this appeared in *Crown Jewels of Iran*, published in 1968 by the University of Toronto Press. From the gemmological aspect the most interesting fact that emerged was the revelation that the principal diamond among the jewellery, the Darya-i Nur, constitutes the major portion of the legendary Great Table which Tavernier had seen and drawn when he was in India in 1642. The history of the Great Table is, therefore, discussed under the Darya-i Nur.

Guinea Star

In March 1989 the William Goldberg Diamond Corporation of New York, and its partner, the Chow Tai Fook Jewellery Co. Ltd of Hong Kong, purchased a rough stone of 255.1 carats. It is one of the largest diamonds to have been recovered in Guinea. The seller was IDC (Holdings) Ltd, the London firm which holds the sole marketing rights to diamonds found in the Aredor mine in Guinea.

After months of painstaking decision-making and careful scrutiny of the complex rough, the work of sawing was begun. Three weeks of sawing resulted in three pieces, the centre stone of which was anticipated to yield a large gem of an

unprecedented shape. Ultimately three gems were polished: an 89.01-carat shield shape, which now bears the name 'Guinea Star', and two satellites, an 8.23-carat pear shape and a 5.03-carat heart shape. All are 'D' colour flawless gems.

Guise

A rectangular-shaped diamond weighing 33¼ carats was once the property of the House of Guise, a branch of the House of Lorraine, which played an important part in France during the sixteenth-century Wars of Religion. In 1665 Louis XIV of France bought it with some other diamonds from his cousin, Marie de Lorraine. In 1786, during the reign of Louis XVI, the Guise was recut: it retained its rectangular shape but now with slightly rounded corners and a large culet. Its weight became 28⅛ carats (29.1 metric carats) and it was described as faultless, white and fiery. Valued at 250,000 livres, the Guise was mounded in a setting for Queen Marie Antoinette. In 1792 the diamond was stolen during the robbery of the Garde Meuble but fortunately it was recovered shortly afterwards, along with lesser diamonds, from the house of one Tavenal. French sources have stated that the Guise was among the former Crown Jewels that were sold by the Third Republic in 1887 but it does not appear in Lord Twining's list of the contents that were disposed of on that occasion. Nor is the diamond among the items that were specifically excluded from that sale and which are on display today in the Louvre. The whereabouts of this jewel are, therefore, unknown.

Heart of Eternity

No diamond of recent times has been blessed with as poetical a name as this beautiful dark blue heart shape weighing 27.64 carats. The intensity of its colour has been described by experts as 'vivid blue'.

The Heart of Eternity is the largest of a unique collection of eleven blue diamonds, polished by the Steinmetz Group, which comprised the 'De Beers Millennium Jewels', displayed at the Millennium Dome in London throughout the year 2000. They range in size from 5.16 carats to the weight of this diamond; each diamond has been especially inscribed with a De Beers Millennium number, using De Beers' proprietary branding technique.

All of these diamonds originated from the Premier mine in South Africa which, in modern times, has become the only important source of blue diamonds, even though they make up less than 0.1 per cent of diamonds recovered at this mine. In the words of Mr Nicholas Oppenheimer, Chairman of De Beers, 'Blue diamonds of this size and quality are so rare that a collection of this size is indeed unparallelled.'

Kirti-Noor

News of a notable diamond often constitutes an exciting event, whether it marks the unveiling of a fine, newly-cut gem or the appearance of a long lost or previously unknown stone. The Kirti-Noor belongs to the second category. Before its recent acquisition by a Western dealer the diamond had never left the shore of India and probably only a few people had been aware of its existence. For long it was an item among the vast collection of jewels owned by a prominent princely family, set as a centre-piece in a diamond necklace. It was whispered that the pink diamond had been the Maharani's favourite gem.

The Kirti-Noor is a Golconda stone of a beautiful pink hue and was cut and polished approximately in the early eighteenth century. Some have noticed that there is a great similarity of colour, shape, cutting and grain to that of the Condé diamond, but, whereas that gem weighs just over nine carats, the Kirti-Noor weighs 15 carats.

Kimberley

There is an old legend about the finding of diamonds in Griqualand West which George Beet, once known as Kimberley's 'Grand Old Man', recounts in his book on the diamond fields:

'After the passing of many moons, and when there was great sorrow in the land, a spirit, pitying the wants and difficulties of mankind, descended from Heaven with a huge basket filled with diamonds. The spirit flew over the Vaal River, starting beyond Delport's Hope, and dropping diamonds as it sped on; past Barkly West and Klipdam it flew along towards the place now called Kimberley, ever throwing out handful after handful of gems from its huge basket. On reaching Kimberley, where at that time large trees were growing, one of the spirit's big toes got caught in a branch of camelthorn tree, and tripping, it upset the basket, emptying out all the diamonds, and thus forming the Kimberley mines.'

This may not quite aspire to the level of Hans Andersen or the brothers Grimm, but it does go a little way to explain some of the mystery and history that visitors to the unofficial Capital of the Diamond World often come to feel about the place. On a less poetical, more realistic level, Beet also relates an old story told to him by a digger:

'One of my friend's servants, a venerable Griqua, who claimed to have lived in the vicinity of the mines in the days when the land there was virgin veld, told him that the place had been a favourite hunting ground of the Griquas, as it was well covered by 'groot klompies' of camelthorn trees, which the larger game, and even lions, loved to frequent. He stated that immediately after rains a peculiar mist arose from the ground, and the natives came to believe that the place was 'spooked' or haunted. This peculiar mist is easily understandable, as white residents of about 30 years ago, and even later, will recall how during the rainy season, sulphuric fumes arose from the reef on the south side and enveloped the town.'

But it was not so much the mist as the dust and the flies which remained the abiding memory of one of early Kimberley's most distinguished visitors, the novelist Trollope. Locals who hoped that he might report more favourably upon the place were to be disappointed: 'Dust so thick,' he commented, 'that the sufferer fears to remove it lest the raising of it may aggravate the evil, the flies so numerous that one hardly dares slaughter them by ordinary means lest their dead bodies should become noisome.' However, Trollope was impressed by the 'Big Hole' – the Kimberley mine in its early days.

Fourteen years later another distinguished visitor to the diamond fields, Lord Randolph Churchill, father of Winston Churchill, was equally unimpressed by both the town and its product. On one occasion he toured the mines accompanied by the wife of a De Beers official and was shown a pile of diamonds which drew forth his celebrated comment: 'All for the vanity of woman,' to which his companion tartly replied, 'And for the depravity of man.'

Among the pile which Lord Randolph saw would certainly have been yellow octahedrons – 'capes' as they are known in the trade – which have become a trademark of the local output. Doubtless Tavernier's reservations concerning the 'citron' tinge of the Florentine diamond would have been expressed in stronger terms had he seen these specimens. It is, therefore, appropriate that the diamond named after Kimberley should be yellowish in colour. Although this stone, weighing 490 carats, is reported to have come from the Kimberley mine, it is far more likely that it came from the De Beers or Dutoitspan mine. The largest diamond on record to have come from the 'Big Hole' weighed merely 213½ (old) carats.

The Kimberley was cut to a flawless emerald cut of 70 carats in 1921. Then in 1958 its owners, the celebrated New York firm of Baumgold Bros, recut it to its existing weight of 55.09 (metric) carats in order to improve the proportions and increase the brilliancy of the gem. It was then valued at $500,000. The Kimberley returned to South Africa in 1966 when it featured in the Diamond Pavilion in Johannesburg. In 1971 Baumgold Bros sold it to a private collector in Texas.

La Belle Hélène

The rich diamond deposits situated along one of the world's most inhospitable coastlines, aptly named the Skeleton Coast, in the extreme south-west corner of Africa, have yielded no diamond finer than the one weighing 160 carats found early in 1951. Of a perfect, blue-white colour, the gem was wedge-shaped and had a cleavage plane that suggested it was part, possibly the bigger part, of an even larger diamond. Interestingly, it was a Type IIa diamond. It was found in the region known as Area G, one of the southernmost workings of the mine, at a spot some 640 metres from the Atlantic Ocean. At this point the workings were approximately 5 metres above sea level, an ancient marine terrace containing diamondiferous gravel. The gem lay in a depression in the bed-rock in an area from which a number of other diamonds had been recovered by the same working shift on that day.

Romi Goldmuntz, a leading Belgian diamantaire, who chanced to be visiting South Africa at the time, bought the diamond at a price of £500 per carat, as part of a deal totalling £80,000. He named it 'La Belle Hélène' after his wife, thereby disappointing several who had suggested that it might be named the Van Riebeek, so commemorating the 500th anniversary of the founding of the Cape. The diamond was eventually cut in New York where it yielded three fine gems: two matching pear shapes of 30.38 and 29.71 carats, and a marquise of 10.50 carats, which were sold through Cartier to private buyers.

La Luna

Lists of the World's Largest Cut Diamonds can never be accurate, especially as away from the auction rooms such sales are private and take place unannounced. Previously unknown, however, is a South American diamond, the largest heart-shaped diamond ever fashioned, weighing 200.07 carats. The La Luna, as it is now called, was purchased as a 453-carat rough of a beautiful colour and fine quality in 1991 by that same senior De Beers buyer who had acquired the Incomparable in Antwerp a decade earlier.

Alas, the country of origin of this gem is unknown for when rough diamonds are traded in a major centre, such as Antwerp, there can be no certainty as to where they were found. One suspects Brazil, because of the 726.60-carat President Vargas and the Darcy Vargas of 460 carats found almost sixty years ago, but either Venezuela or Guyana could have been its source.

What is known is that Mr Beny Steinmetz, an international diamantaire, gave the diamond its name and then had it fashioned in New York. There, on 15 August 1995, the GIA's Gem Testing Laboratory described La Luna as 'a heart-modified brilliant, 'D' colour, internally flawless' and of 'excellent' symmetry. Later, it is understood that La Luna was sold to a private collector, whose anonymity has been preserved. Evidently, this is a most elegant diamond and one that deserves to be recorded, for it far outdistances the largest heart-shaped diamond of similar colour and quality ever to appear at auction.

Liberator

The name Venezuela, meaning 'little Venice', is said to have been bestowed by Portuguese explorers, because the Indian villages built along the swampy shores of Lake Maracaibo reminded them of Venice. Nowadays, the entire basin of the lake and, indeed, the whole of the eastern part of the country is pitted with oil derricks, yielding more than 80 per cent of all Venezuela's export earnings. Less well known is the fact that it is also a small alluvial diamond producer with an estimated annual output of some 450,000 carats.

It was in 1887 that diamonds were first identified in Venezuela – in the Pavichi area north of San Pedros de los Bocos on the Caroni River in the State of Bolivar. Later, in 1925, further discoveries were made on the Gran Sabana, near the head-waters of the Caroni and its tributaries

on the borders of Venezuela and Brazil.

By 1943, over 1,000 people were known to be digging for alluvial diamonds, before a long series of rushes or 'bomba' occurred. One, in 1969, resulted in more than 15,000 entering into the inhospitable jungles of the south-eastern region. Several thousands are now working there in humid conditions and in 40°C temperatures, while braving deadly snakes, spiders larger than a man's hand and malaria-carrying mosquitoes. This is yet another instance of diamonds almost invariably being found in either inaccessible or unfavourable terrain.

Because so many individuals are involved in searching for diamonds, control of their activities is difficult and accurate reporting of their finds is almost impossible. A 75-carat rough diamond, estimated to have been worth $250,000, was reported to have come from the San Salvador de Paul diggings in February 1970.

The most outstanding diamond to have been discovered in Venezuela, however, remains the fine pear-shaped stone that, in the rough, weighed 155 carats. Found in the Gran Sabana, in November 1942, by three prospectors – James Hudson, Rafael Solano and Israel Jaime – it was named the 'Solano'. This was later changed to the 'Liberator' at the request of the Minister of Mines to lend greater significance to the remarkable find.

The liberator was, of course, Simon Bolívar (1783–1830), the South American soldier and statesman, who had been the outstanding leader in freeing northern South America from Spanish Imperial rule. It was not until November 1823 that the last Spanish stronghold in Venezuela capitulated. Once free of the Spanish yoke, Venezuela, together with New Granada and Ecuador, formed the state of Great Colombia with Bolívar as President. Seven years later Venezuela withdrew and set itself up as an independent republic under Jose Antonio Paez, an outstanding general in the wars of independence. Bolívar himself died of tuberculosis in December 1830, a disillusioned man.

In due course, the Liberator diamond was shipped by air mail for forty cents from Caracas by the Banco Holandes Unido, who held it on deposit at the Chase National Bank in New York.

There, a number of diamond dealers inspected it, but it was Harry Winston who outbid them, at a reputed price of $200,000. Since there were many complications involving several owners, final settlement was only reached upon the intervention of the Minister of Mines in Caracas.

A New York cleaver, Adrian Grasselly, split the diamond into two pieces, weighing 115 and 40 carats, at Mr Winston's instruction and only after several hours of study. The resultant yield was four gems – three emerald cuts, weighing 39.80, 18.12 and 8.93 carats, and a marquise of 1.44 carats.

The four gems were sold privately. May Bonfils Stanton, daughter of the publisher of the *Denver Post*, purchased Liberator I. When her jewellery collection was auctioned on 14 November 1962, by Parke-Bernet Galleries, Inc., the gem was set in a platinum ring with two tapering baguettes. Then, Harry Winston paid $185,000 to re-purchase it. Later, Liberator I was sold to a private buyer.

Light of Peace

In 1969, Zale Corporation of Dallas purchased in Antwerp a fine blue-white gem weighing 434.6 carats, the source of which was stated simply as West Africa. More specifically it had almost certainly come from Sierra Leone. After two years' work in New York the outcome was thirteen gems totalling 172.46 carats. The biggest, a pear shape cut with 111 facets, weighs 130.27 carats and has been named the 'Light of Peace'. The twelve smaller gems are the marquise (9.11 carats), marquise (9.04 carats), brilliant (6.93 carats), heart (3.63 carats) oval (3.55 carats), marquise (2.73 carats), pear (1.83 carats), pear (1.55 carats), pear (1.51 carats), pear (1.13 carats), marquise (0.81 carats) and pear (0.37 carats).

The choice of name for the large diamond was explained by Morris Zale, one of the two brothers who had founded Zale Corporation. He stated, 'Once we acquired the diamond, it was suggested that perhaps we could use this great find to make a small contribution to promoting peace. We also felt that it was time for private industry to begin taking a more active role in

The Mouna Diamond

Mirror of Naples

European politics dominate the history of this long-lost diamond connected with the Italian campaigns of Louis XII of France (reigned 1498–1515). Having pursued the claims of his predecessor, Charles VIII, to the Kingdom of Naples, in 1500 Louis XII concluded the Treaty of Granada with Ferdinand II of Aragon for the partition of the kingdom. In the following year Naples was conquered but a dispute, eventually leading to war, broke out between France and Spain over the partition. By 1504 the French king had lost all Naples: in the following year he renounced his claims in favour of a niece. Louis XII became a widower in 1514 and in November of that year he married Mary Tudor, sister of Henry VIII, King of England. It was a match between a man of 52, broken in spirit and ailing in health, and a young and beautiful bride of 18, who was already in love with another man. This was Charles Brandon, Duke of Suffolk, who after the death of Louis XII on New Year's Day 1515, headed the delegation from England to congratulate the new king, Francis I, upon his accession to the throne of France.

Suffolk used the opportunity to win the hand of the young widow. However, she feared opposition to the marriage, above all from her brother. Despite Suffolk's promise to Henry VIII to delay any action until his return from France, he secretly married the Queen, thereby incurring the wrath of the English King. Through the intercession of Cardinal Wolsey, Suffolk was ultimately pardoned on payment of a heavy fine and the surrender of all the former Queen's jewels and plate. The jewels included the diamond known as the Mirror of Naples, then considered a gem of fine quality and valued at 60,000 crowns. Nothing has been heard of it since the time of Henry VIII.

Moon of Baroda

The early history of this pear-shaped, light yellow diamond, weighing 24 carats, is obscure. The gem is said to have been owned by an Indian prince who, at the conclusion of the Second World War, found himself in financial difficulties following the confiscation of much of his property by the Japanese and then the Indian governments.

In 1944 Samuel H. Deutson, President of a firm of diamond cutters and manufacturing jewellers in Cleveland, Ohio, acquired the Moon of Baroda; six years later Meyer Rosenbaum, President of Meyer Jewelry Company of Detroit, Michigan, bought it and it was during his ownership that the stone became well known on account of its assocation with Marilyn Monroe.

In 1952 20th Century Fox made the film version of Anita Loos' *Gentlemen Prefer Blondes*, starring Marilyn Monroe and Jane Russell, during which the former put across in her own inimitable style the song 'Diamonds Are a Girl's Best Friend'. She did not wear the diamond in the picture but wore it instead to promote the film. Her breathless gasp of 'It's gorgeous' when she first set eyes on the diamond was more than enough to ensure adequate publicity both for the film and for the diamond.

In April 1990, Christie's auctioned the Moon of Baroda in New York where it fetched $297,000, compared with the pre-sale estimate of $120,000.

Mouna

The Mouna Diamond weighs 112.53 carats and is VS1 clarity. When it was submitted to the Gemological Institute of America on 9 November 1995, they stated that up until this date it was the largest fancy intense yellow diamond that they had ever graded. The cushion-shaped stone is 26 mm in diameter and set in a baguette-cut diamond mount by Bulgari, which with the diamond has a height of 36 mm. It was sold by Christie's in Geneva on 16 November 1998, lot 161, and fetched US$3,258,000, being purchased by a private collector.

promoting peace which has, up to now, been essentially a governmental function.'

Accordingly Zale Corporation set up a fund with money received from the many showings of the diamond, the proceeds being donated to a cause for peace. In 1980 Zale Corporation sold the Light of Peace to an undisclosed buyer. Explaining the decision to dispose of the diamond, Donald Zale said: 'Over the years we had so many enquiries about the diamond that we put a price on it and said not to call unless the enquirer were willing to pay the price … Somebody called.'

Marie-Antoinette Blue

The early history of this greyish-blue heart-shaped diamond, of 5.46 (metric) carats, must be viewed with a degree of suspicion. It is said that the future Queen brought it with her when she arrived in France, despite the absence of any known inventory or list of her jewels at the time of her marriage. Then the gem is stated to have remained the Queen's private property until shortly before her execution, when she gave it to Princess Lubomirska, one of her closest confidantes. But it is difficult to understand how the Queen could have effected this because she was imprisoned and at all times closely guarded.

From Princess Lubomirska, the diamond apparently passed to one of her four daughters, three of whom married into the Potocki family. It is recorded that the blue diamond was once owned by Count Vladimir Potocki. Next it turned up in the possession of a Mr Poplavisky who gave it to his wife, Nina; subsequently she married a Mr Godovannikov.

In 1955 the diamond was shown at the exhibition 'Marie-Antoinette, Archduchesse, Dauphine et Reine' staged at the Château de Versailles. Prior to that it had also been displayed at earlier exhibitions, notably those held in Paris in 1892 and 1900. In 1967 the Marie-Antoinette Blue was sold at the Palais Galliera in Paris to a private European buyer. Finally Christie's auctioned it in Geneva on 12 May 1983. On that occasion it remained unsold.

Nepal

'The Ageless Diamond' exhibition sponsored by Christie's and De Beers in London in 1959 provided few exhibits as breathtaking as this very beautiful pear-shaped diamond, weighing 79.41 metric carats, mounted as a pendant with a diamond chain. Little is known of its early history, though it is believed to have come to light in the alluvial diamond fields in the vicinity of Golconda. Certainly both the colour and quality of the gem were worthy of this source. Unlike so many fine Indian diamonds this one did not travel westwards but instead went to Nepal, situated on the north-eastern frontier of India, where it remained for several generations, passing from one ruler and one potentate to another.

In 1957 Harry Winston purchased the Nepal from an Indian dealer, and had it slightly recut from its original weight of 79.50 carats. After 'The Ageless Diamond' exhibition he sold the diamond to a European client. It was set as a pendant to a V-shaped diamond necklace that also contained 145 round diamonds weighing a total of 71.44 carats.

Nur ul-Ain

The identification of this lovely diamond came about during the examination and documentation of the Iranian Crown Jewels undertaken by a team of distinguished Canadian gemmologists in 1966. Their most significant discovery had been the realization that the most important diamond in the collection, the Darya-i Nur, comprised the major part of the Great Table diamond which Tavernier had seen in a merchant's hands at Golconda and tried unsuccessfully to buy. But whereas the Great Table had weighed the equivalent of more than 250 metric carats, the Darya-i Nur was estimated to have weighed merely between 175 and 195 carats (due to its setting in a diamond-encrusted ornament its weight could not be gauged with total accuracy). What then had become of the rest of the Great

Table? It was unlikely that the remaining portion of such a remarkable stone did not exist in some form or another.

The answer was supplied by the discovery in a tiara of the Nur ul-Ain, meaning 'Light of the Eye', a pink, slightly drop-shaped oval brilliant cut, estimated to weigh about 60 metric carats. A comparison of the Nur ul-Ain with the Darya-i Nur showed that they possessed identical colour and clarity. Models that were made by the gemmologists showed not just the probability but the certainty that they had been fashioned from the same source. It was considered that the Nur ul-Ain had most likely been cut during the reign of Nasir ud-Din (1848–96), who was responsible for the addition to the Crown jewels of a number of large South African diamonds, which were cut and polished in the workshops in the Golestan Palace in Teheran.

The Nur ul-Ain, which measures 30 × 26 × 11 mm, has been set as the central ornament in a magnificent tiara created by Harry Winston; the tiara was one of a number of important pieces of jewellery designed for the marriage of Muhammad Reza Shah in 1958. The diamond is surrounded by a mixture of yellow, pink, blue and white diamonds. Several exceed 10 carats, the most notable being a pink cushion-cut, estimated to weigh 19 carats. One can only hope that this beautiful tiara, last heard of when housed in the National Bank in Teheran, has survived the turbulent events of recent Iranian history.

Pasha of Egypt

The diamond takes its name from Ibrahim Pasha (1789–1848), Viceroy of Egypt under Ottoman rule. He purchased the gem for £28,000. The London jeweller, Emanuel, described it as of octagonal shape, excellent colour and quality and weighing 40 carats (41.06 metric). It became the finest stone in the Egyptian Treasury.

In 1863 Ismail Pasha (1830–1895) became the ruler of Egypt. Under him the country experienced a period of accelerated economic

development – but at a cost. By 1876, Egypt's debt amounted to £1 million, for which the policies adopted by Ismail Pasha were largely responsible. Eventually the Sultan of the Ottoman Empire deposed him and he went into exile in 1879. Contemporary historians recorded that when Ismail Pasha left Egypt he carried with him a huge hoard of valuables, amongst which was the Pasha of Egypt. Subsequently the diamond was reported to have been sold to an Englishman, a likely happening because Britain and France were the two powers with which the Pasha had had most dealings during his reign.

The Englishman is stated to have put the diamond up for sale. In 1933 the London firm of T. M. Sutton offered it to Cartier. Then the Pasha of Egypt returned to Egypt in the possession of King Farouk. The Italian jewellers, Bulgari, bought it from him before selling it to the American millionairess Barbara Hutton. However, the octagonal shape of the diamond displeased her so that she had it recut at Cartier's to 38.19 carats and set into a ring. When it was re-cut in the early 1980s to 36.22 carats and subsequently submitted to the GIA, they reported that it was the largest circular-cut 'D' flawless diamond they had ever graded.

Pindar

There are parallels between the history of this diamond and that of the Sancy: Paul Pindar and Nicholas Harlay de Sancy both pursued careers as diplomats and financiers; both of their eponymous diamonds were bought in Constantinople, sold to kings of England, and eventually entered the French Treasury. Paul Pindar (1565–1650) early on rather inclined to be a tradesman so that at 17 his father apprenticed him to a London merchant who, in turn, sent him to be his factor at Venice. Pindar remained in Italy for about 15 years during which time he amassed a substantial fortune. He then became consul for the English merchants at Aleppo. In 1611 James I appointed him Ambassador to Turkey. He received a knighthood in 1623.

Pindar brought home from the East several notable jewels. When the Duke of Buckingham accompanied the future king, Charles I, abroad in 1623 he carried off Sir Paul Pindar's great diamonds, promising to talk with him about paying for them. One exceptional jewel, valued in 1624 at £35,000, was lent by Pindar to James I to wear on state occasions. Known as the Great Diamond, it was purchased by Charles I in 1625 for £18,000, though payment was deferred. In 1646 Pindar's diamond was among the jewels which Queen Henrietta Maria, consort of Charles I, pledged in Amsterdam to raise funds for the Royalist cause in the Civil War in England: her agent was Thomas Cletscher of the Bank of Lombardy, Rotterdam, and Court Jeweller to Prince Frederic Henry of Orange. The Pindar featured in Cletscher's famous sketchbook where its weight was estimated at around 36 carats and where it was described as being very pure, perfectly proportioned and of very fine water. The drawing depicted a fine, rather long square classical table-cut. Cletscher also disclosed that it was his father-in-law, Niccolò Ghyberti, the representative of the United Provinces in Constantinople, who had originally bought the diamond for Sir Paul Pindar.

The French historian Bernard Morel has pointed out that Cletscher's description of the Pindar corresponds exactly with that of the second Mazarin diamond. This was among the jewels stolen during the theft of the Crown Jewels of France in September 1792 and never recovered.

Princie

When this 34.64-carat pink diamond came up for sale at Sotheby's in London on 17 March 1960, the name of the vendor was not disclosed. It was reported at the time that it might have come from the Nizam of Hyderabad's collection of jewels. However, it is of interest to read of an extract from *Memories of a Diamond Dealer of the Good Old Days* by Etienne G. Fallek of Paris. In 1927 he drew up a 23-page report on the State Jewels of

the Republic of Turkey; among the rare diamonds which he handled was 'The Rectangular', old-cut brilliant, weighing 36 carats, of pure rose or salmon-rose hue, from Golconda, in India.

Despite the reported difference in the weights of the two diamonds and the fact that rectangular may not mean cushion-shaped, large pink diamonds from Golconda have not been found in such abundance as to exclude the possibility that the gem which M. Fallek saw may have been the same one which came up for auction in London in 1960. Certainly the Princie was a very beautiful diamond of Indian origin containing a single inclusion. What was remarkable about it was that when exposed to ultraviolet rays it had an orange fluorescence and phospherescent after-glow.

Van Cleef & Arpels bought the diamond for £46,000. They sent it to their Paris branch where it was christened at a party in its honour. The guests included the Maharanee of Baroda and her fourteen-year-old son, whose pet family name was 'Princie'. Mounted as a pendant on a necklace of baguette-cut diamonds, the diamond was later sold by Van Cleef & Arpels to an undisclosed buyer.

Star of Arkansas

Before diamonds were recently found at Kelsey Lake, the only known diamond pipe of significance in the United States was in the Crater of Diamonds State Park, 4 km south of Murfreesboro, Arkansas. The discovery of this pipe took place in the latter part of the nineteenth century when the owner of the land was a handyman-farmer, John Wesley Huddleston. He worked in partnership with one John Branner, who became interested in the many luminous pebbles that could be seen on the farm. Early one morning Huddleston decided to venture out alone. He searched the land thoroughly, finding a few of the small stones, but he noticed that many more were to be located on the ground of a neighbouring farm. He rushed over to the startled owner, asked for, and received an option on the nearly 73 hectares adjoining his own property. The

price was $1,000. Although Huddleston's entire capital then consisted of two tired old mules, he talked so fast that the neighbouring farmer finally agreed to take one of the animals as a downpayment.

Later that day Huddleston was in town carrying a couple of the larger stones that he had found on his newly acquired land. At the County Bank he showed them to the cashier and asked how much they were worth. 'Oh, I'd say about fifty cents', the cashier laughed, to which Huddleston retorted, 'Know what them stones are? Them's diamints, and I got a hull crop of 'em.'

Huddleston was sure of his discovery but he still wanted substantial proof, so after consulting the equally incredulous County Bank president and a local jeweller he packed the stones off to Tiffany's in New York for appraisal. There the famed gemmologist and vice-president of the company, George F. Kunz, together with a government expert in rare gems, pronounced them to be genuine diamonds of a fine quality. One weighed 2.75 carats, the other 1.35 carats. The deposit in Murfreesboro was identified as a kimberlite pipe. Huddleston later sold his holdings, after days of haggling, to the Union Trust Company for $36,000. His subsequent mode of living is not known for sure: some say he died soon after the sale, while others have stated that he passed away 27 years later as a pauper, having lost everything in a series of ill-fated investments and reckless gambling.

After it had changed hands several times the Crater of Diamonds came into the ownership of Austin Q. Millar, who bought it with his son Howard in 1912 and operated a test plant there for five years. But in 1919 the operating plant was destroyed by a series of mysterious fires. The Millars' investment of more than $250,000 was burned up and they were unable to rebuild. Thereafter the land was opened to visitors to look for diamonds on payment of a fee. On 4 March 1955, a Mrs A.L. Parker, of Dallas, Texas, turned over a clod of dirt and discovered a diamond weighing 15.33 carats. Flawless and colourless, it was an elongated stone measuring 38.1 × 11.1 × 6.3 mm. The New York firm of diamond cutters,

Schenk & Van Haelen, cut it into a marquise of 8.27 carats, which was named the 'Star of Arkansas'. The value of the gem was originally established at $11–15,000 but its fine quality and unusually large size for an Arkansas gem ultimately led to several jewellers reappraising its value. In 1968 the Star of Arkansas was purchased by a jeweller from Tucson, Arizona, and later sold to a private collector for $50,000.

Star of Este

Weighing approximately 25 (old) carats, this diamond was once owned by the House of Este, one of the oldest Italian princely families. It was reputed to have been of perfect form and quality. The Star of Este became a jewel of the Habsburgs when the daughter of the last Duke of Este married Archduke Ferdinand of Austria, third son of the Emperor Francis I. This branch of the Habsburgs died out in 1875 and the title and possessions passed to Archduke Francis Ferdinand, whose murder at Sarajevo in 1914 was the spark that touched off the First World War. According to a reliable source the Star of Este, together with other Habsburg jewels, was sold in order to help pay the expenses of the exiled Imperial family. The diamond may have come to light in 1951. In that year agents acting on behalf of King Farouk of Egypt purchased in San Sebastian, Spain, a diamond whose description matched that of the Star of Este; it weighed 26.16 metric carats, equivalent to 24.48 old carats. But it was never officially confirmed that it was the same diamond.

Stewart

Weighing 296 (metric) carats, the light yellow octahedron was for many years the biggest alluvial diamond found in South Africa. It was discovered in July 1872 at Waldeck's Plant – alluvial diggings on the Vaal River some 48 km from Kimberley – in a claim considered almost valueless, which the original owner, F. Pepper, had sold for £30. The buyer, named Spalding, did not have high hopes of it either, but as other diggers were finding diamonds nearby he thought it possible that something might turn up. Spalding handed the claim over to Antony Williams to work. One day while showing a labourer where and how he wanted him to work, Williams's pick struck a rock so hard that it bounced: suddenly he was spellbound by the sight of this diamond. It is said that he was so excited he could not eat for two days. Spalding and Williams sold the stone for £6,000 to a Port Elizabeth merchant named Stewart; he sold it shortly afterwards to Messrs Pittar, Leverson & Co for £9,000. The cutting, most likely carried out in Amsterdam, yielded a brilliant of 123 carats, and when last heard of the Stewart was in private hands.

Sultan of Morocco

The Youssoupov family is said to have owned this 35.27-carat bluish-grey cushion cut since 1840: if that is so then clearly it is not of African origin. Cartier, who handled the sale of many of the Youssoupov jewels, purchased the Sultan of Morocco from Prince Felix Youssoupov in 1922. Sometime towards the end of that decade they sold it to a buyer in the United States. In 1969 Cartier loaned the diamond to the New York State Museum for their exhibition entitled 'The World of Gems'. In July 1972 F. J. Cooper Inc., the Philadelphia jewellers, acquired the gem before selling it in the following November to a private American buyer. At some stage in its history the

diamond was presumably owned by a Moroccan ruler, but his identity does not appear to be known. It may have been Moulay Abd al-Hafidh who is said to have been in possession of the Moon of the Mountain diamond – evidence, perhaps, that he was a collector of diamonds. This Sultan signed the Treaty of Fez which established Morocco as a French protectorate.

Taj-i Mah

When the contents of the Iranian Treasury were opened up in the 1960s, the existence of three legendary Indian diamonds was revealed. They are the Darya-i Nur, the Nur ul-Ain and the Taj-i Mah. It has been conclusively proved that the first two diamonds had been cut from the same stone. The Taj-i Mah, meaning 'Crown of the Moon', is an imposing stone and the largest unmounted Indian diamond in the collection. Most certainly of Golconda origin, it is irregular, Mogul-cut, colourless and of the finest quality, slightly worn on top. The diamond weighs 115.06 metric carats and measures 32.0 × 24.3 × 14.7 mm.

The presence of the Taj-i Mah among the Crown Jewels in the Iranian capital had been known for a long time. The British administrator and diplomat Sir John Malcolm, who visited Persia early in the nineteenth century, was allowed by Fath Ali Shah (1797–1834) to inspect the Regalia. He wrote: 'Darya-i Nur, or 'Sea of Light' weighs 186 carats, and is considered to be the diamond of the finest lustre in the world. The Taj-i Mah, or 'Crown of the Moon' is also a splendid diamond. It weighs 146 carats. These two are the principal in a pair of bracelets, valued at near a million sterling. Those in the crown are also of extraordinary size and value.'

The diamond content of these bracelets, or armbands, is somewhat puzzling. Other travellers have specifically stated that the Koh-i-noor was worn by Fath Ali Shah in one of his armbands. In this connection it is of interest to recall the fact that before the Koh-i-noor was recut to its existing weight it weighed approximately 186 carats. Could it, therefore, have been the Koh-i-noor rather than the Darya-i Nur which was the companion diamond to the Taj-i Mah in the ornament? It has always been stated that the Darya-i Nur and the Taj-i Mah were sister stones. This may have been true from a historical point of view, but certainly not from a gemmological one, since the Darya-i Nur is light pink in colour while the Taj-i Mah is colourless. Indeed the colour of the latter is not unlike that of the Koh-i-noor, so that they would have been well matched.

Whatever may have been the truth about the jewel of Fath Ali Shah, there is no doubting the existence of three separate diamonds today. With regard to the discrepancy between the past and present weights of the Taj-i Mah, it is quite possible that at some stage in its history the stone may have undergone recutting. This is most likely to have taken place during the reign of Nasir ud-Din Shah (1848–96), the ruler who was responsible for the purchase of numerous large diamonds, clearly of later South African origin, that are among the Iranian Crown Jewels, and for the recutting of some of his predecessor's acquisitions.

Vainer Briolette

When considering which diamond cutting centres are the most important, it would be unlikely if London sprang to mind as one of them. The city's role in the diamond trade has been as the major point of distribution of rough diamonds. The London Diamond Syndicate, formed in 1890 as a joint buying and selling organization for the output of the De Beers mines, was succeeded by the modern Central Selling Organisation, now the Diamond Trading Company, so that most of the

leading diamantaires the world over are still obliged to consult travel schedules to London. At the same time, for almost two centuries a small cutting industry has contrived to exist in the British Isles and the greatest diamond which it had worked on was the Regent, or the 'Pitt', as it was then known. The largest rough gemstone handled has been the Woyie River, cut in the early 1950s by Briefel & Lemer, who had also been entrusted with the Williamson. With the Vainer Briolette, London was recognized as a cutting centre again.

In the autumn of 1984 associates of M. Vainer Ltd informed them of the existence of a 202.85-carat diamond, yellowish, lightly spotted but of almost perfect octahedral shape. Instead of cutting the customary brilliant from such a stone Milosh Vainer and his master cutter, Michael Gould, had other, more audacious ideas: they decided to fashion a briolette. This is a comparatively rare diamond cut. One older specimen was owned by Henry Philip Hope, the banker whose collection of unique gems included the famous gem named after him. The Briolette of India, weighing 90.38 carats, was thought to have a history extending to the Middle Ages; unfortunately recent research has revealed that it was cut in Paris in 1908–9. Four more briolettes, all yellowish, are the so-called June Briolette of 48.42 carats and three sold in Geneva by Christie's in May 1984 that weighed 44.61, 32.32 and 29.17 carats. These have all been surpassed by the Vainer Briolette weighing 116.60 carats, and with 192 facets. The GIA certified that both the polish and symmetry were excellent and the colour was a light fancy yellow. The diamond also enjoys, therefore, the distinction of being the largest diamond to have been cut in London since the Regent. It was purchased by the Sultan of Brunei. In addition the rough stone yielded five smaller gems weighing a total of 14.93 carats, all of which were polished in keeping with the historical cutting of the principal stone.

Fancy Coloured Diamonds

Eric C Emms, FGA DGA

Diamonds have been appreciated for centuries and valued for their rarity and superb beauty. Acquired as a symbol of wealth and status, as an individual treasure or presented as a token of love, the diamond continues to exert an unparalleled influence upon our emotions and imagination. The finest gem quality diamond is often considered to be representative of the perfectly colourless, transparent gem. However, nature does provide a very small number of diamonds of an attractive definite yellow, orange, pink, blue, green or red colour. The rarity of such diamonds, known as 'fancy' coloured diamonds, has been recognized ever since diamonds have been recovered from the ground. Today the paucity of supply and the increased demand for coloured diamonds are reflected in the high prices these gems attain in the market-place.

Diamond is composed of carbon atoms packed rigidly together to form a three-dimensional pattern. Each carbon atom is tightly bonded to a further four surrounding carbon atoms. It is this close packing of the atoms and the regularity of the diamond crystal structure that are responsible for its superb optical and physical properties; the extreme hardness, remarkable transparency, adamantine lustre, strong refraction and dispersion of light, are characteristics that elevate diamond to the highest rank of gems.

The colour of a diamond is an attribute also determined by its atomic structure. Pure white diamonds are rare; the yellowish and brown tints present in the majority of diamonds are so faint that an inexperienced observer, unless able to compare such diamonds with an absolutely colourless diamond, will fail to recognize the stone has any trace of colour at all. Such diamonds are rather lower in value than absolutely colourless examples of the same clarity and size.

The hint of yellow colour seen in most diamonds is caused by the presence of the element nitrogen incorporated within the crystal structure. For every one million carbon atoms, one thousand may be replaced with nitrogen atoms. Scientists classify diamonds that contain nitrogen as Type I. Prolonged exposure to extreme high temperatures and pressures, which most diamonds experience deep in the earth following their formation,

favours the formation of nitrogen groups or aggregates. Diamonds containing aggregated nitrogen atoms are classified as Type Ia and account for the great majority of all diamonds. Three different nitrogen aggregates are known: a pair of nitrogen atoms called the A-aggregate; four or more nitrogen atoms, termed the B-aggregate, and a triangular group of three nitrogen atoms called the N_3 centre. The N_3 centres absorb particular wavelengths of white light passing through the diamond. In response, our eyes see a near colourless to yellow colour; the intensity of the yellow will depend, in part, upon the concentrations of the N_3 centres within this type of diamond. The A and B aggregates do not absorb visible light, thus are not involved in the cause of colour.

Type Ia near-colourless gems graded as 'D' colour through to 'Z' colour are sometimes called diamonds belonging to the 'Cape' series. Diamonds toward the top end of the series are only just faint yellow or 'near-colourless' and rare in number. Diamonds towards the lower end of the series are light in colour and are referred to simply as 'Capes' by some quarters of the diamond industry because many yellowish diamonds were imported from the Cape of Good Hope in South Africa following the discovery of diamonds there in the 1860s. If the yellow colour is so intense as to be seen as an attractive definite colour when viewed from the top of the stone, the yellow diamond is called 'fancy'.

Other fancy yellow diamonds also owe their colour to nitrogen, but the nitrogen in these gems is present not in groups, but as single isolated atoms replacing the carbon atoms in the diamond structure. These diamonds, classified as Type Ib, tend to be a highly saturated yellow and contain relatively small amounts of nitrogen atoms, perhaps 50 nitrogen atoms for every million carbon atoms. Type Ib diamonds are rare in nature – perhaps less than one per cent of all diamonds are of this type. The term 'Canary' diamond was once reserved for Type Ib yellow diamonds but today this word is used to describe any fancy yellow diamond of intense saturation.

Although it is believed that India has produced a small number of important yellow diamonds, for

example the Florentine, it is South Africa that has dominated the production of yellow gems, ever since the first diamond crystal was discovered by the banks of the Vaal River in 1866. This stone was fashioned into the yellowish 10.73-carat Eureka diamond. Notable large yellow diamonds discovered in South Africa include the De Beers, the Tiffany, the Red Cross and a yellow 616-carat rough.

Diamonds lacking in detectable nitrogen atoms are very rare and are called Type II diamonds. A sub-division termed Type IIa diamonds are the purest form of diamond. They have a perfect internal crystal structure, lacking any foreign atoms replacing carbon atoms, and tend to form large crystals, usually of exceptional transparency and without any trace of colour. These attributes are believed to be characteristic of the finest Indian diamonds traded in the past from Golconda. However, the most famous example of such a Type IIa diamond is the Cullinan diamond discovered at the Premier mine in South Africa.

In a small proportion of Type II diamonds, the element boron is present in the structure, replacing carbon atoms in concentrations of one boron atom per one million carbon atoms. The replacement causes an absorption of the longer wavelengths of white light passing through the diamond, so we see the diamond as greyish-blue to blue in colour. These blue diamonds are extremely rare and are classified as Type IIb diamonds. They will conduct electricity, making them unique amongst diamonds, which are normally electrical insulators. The Hope diamond, 45.52 carats and, owing to its eventful history, the most famous fancy coloured diamond, and the 35.50-carat Wittelsbach are important examples of blue diamonds mined in India. A very small number of blue diamonds are known that do not contain boron. These gems do not conduct electricity, are of Type Ia, and usually contain large concentrations of hydrogen as an impurity. They have a strong grey to violet component to their colour and originate from the Argyle mine in north-west Australia.

Pink diamonds are known to have been found in only a few mines. In India, the river deposits east of the Deccan Plateau highlands have produced

notable pink diamonds such as the Darya-i Nur, the Condé and the Agra, during the many centuries of mining. India was the sole reliable and consistent source of diamonds until the discovery of Brazilian deposits in the 1720s. River deposits near the Brazilian town of what is now called Diamantina reputably became known as an infrequent but notable source of pink and other fancy coloured diamonds. In Africa, the Mwadui mine in Tanzania is known as a source of pink diamonds – the famous example being the Williamson diamond. No single mine produced a steady supply of pinks until the discovery of the Argyle mine in the 1970s. In addition to being a major source of small diamonds, the mine has marketed through an annual tender each year since 1985, a small number of fancy pink diamonds of a saturation range from light rose to full bodied purple-red.

There appear to be at least two types of pink diamond, each having a different cause of colour. The first kind are light pink diamonds of an even colour distribution, extremely transparent and notable for their lack of inclusions. Faint internal whitish banding may be observed under high magnification. These pink diamonds are of Type IIa and the cause of their colour is at present unknown. The other kind of pink diamonds, smaller in size, are of Type Ia and their colour is unevenly distributed within the gem, being confined to internal straight planar bands or lines that run parallel to specific directions of the diamond crystal. The colour intensity of these 'grain lines' and their proximity to each other appear to determine the saturation of the pink colour seen when the gem is viewed through its crown. Pink grain lines are seen in all Argyle pink diamonds and their variety gives rise to the range of colour intensities seen. To the present date, only eight polished Argyle pink diamonds larger than three carats have been offered by tender since the mine opened in 1979.

Diamonds with red as part of their colour description are the rarest of all fancy coloured diamonds. Few pure red diamonds have been documented, examined or are known to exist. The 0.95-carat round purple-red diamond sold by

Christie's in April 1987 is believed to be of Brazilian origin and is of Type Ia, and, as with many other pink and purplish-pink diamonds contains straight planar coloured grain lines. The De Young diamond is a 5.03-carat round gem of red-brown colour. It exhibits internal grain lines that are of a brownish-red hue.

Brown parallel internal grain lines are observed in a range of brown diamonds; from diamonds that are of a faint brown tinge but appear near colourless when viewed through the crown, to true fancy brown diamonds. Most large brown diamonds originate from southern Africa. The largest faceted diamond, the 545-carat Golden Jubilee is golden brown, polished from a huge crystal recovered from the Premier mine of South Africa in 1986. The gem is notable for the presence of noticeable brown planar grain bands.

The presence of internal parallel coloured grain lines and bands in the brown, pink and red range of diamonds suggests a common cause of colour. It is thought to be due to a deformation of the diamond crystal structure occurring deep in the earth after the diamond crystallized. Sub-microscopic-sized planes of carbon atoms slipped over each other as a result of the deformation, producing the visible internal planar coloured grain lines. This 'plastic' deformation to the diamond crystal may have been the result of general stress occurring during the diamond's long history in the earth or that experienced during the eruptive processes that brought the diamond to the surface. Exactly how colour is produced along the grain lines at the time of the deformation remains unknown.

There are a number of different kinds of green diamond crystals recovered from the ground. The majority show isolated green stains or spots that barely penetrate the surface of the crystal. In addition, a number of rough diamonds that show a uniform green colour over their entire surface are known. Unfortunately, during the polishing process both kinds of rough diamonds lose their colour. The green 'skin' of the crystal is polished away revealing, not a green, but a white faceted gem. Green colouration is due to the diamond crystal coming into contact with natural

radioactive sources during the time following its ascension to the surface from the interior of the earth. The natural radiation is usually in the form of alpha-particle energy emitted from uranium compounds or radioactive fluids present in the ground. Irradiation is more common on diamond crystals found in river and other alluvial sources, such as those in Brazil, India and central Africa, reflecting the greater amount of uranium compounds in sedimentary deposits compared to their presence in primary sources such as the diamond-bearing deposits of South Africa and Australia. Apart from the prolific Jwaneng mine in Botswana, few, if any, green 'skinned' diamond crystals have been recovered from the mines of southern Africa or from Argyle.

The radioactivity emitted by the uranium compounds bombard the diamond crystal over millions of years, resulting in a number of carbon atoms being dislodged from their proper sites in the diamond structure. At these damaged sites, a disturbance in the equilibrium of the crystal occurs, resulting in an absorption of the red and, to a lesser extent, the blue wavelengths of white light. Our eyes register this absorption as a green colour.

A diamond crystal requires millions of years of exposure to a radioactive source in the ground to produce the damage that would extend throughout the entire crystal to produce an even green coloration. In this case, the green colour remains when the crystal is fashioned into the gem. Such true green faceted diamonds are extremely rare.

The most famous green diamond is the 40.70-carat Dresden Green. Of exceptional transparency and even colouration, the gem displays evidence of having been subjected to natural irradiation and it is of the very rare Type IIa category. The diamond is widely believed to have originated from India. However, as the history of the gem prior to 1741 is unknown, it may have been discovered in the rivers of Brazil, exploited from the 1720s.

There are a number of green diamonds that exhibit a spectacular change of colour. These are known appropriately as chameleon diamonds. If such a diamond is kept in the dark for several hours then brought into the light, it will appear not green

but a distinct yellow colour. Gradually the chameleon changes its colour through hues of yellow-green until its original green colour is restored. Gentle heating of a chameleon diamond in a flame will also promote the change of colour – the colour reverting to the original green upon cooling.

Because fancy coloured diamonds are so scarce and command such high prices, there has been a development of methods designed to alter the colour of off-white diamonds by artificial means, to induce attractive colours similar to those of natural fancy diamonds. By using irradiation generated by nuclear reactors or other similar machines, it is possible to bombard diamonds to promote damage to the crystal structure, so producing a green to greenish-blue colour. By selecting particular types of diamond for irradiation and by varying the temperature of any subsequent heat treatment, a range of artificial colours of pink, yellow, green, brown or even black can be produced. These colours can be similar in appearance to natural fancy diamond colours so it important that the colour origin of any fancy diamond is established. Detecting whether the colour of a diamond is of natural origin or due to artificial irradiation is a task for a specialist gemmologist who does so by examining the manner in which the fancy diamond under investigation absorbs different wavelengths of light.

The value of natural coloured diamonds depends considerably upon the rarity of its colour much more than its clarity, perfection of cutting style and often even its size. Pure colours are the most prized; however, many fancy diamonds show a secondary hue that may modify the appearance of the gem. Yellow diamonds may possess a brown hint that may detract from its beauty and blue gems may have a grey modifying tint. Therefore in commerce there is a need to describe precisely the colour of fancy diamonds.

Specialists describe colour precisely by using three distinct elements called Hue, Tone and Saturation. Hue is the basic colour seen: for example, red, orange, yellow, green or blue. How light or dark the colour appears is referred to as tone, whereas saturation describes the strength or intensity of the hue.

In theory, any colour can be visualized as occupying a point in an imaginary three-dimensional space called the 'colour space'. Hue, tone and saturation are the three co-ordinates that describe any point within this space. Reference to the three co-ordinates will describe the colour precisely. However, at the present time, so that colour communication may be easier for all to understand, terms are employed to describe areas or 'volumes' of the colour space. The gem industry uses phrases such as Fancy Light, Fancy, Fancy Dark, Fancy Deep, Fancy Intense and Fancy Vivid to describe the tone and saturation of each colour and so communicate the colour description or 'grade' of any fancy diamonds.

For generations, there has been a prevailing belief that the perfect colour of a diamond is a pure white, or in other words, a total absence of colour. Diamond is singular amongst precious gems in this respect. During the last few years there has been a tremendous interest aroused by fancy coloured diamonds. High prices paid for these gems recently at auction have focused public attention upon this small but important area of diamond commerce. For many years, fancy coloured diamonds were little known to the public and to most members of the jewellery industry. Today, we can appreciate their beauty and under-stand their rarity. The conditions in which fancy coloured diamonds crystallize and acquire their coloration are not constant. Each one is unique.

Previous page, from left to right:
1. A fancy orange-pink diamond ring, 18.65 carats. Sold at Christie's Geneva, 18 May 1995, for US$2,102,800;
2. The heart-shaped fancy intense purplish-red Mikimoto Red diamond, 1.03 carats. Purchased in the 1994 Argyle Pink Diamond Tender. *Courtesy K. Mikimoto & Co.;*
3. A fine unmounted fancy dark grey-yellowish green diamond, 2.02 carats. Sold at Christie's Geneva, 20 May 1997, for US$88,000.

Above, from left to right:
1. A fancy intense yellow diamond ring, 16.34 carats. Sold at Christie's Geneva, 15 November 1995, for US$576,400;
2. The Begum Blue diamond. A heart-shaped fancy deep blue diamond, 13.78 carats. Sold at Christie's Geneva, 13 November 1995, set in a necklace, for US$7,474,00;
3. A fancy intense purple-pink diamond ring, 3.03 carats, VVS1. Sold at Christie's New York, 24 October 1995 for US$882,500.

Note on the Carat

Over the centuries, diamonds have been weighed in several different types of units. When the Mogul Emperors of India collected them, their inventories apparently gave the weights in ratis or mangelin, although before this tandulas, sarsapas, masas and surkhs were also in common use. Indeed, it takes some considerable detective work to determine how they would relate to the metric carat today. When Tavernier made his travels to India in the seventeenth century, he took a pair of hand scales with him recording carats, so we know the relationship between an old carat and a rati. But the old carat weight varied considerably, ranging from 188.5 milligrams in Bologna to 206.1 mg. in Vienna. They were not measured in decimals as now, but in fractions from a quarter to a sixty-fourth. There was also another measure, the grain, which was 3.1783 of a carat; 480 grains made a troy ounce.

In 1907 the French decided to rationalize gem weights and introduced the metric carat that is exactly one fifth of a gram (0.2 gm). Spain followed in the same year, but it was not until 1914 that Great Britain, the United States, and two more Continental countries followed suit. Consequently when weights of famous diamonds were recorded in the past, it is often only possible to give the stated weight at the time and to estimate its weight in metric carats. For example, the weight of the recut Koh-i-noor has long been stated as 108.93 carats, but only recently has the diamond been taken out of its setting and re-weighed on a modern, standards-verified, electronic balance. Then it was found to weigh 105.60 metric carats. It follows that books published before the year 1914 will have recorded the weights of diamonds in old carats. However, since that date some publications have maintained this practice and chosen to ignore the metric carat, which is universally employed in the diamond industry today. In order to clarify the situation, where the weight of a diamond in metric carats is certain, this is the weight given in the text. In other instances, the weight has been recorded in old carats together with the calculated weight in metric carats.

The World's Largest Cut Diamonds

308

Polished weight in metric carats	Name	Colour	Shape	Country	Last Reported Owner or Location
–	Braganza (see note I)	–	–	–	(see note I).
545.67	Golden Jubilee	Dark brown	Fire-rose cushion	South Africa	Thailand.
530.20	Cullinan I	White	Pear	South Africa	Tower of London. Crown Jewels of Great Britain.
407.48	Incomparable	Brownish yellow	Triolette	Dem. Rep. of Congo	Auctioned in New York, October 1988.
–	Matan (see note II)	–	–	Borneo	(see note II).
317.40	Cullinan II	White	Cushion	South Africa	Tower of London. Crown Jewels of Great Britain.
–	Nizam (see note III)	–	–	–	–
273.85	Centenary	White	Modified heart	South Africa	Privately owned
245.35	Jubilee	White	Cushion	South Africa	Robert Mouawad.
234.65	De Beers	Light yellow	Cushion	South Africa	Auctioned in Geneva, May 1982; now repolished and recertified.
205.07	Red Cross	Yellow	Square brilliant	South Africa	Auctioned in Geneva, November 1977
203.04	Millennium Star	White	Pear	Dem. Rep. of Congo	De Beers, London
202 (old cts?)	Black Star of Africa	Black	–	–	Exhibited in Tokyo, 1971.
200.87	Anon	Yellow	Pear	–	Cut by William Goldberg Diamond Corporation of New York.
200.07	La Luna	White	Heart shape	South America	Privately owned.
189.6	Orlov	Slightly tinted white	Half of an egg: rose cut above, flat and unfaceted below	India	Kremlin Museum, Moscow.
175 to 195 (estimated)	Darya-i Nur	Pale pink	Rectangular step-cut	India	Teheran, Crown Jewels of Iran.
184.5	Victoria, also called Jacob, Imperial or Great White	White	Oval	South Africa	Late Nizam of Hyderabad (died 1977).
183.00	Moon	White with faint yellow tinge	Round	South Africa	Auctioned in London, August 1942.
180.85	Anon	Yellow	Briolette	–	Privately owned.
170.49	Star of Peace	Brownish yellow	Pear	–	Privately owned.
160.18	Tablet of Islam	Black	Emerald cut	–	Reported for sale in January 1992.
152.16	Anon	Silver Cape	Rectangular old brilliant cut	South Africa (?)	Teheran, Crown Jewels of Iran.
150 (old cts?)	Anon	Yellow	Emerald cut	–	SIBA Corporation.
–	Turkey I (see note IV)	–	–	–	–
141.23	Anon	–	–	–	Privately owned.
140.50	Regent	White with blue tinge	Cushion	India	Musée du Louvre, Paris.
137.82	Paragon	White	Kite	Brazil	Graff Diamonds, London.
137.27	Florentine	Light yellow	Irregular nine-sided double-rose cut	India	Stolen in 1920 from the Imperial family of Austria.
137.02	Premier Rose	White	Pear	South Africa	Sold by William Goldberg Diamond Corporation to an undisclosed buyer in 1979.
137	Anon (see note V)	–	–	–	Saudi Arabia.
135.92	Queen of Holland	White with blue tint (intense blue)	Cushion	India (?)	Sold by William Goldberg Diamond Corporation to an undisclosed buyer in 1978.
135.75 (old cts)	Anon	Yellow	Cushion?	South Africa (?)	Auctioned in London, May 1905.
135.45	Anon	Cape	High (old) cushion cut	South Africa (?)	Teheran, Crown Jewels of Iran.
135 (old cts)	Mountain of Splendour (see note VI)	–	–	India (?)	Iran.
133.03	Algeiba Star	Yellow	Square antique modified brilliant	South Africa (?)	Privately owned.
132.42	Golden Hue	Yellow	Cushion	South Africa (?)	Auctioned in Geneva, November 1983.
130.00	Great Brazilian	White	–	Brazil (?)	Shown at Sears Roebuck Stores in 1956.
129	Star of the South	White	Elongated cushion	Brazil	Rustomjee Jamsetjee, Bombay.
128.51	Tiffany	Yellow	Cushion	South Africa	Tiffany & Co., New York.
128.25	Niarchos	White	Pear	South Africa	Stavros Niarchos.
128	Anon	Yellow	Emerald cut	South Africa (?)	Tiffany & Co., New York.
127.01	Portuguese	White	Cushion	Brazil (?)	Smithsonian Institution, Washington DC.
126.76	Light of Peace	White	Pear	Sierra Leone	Privately owned.
126 (old cts)	Moon of the Mountains (see note VII)	–	–	India (?)	–

125.65	Jonker	White	Emerald cut	South Africa	Privately owned.
123.93	Anon	Silvery Cape	Cushion	South Africa	Teheran, Crown Jewels of Iran.
123.00 (old cts)	Stewart	Yellow	Brilliant	South Africa	–
123.00	Julius Pam	Yellow	–	South Africa	–
121.90	Anon	Yellow	Multi-faceted octahedron	South Africa	Teheran, Crown Jewels of Iran.
120.20	Tear of the Emperor	White	Pear	–	Privately owned, Asia.
118.00	Meister	Yellow	Cushion	South Africa (?)	Walter Meister, Zurich.
116.60	Vainer Briolette	Yellow	Briolette	South Africa	Sultan of Brunei.
115.83	Al-Nader	White	Pear	–	–
115.06	Taj-i Mah	White	Mogul cut	India	Teheran, Crown Jewels of Iran.
115.00	Edna Star	White	Emerald cut	–	Sold by Harry Winston Inc. to an Arabian client in 1957.
114.64	Anon	Yellow	Briolette	India	Privately owned.
114.63	Anon	Yellow	Cushion	South Africa	Privately owned.
114.28	Anon	Silvery Cape	High (old) cushion cut	South Africa (?)	Teheran, Crown Jewels of Iran.
114.03	Anon	Yellow	Cushion	South Africa (?)	Purchased by W. Jackson at auction London, October 1962.
112.53	Mouna	Yellow	Cushion	South Africa	Sold Christie's, Geneva, November 1998
112 (old cts)	African Yellow	Fancy intense yellow	–	South Africa	(see note VIII)
111.59	Earth Star	Coffee	Pear	South Africa	Purchased by Stephen Zbova of Naples, Florida in 1947.
111.22	Anon	White	Heart	–	Privately owned.
109.26	Cross of Asia	Champagne	–	–	Exhibited at Joske's, San Antonio, Texas in 1983.
108.81	Mouawad Magic	White	Emerald cut	Guinea	Robert Mouawad.
108.04	Anon	Yellow	Emerald cut	–	–
107.65	Anon	Yellow	'Starburst' cut	–	Displayed at the Basle Fair 1990.
107.46	Rojtman	Yellow	Cushion	South Africa (?)	Mrs Mark Rojtman, New York, in 1966.
107.10	Anon	Brown	Cushion	–	Privately owned.
107.07	Louis Cartier	White	Pear	South Africa	Sold to a European collector in 1975 by Cartier, Paris.
106	Nameless polygonal	–	Modified pear shape	–	Robert Mouawad.
105.60	Koh-i-noor	White	Oval	India	Tower of London, Crown Jewels of Great Britain.
105.54	Soleil d'Or	Yellow	Emerald cut	–	Privately owned in America.
104.53	Deepdene	Yellow (treated)	Cushion	South Africa (?)	Purchased at Christie's by Laurence Graff, Geneva, November 1977
105.51	Star of Egypt	White	Emerald cut	India (?)	Privately owned.
104.95	Golden Door	White	Modified pear	–	Privately owned.
104.15	Great Chrysanthemum	–	Pear	South Africa	Julius Cohen, New York.
104.02	Mouawad Monolith	–	Emerald cut	–	Robert Mouawad.
102.65	Anon		Antique round cut	–	Privately owned.
102.61	Anon		Cushion	–	Privately owned.
102.48	Ashberg	Amber	Cushion	–	Auctioned in Geneva, May 1981.
102.42	Anon	Light brown	Pear	–	Privately owned.
102.41	African Queen	White	Pear	Afria	–
102.07	Allnatt	Fancy intense yellow	Cushion	South Africa	Auctioned by Christie's, Geneva, May 1996
102.04	Anon	–	Emerald cut	–	Robert Mouawad.
101.84	Mouawad Splendour	White	Eleven-sided pear	–	Robert Mouawad.
101.25	Anon	Yellow	Briolette	–	M. Vainer Ltd, London.
101.25	Anon	–	–	India	Privately owned.
101.14	Anon	White	Kite	–	Privately owned.
100.52	Sunrise	Yellow	Emerald cut	–	Privately owned.
100.36	Star of Happiness	White	Rectangular modified brilliant cut	–	Purchased at auction in Geneva, November 1993 by Sheikh Fitaihi.
101.31	Anon	White	Heart	–	Privately owned, offered by Christie's New York, October 1996.
100.10	Star of the Season	White	Pear	–	Purchased at auction in Geneva, May 1995, by Sheikh Fitaihi.

Notes

I. The Braganza, weighing 1,860 old carats, is considered most likely to have been a white topaz, not a diamond.

II. The Matan, weighing 367 old carats, is generally thought to have been a rock crystal.

III. The Nizam is believed to be only a partially cut diamond: its weight has been variously reported as 340 or 277 old carats.

IV. According to Streeter, the larger of two diamonds formerly in the Turkish Regalia weighing 147 old carats. Nothing is known today of this stone.

V. Diamond Selection Ltd's *Diamond Digest* reported the sale of a finest quality diamond of this weight to a Saudi Arabian client. It is assumed that this is the Premier Rose.

VI. Murray mentions in his *Sketches of Persia* the existence of a diamond of this name weighing 135 old carats. It cannot be identified for certain with an existing diamond today.

VII. A diamond weighing 126 old carats is known to have been among the Russian Crown Jewels in the 19th century but has since disappeared.

VIII. Streeter listed a diamond of this name of 112 old carats. It was obviously one of the earliest large South African diamonds, the location of which remains unknown today.

The Cutting of the Cullinan diamond

6 February 1908–13 October 1908
Asscher's Manufactory, Amsterdam

'On this the sixth day of February the year nineteen hundred and eight

Appeared before me Hendrik Wertheim, Notary, residing in Amsterdam, in the presence of the witnesses hereafter named Mr Abraham Asscher and Mr Joseph Asscher diamond cutters, the first living in Amsterdam, the other living in Paris, members of the firm Joseph Asscher en Co and Mr Alexander Michael Levy, broker in diamonds, member of the firm M J Levy and Nephews of London, living in London.

The appeared gentlemen are personally known to me.

The gentlemen present showed me the Cullinan Diamond.

The gentlemen present have weighted the said diamond in the presence of me and the witnesses and they requested me to certify that the said diamond has a weight of three thousand nineteen and three quarter Carats – 3019¾ Dutch weights (three thousand twenty five and three quarter Carats English weight 3025¾). And that also by me the notary is certified.

Of all which the present deed is drawn up at Amsterdam, in the manufactory of Mr Asscher in Amsterdam Tol straat number 127 and 129, the day of the month and the year aforesaid by me the undersigned Notary in the presence of Mr Johannes Pieter Smits public notary and Mr Mari van Riel prospective notary both living in Amsterdam both personally known to me.

After having read the gentlemen present the witnesses and I, myself the notary have immediately signed this present deed which will be retained by me.

Signed
A Asscher Joseph Asscher, Alexander M Levy
J P Smits, M van Riel, H Wertheim
Notary

No 42 *Geregistreerd te Amsterdam den zevenenden Februari 1900 acht deel 266 folio 57 recto vak 2 een blad geen renvooi Ontvangen voor recht een gulden twintig cent.*

De Ontvanger B. Ct no 1 Holtersom
Signed

Delivered by the undersigned Notary as a true copy of the above mentioned deed
[signature and stamp of Wertheim]

Bij proces verbaal d.d 30 October 1908 voor mij notaris verleden is de inflating van het woord Februari geconstateerd en gerectificeerd.

'On this tenth day of February of the year nineteen hundred and eight, at three fifteen o'clock in the afternoon appeared before me Hendrik Wertheim, Notary residing in Amsterdam in the presence of witnesses hereafter named

Mr Abraham Asscher at Amsterdam
Mr Joseph Asscher, at Paris
Mr Lodewijk Asscher living at Paris
Mr Elie Asscher living at Paris all merchants and diamond cutters

Mr John Arthur Levy and Mr Alexander Michael Levy, both diamond brokers living at London, members of the firm Mr J Levy and Nephews at London, acting in their quality as Inspectors designated as experts for this purpose by the British Crown nominees

These gentlemen present are all personally known to me, the undersigned notary.

The gentlemen present produced to me the undersigned notary in the presence of the witnesses the Cullinan Diamond which was ready to be cloven.

Immediately thereafter the Cullinan diamond was cloven in two pieces by Mr Joseph Asscher and which pieces laid together on their respective cleaved surfaces had still exactly the form of the Cullinan diamond, before it was cloven.

These two stones when the cement was removed weighed respectively nineteen hundred seventy three and three Quarter carats Dutch weight (nineteen hundred seventy seven and a half carats English weight) and one thousand thirty eight and one quarter carats Dutch weight (one thousand fourth and a half carats English weight).

The splinters consisting of small fragments weigh six carats (Dutch and English weights).

The above mentioned Inspectors declare that the cleaving has been executed exactly in conformity with all rules of the art of splitting and as they anticipated having approved of the mode of cleaving the operation has given the best possible results.

Of all which the present deed is drawn up at Amsterdam in the manufactory of Mr Asscher in Amsterdam Tol Straat numbers 127 and 129 the day of the month and the year aforesaid by me the undersigned Notary in the presence of Mr Herman Louis Israels, doctor in law, barrister and Mr Mari van Riel prospective notary, both living in Amsterdam and both personally known to me.

After having read this the gentlemen present the witnesses and I myself the notary have immediately signed this present deed which will be retained by me the undersigned notary.

Signed
A Asscher, Joseph Asscher, Lodewijk Asscher
Elie Asscher, J A Levy, Alexander M Levy
Mr H Louis Israels, M van Riel, H Wertheim
Notaris
No 66 Geregistreerd te Amsterdam, den Elfden Februari 1900 acht deel 266 folio 58 verso vak 8 een blad een renvooi Ontvangen voor recht een gulden twintig cent
f.120 De Ontvanger B A no 1
Woltersom
Delivered by the undersigned Notary as a true copy of the above mentioned deed
[signature and stamp of Wertheim]

'On this eighteenth day of February of the year ninteen hundred and eight appeared before me Hendrik Wertheim Notary residing in Amsterdam in the presence of the witnesses hereafter named.

Mr Joseph Asscher and Mr Abraham Asscher diamond cutters the first living in Paris the other living in Amsterdam, Mr Lodewijk Asscher merchant living at Paris and Mr John Arthur Levy, broker in diamonds, member of the firm M J Levy and Nephews of London. Living in London.

The appeared gentlemen are personally known to me.

These gentlemen present showed me three pieces and some splinters that they declared to represent the entire result after splitting of the Cullinan Diamond and which they have weighed in the presence of myself and the witnesses and they requested me to certify the weight of the said three pieces and the splinters, which have respectively the weights of

one piece weighing fifteen hundred and eighty one carats (1581) Dutch weight

one piece weighing one thousand thirty eight and one quarter carats (1038¼) Dutch weight

one piece weighing three hundred and eight carats (308) Dutch weight

one splinter weighing seventy two and a half carats (72½) Dutch weight

small splinters weighing fourteen carats together Dutch weight

Of all which the present deed is drawn up at Amsterdam, in the manufactory of Mr Asscher in Amsterdam Tolstraat numbers 127 and 129 the day of the month and the year aforesaid by undersigned notary in the presence of Mr Mari van Riel prospective notary and Mr Christianus Stephanus Johannes Dordregter clerk, both living in Amsterdam, both personally known to me.

After having read the gentlemen present the

witnesses and I myself the notary have immediately signed this present deed which will be retained by me.

Signed

Joseph Asscher, A Asscher, Lodewijk Asscher
J A Levy, M van Riel, C. Dordregter, H Wertheim
Notary

No 119 *Geregistreerd te Amsterdam den Negentienden Februari 1900 acht deel 267 folio 68 verso vak 3 een blad drie renvooien. Ontvangen voor recht een gulden twintig cent fl.20 De Ontvanger B.A. no 1*

Woltersom

<u>Delivered by the undersigned Notary as a true copy of the above mentioned deed</u>
[signature and the stamp of 'H Wertheim Notaris te Amsterdam']

'On this the twentieth day of February of the year nineteen hundred and eight appeared before me <u>Hendrik Wertheim</u>, Notary residing in <u>Amsterdam</u>, in the presence of the witnesses here after named.

<u>Mr Abraham Asscher … Mr John Arthur Levy</u>
The appeared gentlemen are personally known to me,

These gentlemen present showed me the following stones product of the <u>Cullinan diamond</u>.

The piece of fifteen hundred and eighty one carats Dutch weight (fifteen hundred and eighty four and a half carats English weight).

And the piece of one thousand thirty seven and three quarters carats Dutch weight (one thousand and fourth carats English weight) are both still intact.

The gentlemen present find that a small piece of cleavers cement has come away from the piece of one thousand thirty seven and three quarter carats Dutch weight, which accounts for the difference of one half carats between the firt and present weighing.

The gentlemen present declared that the piece of the three hundred and eight carats Dutch weight has had one piece split off of it which weighs fourty six carats Dutch weight (fourty six and one eighth carats English weight) and the

piece formerly weighing three hundred and eight carats Dutch weight now weighs two hundred sixty and a half carats Dutch weight (two hundred sixty one and one quarter carats English weight), the splinter of seventy two and a half carats Dutch weight has been split into three pieces namely one piece weighing thirty two and three quarter carats Dutch and English weight.

the second piece weighing twenty four and three quarter carats Dutch and English weight

the third piece weighing thirteen and one quarter carats Dutch and English weight.

While the smaller splinters of fourteen carats together Dutch and English weights are still intact.

The declarations of the gentlemen present are certified by me the under signed notary.

The gentlemen present declared that the operation of splitting is now entirely completed.

Of all which the present deed is drawn up at <u>Amsterdam</u>, in the manufactory of <u>Mr Asscher</u> in Amsterdam…in the presence of <u>Mr Mari van Riel</u> prospective notary and <u>Mr Isaac Sammes</u> clerk both living in <u>Amsterdam</u>, both personally known to me.

After having read the gentlemen present the witnesses and I myself the notary have immediately signed this present deed which will be retained by me.

Signed

A Asscher, J A Levy, M van Riel, I Sammes, H Wertheim Notary

No 198 <u>Geregistreed</u> …
<u>Delivered by the undersigned Notary as a true copy of the above mentioned deed</u>
[signature and H Wertheim's stamp]

'On this nineteenth day of March of the year nineteen hundred and eight appeared before me <u>Hendrik Wertheim</u>…in the presence of the witnesses here after named

<u>Mr Abraham Asscher</u>…and <u>Mr John Arthur Levy</u>…
The appeared gentlemen are personally known to me

These gentlemen present showed me a piece, which they declared to be the piece described in the deed drawn up on the twentieth day of February of the year nineteen and eight by me the undersigned notary, formerly weighing fifteen hundred and eighty one carats Dutch weight (fifteen hundred and eighty four and a half carats English weight) product of the <u>Cullinan diamond</u>.

This piece now in the process of polishing has been weighed by these gentlemen present in the presence of me and the witnesses here after named, and it is certified by me in this present deed that the piece now weighs fourteen hundred and sixteen and a half carats (Dutch weights) or fourteen hundred and nineteen and a half carats (English weight)

Of all which the present deed is drawn up at <u>Amsterdam</u> … by me the undersigned notary in the presence of <u>Mr Mari van Riel</u> … <u>Mr Christianus Stephanus Johannes Dordregter</u> clerks…After having read the gentlemen present the witnesses and I myself the notary signed this present deed, which will be retained by me.

Signed

A Asscher, J A Levy, M van Riel, C Dordregter
H Wertheim

No 155…
<u>Delivered by the undersigned Notary as a true copy of the above mentioned document</u>
[signature and stamp of Wertheim]

'On this twenty sixth day of May the year nineteen hundred and eight appeared before me <u>Hendrik Wertheim</u> Notary…in the presence of the witnesses hereafter named

<u>Mr Joseph Asscher…Mr Abraham Asscher…Mr John Arthur Levy</u>
The appeared gentlemen are personally known to me.

These gentlemen present showed me the pieces hereafter described, all products of the Cullinan diamond.

I. a piece, now in the process of polishing which originally weighed fifteen hundred and eighty one carats Dutch weight (fifteen hundred and eighty four and a half carats English weight) and weighed on the nineteenth day of March fourteen hundred and sixteen and a half carats Dutch weight (fourteen hundred nineteen and a half carats English weight) now weighs nine hundred fifty one carats Dutch weight (nine hundred and fifty three carats English weight)

II. a piece originally weighing one thousand thirty seven and three quarter carats Dutch weight has been cleaved and produced one piece weighing eight hundred and nineteen carats Dutch weight (eight hundred twenty and a half carats English weight) and one other weighing two hundred sixteen and a half carats Dutch weight (two hundred sixteen and three quarter English weight).

III. one drop brilliant weighing ninety four and three eighth carats Dutch weight (ninety four and a half carats English weight) this the product of the cleaved piece originally weighing two hundred sixty and a half carats. This brilliant has still to have some work done on the back (culette) and will lose a little weight.

IV. one heart shaped brilliant eightteen and three eighth carat (Dutch and English weight) product of the cleaved piece originally weighing forty six carats.

V. one marquise brilliant weighing eleven and a quarter carats (Dutch and English weight) product of the cleaved piece originally weighing thirty two and three quarter carats.

VI. one marquise brilliant weighing eight and nine sixteen carats (Dutch and English weight) product of the cleaved piece originally weighing twenty four and three quarter carats.

VII. one drop brilliant weighing four and a quarter and a thirty-second carat [sic] (Dutch and English weight) product of the cleaved piece originally weighing thirteen and a quarter carats; also a few small splinters weighing together fifteen carats.

Of all which the present deed is drawn up at Amsterdam, in the manufactory of Mr Asscher…

by me the undersigned Notary in the presence of Mr Mari van Riel… and Mr Cornelius Arnoldus van Reen, clerk…

After having read the gentlemen present the witnesses and I myself the notary have immediately signed this present deed which will be retained by me.

Signed Joseph Asscher – A Asscher – J A Levy – M van Riel – C A van Reen – H Wertheim Notary…

No. 274 *Geregistreerd*…

Delivered by the undersigned Notary as a true copy of the above mentioned deed
[signature and stamp of Wertheim]

[Red wax seal of Stumphius in the margin.]

'Official Report
On this the twelfth day of August of the year nineteen hundred and eight appeared before me Anthon Diederich Stumphius, Notary, residing in Amsterdam in the presence of the witnesses here after named.
Mr Abraham Asscher… and Mr Joseph Asscher…
And Mr Alexander Michael Levy…
These gentlemen are personally known to me.
These gentlemen present showed me the piece hereafter described, all products of the Cullinan Diamond and declared them to be:

I. a piece, now in process of polishing, which originally weighed fifteen hundred and eighty one carats Dutch weight (fifteen hundred and eighty-four and a half carats English weight) and weighed on the sixth day of May nine hundred and fifty one carats Dutch weight (Nine hundred and fifty three carats English weight) and now weighs six hundred and thirty-five and one quarter carats Dutch weight (six hundred and thirty-six carats and one half carat English weight). In this piece there is still a small white imperfection on the table side and a small black spot in the side of the culette;

II. a piece now in process of polishing, which originally weighed eight hundred and nineteen carats Dutch weight (eight hundred and twenty and a half carats English weight) now weighs four hundred and three and one quarter carats Dutch weight (four hundred and four carats English weight). This piece has still a hole in the girdle, also a small hole and slight imperfection on the culette side.

III. a piece originally weighing two hundred sixteen and a half carats Dutch weight (two hundred sixteen and three quarters English weight).
This stone has this day been cloven and has produced: one piece weighing one hundred seventy one and three quarters carats Dutch weight (one hundred seventy-two carats English weight); one piece weighing fifteen and one eighth carats Dutch and English weight, eleven pieces weighing twenty-four and five eighth carats Dutch weight and English weight; some splinters weighing two carats Dutch and English weight. The loss of three carats in splitting the two hundred sixteen and a half carats stone is to be accounted for by it having had windows polished upon it previous to the cleaving operation for the purpose of careful inspection.

IV. one drop brilliant weighing ninety four and three eighths carats Dutch weight (ninety four and a half carats English weight). This is the product of the cleaved peice originally weighing two hundred sixty and a half carats. This brilliant has still to have some work done on the back (culette) and will lose a little weight;

V. one heart shaped brilliant weighing eighteen and three eighths carats (Dutch and English weight) product of the cleaved piece originally weighing forty-six carats;

VI. one marquise brilliant weighing eleven and a quarter carats Dutch and English weight, product of the cleaved piece originally weighing thirty-two and three quarter carats;

VII. one marquise brilliant weighing eight and nine sixteenths carats Dutch and English weight, products of the cleaved piece originally weighing twenty-four and three quarters carats;

VIII. one drop brilliant weighing four, a quarter and a thirty-second carats Dutch and English weight product of the cleaved piece originally weighing thirteen and a quarter carats; also a few small splinters weighing together fifteen carats;

the weighing of all these pieces having been done in the presence of me the Notary and the witnesses.

Of all which the present deed is drawn…the day of the month and the year aforesaid by me the undersigned Notary in the presence of Mr Thoedorus Cornelius Leo Smit, prospective Notary…and Mr Mari van Riel…both personally known to me as witnesses.

After having read the gentlemen present, the witnesses and I myself the notary have immediately signed this present deed, which will be retained by me.

<u>Signed</u>
A Asscher, Joseph Asscher, Alexander M Levy
TCL Smit, M van Riel, Stumphius
Notaris

Geregistreerd…
<u>Delivered by the undersigned Notary as a true copy of the above mentioned deed</u>
[Signed by Stumphius and accompanied by his stamp]

'On this thirteenth day of October of the year nineteen hundred and eight, appeared before me Hendrik Wertheim Notary…in the presence of the witnesses hereinafter named

    Mister <u>Joseph Asscher</u>…
    Mister <u>Abraham Asscher</u>…
    Mister <u>John Arthur Levy</u>…
    Mister <u>Alexander Michael Levy</u>…

The appeared gentlemen are personally known to me.

These gentlemen present showed me the pieces hereinafter described, the entire and final product of the <u>Cullinan Diamond</u> on which all operations are now finished and declared them to be

I. One piece now polished in the form of a Pendeloque Brilliant weighing five hundred and fifteen and one half carats Dutch weight (five hundred and sixteen and one half carat English weight) product of the piece originally weighing fifteen hundred and eighty one carats Dutch weight (fifteen hundred and eighty four and one half carats English weight) and having a length of fifty-nine and a breath [sic] of forty five and one half millimetres.

II. One piece now polished in the form of square brilliant weighing three hundred and eight and five eighths carats Dutch weight (three hundred and nine and three sixteenths carats English weight) product of the piece originally weighing eight hundred and nineteen carats Dutch weight (eight hundred and twenty and one half carats English weight) and having a length of forty-five and a breath of forty and one half millimeters.

III. One piece now polished in the form of a Pendeloque brilliant weighing ninety one and three quarters carats Dutch weight (ninety two carats English weight) product of the piece originally weighing two hundred and sixty one and a half carats Dutch weight (two hundred and sixty one and one eighth carats English weight) and having a length of thirty-nine and one half and a breath of twenty-six millimeters.

IV. One piece now polished in the form of a square Brilliant weighing sixty one and seven eighths carats Dutch weight (sixty two carats English weight) product of the piece originally weighing one hundred and seventy one and three quarters carats Dutch weight (one hundred and seventy two carats English weight) and having a length of twenty-six and a breath of twenty-six millimeters.

V. One piece now polished in the form of a Heart Brilliant weighing eighteen and three eighths carats Dutch and English weights, product of the piece originally weighing forty six carats Dutch weight (forty six and one eighth carats English weight) and having a length of seventeen and a breath of eighteen and one half millimeters.

VI. One piece now polished in the form of a Marquise Brilliant weighing eleven and one quarter carats Dutch and English weights product of the piece originally weighing thirty two and three quarter carats Dutch and English weight and having a length of twenty-eight and one half and a breath of twelve millimeters.

VII. One piece now polished in the form of a Marquise Brilliant weighing eight and nine sixteenths carats Dutch and English weights product of the piece originally weighing twenty-four and three quarters carats Dutch and English weight and having a length of twenty-two and a breath of eleven and one half millimeters.

VIII. One piece now polished in the form of a Square Brilliant weighing six and five eighths carats Dutch and English weight product of the piece originally weighing fifteen and one eighth carats Dutch and English weight and having a length of fifteen and a breath of ten and one half millimeters.

IX. One piece now polished in the form of a Pendeloque Brilliant weighing four and nine thirty seconds carats Dutch and English weight product of the piece originally weighing thirteen and one quarter carats Dutch and English weight and having a length of fourteen and a breath of nine millimeters.

X. Ninety six small Brilliants weighing seven and three eighths carats Dutch and English weights product of the splinters, the rough weight having been twenty and three quarter carats Dutch and English weight.

XI. Nine carats of rough ends.

The difference in weight being twenty five and seven eighths carats Dutch and English weight is accounted for by both Messieurs <u>Levy</u> and Messieurs Levy as having occurred in the process of splitting and rubbing surfaces entailed by the different splitting operations.

The weight of all these pieces having been made in the presence of me the Notary and the witnesses.

314   Of all which the present deed is drawn up at
Amsterdam in the manufactory of Mr Asscher in
Amsterdam Tol straat numbers 127 to 129 the day
of the month and the year aforesaid by me the
undersigned Notary in the presence of Messieurs
Herman Louis Israels barrister LLD and Mari van
Riel prospective notary, both living at Amsterdam
and both personally known to me, as witnesses.
    After having read the gentlemen present, the
witnesses and I myself the Notary have
immediately signed this present deed, which will
be retained by me.

Signed
Joseph Asscher, A Asscher, J A Levy, Alexander M
Levy, Mr H Louis Israels, M van Riel, H Werheim
Notary

*No9 Geregistreerd te Amsterdam den Tweeden November
1900 acht deel 169 folio 60 verso, vak 6 twee bladen geen
renoovi. Ontvangen voor recht een gulden twintig cent.*

f1.20 De Ontvanger B.A. no1
Signed/Woltersom
Delivered by the undersigned Notary as a true
copy of the above mentioned deed.
[Signature and stamp of Wertheim.]'

Bibliography

AMINI, Iradj. *Koh-i-noor*, Lotus Collection, Roli Books, New Dehli, 1994.

BAIRD, J.G.A. (Editor). *Private Letters of the Marquess of Dalhousie*, William Blackwood and Sons, Edinburgh & London, 1910.

BEET, George. *The Grand Old Days of the Diamond Fields*, Maskew Miller Limited, Cape Town.

BLAKEY, George G. *The Diamond*, Paddington Press Ltd, New York & London, 1977.

BRUTON, Eric. *Diamonds*, N. A. G. Press Ltd, London, second edition, 1978.

BRUTON, Eric. *Legendary Gems or Gems that made History*, Chilton Book Company, Radnor, Pennsylvania, 1986.

CATTELLE, W. R. *The Diamond*, John Lane Company, New York, 1911.

CHILVERS, Hedley A. *The Story of De Beers*, Cassell & Company Ltd. London, Toronto, Melbourne & Sydney, 1939.

COPELAND, Lawrence L. *Diamonds: Famous, Notable and Unique*, Gemological Institute of America, 1965.

DESAUTELS, Paul E. *Treasures in the Smithsonian. The Gem Collection*, Smithsonian Institution Press, Washington, DC, 1979.

DE SMET, K. *The Great Blue Diamond*, Standaard-Boekhandel, Antwerp-Amsterdam, 1963.

DUVAL, D.; GREEN, T.; LOUTHEAN, R., *New Frontiers in Diamonds, The Mining Revolution*, Rosendale Press Ltd, London, 1996.

EMANUEL, H. *Diamonds and Precious Stones*, John Camden Hotten, London, second edition, 1867.

FOX, George. *An Account of the Firm of Rundell, Bridge and Rundell*, written between 1843–6, typed copy of the manuscript in the Victoria & Albert Museum Library.

GIARD, Maurice E. *Les Diamants Célebres*, Société d'Éditions Millot et Cie, Besançon.

GLEASON, Barbara (ed.). *Notable Diamonds of the World*, Diamond Promotion Service, New York.

GOLDBERG, William Diamond Corp. *The Story of the 'Premier Rose'*, New York, 1980.

GORDON, W. T. A. *Note on Some Large Diamonds*, The Imperial Institute, London, 1945.

GREEN, Timothy. *The World of Diamonds*, Weidenfeld & Nicolson, London, 1981.

HANOVER. *Letters of the King of, to Viscount Strangford*, Williams & Norgate, London, 1925.

HARRIS, Harvey; HAMMID, Tino. *Fancy-Color Diamonds*, Fancoldi Registered Trust, Liechtenstein, 1994.

HEIDGEN, Heinz. *The Diamond Seeker. The Story of John Williamson*, Blackie, London & Glasgow, 1959.

HELME, Nigel. *Thomas Major Cullinan*, McGraw-Hill Book Company, Johannesburg, 1974.

HOWARTH, Stephen. *The 'Koh-i-noor' Diamond. The History and the Legend*, Quartet Books, London, Melbourne, New York, 1980.

JOBBINS, E. A.; HARDING, R. R.; SCARRATT, K. 'A Brief Description of a Spectacular 56.71 carat Tabular Diamond', *Journal of Gemmology*, Vol 19, No 1, 1984.

KAPLAN, Lazare. *Cutting the 'Jonker' Diamond*, The American Museum of Natural History, New York, 1936.

KOCKLEBERGH, I.; VLEESCHDRAGER, E.; WALGRAVE, J. *The Brilliant Story of Antwerp Diamonds*, MIM n.v., Antwerp, 1992.

KRASHES, Laurence S. *Harry Winston. The Ultimate Jeweler*, Harry Winston Inc. & the Gemological Institute of America, New York & Santa Monica, California, second edition, revised 1986.

LEGRAND, Jacques. *Diamonds. Myth, Magic and Reality*, English translation, Crown Publishers Inc, New York, 1980.

LENZEN, Dr G. *The History of Diamond Production and the Diamond Trade*, Barrie and Jenkins Ltd, London, 1970.

LIDDICOAT, Richard & Dr John HUMMEL. *The GIA Diamond Dictionary*, third edition, Gemological Institute of America, California, 1993.

LORD, John. *The Maharajahs*, Hutchinson, London, 1972.

MAWE, J. *A Treatise on Diamonds and Precious Stones*, Longman, Hurst, Rees, Orme & Brown, London, 1823.

MEARS, Brigadier Kenneth C. B. E. *The Crown Jewels*, Tower of London, Department of the Environment, London, 1986.

MEEN, V. B.; TUSHINGHAM, A. D. *Crown Jewels of Iran*, University of Toronto Press, 1968.

MEEN, V. B.; TUSHINGHAM, A. D.; WAITE, G. G. 'The Darya-I Nur Diamond and the Tavernier Great Table', *Lapidary Journal*, November 1967, San Diego, California.

MEHTA, Kantilal Chhotalal. *Diamonds, a Century of Spectacular Jewels*, Harry N. Abrams Inc., New York, 1996.

MENKES, Suzy. *The Royal Jewels*, Grafton Books, London, 1985.

MILLER, Peter. *Diamonds, Commencing the Countdown to Market Renaissance*, Yorkton Securities, Inc., London, 1995.

MONNICKENDAM, A. *The Magic of Diamonds*, Hammond, Hammond & Company, 1955.

NADELHOFFER, Hans. *Cartier, Jewellers Extraordinary*, Thames & Hudson, London.

PATCH, Susanne Steinem. *Blue Mystery. The Story of the Hope Diamond*, Smithsonian Institution Press, Washington, DC, 1976.

PRODDOW, Penny; FASEL, Marion. *Diamonds, a Century of Spectacular Jewels*, Harry N. Abrams, Inc., New York, 1996.

PURTELL, Joseph. *The Tiffany Touch*, Random House Inc., New York, 1971.

REIS, Esmeraldino. *Os Orandes Diamantes Brasileiros*, Departamento Nacional Da Producao Mineral, Divisao De Geologia E Mineralogia, Rio De Janeiro, 1959.

ROBERTS, Brian. *Kimberley. Turbulent City*. David Philip: Publisher. Cape Town. 1976.

316 ROBERTSON, Marian. *Diamond Fever. South African Diamond History 1866-69. From Primary Sources.* Oxford University Press, Johannesburg, London, New York, 1974.

SEN, N. B. *Glorious History of the Koh-i-Noor Diamond,* New Book Society of India, Delhi, 1970.

SHIPLEY, Robert M. *Famous Diamonds of the World,* Gemological Institute of America. Los Angeles, California, sixth edition, June 1955.

SHOR, Russell, *Connections, a Profile of Diamond People and their History.* International Diamond Publications, Tel Aviv, 1993.

STREETER, Edwin W. *The Great Diamonds of the World,* George Bell & Sons, London second edition, 1882.

STREETER, Edwin W. *Precious Stones and Gems,* George Bell & Sons, London, sixth edition, 1898.

STRONGE, S.; SMITH, N.; HARLE J.C. *A Golden Treasury, Jewellery from the Indian Subcontinent,* Victoria & Albert Museum/Mapin Publishing Pvt. Ltd., London, 1988.

STRONGE, Susan. 'The Myth of the Timur Ruby', *Jewellery Studies,* Vol. 7, The Society of Jewellery Historians, London, 1996.

SUTTON, J. R. *Diamond. A Descriptive Treatise,* Thomas Murby & Co., London, 1928.

SYKES, Sir Percy. *A History of Persia, in Two Volumes,* Macmillan & Co., Limited, London, 1930.

TAVERNIER, John Baptista. *The Six Voyages of John Baptista Tavernier through Turkey into Persia and the East-Indies,* English translation, London, 1678.

TAVERNIER, Jean Baptiste. *Travels in India,* translated from the French edition of 1676 with a biographical sketch by V. Ball. Macmillan and Co, London, 1889, second edition, edited by William Crooke, Oxford University Press, 1925.

TILLANDER, Herbert. *Diamond Cuts in Historic Jewellery, 1381–1910,* Art Books International Ltd, London, 1995.

TILLANDER, Herbert. *The Hope Diamond and its lineage. A challenge for further research,* presented at the 15th International Gemmological Conference held in the Smithsonian Institution, October 1975.

TOLANSKY, S. *The History and Use of Diamond,* Methuen & Co. Ltd, London, 1962.

TOLANSKY, S. 'The Great Table Diamond of Tavernier', reprinted from the *Journal of Gemmology,* Vol III No 5, January, 1962.

Treasures of the Kremlin Diamond Fund, Moscow.

TWINING, Lord. *A History of the Crown Jewels of Europe,* B. T. Batsford Ltd. London. 1960.

WANNENBURG, A. J.; JOHNSON, P. *Diamond People,* Norfolk House Publishers, London, 1990.

WILLIAMS, A. F. *The Genesis of the Diamond,* 2 volumes, Ernest Benn Limited, London, 1932.

WILLIAMS, A. F. *Some Dreams Come True,* Howard B. Timmins, Cape Town, 1948.

WILSON, A.N. *Diamonds from Birth to Eternity,* Gemological Institute of America, California, 1982.

YOGEV, Gedalia. *Diamonds and Coral,* Leicester University Press, 1978.

ZUCKER, Benjamin. *Gems and Jewels, A Connoisseur's Guide,* Crown Publishers Inc., New York, 1984.

Sale catalogues:

Christie's, New York. *The Emperor Maximilian Diamond;* New York on 20th April 1982.

Christie's. *A Casket of Magnificent Jewels. The Collection of the late Lydia Deterding;* Geneva on 14th November 1984.

Christie's. *An Important Collection of Moghul Jewellery,* by Diana Scarisbrick; Geneva on 16th May 1991.

Christie's. *A Rare Jewel of the World;* Geneva on 14th November 1984.

Christie's. *A Spectacular Historic Table-Cut Diamond;* Geneva on 16th May 1985.

Parke-Bernet Galleries Inc. *The Fabulous Collection of Precious Stone Jewelry formed by the late May Bonfils Stanton;* New York, 1962.

Sotheby Parke Bernet S. A. *The De Beers Diamond;* Geneva on 6th May 1982.

Sotheby & Co. London. *Catalogue of Highly Important Jewels including the Two Historic 'Arcot' Diamonds;* London on 25th June 1959.

Sotheby's. *The Jewels of the Late Duchess of Windsor;* Geneva, 2nd and 3rd April 1987.

A Kaleidoscope of Colours – Indian Mughal Jewels of the 18th and 19th Centuries. Exhibition catalogue, Provincial Diamond Museum, Antwerp, 1997.

The Ageless Diamond. Exhibition catalogue, London, 1959. Sponsored by Christie's and De Beers Consolidated Mines.

Dix Siecles de Joaillerie Francaise. Exhibition catalogue, Musée du Louvre, 1962. Ministère d'État Affaires Culturelles.

Catalogue de brillants et les autres pierres precieuses, Son Altesse monseigneur le duc souverain de Brunswick-Lunebourg. Chauvet, Paris.

Acknowledgements

This fourth edition of *Famous Diamonds* is to a large extent based on the excellent work done by the team that put together the third edition. I would like to thank the following for all the effort they put into compiling the previous edition: the late Mr Howard Vaughan, who revised the Introduction, updated other areas of the book and assisted me throughout its production; Mr Eric Emms, who has written the interesting section on colour in diamonds; Mr Robin Walker of the Diamond Trading Company (DTC), who has kept me informed of press reports pertaining to important diamonds; the editor Ms Sophie Henley-Price, who created an edition very different from the previous, to great admiration; and Mr Raymond Sancroft-Baker of Christie's for his advice and invaluable assistance. I would also like to thank Mr Paul Holberton, the editor of the new edition, and Ms Lesley Coldham of DTC for her help in preparing the new entries for it.

I would also like to thank Mr René Brus for his kindness in allowing me to make use of his research into the Holland diamond, and Mr Edward and Mr Joop Asscher for their kindness in allowing me to study the daily record which his family firm kept while the Cullinan diamond was being cut and polished.

On the other side of the Atlantic, I wish to thank Mr John Nels Hatleberg for his help in updating some of the information and his invaluable contribution to the visual enhancement of this book. My thanks also to Mr Jeffrey E. Post, curator of the Gem and Mineral Collection at the Smithsonian Institution, Washington DC, as well as to his predecessor, Mr John Sampson White, both of whom have been of great assistance in trying to unravel the complicated history of the Hope diamond.

I should like to thank the late Harry Oppenheimer for so kindly agreeing to write a new Foreword to this book. Together with his father, Sir Ernest Oppenheimer, he has been the guiding hand behind the diamond industry for over sixty years. I am grateful for his contribution. I am also thankful to Mr Nicholas Oppenheimer, Chairman of De Beers, and Chairman of the DTC in London, who, together with his cousin and its President Mr Anthony Oppenheimer, have been constant in their support of this fourth edition.

Further thanks are also due to M. François Curiel, Christie's International Jewellery Director and Group Vice-Chairman, for the important role he has played throughout its production. Also to Mr David Warren, and, finally, to Ms Helen Teicher for her help in obtaining several images that appear.

I should also like to thank all of the following who have provided information, material, suggestions or encouragement in the preparation of this and previous editions: Mr Ronald Winston; Sheikh Ahmed H. Fitaihi; Mr Robert Mouawad; Mr Laurence Graff; Mr Marvin Samuels; Mr William Goldberg; Mr Sergei Oulin and Ms Elena Afinoguenova of Almazy Rossii Sakha; Mr Nick Pleasance, formerly of the De Beers Moscow office; Mrs Joan Braune and Mrs Kate Evan-Jones of the DTC; Mr Nigel Jones, Mr Andrew Murray and Ms Terese Denisen, curator of the Antwerp Diamond Museum; Mr and Mrs Rajesh Mehta and Mr and Mrs Rashmi Mehta of Antwerp's Indian diamond community; Mr Hans Wins of Braaschat and Mr Walter Baert, formerly of Belgium's Hoge Raad voor Diamond (Diamond High Council); Mr Richard Edgecumbe, deputy curator (documentation) of the metalwork collection at the Victoria and Albert Museum in London; Mr Nigel Israel, chairman of the Society of Jewellery Historians, and its founder, Dr Jack Ogden; Mr Alan Jobbins, formerly curator of Minerals and Gemstones, London's Geological Museum; Mr Kenneth Scarratt, former director of the Asian Institute of Gemological Sciences, Bangkok; Mr Adrian Klein, Precious stones sector chairman of the CIBJO organisation, and his predecessor, M. Gerard Grospiron; Mr Eric Bruton, author and past President of the Gemological Association and Gem Testing Laboratory of Great Britain, and its director, Dr R.R. Harding, previously curator of Gems at the British Museum; Mr Roy Huddlestone of Gemmological Consultants Ltd; Mr. Russell Feather at the Smithsonian Institution; Ms Linda Buckley at Tiffany & Co.; Ms Carolyn Brodi and Ms Vanessa Neueunhaus at Harry Winston Inc.; Ms Suzanne Waugh at Sotheby's; Mr George Burne, a former director of De Beers, and to his longterm colleague, Mr Michael Grantham, a former DTC director; also Mrs Suzanne Spencer, Ms Susan Farmer, Mrs Elaine Tipping, and Messrs Harry Garnett, Martin Cooper, Bill Lear, Rory More O'Ferrall, Richard Williams, Dr Chris Welbourne, Peter Cooke, Geoffrey Chessum, Duncan Christie, Andrew Bone, Michael Thomas and John Esslemont; Mr Peter Brandon of Design for Print; Mr Beny Steinmetz of R. Steinmetz and Sons; and several people at the Gemological Institute of America (GIA). They include Dr. John Hummel, Shane McClure and Mrs Alice Keller – editor of *Gems and Gemmology* – in California, and Tom Yonelunas, John King, Tom Moses and Ms Pattie Singh of its Gem Trade Laboratory in New York.

A final word of thanks is due to Mr Omer Khalidi for supplying me with supportive information on Golconda which has been usefully incorporated into the text.

Index

320